T0323681

Hedge Fund Activism in Japan

Hedge fund activism is an expression of shareholder primacy, an idea that has come to dominate discussion of corporate governance theory and practice worldwide over the past two decades. This book provides a thorough examination of public and often confrontational hedge fund activism in Japan in the period between 2000 and the full onset of the global financial crisis in 2008. In Japan this shareholder-centric conception of the company espoused by activist hedge funds clashed with the alternative Japanese conception of the company as an enduring organisation or a 'community'. By analysing this clash, the book derives a fresh view of the practices underpinning corporate governance in Japan and offers suggestions regarding the validity of the shareholder primacy ideas currently at the heart of US and UK beliefs about the purpose of the firm.

JOHN BUCHANAN is a research associate at the Centre for Business Research, Judge Business School, University of Cambridge. His first degree was in oriental studies and subsequently he worked as a commercial banker in Brazil, Japan, and Spain, and then as an investment banker in the UK and Japan, at both British and Japanese banks. He has been studying Japanese corporate governance since 2002.

DOMINIC HEESANG CHAI is Assistant Professor of Strategy and International Management at the Graduate School of Business, Seoul National University. He has held a faculty position at Manchester Business School, The University of Manchester, and a research fellowship at the Centre for Business Research, Judge Business School, University of Cambridge.

SIMON DEAKIN is Professor of Law in the Faculty of Law and Fellow of Peterhouse at the University of Cambridge. He has directed an interdisciplinary programme of research on corporate governance at the Centre for Business Research in Cambridge since the early 1990s. He was elected a Fellow of the British Academy in 2005.

Hedge Fund Activism in Japan

The limits of shareholder primacy

JOHN BUCHANAN

DOMINIC HEESANG CHAI

SIMON DEAKIN

CAMBRIDGE
UNIVERSITY PRESS

CAMBRIDGE UNIVERSITY PRESS
Cambridge, New York, Melbourne, Madrid, Cape Town,
Singapore, São Paulo, Delhi, Mexico City

Cambridge University Press
The Edinburgh Building, Cambridge CB2 8RU, UK

Published in the United States of America by Cambridge University Press, New York

www.cambridge.org
Information on this title: www.cambridge.org/9781107016835

First published 2012

Printed in the United Kingdom at the University Press, Cambridge

A catalogue record for this publication is available from the British Library

Library of Congress Cataloguing in Publication data
Buchanan, John, 1951–
    Hedge fund activism in Japan : the limits of shareholder primacy / John Buchanan,
    Dominic Heesang Chai, Simon Deakin.
        pages   cm
    Includes bibliographical references and index.
    ISBN 978-1-107-01683-5 (hardback)
    1. Corporations–Investor relations–Japan.   2. Stockholders–Japan.
    3. Hedge funds–Japan.   4. Corporate governance–Japan.   I. Chai, Dominic
    Heesang.   II. Deakin, S. F. (Simon F.)   III. Title.
    HD2744.B83 2012
    332.64'5240952–dc23
    2012002155

ISBN 978-1-107-01683-5 Hardback

Contents

Figures

Tables

Acknowledgements

The authors wish to acknowledge the many parties who have supported their research for this book.

We are grateful to the Japanese Ministry of Education, Culture, Sports, Science and Technology (MEXT 21st. Century COE Programme) and the Belgian Federal Science Policy Department (Belspo grant IAP VI/06, *Democratic Governance and Theory of Collective Action*) for their financial support, which enabled us to undertake important elements of our empirical research in Japan. We are also grateful for the support received from two interdisciplinary research centres which helped us to set up and complete the research: the Centre for Business Research at the University of Cambridge and the Institute for Technology, Enterprise and Competitiveness at Dōshisha University. Dominic Chai is grateful also for the support given to him by Manchester Business School.

We also wish to express our appreciation to the many officers of industrial companies, financial investors, official bodies, and other entities, as well as many private individuals, who kindly spared their time to meet us and respond to our questions in the course of our research; with certain exceptions, most of these responses were provided on a confidential basis and therefore are not directly attributed.

We are especially grateful to Uchida Kensuke, formerly Senior Managing Director of The Sumitomo Bank, Deputy President of Daiwa Securities SMBC, and President of Ōtemachi Tatemono, for his help in arranging many informative meetings that might otherwise not have been possible, to Kobayashi Kōichi, formerly Chief Representative Europe of Toray Industries and Senior Managing Director of Du Pont-Toray for his kindness in making numerous introductions, and to Nakajima Yūichirō, Managing Partner of Crimson Phoenix, for his introductions and comments on our manuscript.

We have relied throughout on the excellent research support supplied to our project over several years by Kobayashi Eku and Aleksandra Polanska.

We are grateful to Curtis Milhaupt and Hugh Whittaker for reading and commenting on a draft of the book.

Finally we would like to thank the officers of several companies, investors, and hedge funds who provided comments on our drafts, and the anonymous reviewers who provided guidance on our first draft.

Note on transcription of Japanese words

Japanese words are transcribed using the Hepburn Romanisation, with macrons to indicate long vowels except where place names are considered to have become adopted into the English language through frequent use (e.g. 'Tokyo' and 'Osaka' rather than the strictly correct 'Tōkyō' and 'Ōsaka'). Where corporate names currently exist in a Romanised version promoted by the company which does not follow this orthography we have generally followed their usage (e.g. 'Sotoh' rather than 'Sotō' and 'Nihon Keizai Shimbun' rather than 'Nihon Keizai Shinbun') although we have added macrons to some company names to indicate pronunciation where it is not already evident. Japanese personal names are shown in Japanese order, with surname first.

1 | *Introduction: hedge fund activism, Japanese corporate governance, and the nature of the company*

This book is about corporate governance in Japan, as it was revealed through a particular series of interactions between activist hedge funds, target boards, and other interested parties between roughly 2000 and the full onset of the global financial crisis in 2008. At the same time it is an account of a clash between two different conceptions of the company: the view promoted by activist hedge funds of the company as the shareholders' property, which we call 'shareholder primacy', and the view predominant in Japan of the company as an enduring organisation or a 'community'. This was an unusual instance of two distinct conceptions of corporate governance encountering one another within a single national market. Where the disagreements became public, they brought fundamental and often hitherto tacit assumptions about the purpose of the company into the open. The result was in many ways a demonstration of the strengths and weaknesses of both approaches, making it also a story with a wider significance, with implications for regulatory policy and corporate practice beyond Japan.

The tension between the idea of the company as property and the idea of it as community originates in the nature of the institutional form which describes the business enterprise in modern market economies: the joint stock company.[1] This is a legal form which has evolved over time and in a number of different national and commercial contexts to meet business needs. Its nature cannot be understood without taking into account certain of its features, which include separate personality and limited liability, which would not exist without a legal underpinning

---

[1] In this book we use the expression 'joint stock company' as a generic term to refer to companies which are limited by share capital and either have, or legally could have, at least some shareholders who are not directly engaged in the management of the business. Different legal systems use various terms to describe this widely observed business form. The Japanese expression 'kabushiki kaisha' approximately translates as 'joint stock company'.

of some kind. The joint stock company is, however, more than just the legal model of the firm. That legal model is a response to and reflection of organisational practices, market pressures, and political forces which have shaped the law. How companies are governed is the result not just of a certain legal framework, but depends additionally on institutional norms and practices of differing degrees of formality, which vary from country to country and from one market context to another. These practices may complement the formal rules of company law, but they may also contradict them, or render them irrelevant. Outward resemblances among formal laws and regulations may be misleading as a guide to corporate governance on the ground. In this book, while we take account of the law in shaping corporate experience, our main focus will be on practice as revealed by empirical investigation.

Against the background of a corporate governance system incompletely defined by law and necessarily supplemented and amended by institutional practice, solutions to the long-standing problem of the 'separation of ownership and control' in the structure of the joint stock company were pioneered in the USA and UK. The rise of shareholder primacy in those markets can be traced to intellectual currents in financial economics and the theory of the firm in the 1970s, which found a practical manifestation in the hostile takeover movement and growing role of independent boards in the following decades. Underpinning these solutions was the view that shareholders were the ultimate or 'residual' owners of the company and that the directors and managers were their agents, whose duty was to generate 'shareholder value' before all other considerations. Other so-called 'stakeholders', such as employees and customers, were acknowledged to be of importance to the success of the company as a business, but they had no direct role in its governance. The emergence of these ideas and practices was triggered by corporate scandals in America and Britain, and assisted by the lobbying of influential groups, including institutional shareholders such as pension funds, insurance companies, and other collective investment vehicles which were coming to prominence as owners of corporate stock at this time. Because of their similarities, the US and UK approaches to corporate governance are often discussed in tandem as 'Anglo-American' but they are not identical. We look at the UK market's response to hedge fund activism in Chapter 5 but generally focus on American patterns of corporate governance because these have had a greater international impact. It was specifically the success of the US economy in the 1990s that helped to spread these ideas worldwide, often to the point of eclipsing prior traditions of the company as a socially embedded entity which produced value for a range of different stakeholders including the shareholders, sustained over time by a management devoted to preserving the organisational identity of the firm.

In Japan, the search for mechanisms to deliver effective corporate performance had taken a different path since the late 1940s. Then, the priority had been national economic recovery, and the company was seen as a vehicle for achieving sustained growth of the kind needed to bring this about. A government bureaucracy accustomed to intervening in the economy encouraged a revival of industry with firms under the control of largely autonomous management, funded by bank finance rather than by equity capital. Shareholders, or at least pure portfolio shareholders investing for returns, played little part in this process. Their legal position as owners of shares, with the right to appoint and remove directors and thereby to hold management to account, was little different from that which prevailed in the USA and UK at this time. In some respects, the formal rights of Japanese shareholders were stronger and clearer than, for example, those of their American counterparts. Yet there developed in Japan a model of the 'community firm' which led to the almost complete marginalisation of shareholder voice. Initially motivated by the need to control labour unrest and later by the economic advantages, in terms of enhanced productivity, which were seen to flow from workforce involvement in the organisation of the firm, Japanese managers set out to cultivate a communitarian ethos, encouraging employees, up to and including the mostly executive boards, to identify with the company and to internalise its values. By the 1980s, bureaucratic intervention had receded and bank-led finance was less important for the larger and richer firms, leaving management effectively unsupervised, except by reference to the internal corporate ethic of the community firm. Directors and other senior managers tended to see themselves as representatives of the extended corporate community, which included past and present employees and long-term suppliers and customers. Retaining employee trust and loyalty on the one hand, and producing value for the firm's customers and for the firm itself on the other, were the twin objectives which, if met, would ensure the sustainability of the company over time.

The American and Japanese models were both, in their ways, responses to crisis, although crises of very different kinds and of different eras. US corporate governance took a pro-shareholder turn in response to scandals related to management behaviour, economic recession, and concerns over a loss of international competitiveness in the 1970s. Japan's system, which originated in the period of post-war reconstruction in the 1940s, proved remarkably robust even in the changed circumstances of the later decades of the last century, including the period of economic stagnation which began with the bursting of the real estate and stock market bubble at the beginning of the 1990s. The Japanese system drew a veil over shareholders' property rights and was mostly conducted as if their legal status within the company simply did not matter. It provided few mechanisms to hold management to account should it abuse its position of trust. The growing contrast between the US emphasis on shareholder value and the Japanese indifference to shareholder rights was widely remarked on, but had few practical effects because the two systems had few opportunities to impact on one another. Beginning in the 1980s, the Structural Impediment Initiative talks between the US and Japanese governments created a degree of friction, as the US side called for changes in Japanese retailing practices, land use, and investment in public works, some of which touched on corporate governance issues. But the talks had few direct implications for the way companies in Japan were run. The growing international reach of institutional investors also had limited impact at this time, as senior Japanese managers reiterated the virtues of their model in the face of calls for heightened sensitivity to shareholder concerns.

All of this changed with the emergence of hedge fund activism in Japan. Activist hedge funds had appeared in the USA in the aftermath of the 'deal decade' of the 1980s. As the hostile takeovers of that period receded, new types of shareholder activism came to the fore. American activist hedge funds were often confrontational investors who targeted companies which they believed were squandering shareholder value. Through public engagement with the boards of companies in which they took important but not normally controlling stakes, the funds frequently succeeded in facilitating the release of free cash flow to shareholders in the form of increased dividends and share buy-backs. This often necessitated asset sales and restructurings, which, notwithstanding their negative implications for employees and other stakeholders, were justified by the activists as enhancing capital efficiency. As this strategy was successful in generating above-market rates of return for the funds and their own investors, they turned to other markets, in Europe and in Japan. In Japan, the approach of the funds came into immediate conflict with the idea and practice of the community firm which still retained widespread support among managers, bureaucrats, and politicians in the early 2000s, despite the economic vicissitudes of the post-bubble period.

What followed was a tournament of corporate governance beliefs. Activist hedge funds, often of foreign origin, but sometimes Japanese, used the formal legal rights conferred on shareholders by Japanese company law and by companies' own articles of association to mount a fundamental challenge to the core of management practice in the community firm. In doing so, they drew out into the open a range of issues that had previously been uncontroversial concerning managerial autonomy and accountability, the balance in dividend policy between the distribution of income and the accumulation of reserves, and the optimal level of financial gearing for companies. Above all, hedge fund activism crystallised the debate over competing conceptions of the company as shareholders' property on the one hand and as the community firm on the other. With money and power at stake in these contests, and against a backdrop of sustained media and public interest, the debate was carried out at an unusually heightened level of engagement.

In this book we chart the progress of this debate, as it was conducted over several years through public dialogue between funds and boards, tender offers, litigation, and regulatory and bureaucratic responses. In particular, we examine why not just corporate managers but also many institutional investors in Japan resisted the activist hedge funds, and how they went about constructing their defence. We also make an assessment of why that defence, which was initially uncertain, was, in the end, largely successful. Because two diametrically opposed approaches to corporate governance were set against each other in an unusually clear way, the Japanese experience of hedge fund activism provides a rare opportunity to study, in a concrete setting, a clash of ideas which is otherwise only indirectly observable, or must be considered at a theoretical level, several removes from practice.

Our account of hedge fund activism in Japan is thus located in the context of the global development of the joint stock company as the principal legal form of business enterprise in market economies. We note its dynamic strengths as well as its inbuilt anomalies and weaknesses, and its need for complementary mechanisms of corporate governance, expressed through formal and informal norms and practices beyond the law. We focus on the tension between the two divergent threads of corporate governance that we have referred to above, namely the property-rights, shareholder-orientated model of the company that has emerged from the historical experience of a number of countries but in particular the USA and UK, and the firm-centric, communitarian strand that emerged from Japan's period of post-war reconstruction. We see this tension as not just a consequence of the divergent experience of different national systems, but as inherent in the original form of the joint stock company itself. The rise of the activist hedge fund phenomenon, as it began in the USA and spread from there, can be seen as the drawing out, under contemporary conditions, of this inherent conflict of models. Hedge funds, despite their recent rise to prominence and the widespread attention given to them, represent only a small part of the total funds under professional management, even in the USA, and activist funds are a fraction, in turn, of the wider hedge fund category. Their importance lies not in the scale of their holdings, but in their conscious adoption of the language and strategy of shareholder primacy as the foundation of their investment approach. They were seen, and saw themselves, as the shock troops of shareholder primacy. That is why we are studying them.

Hedge fund activism in Japan during the period of our study was a calculated venture by professional fund managers; it is important to bear in mind that the funds did not set out primarily to reform Japanese management but to make a profit from their investments. Demanding reform was nevertheless a means to this end and the reactions that it provoked were often instructive. Thus, for our purposes, what matters is not whether particular funds were successful or made money for their investors, but what they revealed about corporate governance ideas in Japan and how far they brought about wider change in the Japanese corporate governance system. In addition to charting broad trends in hedge fund interventions across the period we are studying, we therefore look in detail at a small number of more confrontational funds which attracted the most interest in the Japanese press and whose activities had a marked impact on corporate practice and on the responses to activism of the courts and bureaucracy.

Chapter 2 continues our introduction by explaining the methodology we adopted for this study.

Chapters 3–7 establish the framework of our discussion, taking us through the development of the company to the split between property rights and communitarianism, as it was played out in different markets, to the emergence of activist hedge funds. In Chapter 3 we look at the legal form of the joint stock company, the concept of corporate governance, and the way in which informal practices permeate and influence the ways that corporate governance is conducted. In Chapter 4 we look at the American and British experience of the rise of shareholder primacy from the 1970s onwards, and consider its significance for corporate governance at a global level. In Chapter 5 we look at the development of the hedge fund sector and its activist subsector in the USA, in the UK, and in Continental Europe. In Chapter 6 we look at the contrasting experience of Japan and the style of communitarian corporate governance that emerged there after the Second World War. In Chapter 7 we consider what attracted activist hedge funds to Japan, despite the existence of so many outwardly hostile factors.

Chapters 8–12 contain the core of our empirical analysis. Here we use a narrative approach to give a sense of the chronological unfolding of events. Chapter 8 looks at the emergence of hedge fund activism in Japan, beginning with the most prominent of the early Japanese funds, the so-called 'Murakami Fund', and describes the arrival of foreign funds in the early 2000s. We then provide an overview of the state of hedge fund activism in Japan at its height in late 2007, and look at the styles of activism pioneered by the five most high-profile funds during 2001–8. In Chapter 9 we provide more detailed accounts of two interventions which we consider confrontational and which proved to be turning points: Steel Partners' intervention in Bull-Dog Sauce and TCI's intervention in J-Power. Chapter 10 reports on the reactions to activism of managers, shareholders, the courts, the bureaucracy, the public, and the media, particularly the financial press in Japan and overseas. In Chapter 11 we look at the record and prospects of other activist hedge funds in Japan, which did not attract the same publicity as the more confrontational ones, but whose strategies may prove to be more enduring in a Japanese setting. In Chapter 12 we offer our conclusions. We consider what confrontational hedge fund activism revealed about Japanese corporate governance, review its significance for Japanese corporate and managerial practice, and discuss its wider implications for the nature of the company and the dynamics of global corporate governance.

2 | Perspectives, methods, and data

2.1 Studying hedge fund activism in context

The basis of our study is an empirical inquiry into the dynamics of Japanese corporate governance during the 2000s. Our empirical research was conducted from an *institutionalist* theoretical perspective, and employed a *multiple methods approach* combining qualitative, quantitative, and narrative elements.

By an 'institutionalist' perspective we mean one which sees individual behaviour as both shaping and being shaped by enduring institutional features of a given societal context or environment. At their simplest, institutions consist of behavioural regularities or practices which, through repetition and routinisation, achieve a certain level of stability. The organisational practices of a business enterprise – the routines associated with the allocation of tasks between individual employees, team working, the exercise of supervisory authority, and so on – can possess this institutional quality on the basis of repeated behaviour. At a further level, when routines which are still largely tacit and informal acquire a certain degree of legitimacy in the eyes of those who observe them, they become norms which provide a benchmark for behaviour. Many of the practices of the large Japanese enterprise or community firm that we will be studying in this book, ranging from so-called 'lifetime' or stable employment for core employees to the marginalisation of external shareholders in corporate decision-making, make claims on the behaviour of corporate actors which are normative in this sense: claims which were contested by activist hedge fund managers who had a quite separate set of normative reference points. Norms, in their turn, can be formalised as written rules contained in texts which claim to offer authoritative guidance for behaviour and which, if they are embodied in a legal form, can be backed up by sanctions of various kinds. The terms of corporate articles of association, the standards set out in codes of practice, and the contents of company law, are examples of formal institutions which are relevant to our study.

Institutions in each of the senses that we have just set out – routines, norms, and rules – do not mechanically predetermine individual choices, and they do not eliminate the central role of human agency in shaping behavioural outcomes. They do, however, have the potential to channel and influence those outcomes, which is why they merit empirical study in their own right, alongside the study of more purely behavioural traits and trends.

In the short run, institutions influence and structure behaviour, and so appear as an exogenous constraint on individuals' choices. In the longer run, however, they are the consequence of behavioural outcomes, and hence endogenous to a given societal setting (Aoki, 2010). Institutions are path-dependent, in the sense of being the result of evolutionary processes which have been shaped by particular contextual influences, possibly in contingent or accidental ways (Roe, 1996). Institutions reflect their societal contexts to a large degree, but the fit is not exact, and more formal institutions may become rigid to the point where they diverge from actual behaviour, particularly in fast-changing environments. Such a view suggests the need for an historical perspective on institutions, that is to say, one that can explain how particular institutions came to be as they are. Institutions may be the result of conjunctions of features of the economic or political environment which no longer hold, which is not to say that the institutions in question cannot be adapted to a new context.

It follows from what we have said that we should think of individuals as acting with bounded rationality and as institutions as being qualifiedly efficient. To say that individuals act with bounded rationality implies that they tend to act in an instrumental way and with the aim of improving their well-being, but in an environment which is complex and open-ended where they cannot consistently foresee the consequences of their actions (Gigerenza, 2010: ch. 1; Simon, 1955). Very often the most important information for an actor concerns what other actors are likely to do, but this information may not be readily available. In a theoretical world of fully competitive markets, such information would, by definition, be costlessly available and fully incorporated into prices. In the real world, such information is often costly to obtain, and is not always embedded in prices. Some of the information that actors need to coordinate their behaviour in complex environments is available to them through direct observation, but much more of it is embedded in institutions of different kinds. The market is one such institution, and its prices are the means by which the market conveys information of a certain kind to actors (principally, information on the preferences of other actors). The legal system is also an institution in this sense: the rules which it produces can be thought of as disseminating information concerning expectations of behaviour which are widely held in a given society and which, by virtue of their legal status, have acquired normative force. Informal institutions in the form of routines and norms perform similar functions of aiding coordination. For actors engaged in any collective social activity, including but not limited to economic exchange, accessing the information they need to coordinate their actions is a matter of interpreting their environment, and thus engaging in a search for shared meaning in objects, events, and ideas, as much as it is a question of responding in an instrumental way to signals they receive from that environment.

To say that formal institutions are qualifiedly efficient is to take the view that whatever stability or 'fitness' for their environment they may possess is contingent and contestable rather than being fixed or complete. All institutions are in a state of flux, responding mostly incrementally to shifts in their environment, but sometimes being impacted by exogenous shocks. While formal institutions reflect their environment, their separation from it, which is the precondition for their stability, is also a source of rigidities which can sometimes only be addressed through radical readjustments. To that extent, shocks are never entirely external events, but are endogenously generated whenever formal institutions cease to reflect the wider institutional environment.

The perspective we have taken on the role of institutions in responding to and, in their turn, shaping behaviour in the context of the business enterprise, has influenced the methodological choices we have made in our empirical research. A 'multi-methods approach', of the kind we have used, is appropriate for the study of societal phenomena involving complex causal processes, and in contexts where the relevant data are scarce and difficult to access (Poteete, Janssen, and Ostrom, 2010: 33). Both are the case here. To understand cause and effect in the case of hedge fund activism in the Japanese setting, it is necessary to consider several features of the institutional context of corporate governance in

Japan: the underlying legal structure of the joint stock company form, transplanted from Western legal systems; the adaptations to that model which had occurred in Japan over a century or more of legal and economic development; the further adjustment of the corporate form by the organisational practices of the so-called community firm in the post-1945 period; the political and economic pressures for reform of the corporate governance system and for wider changes to the practices of the community firm throughout the 1990s and 2000s; the origins of hedge fund activism in the very different corporate governance context of the USA in the 1980s; and the conditions which facilitated the entry of activist hedge funds into the Japanese market in the early 2000s. These contextual factors all had some influence over the strategies of the actors involved, in one form or another, in the process of hedge fund activism in Japan. But, as we shall see, the institutional framework did not just supply a set of incentives or constraints to which agents responded in a more or less 'rational' way. The advent of hedge fund activism in Japan affected those institutions, and altered their evolutionary path, but in ways that could not have been anticipated at the outset of the process. Because the institutions (practices, norms, rules) of corporate governance were themselves in a state of flux throughout this period, it is far from straightforward to disentangle cause and effect in this process. As we shall see, confrontational activism failed to bring about the kind of changes that would have aligned Japanese practices with the shareholder primacy model. However, this does not mean that confrontational activism was without effects. These effects included a greater acceptance, on the part of the managers of large Japanese companies, of the merits of dialogue with shareholders, but also a growing accommodation of shareholder activism to the organisational priorities and values of the community firm, a phenomenon we describe in terms of 'quiet activism' (see Chapter 11).

Where causal relations are complex in the sense just described, accessing and analysing the data needed to unravel them becomes particularly problematic. At one level, there is no shortage of data on corporate governance phenomena. Listed companies, which are the main focus of corporate governance research, are required by a combination of legal rules and stock exchange requirements to publish information concerning their operations and performance. This information is collated by commercial and other suppliers of financial data. A certain amount of data is also available on the structure and activities of hedge funds. Together, these data sets on companies and funds provide a basis for quantitative analysis of the effects of hedge fund interventions in listed companies. Quantitative analysis based on a representative sample of cases holds out the prospect of identifying correlations and, possibly, causal relationships between the variables of interest, in a way which makes the results more robust and generalisable. Econometric techniques make it possible to examine overall trends within a population or sample, and to isolate correlations between variables in a way which controls for background factors and for the possibility of interactions between the different variables of interest. We employ statistical testing and logistic regression analysis, as explained in Chapter 8, to identify the predominant features of target firms and the impact of hedge fund interventions on the targets' continuing profitability and strategy.

However, quantitative analysis has limitations. The data on companies and funds that can be drawn from the financial data sets which are widely used in corporate governance studies provide only a limited picture of hedge fund activism. The terms 'hedge fund' and 'activist hedge fund' are not legal terms of art and, although we present definitions in Chapter 5, there are no universally accepted understandings of these terms that would ensure that data sets consistently represented what was expected of them. In the Thomson Reuters data set that is our main source of financial data on companies and investments in Japan and elsewhere, and which we use in Chapter 8, funds are selected on the basis of being 'hedge funds' with an 'active orientation'. Some of these meet our definition of activist funds but some do not. To identify which of these funds can be classified as activists for the purposes of our analysis, and which of the activists, in turn, can be understood to have taken a confrontational stance with regard to their dealings with the management of the target companies, further contextual information is required. We use a range of other data sources, including press reports and interviews with funds and companies involved in various activist interventions, to draw the necessary distinctions within the wider sample of funds. As we explain further in Chapter 8, without these additional sources, we could not have arrived at an appropriate identification of the sample of hedge fund investments which forms the basis of our quantitative analysis.

The benefits of contextualising quantitative data through background documentary research and interview-based fieldwork are not confined to refining the scope of econometric analysis. There are a number of reasons for carrying out interview-based fieldwork in institutional studies. Interviews can offer access to data on informal institutional phenomena, such as routines and norms, which are not otherwise available. When used in the framework of case studies of particular events, such as the activist hedge fund investments that we have studied, they also permit 'sequence tracing', clarifying chronologies and specifying the direction of causal relations (Poteete *et al.*, 2010: 33).

Qualitative methods are of particular value where there are multiple causal variables in play, and where causal relationships are cumulative and non-linear in their effects. These effects may not be captured adequately by econometric analysis in contexts where variables are interdependent, and where statistical techniques do not readily allow causation to be distinguished from correlation. Thus while qualitative work will always, to some degree, be affected by problems of selection bias in the construction of samples, indeterminacy of results, and limited opportunities for replication, the limitations of quantitative methods also need to be acknowledged (Poteete *et al.*, 2010: 37). A multi-methods research design which seeks to integrate data from different methods, and to take account of contradictions as well as confirmatory trends in the evidence, offers the best prospect of overcoming the limits of individual techniques (Kritzer, 1996; Nielsen, 2010).

We began our fieldwork in 2003 by looking at the adoption of new, formal structures among Japanese listed companies that involved changes to board membership and function, and their impact on managerial behaviour and practice. From 2006 we began to look also at interventions by activist hedge funds, which had commenced roughly from early 2000, but had gained fresh momentum with the entry of assertive foreign funds by 2001, and soon seemed poised to become a major destabilising element in the Japanese corporate governance environment. Our interview data provided us with insights into the beliefs and perceptions of managers, investors, and other relevant actors concerning the phenomenon of hedge fund activism. We had the benefit of obtaining direct access and thereby receiving a more immediate and complete impression of interviewees' beliefs and perceptions than those available from third-party accounts. On several occasions we were given information that corrected apparently misleading or partial versions of events that had been reported in the press.

Interview data consist of subjective perceptions of the respondents. As such, there is a danger that they are neither generalisable, nor perhaps even reliable. Data drawn from a limited sample of interviews cannot be said to be representative in the same way that data drawn from a randomly drawn survey sample might be. However, the reliability of interview data, and their generalisability, can be enhanced in various ways. One is to construct an interview sample explicitly not on the basis of the representativeness of the respondents, but on the degree of salience of the research issue for the interviewees themselves (Webley, 2010: 934). In this vein, we sought out the views of managers in companies which had undergone some kind of alteration or adjustment to their internal corporate governance arrangements, on the grounds that the experiences of this group would reveal more about the dynamics of change in the Japanese corporate governance system during the 2000s than would be the case of a sample of interviewees that was more representative of the listed company sector as a whole. Another method for enhancing the validity of interview data is to obtain multiple views of the same phenomenon or event. In our case this took the form of interviews with funds and the specific companies they targeted. As we shall see in later chapters, these interviews provided evidence of widely divergent perspectives and interpretations of the same events, as well as shared understandings on certain points.

With a multi-methods approach, the limitations of one method can be overcome through the use of another. Thus qualitative techniques can help to supply part of the answer to the question, 'what does rationality mean?' when we are seeking to understand the basis for agents' behaviour, at the point when formal models and related quantitative methods cannot take us any further. The 'basic microeconomic foundations [of] rational self-interested people, profit-maximizing firms, and competitive markets' may provide a starting point for studying the Japanese economy, on the grounds that it is a market-based system like any other (Miwa and Ramseyer, 2006: 160). However, the 'rationality' of the corporate officers, investors, and other parties to whom we spoke was conditioned by the environment in which they were acting. Where, as here, rationality is structured by context, a close analysis of that context is required: 'the specific attributes of the situation in which individuals interact are more important in predicting outcomes than is the model of rational behaviour' (Poteete *et al.*, 2010: 221–2). Without our interview material, it would have been possible to speculate, with some accuracy, that the career structure, promotion patterns, and limited mobility of senior Japanese managers would give them strong incentives to oppose confrontational hedge fund interventions. But it would have been difficult to explain why, as we shall see, many Japanese shareholders and also some overseas investors were reluctant to support hedge fund strategies that were apparently in their best interests as portfolio investors.

2.2 Sources of data

Interview-based data

We carried out 116 interviews in Japan with directors and senior managers at listed companies, institutional investors, regulators, officers at providers of market infrastructure and commercial associations, politicians, lawyers, and commentators. We also met officers of prominent activist hedge funds and representatives of some of the companies they had targeted. Just over half of these interviews (54 per cent) were repeat meetings to explore attitudes to the developing situation. The most recent interviews were conducted in early 2010 when we investigated prospects for activist hedge funds after the financial crisis of 2008 amid expectations of legislative reforms to corporate governance following the change of government in Japan from late 2009. In addition, we carried out several meetings with activist hedge funds and institutional investors in the UK. The interviews were conducted face-to-face, usually at the interviewee's office. In each case we used a semi-structured questionnaire to provide a basis for a discussion which was often more wide-ranging than the initial topics presented. The interviews in Japan were mostly conducted in Japanese, and occasionally in English. The majority were recorded electronically (although some were noted by hand where the meeting place did not facilitate recording), transcribed and, in the case of the Japanese interviews, translated into English. Most of them lasted around one hour. The interviews were all conducted on the basis of anonymity, in that we undertook not to reveal the identity of the organisations or individuals concerned in any published work drawing on the interview material. In a few cases we have subsequently been authorised to attribute comments.

The companies in our sample represented the main manufacturing, utility, and service sectors. They varied in size, from very large multinationals to small, family-run businesses but all of them were listed. As explained above, we intentionally sought interviews at companies where a change of corporate governance practices or pressure to change their practices was proving to be an issue at the time we spoke to them. The majority were active in global markets and most had some degree of foreign share ownership. Many had external directors, and several had adopted the 'company with committees' structure of corporate governance, with a majority of outside directors required for the three board sub-committees dealing with nomination, remuneration, and audit, respectively. Most of our respondents' companies had active investor relations departments.

The investors whose officers we interviewed included major institutional investors active in the Japanese market, both Japanese and non-Japanese, and also some of the hedge funds whose strategies we discuss in this book. The funds we spoke to covered the range of confrontational and non-confrontational strategies. Some did not accept the description 'activist', partly because of its unfavourable connotations in Japan, but all professed to some degree of engagement with at least some of the boards of companies in which they invested.

The other interviews we conducted, as indicated above, were with parties interested in corporate governance developments by virtue of their work as providers of market infrastructure, or with politicians, civil servants, lawyers, or commentators. These interviews helped to focus our research on particular issues that were being debated in Japan and to understand how they were seen more generally.

The Data Appendix at the end of the book contains further details of the sources of our interview data. Table A.1 presents details of the entities visited, broken down by sector, and shows data on the number of meetings for each sector. Table A.2 provides specific information on the corporate visits, in an anonymised form.

Documentary sources

We used press and documentary sources to build up a picture of the wider environment within which the events we were examining occurred. Press reports, despite the inaccuracies noted above, were an important supplement to our research. Financial and other journalists often have direct access to senior managers and officials, and are able to relay the positions taken by their interviewees to a wider audience.

We found this a valuable source of information on the progress of events and on the formal stances that players had adopted.

Documentary and other archival sources provided an understanding of more formal institutions, including legal rules. Our interpretive analysis from these sources has the objective not of offering systematic interpretations of legal rules in the manner of doctrinal legal scholarship, but of charting the influence of ideas and concepts in the official discourse of the courts and bureaucracy. We do not offer, for example, a legal-doctrinal interpretation of the concept of *kigyō kachi* or 'corporate value' which was used in legal discourse as well as more widely in debates concerning hedge fund activism, but instead trace the use of the idea in court judgments and official documents, and examine its impact on corporate practice, evidence for which we found in the statements issued by corporate boards seeking to justify the use of poison pills and other defensive mechanisms.

Quantitative data

In using quantitative methods to understand why activist hedge funds target some companies and not others, and what the results of their interventions are, it was necessary either to have a fully representative sample of target companies or one which approximated as closely as possible to the actual population of targets. We adopted the latter approach. We identified targeted companies and the principal hedge funds involved by combining financial data from the Thomson Reuters[1] and Tōyō Keizai data sets[2] with data from our own, 'hand collected' data set of interventions which we compiled mainly using information from the Japanese FSA's EDINET database (which is described in the Data Appendix), websites, and press reports.

---

[1] We have used various sources provided by Thomson Reuters, the business information services company. Our financial data come from the *Worldscope* database. Our firm level ownership data are from *Thomson ONE Banker*'s ownership module which provides corporate filings and ownership profiles, and basic fund information and profiles.

[2] Tōyō Keizai is a financial magazine and data publisher founded in Tokyo in 1895 which publishes a weekly magazine *Shūkan Tōyō Keizai* on financial topics and has published the *Shikihō* compendium of corporate financial data since 1936. The *Shikihō*, which is also available electronically, draws together data from official returns submitted by companies in Japan to present information on their accounts and share performance in a common format.

For our quantitative research we used as our starting point Thomson Reuters' database of 145 Japanese companies targeted by 'hedge funds' with 'active orientation', whose limitations we have already discussed. After removing targets that we considered, on the basis of the Thomson Reuters classifications, to be financial or real estate investment vehicles, and drawing on other data, from EDINET, press reports, and our interviews, we refined this into a list of 119 companies targeted by a total of 19 funds. We further divided this list, using the criterion of the degree of attention that each of these funds had received from *Nikkei*, into 39 interventions by five funds following 'public' strategies (as defined by the intensity of *Nikkei*'s coverage), and a further 80 investments by the remaining 14 funds that we characterised as 'non-public'. We describe the process of refining the data in detail in Chapter 8. The list of 119 targets and the 19 funds involved is shown in Table A.3 in the Data Appendix.

This sample, even in its reduced format of 119 targets, was known to include funds that were not recognised by practitioners as being activist, and indeed included some funds that specifically rejected such a description. In order to investigate the impact of explicitly confrontational activism, whose impact interested us most, we refined our study further by looking laterally at 34 interventions during the full period 2001–8 by two of the 'public' funds which we considered, from the evidence of press reports, website data, and interview material, to fall into this category (30 of these interventions appeared within the 119 of our original sample but four were omitted because they ended before 31 December 2007), together with observations on the progress of those investments among them that continued to the end of 2010. To produce these data we used mostly EDINET and press reports. Using the same methods, we also identified 44 major interventions by the Murakami Fund between 2001 and 2006 (there were more, but many were not picked up by the EDINET database because they fell below the threshold for public disclosures) and presented these in the same lateral format.

Becht, Franks, and Grant (2010), using a similar basic methodology, identified slightly more investments by activist hedge funds (180) in Japan over the same period. Hamao, Kutsuna, and Matos (2011) identified 759 investments at non-financial companies by what they characterise as US-style activist investors in Japan between

1998 and 2009, involving a total of 34 funds, of which 26 were non-Japanese. These studies appear to interpret activism broadly to include some funds that we consider to be largely passive investors ('value funds' or 'stock pickers') and which we have not categorised as activists.

2.3 Chronological note

Our main research was completed in early 2010. Thereafter, we continued to observe developments and to update information from publicly available sources until the end of December 2010 and carried out further limited updates of particularly relevant matters until the end of September 2011, when our manuscript was finalised (apart from some later internet source confirmations). Events after September 2011 and any implications they may have for corporate governance in Japan or elsewhere are therefore not covered.

3 | Companies, company law, and corporate governance

3.1 Introduction

Our analysis in this book focuses on companies and the processes by which they are governed. The terms 'company' (or in some jurisdictions 'corporation') and 'corporate governance' are, however, ambiguous and contested. Our aim in this chapter is to clarify their meaning and to set out how we intend to use them. We first highlight the distinction between two distinct, if intertwined, notions: one is the legal form, the 'company', which facilitates and underpins concerted commercial activity; the other is the social and economic structure, the 'business firm' or 'business enterprise', through which production is organised. The term 'company' is widely (and to some degree unavoidably) used in both senses, but the two meanings are distinct (Robé, 2011). Failure to distinguish between them, or to be clear about which of them is being used in a given context, is a source of confusion in the corporate governance literature, particularly when the role of the law in shaping corporate activity is being described.

This observation leads on to our second aim in this chapter which is to specify the nature of the relationship between company (or corporate) law and corporate governance. Company law provides an account of the business enterprise which is in significant respects incomplete. The way that company law describes business firms is not necessarily a good guide to the way that they operate as social or economic organisations. Corporate activity and behaviour is shaped, beyond the law, by institutionalised practices of varying degrees of formality. These practices can fill in the gaps left by legal rules and thereby complement their operation, but they can also, on occasion, defeat their purpose, or otherwise render them ineffective. The law is just one part of that wider set of routines, norms, and rules which make up 'corporate governance' in the context of a given national system or individual enterprise.

3.2 The company as a legal form

While the term 'company' can be used to describe a large variety of organisational forms, not all of which have a business purpose, it is most commonly applied to the type of business entity known as a 'joint stock company'. Joint stock companies are widespread throughout the world. In 2010 the World Federation of Stock Exchanges (www.world-exchanges.org) counted 45,508 such companies listed on its 52 member exchanges, with an estimated market capitalisation of over US$54,953,615 million; there are many more which are not listed on any exchange.

Joint stock companies are organisations which engage in industrial or commercial activity, the capital for which is initially supplied by investors who receive, in return, securities ('stocks' or 'shares') which are freely tradable. In a joint stock company, the management of the company's business is the responsibility of its board of directors, which delegates most operational matters to salaried officers. It is possible for a dominant shareholder or group of shareholders, such as a founding family or team of entrepreneurs, to utilise this structure to draw in capital from external shareholders while still maintaining effective control of the company at all levels, in some cases managing the business directly. However, one of the distinctive features of the joint stock company is that it is capable of enduring beyond the lifespan or contribution of its founding members. Many joint stock companies become, within one or two generations, 'widely held' or 'public' entities in which there is no single, dominant shareholder. Such companies will generally offer liquidity of share transfer in order to attract a wider range of investors. By listing its shares on a regulated or public exchange, a joint stock company facilitates the trading of those shares at transparent prices.

Joint stock companies, in the sense that we have just defined them, are the product of a particular legal structure or template which is supplied by systems of company law in a form which is relatively uniform across different national jurisdictions. This template has five central features which are generally referred to as corporate personality, limited liability for shareholders, delegated management, free transferability of shares, and shareholder ownership (Armour, Hansmann, and Kraakman, 2009b; Davies, 2010; Hansmann and Kraakman, 2000, 2001; Pistor, 2011).

The first and most important of these features, *corporate personality*, provides that the company is a legal person in its own right, distinct from its shareholders or members. The company can own property, undertake legal commitments, and be held liable for its trading debts and other obligations in the same way that human persons can. The attribution of legal capacity to the corporate form is the basis for its enduring organisational identity, sometimes called its 'permanence'. By these legal means, the company is separated from its founders, from the initial subscribers of its capital, and from those who hold its tradable securities at any given time, and enabled to hold enduring contractual relationships with its employees and other parties.

The legal personality of the company is not just a 'fiction' or figure of speech. It permits 'entity shielding', or the separation of the company's business assets from the property of its members (Hansmann and Kraakman, 2000; Hansmann, Kraakman, and Squire, 2006; Armour *et al.*, 2009b: 6–9). Formally, this means that the company is not liable for the personal debts (trading or otherwise) of its members. Legal personality is not the only means by which this effect can be achieved, but it is the simplest and most effective one from the point of view of ring-fencing the company's assets. In economic terms, entity shielding facilitates 'bonding', or the exchange of credible commitments, between the suppliers of the different inputs, including those supplying labour and credit, which the firm requires for its business. From an organisation-theory perspective, corporate personality is the foundation of what might be called the firm's organisational capacity, that is, its ability to undertake concerted productive or commercial activity.

The second feature of the legal template of the joint stock company is that shareholders are protected from liability for the company's trading debts. This, the legal rule of *limited liability for shareholders*, is not simply the converse of the entity shielding which the company enjoys by virtue of its separate legal personality (Armour *et al.*, 2009b, 9–11). Limited liability for shareholders adds nothing to the 'bonding' effect of separate corporate personality. Limited liability seems to have played only a minor role, historically, in the emergence of industrial firms in Europe and North America during the course of the eighteenth and nineteenth centuries, many of which were constituted as partnerships or unincorporated associations whose members were directly liable for their business's trading debts (Harris, 2000). Limited liability serves other, important, purposes. The first is to enable shareholders to take a passive role in the management of the firm (Easterbrook and Fischel, 1991: 41–2). Their legal obligations are limited to supplying the capital which is the condition of their initial subscription. This means that shareholders can act as pure retail or portfolio investors, investing solely for returns. They can also diversify their holdings across a wide range of companies without the need to be engaged in the management of all or any of them.

A further effect of limited liability is that individual shareholder wealth becomes irrelevant to investment decisions. In a world of unlimited liability, the company's ability to raise capital and the conduct of its wider business would be dependent in part on the extent of its members' personal assets. As late as the final quarter of the nineteenth century, some companies, such as certain private banks in Britain, were structured in this way, with the result that their wealthy members acted, in effect, as guarantors of their trading commitments (Acheson, Hickson, and Turner, 2011). This structure had the advantage of minimising the risk of moral hazard – referring, in this context, to the ability of shareholders to shift risk onto third parties including the firm's creditors and employees – which was then still widely associated with the limited liability form. It had the disadvantage of limiting the liquidity and tradability of shares, while also preventing all but the very wealthy from participating in share ownership. By the turn of the twentieth century, the large majority of manufacturing and financial enterprises in the leading industrial economies were constituted as joint stock companies with limited liability (Hannah, 2007). This trend responded to, while in turn facilitating, the growth of stock markets based on the participation of retail and portfolio investors. The wide dissemination of share ownership across a range of income groups, and the trading of shares on an impersonal, anonymised basis, which are taken for granted in modern capital markets, would not be possible on their current scale without the legal rule of limited liability (Easterbrook and Fischel, 1991: 43–4). At the same time, concerns remain over its moral hazard implications (Strine, 2008).

The third feature of the legal form of the joint stock company is the rule of *delegated management* (Armour *et al.*, 2009b: 12–14). This is complementary to limited liability which, as just explained, allows shareholders to play no role in the management of the firm. The rule of delegated management goes one step further in stipulating that shareholders have no *right*, merely by virtue of their shareholdings, to be engaged in management. Management – understood as the strategic control of the firm's operations and activities – is vested in the board of directors which, in turn, has the power to delegate operational matters to the company's officers and employees. While shareholders may have certain rights (the content of which differs from one context to another) to nominate, elect, and remove directors, these rights do not confer on them powers of management. Even a dominant shareholder with a majority stake does not, merely by virtue of that status, have the right to intervene directly in management issues.

The rule of delegated management reflects the sense in which the form of the joint stock company involves a division of labour between the suppliers of capital on the one hand and the suppliers of labour on the other. It facilitates managerial specialisation and underpins the operational autonomy of management. The managerial team is insulated from day-to-day shareholder pressure. This creates a space for strategic planning over the medium to long term. At the same time, management remains accountable, through the board, to the shareholders: the shareholders, as a body, can change the strategic direction of the company by voting to replace the board or, in certain circumstances, by endorsing a change of corporate control. The tension between managerial accountability and operational autonomy, sometimes referred to in terms of the separation of ownership and control, is built into the structure of the joint stock company.

The fourth feature of the joint stock company is the legal principle of *free transferability of shares* (Armour *et al.*, 2009b: 11–12). This means that the legal system does not normally impose restrictions on the transfer of shares from one party to another. Shareholders cannot demand the return of the capital which they have invested with the company, but they are generally free to sell their shares to third parties for cash or other consideration. However, the initial subscribers of a company's share capital can contract between them to limit the right of free transfer. More generally, the shares of a company which is a 'closed' or 'private' corporation may not normally be traded on a public exchange. For a company's shares to be traded publicly, it must, as a first step, become what some legal systems describe as a 'public' or 'public limited' company, a move which entails compliance with certain regulatory requirements such as attaining a minimum paid up share capital. The company's listing on a public stock exchange will then involve a further round of regulatory compliance. Listing rules (the rules set initially by the exchanges themselves, which in some jurisdictions have been subsumed into regulatory frameworks underpinned by law) and the rules of securities law (the law regulating trading in capital markets) generally have the purpose of ensuring transparency of share trading and pricing. By proscribing insider dealing and other forms of so-called 'market abuse' they aim to put in place a level playing field between retail and portfolio investors on the one hand and corporate insiders (those with privileged knowledge of corporate transactions and managerial strategy) on the other. In protecting these non-insider investors – often referred to as 'minority shareholders' in contrast to those holding majority or controlling stakes, although minority shareholders can equally become insiders – these forms of regulation also serve to strengthen the mechanisms through which shareholders can hold managers to account. In this way, securities laws, broadly understood to include stock exchange listing rules, complement the phenomenon of the 'widely held' joint stock company.

The fifth and final main feature of the legal form of the joint stock company is sometimes referred to as the principle of *shareholder ownership* (Armour *et al.*, 2009: 14–16). What exactly 'ownership' means in this context is, however, controversial in theory and contested in practice. Shareholders in a joint stock company normally have significant income and control rights which other suppliers of inputs (such as employees and creditors) do not have. These include the right to share in the surplus from production through dividends and share repurchases, the right to determine the composition of the board and hence, in principle, the long-term strategic direction of the company, and rights of decision-making in respect of change-of-control transactions, including mergers and takeovers. These rights are incidents of share ownership, and, at least in systems which require or encourage the practice of one share, one vote, they are proportionate to the size of the financial investment made by a given shareholder. The joint stock company can therefore be thought of as a 'capital cooperative' (Armour *et al.*, 2009: 16), in which there is an underlying symmetry between the risk to which individual shareholders, and shareholders as a class, are exposed, and their control and income rights.

However, these rights do not stem from ownership of the company or of its assets. Ownership of a share does not in itself confer a pro rata interest in or control over an equivalent part of the company's assets. It may well be efficient, from the point of incentives for monitoring, for residual control and income rights to be vested in the shareholders as a class (Easterbrook and Fischel, 1991; Fama and Jensen, 1983; Jensen and Meckling, 1976), but this type of justification or explanation of the legal structure of the joint stock company in no way depends upon the shareholders being constituted as the company's owners.

Nor does the legal structure of the joint stock company require managers to give priority to the interests of shareholders over those of other corporate constituencies. On the contrary, company law recognises, in various ways, the nature of the joint stock company as an exercise in group cooperation for the purposes of which the contributions of the different suppliers of inputs are all of importance. This is reflected, for example, in the way that different legal systems express the duties of directors. In all systems, more or less without exception, the duty of the board is stated in terms of an obligation to act in the best interests of the company. In common law countries this tends to be interpreted as a duty to have regard to the long-term interests of the shareholders (Davies, 2010: 155–7). The concerns of other constituencies or stakeholders can only be taken into account in so far as doing so serves the goal of returning value to the shareholders. In civil law countries, the duty is interpreted somewhat differently, as an obligation to ensure the sustainability of the enterprise over time, with a view to returning value to each of the groups with an interest in its continuing success (Viénot, 1995). In practice, these two conceptions converge (Siems, 2008). In the civil law, there is no legal obligation to place the concerns of shareholders above those of other groups. The common law position is outwardly more supportive of the idea of shareholder primacy, but it allows boards considerable leeway in setting the timescale over which value is to be returned to shareholders, and substantive discretion in determining what arrangements to make with employees and creditors in order to achieve an appropriate shareholder return. Neither legal approach requires the board to *maximise* shareholder value at the expense of other constituencies or interests.

3.3 The incompleteness of the legal model of the company

The legal model that we have just outlined is foundational to the operation in practice of the modern public or joint stock company, but it is also incomplete as an account of the way companies function in contemporary market economies. This dual aspect of company law needs to be borne in mind when considering the role of the legal system within the wider framework of corporate governance.

The legal model is foundational in the sense that it provides the basic framework for the operation of modern joint stock companies. Some of the legal features of the joint stock company could be reproduced by private contract and, indeed, many of the rules of company law are 'default terms' of an implicit corporate contract that the parties can modify if they wish to. Large parts of the legal structure are facilitative rather than directive. However, many of the defaults contained in the corporate 'contract' are regularly applied and observed as a matter of course, thereby achieving a de facto mandatory status (Deakin and Hughes, 1999). In addition, all systems of company law recognise a hard core of rules that cannot be waived (Eisenberg, 1989).

As we have seen, certain institutions that tend to be taken for granted in modern economies, such as stock markets with anonymised trading, would most likely be impossible to recreate without the legal model of the joint stock company in place. But even if it were possible to reconstruct the joint stock company and associated institutions using the raw materials of contract and property law alone, there would be no need to do so given that the legal template of company law has evolved to meet business needs in the way that it has. The result is the complex intertwining of legal form and business practice that can be observed on an everyday basis in the conduct of corporate affairs. In these circumstances, it is not particularly interesting to ask whether company law is irrelevant to the operation of business firms. A more relevant question is how the company law systems that we can observe in contemporary market economies actually shape business activity.

The suggestion that company law plays a foundational role with regard to the constitution of business activity is not equivalent to saying that the company is first and foremost a legal phenomenon before it is an economic or organisational one. This is true neither analytically nor empirically. Analytically, the 'company' (and not just the 'firm') can be defined independently of the legal system. In this vein, Aoki suggests that 'corporations are voluntary, permanent associations of natural persons engaged in some purposeful associative activities, having unique identity, and embodied in rule-based, self-governing organizations' (Aoki, 2010: 4). The features of the legal model of the company which correspond to the elements of this definition can be viewed as functional responses to the needs of associational forms of various kinds. In the more specific context of the business enterprise (which is a subset of the generic form of the 'corporation' or 'company' as defined by Aoki), this relationship can be understood historically as the outcome of a process of co-evolution between legal and economic forms (Deakin and Carvalho, 2011; Pistor, 2011).

The rules of company law can be understood in broad terms as a functional response to the needs of the business enterprise as it has evolved over time. If the process of matching company law to economic conditions were entirely unproblematic, the content of particular legal rules could be assumed to be perfectly aligned with business needs. We have seen already that this is not the case: the legal model of the joint stock company 'solves' certain economic problems (such as responding to the needs of firms for external finance by protecting the interests of minority shareholders) while creating others (the moral hazard implications of shareholders' limited liability). The 'solutions' arrived at by company law are imperfect, incomplete, and contested. This is because the legal form of the joint stock company has evolved over many centuries in a way which reflects the conditions of industrialisation in different countries, as well as their common experience of the rise of the market economy. Its evolution has been marked by historical accident and contingency, and hence by path dependence (Roe, 1996), as much as by pressures from industry and finance for workable rules.

The institution of joint stock can be traced back to commercial ventures designed to share the risks and rewards of overseas trade in the late sixteenth and early seventeenth centuries. The trading ventures organised by Dutch and English merchants were initially structured as discrete projects; each expedition was a separate exercise and the assets were liquidated when the ships returned to their home ports in order to provide the greatest possible return to investors (Vergne, 2008). The first state-sponsored trading companies, including the English and Dutch East India Companies, were set up to channel such investments into a series of voyages. These early joint stock companies were not, however, characterised by the same kind of organisational continuity which we have come to associate with the modern company.

In the British industrial revolution of the eighteenth century, the corporate form was widely used by utilities and banks. Most manufacturing firms, on the other hand, took the form of partnerships or unincorporated associations (Harris, 2000). In the absence of a developed system of company law, trust law and contract law were used to structure the rights and claims of investors and creditors. Although reforms of the 1840s and 1850s made incorporation with limited liability generally available to the founders and operators of businesses, this option was not taken up by most industrial firms until later in the nineteenth century. By contrast, in the USA, France, and Germany, which began to industrialise at a point when legal rules embodying the principles of separate corporate personality and limited liability were already in place, the corporate form was more widely used from the outset. By the end of the nineteenth century the leading industrial economies had more or less converged on the practice of manufacturing and financial firms using the legal form of the joint stock company to structure their activities. However, national company law regimes, their common elements notwithstanding, had already begun to diverge in ways which reflected differences in the initial conditions of industrialisation in those countries (Ahlering and Deakin, 2007).

This process of divergence from a common legal inheritance can be seen in the evolution of the rules governing the relationship between the main organs of the company, namely the board of directors and the shareholders acting in general meeting. In all systems, the growing needs of industrial firms for outside capital, combined with the increasing popularity and availability of share ownership, led to the emergence of legal rules around the turn of the twentieth century which sought to prevent controlling shareholders from deceiving or defrauding other investors and to allow creditors to identify a corporate body to sue (Lobban, 1996). At the same time, the increased specialisation of the management function led to the recognition by the law of the practice of managerial autonomy. In Britain the courts took the view that the board of directors and shareholders' meeting were two separate bodies unable to interfere with each other provided that each acted within the scope of the company's articles of association (Davies, 2008: 368–72). In France and Germany, on the other hand, managerial autonomy was expressed in the legal clarification of the powers of the chief executive (*président-directeur général*) and management board (*Vorstand*) respectively. Thus in their different ways, national systems arrived at a position in which, while shareholders' property rights remained formally intact, the interposition of the legal person of the corporation qualified (and often severely diluted) their ability to exercise these rights. This process enabled legal systems to adjust to the growing organisational presence of business firms within market economies, while leaving many questions concerning the scope of shareholders' control and income rights unresolved.

The modern legal form of the joint stock company is at best a partial and contested solution to the problem of how to reconcile the capital and organisational requirements of firms with the assertion by shareholders of property-type claims. The incompleteness of the legal model of the company is evident in other ways. The lack of an articulated account of the management function within company law is a particularly striking absence. Company law recognises the existence of management largely by limiting the claims of shareholders to intervene in day-to-day decision-making. Aside from stipulating that management is the responsibility of the board and that it can delegate this function, company law has surprisingly little to say about how the firm is organised internally. Employment law partly makes up for this gap by recognising the authority of management to direct production in the form of the open-ended duty of obedience which is implied in the contract of employment. In this way the contract of employment gives juridical expression to the practice of managerial power (Deakin, 2002). The solution is incomplete, however, in part because employment law has an underdeveloped notion of the business enterprise, in which the distinct features of the corporate form are largely invisible (Deakin, 2003).

The law of enterprise liability also casts light on the legal dimension of the managerial function. Health and safety laws and environmental regulations specify in some detail the particular levels of management within firms, even down to specific post-holders, responsible for the delivery of workplace or environmental safety. The appearance of the managerial function of the firm in these areas of law suggests that the legal system is capable of recognising the firm's responsibility for the risks which its activities create for its employees and for third parties. The idea of corporate social responsibility thereby receives a degree of legal expression (Deakin, 2003) but, again, this is incomplete because the law of enterprise liability does not distinguish between business firms according to their corporate form.

The problem here is not so much the failure of the law to acknowledge the various dimensions (financial, organisational, and social) of the activities of the business firm, but rather its inability to provide a unified account of the kind which would enable tensions and conflicts between the firm's multiple roles to be more effectively resolved. There is no integrated legal concept of the firm or enterprise as such (Robé, 2011). The legal concept of the company captures only part of the reality of the contemporary firm. Fragments of a more complete legal model of the firm are to be found scattered across the different areas of law which have a bearing on business activity. Company law, in emphasising the conflicts inherent in the shareholder-manager relation, neglects other, potentially equally important relationships. The emergence of the public company as an enduring entity has made its relationships with its 'stakeholders' – employees, suppliers, and customers who bring valued economic resources to the company and have an interest in its long-term success (Kochan and Rubinstein, 2000) – a critical issue. Some legal systems have incorporated an analysis of the relationship between shareholders and other stakeholders into the core of company law, most notably through the notion of codetermination, involving board-level representation for employees and other groups, in German-influenced systems. The issue is only occasionally recognised in the common law systems and even then in a much diluted form. In 2002 the UK's Company Law Review Steering Committee expressed support for the notion of 'enlightened shareholder value' which it defined in terms of the board's duty 'to achieve the success of the company for the benefit of the shareholders by taking proper account of all the relevant considerations for that purpose', including 'a proper balanced view of the short and long term, the need to sustain effective ongoing relationships with employees, customers, suppliers and others; and the need to maintain the company's reputation and to consider the impact of its operations on the community and the environment' (DTI, 2002: 12). This approach was subsequently embodied in the major reform of company law that was accomplished with the passage of the UK's 2006 Companies Act. It remains an isolated example of an explicit consideration, within the company law systems of the common law, of the position of the company's non-shareholder constituencies, and its impact on corporate practice remains to be seen.

Thus modern company law is the end result of a long process of adjustment to the rise of business firms. The process has been path-dependent and contingent, and the result is a legal template that, while in near-universal use in market economies, is incomplete and contested in numerous respects. The legal model is, however, only one of the institutional influences on the operation of companies. It bears a complex relationship to the wider set of practices, routines, and norms that makes up the system of corporate governance.

3.4 The institutions of corporate governance

Arguably, there has been 'corporate governance' for as long as there have been companies in the modern sense of the term. Today, the term 'corporate governance' is widely used to refer, variously, to aspects of corporate practice, to an area of policy-making, and to a field of research. These usages are all recent. Corporate governance emerged as a focus for debate in policy-making circles in the USA in the 1970s. After the bankruptcy of the railway company Penn Central in 1970, revelations of uncontrolled executive activity led to an enquiry by the US Securities and Exchange Commission and ultimately to New York Stock Exchange requirements for independent audit committees at listed companies (Cadbury, 2002: 7–8). The way in which large companies were governed soon became a topic of general interest but the expression 'corporate governance' itself appears only to have gained acceptance towards the end of the decade, followed by increasingly frequent use during the early 1980s. Fischel, in an article that challenged the prevailing desire for formal controls on management practices in the USA, observed in 1982 that 'the issue of corporate governance has received an enormous amount of attention in the past ten years'. Nevertheless, the earliest reference he cites which uses 'corporate governance' in its title refers to a symposium in 1977 (Fischel, 1982: 1259–60).

Awareness of the concept of corporate governance by this name outside the USA came later. Tricker had specifically discussed it in relation to British corporate practices in the early 1980s (Tricker, 1984), but widespread use in the UK came only after the publication of the Cadbury Report in 1992 – itself a reaction to a series of UK corporate scandals – only slightly before the rise of concern in Japan. As late as 1990, when the National Association of Pension Funds in the UK issued a collection of essays on relationships between the management of public companies and institutional investors (Leigh-Pemberton, 1990) – something that would now be seen as a study in corporate governance – some of the contributors discussed this topic without using the expression 'corporate governance' at all.

The emergence of the corporate governance debate in Japan can be traced to growing unease with prevailing economic and corporate structures in the 1990s as Japanese companies struggled to adjust to harsher economic conditions after the bursting of the equity and land price 'bubble'. As a stream of scandals and corporate collapses shook public confidence in the quality of management at large companies, the idea began to be discussed publicly that weakness in companies' management structures was to blame not only for these immediate problems but also for Japan's wider economic distress (Keidanren, 1997; Morck and Nakamura, 1999: 2). The incidence of articles referring to 'corporate governance' in *Nihon Keizai Shimbun* ('*Nikkei*') illustrates the growth of this awareness.[1] From 1980 until 1991 the term does not appear to have been used at all but thereafter it increased gradually to reach over 150 instances in 1997 – a year when corporate scandals emerged with particular intensity – and has stood consistently in excess of 200 per annum since 2001, although a gradual downward trend has emerged in recent years.

In a highly influential definition, the Cadbury Report on financial aspects of corporate governance of 1992 defined corporate governance as 'the system by which companies are directed and controlled' (Cadbury, 1992: para 2.5). It is significant that Cadbury's definition does not refer to the 'management' of companies. His committee's report was concerned with the mechanisms by which shareholders and others could hold management to account, using the board, among other means, to this end. The Cadbury Report saw management as distinct from and subject to the 'direction' and 'control' which the board and shareholders between them were capable of exercising. The management of the firm was viewed as embedded within a wider governance 'system' consisting of a number of linked elements: company law was one, but widely held assumptions and beliefs about good practice within companies could be equally important as constraints on managerial behaviour. The Cadbury Report helped to popularise the idea of the corporate governance code as a relatively flexible restatement or crystallisation of good practice, which could serve to minimise the conflicts inherent in the shareholder–manager relationship without resort to formal legislation.

---

[1] Our data here refer to usage of the Japanese expression コーポレートガバナンス (*kōporēto gabanansu*) and do not include other expressions such as 企業統治 (*kigyō tōchi*).

Cadbury's definition, and indeed his committee's approach to resolving the problems inherent in the governance of business firms, prompts a number of further issues. It is not clear, first, what is meant in this context by 'good practice'. Second, the process by which practices in the sense of behavioural regularities or routines become instantiated, and thereby legitimated, in codes and laws, remains to be identified. Third, the nature of the feedback loops between these more formal expressions of standards of appropriate behaviour, and the continuously evolving practices of corporate actors, is unclear. To address these issues, a *functional* definition of corporate governance is required, that is to say, one which helps to identify the elements of corporate governance in terms of the functions they perform within the wider system of which they are a part.

Kester, in his discussion of US and Japanese corporate governance practice, offers such a definition when he suggests that corporate governance be understood as 'the entire set of incentives, safeguards, and dispute-resolution processes used to order the activities of various corporate stakeholders, each seeking to improve its welfare through coordinated economic activity with others' (Kester, 1996: 109). This definition is helpful in suggesting that the overall goal or function of governance is to improve coordination among the different corporate constituencies or stakeholders with a view to enhancing the performance of the firm. In this context, it is assumed that the different groups who supply valuable resources to the firm ('stakeholders') have interests which are in principle divergent – they each seek to improve their own welfare – but are capable of being coordinated or reconciled in such a way as to increase the surplus from production. How the surplus is to be divided between the different groups will influence the scope for mutually beneficial cooperation between them. The individual elements or mechanisms of governance are identified by Kester as 'incentives, safeguards and dispute-resolution processes', examples of a wider set which he implies is very broadly defined. We could therefore think of the elements of corporate governance as all aspects of practice (including those instantiated in formal laws or standards) capable of shaping the interaction of the stakeholders. These mechanisms may be derived from the way the legal system allocates residual income and control rights and from the standards contained in corporate governance codes, but also from such factors as the ownership structure of particular firms, the composition and mode of proceeding of boards, and from the way management is conducted within the organisational structure of the firm. As Kester indicates, the shareholder–manager conflict is just one example of the coordination problems to which the elements of corporate governance systems, defined in this broad sense, are seen to respond.

We can go further in identifying more precisely the nature of the types of governance mechanism that operate within the context of the company or business firm. In this regard, Zingales, building on an earlier definition by Williamson (1985: ch. 12), suggests that corporate governance be defined as 'the complex set of constraints that shape the ex-post bargaining over the quasi-rents generated by the firm' (Zingales, 1998: 497). This definition has the merit of locating the analysis of corporate governance within the wider framework of new institutional economics. Zingales' reference to ex-post bargaining implies a functional theory of governance as a response to the incompleteness of contracting in the corporate context. In effect, he supplies an answer to the question of why we need 'governance' of the firm at all. Why is it not sufficient to leave it to the parties themselves to allocate the surplus from production in a way which will maximise their aggregate well-being? The answer is that property rights cannot be costlessly allocated or contracts perfectly enforced. If they could be, there would be no need for the mechanisms of governance. The firm would then be the 'nexus of contracts', centred around the 'legal fiction' of the corporate form, that some accounts suggest (Jensen and Meckling, 1976). The study of corporate governance would consist of the analysis of the equilibrium properties of finance, product, and labour markets at the point, within the firm, where they intersect, while the study of company law would be confined to the listing of the various default terms of a corporate contract that was infinitely adjustable.

If the processes and mechanisms of corporate governance are worth studying in their own right, it must be because the contracts, implicit and explicit, which make up the complex web of relationships that is the business firm, cannot be completely specified. There are three interrelated reasons for thinking that is the case. First, the corporate environment is complex and open-ended (Williamson, 1985: ch. 12). Companies operate in a context where future contingencies can, within limits, be planned for, but cannot be fully anticipated. Financing needs, labour supply constraints, technological requirements, and customer wants and a host of other relevant parameters can all change in ways which are unpredictable, not least in the way they may interact. Second, the subject matter of the exchanges which take place within the context of corporate activity is uncertain. How far this is the case differs from one context to another, but a degree of irreducible uncertainty in the relationship between contracted-for inputs and expected rewards is the rule rather than the exception within the firm. The indeterminacy of expectations of investment returns in a context of shareholder 'lock-in' (Blair, 2003) is a key example, but there are many others, including the open-ended nature of the obligations of the parties to the employment contract (Coase, 1937). Third, alternative mechanisms for resolving contractual uncertainty are only partially effective at best. Markets cannot provide full solutions to incomplete contracting in a context where the parties make relational or 'asset-specific' investments which create the possibility of 'hold up' in the course of performance (Williamson, 1985: chs. 1–2) or where persistent asymmetries of power and information prevent the movement of prices to equilibrium (Greenwald and Stiglitz, 1986). The legal system provides, at best, only imperfect and costly enforcement of contract and property rights (Coase, 1988). This is not to say that market and legal mechanisms are irrelevant in the context of corporate contracting, simply that because the solutions they provide are incomplete, they need to be complemented by mechanisms of governance beyond the legal system (Williamson, 1996: ch. 7).

We may therefore think of corporate governance as a process which is defined to some degree by law and regulation and framed by the market, but which is predominantly influenced by institutionalised practices at firm level, and should be studied, empirically, at that level. These practices have an *institutional* dimension in so far as they acquire a certain regularity through repetition and routine, which may or may not result in their codification in formal contracts, laws, or codes. Institutions, in this sense, represent social practices that have become widely accepted, often to the point of being unquestioned or taken for granted. They are the 'rules of the game in a society' (North, 1990: 3) that emerge on the basis of agents' repeated choices (Aoki, 2001: 26). They capture and condense the generally shared beliefs or common knowledge of a given population of agents. The institutions of corporate governance are not so much imposed on business firms, as representations of corporate practice which emerge from the interactions of the parties to the corporate contract (Aoki, 2010: 12). As such, corporate governance institutions possess the qualities of emergence and complexity: emergence, in the sense that, while originating in the interactions of individuals, they constitute a framework which shapes and directs those interactions, and complexity in the sense of consisting of a number of interlinked and complementary parts, which must be studied in a holistic way and with regard to particular corporate and national contexts if their functioning is to be effectively understood.

A theory of corporate governance institutions should also be capable of providing insights into why and to what extent they differ and how they change. Although corporate law in developed market economies such as Japan and the USA has much in common across national systems, in part thanks to cross-fertilisation and transplants between systems, there are significant differences in corporate law regimes and even more so in corporate practice. There are clear differences in institutional practice between countries; what constitutes 'normal' or taken-for-granted behaviour in a given corporate context is often determined by nation-specific practices. Institutions come to define beliefs, attitudes, and practices in a given national economy on the basis of a co-evolutionary process, though which business firms both shape and respond to their institutional environment: just as 'what organizations come into existence and how they evolve are fundamentally influenced by the institutional framework', so 'as the organizations evolve, they alter the institutions' (North, 1990: 5, 7). Through various pressures for institutional 'isomorphism' (DiMaggio and Powell, 1983), organisations which share a common business environment can converge on the practices which shape the interaction of agents. Thus even across geographically proximate national systems, variety can be observed. Orrù, Biggart, and Hamilton, asking why it was that business groups in Japan, Korea, and Taiwan could be 'so uniform within each market economy, yet so different in comparison with the others', concluded that 'each society creates a context of fiscal, political, as well as social institutions that limit and direct the development of fit organizational forms' (Orrù, Biggart, and Hamilton, 1991: 386–7).

Cross-national variety of corporate governance practices is a consequence in part of the path dependence of institutions. Corporate governance institutions are embedded in the historical processes of development of national market economies. It is because institutions 'cannot be understood completely without an understanding of the environment in which they operate and evolve' that 'researchers studying institutions must place events into historical context' (Galaskiewicz, 1991: 294). Institutions reflect the original conditions of their emergence and their complementarity with features in their environment, to the extent that conscious attempts to alter them, while in principle welfare-enhancing, may not be cost-effective (Roe, 1996: 643–4). Thus some degree of institutional rigidity and autonomy from changes in the environment may be expected, at least in the short run.

Why the issue of corporate governance should have returned to the policy and business agenda as it did in the 1980s, and what the consequences of this have been for corporate practice, will be a theme to which we shall return throughout this book, beginning in the next chapter. At this stage it is sufficient to note the implications of the focus on governance, as opposed to law, in the process of institutional adjustment. The revival of interest in corporate governance has taken place alongside a shift in corporate practice towards the prioritisation of shareholder interests, particularly in the USA and UK (see Chapter 4 below). This move was not determined by the legal system which, as we have seen, recognised the principle of managerial autonomy and acknowledged, if in a qualified way, the interests of non-shareholder stakeholders. The rise of shareholder primacy was, however, a consequence of, and reaction to, the incompleteness of the legal model of the firm. The company law of the final decades of the twentieth century did not dictate that managers in American or British companies should start to see the principal goal of corporate activity as the maximisation of shareholder value, but it did not place significant obstacles in the path of this development. The model of the corporate governance code which used 'soft law' techniques to instantiate the idea of shareholder primacy spread rapidly across developed and developing nations alike in the course of the 1990s and 2000s (Aguilera and Cuervo-Cazurra, 2009). This was a response to a shift in corporate practice to which the legal system was slower to adjust. Some predicted that the shift towards shareholder primacy within corporate practice and corporate governance codes would trigger an eventual move in that direction within the law itself, signifying an end to the debate between shareholder-orientated and managerialist theories of the firm (Hansmann and Kraakman, 2001). However, company law has remained contested terrain, within which a number of different legal conceptions of the business enterprise compete for influence (Armour, Deakin, and

Konzelmann, 2003). As we shall see in more detail in the case of Japan, there has been no 'end of history' for company law.

3.5 Conclusion

This chapter has considered the relationship between company law and the wider system of corporate governance in shaping the activities of business firms. Company law provides a basic template for the operation of the business enterprise which, with respect to its main components, is to be found in a functionally similar form in most national systems. This legal template or model captures the sense in which the enterprise is a complex exercise in group cooperation. Company law evolved in response to the needs of business firms as they, in turn, developed over time within the context of industrialised, market economies. This response has, however, been contingent and partial, and remains incomplete in a number of respects. There is an underlying and unavoidable tension, built into the legal structure of the joint stock company, between the claims of shareholders as external investors, and the organisational need for a specialised and autonomous management function.

To a certain extent, the wider set of institutions which makes up the system of corporate governance is a reaction to the limits of the law. The gaps and ambiguities in the legal model have been filled in by institutionalised practices at the level of the firm, some of which have been captured in the relatively informal and flexible form of the corporate governance codes which many countries have adopted since the 1980s. Increasingly, these codes have stressed the importance of managerial accountability to shareholders as a solution to governance problems at the level of the firm. This move has been associated with the growing acceptance of the principle of shareholder primacy, particularly in the practice of American and British companies. In the next chapter we examine the rise of shareholder primacy in more detail.

4 | *The rise of shareholder primacy in America and Britain*

4.1 Introduction

In this chapter we examine the rise of the concept and practice of shareholder primacy. At the mid-point of the twentieth century, the tension inherent in the structure of the joint stock company, between managerial autonomy and shareholder rights, had been resolved in favour of the former. Large corporations throughout the industrialised world were run by salaried managers against a background of shareholder passivity (Jacoby, 2005a). By the end of the century, at least in the USA and UK, it had become widely accepted that 'the corporation existed to create shareholder value' and that 'other commitments were means to that end' (Davis, 2009: 33). This near reversal in the position of shareholders and managers was not, for the most part, achieved through legal reform. The core legal structure of the joint stock company remained largely unchanged. Takeover regulation and corporate governance codes more clearly reflected growing shareholder influence, but it was above all through a shift in corporate practice, that is to say, in the attitudes of managers and investors, and in the strategic direction of large companies, that the shareholder primacy norm was manifested.

The 'rise' of shareholder primacy could perhaps equally well be called its 'resurgence' from the days of founder shareholders, but this does not entirely capture the sense in which it was a new development. The managerialist firm of the middle decades of the twentieth century was itself a reaction to the control which had been exercised by shareholders over large, publicly held companies prior to that point (Jacoby, 2005a). However, the controlling shareholders of this earlier period were mainly corporate insiders, that is to say, founders of firms, or families which had inherited control from the founders (Hannah, 2007). The revival of shareholder influence in America and Britain which began in the late 1950s and gathered pace in subsequent decades took a different form. In these countries, shareholdings were no longer in the hands of dominant families, but were dispersed across multiple shareholders, in particular pension funds and other institutional or retail investors (Cheffins, 2008). Shareholder influence was increasingly exercised through the mechanisms of the capital market, rather than via the boardroom and the shareholders' general meeting (Davis, 2009). The terms 'shareholder primacy' and 'shareholder value' came into general usage around this time, and as with the expression 'corporate governance', they signified a new phase in the evolution of the modern business enterprise.

In charting the rise of shareholder primacy, we look first of all at its theoretical basis in agency theory and the theory of finance. Then we look at the mechanisms, including independent boards, capital market disclosure rules, and hostile takeover bids, through which growing shareholder pressure on listed companies was expressed in practice in the USA and UK. This is followed by an account of the impact of these pressures on corporate management and strategy. We then consider the nature of the reaction to shareholder primacy, in the form of emerging critiques of the idea and its practice.

4.2 The theory of shareholder primacy

Because 'shareholder primacy' is not a legal or regulatory term of art, but rather an expression used to capture a practice which is only partially encapsulated in regulation, it is not entirely straightforward to define it. We adopt here the definition given initially in the context of the US market by Hansmann and Kraakman to what they refer to as the 'standard shareholder-oriented model' of the firm, or the 'shareholder primacy model' (Hansmann and Kraakman, 2001: 441, 443). This, they suggest, rests on a view which by the early 2000s had become a consensus among business, governmental, and academic elites, based on the following linked propositions:

that ultimate control over the corporation should rest with the shareholder class; the managers of the corporation should be charged with the obligation to manage the corporation in the interests of its shareholders; other corporate constituencies, such as creditors, employees, suppliers, and customers, should have their interests protected by contractual and regulatory means rather than through participation in corporate governance; noncontrolling shareholders should receive strong protection from exploitation at the hands of controlling shareholders; and the market value of the publicly traded corporation's shares is the principal measure of its shareholders' interests. (Hansmann and Kraakman, 2001: 440–1)

What Hansmann and Kraakman call the 'standard model' addresses the tension between shareholders and managers or, as modern agency theory puts it, between 'principals' (the shareholders) and their 'agents' (the managers), within the structure of the modern public company. As we have seen, this is not a new idea. It is inherent in the legal form of the joint stock company, and has led many commentators, from at least Adam Smith in the eighteenth century onwards, to doubt the efficacy of that type of business organisation: 'being the managers rather of other people's money than of their own, it cannot well be expected that [company directors] should watch over it with the same anxious vigilance with which the partners in a private copartnery frequently watch over their own' (Smith, 1776: 330). Interest in the issue reached another high point in the 1930s when Berle and Means advanced the hypothesis of the 'separation of ownership and control' to explain the growing power of a managerial class that had been freed from shareholder influence by the dispersion of ownership in large American companies. Although their classic study argued for a reassertion of shareholder control as one means of limiting managerial power, they also offered the view that 'the owners of passive property, by surrendering control and responsibility over the active property, have surrendered the right that the corporation should be operated in their sole interest', and that 'neither the claims of ownership nor those of control can stand against the paramount interests of the community' (Berle and Means, 1932: 311–12).

In its modern form, the agency-based conception of the shareholder–management relationship can be traced to Jensen and Meckling's influential paper, 'Theory of the firm: managerial behavior, agency costs and ownership structure' (Jensen and Meckling, 1976). This paper used elements of the then emerging new institutional economics, based around the notion of transaction costs, to explain the structure of business firms. In this regard, Jensen and Meckling's account of the shareholder–manager relationship was subtly different from its antecedents. They did not claim that the firm's capital was 'other people's money' or that shareholders' rights were based on their property in the firm (as opposed to their shares). It was, they argued, efficient from the point of view of the minimisation of transaction costs for the large company to be structured in such a way that managers should be exclusively accountable to shareholders. Thus the shareholder-oriented firm was one in which firm value would be maximised, to the benefit of all constituencies or stakeholders, and of the wider community.

The core of the agency–cost argument is the observation that, within the structure of the joint stock company (or, more generally, any company limited by share capital), the shareholders constitute 'residual claimants' whose participation in the surplus from production is entirely contingent on the business success of the firm (see Williamson, 1985: 304–6). All other stakeholders – employees, creditors, suppliers and so on – have income rights which are defined by the contracts they enter into with the firm. The income rights of these other groups are at least partially fixed in the sense that, for example, employment contracts or collective bargaining agreements will set out a given schedule of wages and salaries, and bank loans will stipulate a certain rate of interest. Shareholders who hold 'common stock' have no such guarantee of a return on their investment. Their returns, which may come in the form of dividends or of increases in the market value of their transferable shares, are dependent on the profitability of the enterprise, and, in a basic sense, are proportionate to it. If the firm fails, they will stand last in line to receive any surplus left over after the contractual claims of the other stakeholders have been met. Conversely, if the firm is successful, the surplus it generates will be proportionately reflected in the gains shareholders make through dividends and share price increases.

Jensen and Meckling (1976), in an argument developed further by Hansmann (1996), claimed that within the legal structure of the joint stock company, shareholders had both the means and the incentive to monitor the performance of the firm's management in a way which would ensure an optimal balance between effort and reward on both sides. The structure of the corporate form acknowledged the basic symmetry between risk and return in the 'residual claimant' status of the shareholders by granting the holders of common stock the sole right, within the firm, to hold management to account. This group alone could nominate, elect, and dismiss the members of the board. The holders of 'preference' shares, which conferred priority over the holders of common stock in the event of the company's bankruptcy, had appropriately reduced voting rights, while other stakeholders, such as employees and creditors, had no rights to engage in the governance of the firm, at least as long as it was a going concern.

The argument, so put, was a striking demonstration of the value of the economic theory of the firm in delineating the incentives implicit in legal structures which, at least formally, were described in very different terms. For Jensen and Meckling, the terminology used by company law was mostly just rhetoric and liable to mislead. It was important, they suggested, 'to recognize that most organizations are simply legal fictions which serve as a nexus for a set of contracting relationships among individuals', adding that 'by legal fiction we mean the artificial construct under the law which allows certain organizations to be treated as individuals' (Jensen and Meckling, 1976: 310). It therefore did not matter that company law regarded directors as agents of the company, not the shareholders, or that the board's duty, in legal terms, was to have regard to the company, not the shareholder, interest. Because the company was a 'fiction', it was strictly meaningless to talk of managers acting in its interests. This view was at best a gloss on the complex bundle of rights and obligations which made up the legal concept of the company, and at worst wilfully ignored those elements within company law which supported the practice of managerial autonomy (see Chapter 3 above). However, it was to prove remarkably influential in the evolution of corporate practice and in the formulation of corporate governance standards, to the extent that what was initially presented as a positive or descriptive theory of the widely held company (Jensen and Meckling, 1976: 305–6) became, within the space of a few years, a normative benchmark with the potential to reshape the core of company law itself (Hansmann and Kraakman, 2001: 454).

4.3 The financial model of the firm

Agency theory drew not just on transaction cost economics but also on contemporaneous developments in the theory of financial markets. From the 1960s, the theory of finance increasingly saw capital markets – that is, markets in the issued securities of publicly listed companies – as playing a central role in asserting discipline over management and in ensuring an efficient allocation of society's resources across different corporate projects. The emphasis within agency theory on the efficiency, at the level of the firm, of managerial accountability to shareholders, dovetailed with this broader view on the allocative properties of finance.

From a finance theory perspective, the surpluses or retained earnings of large companies were a potential source of distortions in the process by which scarce resources were allocated by the market to efficient uses within society. Where companies invested their retained earnings in internal projects which produced a lower rate of return than could have been achieved elsewhere, there was a cost to society as a whole. The financial market functioned, among other things, to free up capital from unproductive uses and channel it elsewhere. This was achieved, in the first instance, by self-interested portfolio or retail shareholders putting pressure on firms to release unused or mis-used capital through dividends and share 'buy-backs' (whereby the company purchased issued stock, thereby returning value to shareholders in proportion to their holdings). Such shareholders, who by definition invested purely for profit, would then serve as the conduit for the reallocation of capital to higher value-creating uses.

This idea chimed with the suggestion of agency theory that, within the structure of the joint stock company, self-interested managers were likely to 'appropriate larger amounts of the corporate resources in the form of perquisites' (Jensen and Meckling, 1976: 313). This was particularly likely where firms had substantial retained earnings or, as it was put, 'free cash flow'. The problem was 'how to disgorge the cash rather than investing it at below the cost of capital or wasting it on organizational inefficiencies' (Jensen, 1986: 323). The solution lay in empowering external shareholders and more generally in activating the mechanisms of the capital market.

To this end, the idea gained ground that the surplus generated from production was 'shareholder value' which it was the duty of management first to create and then to distribute to the shareholders as a group. Shareholder value was a 'new standard for business performance', within which generating dividend and share price increases was the 'fundamental objective of the business corporation' (Rappaport, 1986: 12). Shareholder value maximisation provided managers with 'a single objective' (Jensen, 2001: 9) which would enable them more effectively to meet the demands of all the 'various corporate constituencies such as employees, customers, suppliers, debtholders and stockholders' (Rappaport, 1986: 20). This was, then, a precept which was presented as a guide for sound management rather than as a justification for shareholder benefits. It was completely consistent, according to its proponents, with the view that 'managers must pay attention to all constituencies that can affect the value of a firm' (Jensen, 2001: 13).

The assertion of shareholder value was also part of a wider process of growing financial influence over societal decision-making. At the root of this approach was the claim that the prices of publicly traded shares were informationally efficient, at least in the sense of embodying all relevant public information about alternative investments (Fama, 1970). This 'efficient capital market hypothesis' was initially put forward in the 1970s to explain the efficiency of the anonymised trading of shares and the associated trend towards the diversification of shareholders. Investors could generally rely on share prices to provide an accurate picture of investment opportunities, and, conversely, could not expect to 'beat the market', at least over the longer term, through specialised investment strategies. In time, the theory of efficient stock pricing came to acquire a wider significance, as the basis for the argument that a wider set of decisions on resource allocation could best be made by reference to the valuation placed by equity prices on different projects. As this was put by a prominent academic economist and public official around the turn of the millennium:

There are two broadly different views that thoughtful people take about financial systems. I confess that I have become increasingly convinced that while there are elements of truth in both of them, the dominant truth lies in the second that I am going to present. The first view holds that there is production of real things and then there is transacting and financial claims, that real things have real value, that transacting in financial claims is a zero sum gain, carried on by paper entrepreneurs to relatively little social benefit. The second view, and the view that I think increasingly needs to be understood in our body politic, is [that] the task of a financial system is to make the most important decisions that society makes. Where is its capital going to be allocated for the future? How is the use of that capital going to be monitored when it is entrusted to particular individuals or particular institutions? How much of society's resources are going to be allocated to the present and how much are going to be oriented to the future? And that is very much what financial systems are all about … The emphasis on shareholder value, while not always right, and while markets obviously make mistakes, has proved to be a major discipline in bringing about restructuring and change that have very substantially increased the efficiency of our economy. (Summers, 2001)

Thus the shareholder value norm was presented as a necessary step in the modernisation and competitive renewal of the American and British economies. In other words, it was primarily justified in public interest terms. At the same time, an unavoidable part of the rise of shareholder primacy was 'the increasingly strident assertion of the property rights of owners as transcending all other forms of social accountability of corporations' (Dore, 2008: 1098). This was reflected in the regulatory framework for corporate governance and capital markets and in the practice of management at large British and American firms.

4.4 Mechanisms of shareholder primacy: institutional shareholders, takeover bids, and independent boards

The shareholder primacy idea did not emerge in a vacuum. In the USA and UK, the growing assertion of shareholder rights was associated with the rise of an increasingly powerful economic constituency, the institutional investors. Starting from a low base in the 1950s, institutional investors in the USA – a broad category which included insurance companies, mutual funds, and pension funds, all of which invested on behalf of a wider, disparate group of private or 'retail' investors – rose in significance as owners of the shares of listed companies and eclipsed family shareholders. Institutional investors, so defined, held 47% of publicly traded US equities in 1987, a figure which rose to 61% in 2000 and 76% by 2007 (Conference Board, 2008). Changes to pensions law made by the federal Employee Retirement Income Security Act ('ERISA') in 1978 clarified the investment mandate of pension funds in such a way as to emphasise their duty to maximise the financial returns to their beneficiaries and to encourage their investment in equities. In the UK, the dominance of institutional investors was even more clearly felt: by 1981, domestic institutional shareholders and foreign investors (most of which could be assumed to be institutions) held 61% of all issued shares, and by 2006 this had risen to over 81% (ONS, 2010).

The institutions operated somewhat differently as corporate governance actors in the two countries (Armour and Skeel, 2007). In the USA their influence was felt in the form of public pressure on listed companies to return capital through dividend increases and share buybacks, by their support for litigation over takeover bids and other corporate governance issues before the state and federal courts, and via their occasional involvement in 'proxy fights' (voting contests) for the control of publicly listed companies. In the UK, the concentration of financial interests in the City of London, the limited role played by the courts in regulating corporate activity, and the willingness of successive governments to defer to self-regulation by the major financial trade associations and professional bodies, gave the institutions greater scope for direct influence over the regulation and practice of corporate governance. In addition to exercising informal influence over the conduct and strategy of listed companies 'behind the scenes' (Black and Coffee, 1994), the institutions were influential in the emergence and development of a series of self-regulatory codes in the areas of takeover regulation and corporate governance more generally which gave expression to the shareholder primacy norm.

The first hostile takeover bids, which occurred in both countries around the same time in the mid-1950s, were cautiously, even sceptically received, but also initiated a debate about minority shareholder protection which was to lead to the development of takeover regulation as a specialised branch of securities law with wider implications for corporate governance. Before these developments, boards were accustomed to being able to 'just say no' to unwelcome approaches. The board of the company approached by a potential purchaser – the 'target' company's board – had no legal duty to pass on any offer to its shareholders, or to provide them with information on the financial merits or otherwise of a bid. In the course of the takeover of British Aluminium in 1958–9, the target's directors, apparently unconcerned that the company's share price had been trading at an historically low level, were surprised to receive an offer from two industrial bidders for the whole share capital of the company. They rejected the offer and initially planned a sale of shares to a friendly minority investor at a price some 22 per cent below the offer price. When the bidders appealed directly to the company's shareholders and publicised this anomaly, British Aluminium's board arranged a counter-offer from a consortium supported by most of the City of London merchant banks, and informal pressure for the bid to be called off was exerted through the Bank of England. The bid nevertheless went through, at a slightly increased price, as the company's shareholders were clearly in a position to benefit from the offer (Armour and Skeel, 2007). The bidder's adviser, Siegmund Warburg, was subsequently shunned by most of the London financial establishment. As a member of another bank, one of the few still on speaking terms with Warburg, is reported to have said to him at the time, 'no company director whose shares are publicly traded can sleep well from now on, because he must always wake up in the middle of the night and wonder who will make a raid on his company' (Chernow, 1993: 647–54).

The British Aluminium case showed that, in the right circumstances, shareholders could dictate the fate of a company independently of the wishes of its board of directors. However, that case, together with a few other isolated cases of hostile bids, also highlighted the potential for discriminatory treatment of minority shareholders. This triggered the adoption by City financial institutions, with the support of the Bank of England, of the code of practice known as the 1959 Notes on Amalgamations and Reconstructions, which formed the beginning of takeover regulation in the UK. This matured into the City Code on Mergers and Takeovers in 1968, subsequently renamed the Takeover Code (Johnston, 1980). The Takeover Code, which is largely the crystallised expression of the practice of the Takeover Panel, a body which gives guidance and rulings on the conduct of takeover bids, remains in force in a progressively amended form to this day. The Takeover Code sets out a series of principles, together with more detailed and specific regulatory provisions, which express the idea of shareholder sovereignty in relation to public tender offers: the responsibility for deciding the outcome of the bid rests with the shareholders, not the board; shareholders should be treated equally in the course of a bid, to the extent of being given the opportunity to tender their shares in response to a public offer and to participate, in proportion to their holdings, in the premium generated by the bid; boards have a duty to provide financial information to shareholders on the merits of a bid; and boards may not take frustrating action to defeat a bid (see Davies, 2008: ch. 28).

In the USA, takeover regulation took a different path, which reflected the more diffuse influence of institutional shareholders within the US system (Armour and Skeel, 2007). The form of tender offers for the shares of listed companies was regulated from the late 1960s by federal securities legislation, but the main focus of regulatory activity was the legality of takeover defences under state company law. Companies responded to an increase in the volume and scale of hostile bids in the first half of the 1980s by putting in place defences of various kinds, known in the USA as 'poison pills', which were intended to deter or defeat bids by, for example, authorising the board to issue shares at an undervalue to a friendly third party. After some vacillation, the courts of Delaware, the leading state for the incorporation of larger companies, established that poison pills could be triggered where a target board considered that to do so was necessary in order to preserve long-term shareholder value. To this end, the board was entitled to take into account the interests of other corporate stakeholders. Around this time a number of states enacted 'corporate constituency statutes' to much the same end. The Delaware courts, however, in a move followed more generally, ruled that a poison pill or similar defence could not be applied where the sale of a company was held to have become inevitable, as would be the case where more than one bidder entered the fray and an 'auction' began. The 'zig-zags' undertaken by the Delaware courts can be explained by the position of Delaware as the principal state of choice for incorporation; in a context where companies were free to decide in which jurisdiction to incorporate, the Delaware courts and legislature had to strike a balance between shareholder rights and management demands for protection from what some saw as illegitimate shareholder pressure (Roe, 1993).

Takeover waves have come and gone since the mid-1980s, driven partly by fashion and sentiment, and also by factors in the economic environment such as the availability of bank finance, which is related in turn to the level of interest rates and to conditions in the macroeconomy (Winter, 1993). Hostile takeovers – defined as bids which, at least initially, are not welcomed by the board of the target company – can be observed at a significantly higher level in America and Britain than in other industrialised economies (Jackson and Miyajima, 2007). Even in the USA and UK, however, they only account for a few tens of transactions, at most, in a given year (Deakin and Slinger, 1997). The wider importance of the hostile takeover movement lay in legitimating the idea of shareholder primacy and prioritising shareholder value. Increases in dividend payments and, in particular, in share buy-backs have reflected this trend. Thus companies which may never receive a hostile bid or be considered to be a viable target indirectly feel the pressure of the 'market for corporate control'. As Manne had predicted in the early stages of this process in the USA, the takeover mechanism has come to serve as a general disciplinary device, shaping decisions on corporate structure and investment, and providing a backdrop to the evaluation and reward systems of senior executives (Manne, 1965).

A rather different focus is that provided by corporate governance codes setting out standards for the conduct and performance of
boards of directors. Company law in Britain and America imposes
a duty of care on individual directors which can, in exceptional circumstances, result in personal liability. However, traditionally the law
did not define what the precise obligations of a director were, except
in the most minimal terms. A director could in principle act in either
an executive or non-executive capacity. The responsibilities of executive directors stemmed from their managerial positions and duties,
but those of non-executives were not defined. They did not have a
specific duty to monitor the executive directors or the wider management team, and the board as a whole was not seen, in legal terms at
least, as necessarily having a monitoring role. As late as the 1980s
in Britain, non-executives were held to a very low standard of care
according to which their subjective knowledge and capabilities set
limits to their legal responsibilities (Davies, 2008: 475–574; Deakin,
2011a: 527–30).

As we saw in Chapter 3, pressure for the nomination to boards of
independent directors – those with no existing or prior connection to
the company, either as employees or principal customers or suppliers –
began in the 1970s as a result of large-scale corporate failures, beginning with the Penn Central bankruptcy in the USA, which revealed
board-level inertia, ignorance or worse. In Britain, this trend received
impetus from the collapse of several listed companies in the recession
of 1990–1. The failures of Polly Peck and Coloroll led to the establishment of the Committee on Financial Aspects of Corporate Governance
(the 'Cadbury Committee'). While the Committee was sitting, two further scandals, involving the collapse of the BCCI bank in 1991 and
the Maxwell group of printing and publishing companies in 1992,
reinforced the pressure for more effective mechanisms of governance. Cadbury's response was consistent with the British tradition of
financial self-regulation: a code of practice, based on the principle of
'comply or explain', the effect of which was to place a listed company
under an obligation (through the operation of the then listing rules of
the London Stock Exchange) either to observe the standards set out
in the code or to disclose its reasons for not doing so. This approach
was intended to allow companies to tailor the form of compliance
to their own individual circumstances, while providing a market test,
based on the reaction of share prices, to those opting out of the code's

provisions. In terms of substance, at the core of the Cadbury code is the idea of managerial accountability to shareholders: 'The shareholders as owners of the company elect the directors to run the business on their behalf and hold them accountable for its progress. The issue of corporate governance is how to strengthen the accountability of boards of directors to shareholders' (Cadbury, 1992: para. 6.1).

The solution proposed by Cadbury was to encourage companies to appoint non-executive directors to sit alongside executives on corporate boards. Over time, in the case of the UK Corporate Governance Code (as it now is), this has developed into a standard according to which independent directors should comprise at least half of the board at larger companies (UKCGC, 2010: B.1.2), although, consistently with the comply-or-explain approach, the precise definition of independence is to some degree for the board to decide. A related aspect of good practice suggested by Cadbury was for the separation of the roles of CEO and board chairman. Subsequent reports dealt with a number of related corporate governance matters. The most significant, the Turnbull report of 1999, suggested that boards of listed companies should put in place a system of internal audit in order to oversee the company's business, investment, and reputational risks, and report periodically on its operation (Turnbull, 1999). In this way, the basic legal duty of the board to take responsibility for the management of the company's business, if necessary by delegating that task to officers and employees, was amplified into an obligation within the framework of the comply-and-explain approach to monitor the execution of tasks, and to report back on this review of operational matters to the wider shareholder body.

The concepts established by the Cadbury Report have been widely diffused across the world (Aguilera and Cuervo-Cazurra, 2009), and have influenced the content of international restatements of best practice in corporate governance, most notably the OECD's Corporate Guidelines of 2004 (OECD, 2004). They have had least influence in the USA, for a number of reasons. The tradition of regulating through a quasi-voluntary code is less well established in the US context, and the practice of appointing independent directors was in any case well established. By 2005 approximately 75 per cent of directors on the boards of large US-listed companies were independent, an increase from around 20 per cent in the 1950s (Gordon, 2007: 1475). A combination of stock exchange rules and legislation (notably the Sarbanes

Oxley Act of 2002) made it mandatory for listed companies to have a majority of independents on the main board and audit committee.

Cadbury's emphasis on the shareholders as 'owners' and the absence of a role for other stakeholders in the governance process was consistent with the shareholder primacy approach, although this expression does not appear anywhere in the 1992 report. The British government-sponsored review of company law which began in 1997 came down in favour of the principle of 'enlightened shareholder value' (see Chapter 3 above), which can be thought of as a qualified form of shareholder primacy: the board must have regard to the long-term interests of shareholders, while retaining a discretion to take the interests of other stakeholders into account as a means to that end. In the USA, as Gordon (2007) puts it, one of the main functions of independent directors in the US context has been seen as enhancing 'the fidelity of managers to shareholder objectives, as opposed to managerial interests or stakeholder interests' (Gordon, 2007: 1469). As we have seen, Delaware law, in an approach reminiscent of 'enlightened shareholder value', allows the concerns of stakeholders to be taken into account, within limits, in the context of change of control transactions. Thus the principle of shareholder sovereignty is not absolute in either system. However, the practical consequences of shareholder primacy for managerial behaviour and strategy have been profound.

4.5 The impact of shareholder primacy on managerial practice

Consideration for the interests of minority shareholders on the part of management in the USA is still a fairly new phenomenon. Hamilton (2000) suggests that 1950 marked the turning point from the domination of management at large US companies by family interests to the pre-eminence of professional, salaried managers. At this time there was, if anything, a pro-management orientation on the part of shareholders:

Shareholders who were unhappy with management exercised the 'Wall Street Rule' and simply sold their shares into the market. In turn this process of self-selection meant that shareholders of a corporation at any one time tended either to have a favourable view of management's performance or at least an acquiescent attitude towards management – a pro-management bias. With this composition of the body of shareholders, management was assured that shareholders would routinely approve management proposals. (Hamilton, 2000: 350)

In this environment, chief executives enjoyed great autonomy and boards typically found it difficult to remove them, even where they proved incompetent. In the case of the Penn Central bankruptcy, some directors apparently only learned what had happened from the newspapers. In his study of how American boards operated, conducted over the two years prior to mid-1971, Mace found that although some exercised decision-making powers, many of them did not. He reported the opinion of an executive vice president about his company's board meetings as follows: 'Before our one-hour monthly board meeting, I know exactly what is going to happen, and I know that the eight outside directors are not going to ask any questions. They may ask for clarification of some expressed position of the management, but that is all. Hell! I could write the minutes of the meeting before the meeting is held!' One company president told Mace, 'I would never take a capital appropriation request to the board. What in the world would they know about it!' (Mace, 1971: 44, 53).

By the 1990s, there had been an almost complete inversion of this position. The shareholder value norm had become internalised at the level of managerial practice in the USA and UK. As Froud, Haslam, Johal, and Williams (2000) showed, in a study of UK practice, shareholder value metrics measuring the value created by investments against the overall cost of a company's capital, which originated in the work of consultancies in the 1980s, were increasingly being used to evaluate and reward managers, and to benchmark the performance of entire companies. In their view the shareholder value norm had a wide appeal which was to some degree independent of its supposed significance as an indicator of corporate performance:

The idea of financialization as the new kind of competition captures elements of what is going on and has a certain 'that's it' plausibility for corporate managers. This schema appeals strongly to senior managers who often struggle with external requirements without understanding the structural limits of high labour costs, capital requirements or saturated product markets; and must always try to motivate others by at least appearing to plan for emergent reality. As for consultants and business school researchers, they would find this kind of schematicism congenial because they produce interpretations and recipes for success which generally flatter management agency and presume that management can both understand and change the world in a way which realizes intention and capability. (Froud, Haslam, Johal, and Williams, 2000: 104)

The extent of internalisation was such that some of the managers interviewed by Barker, Hendry, Sanderson, and Roberts for their empirical research on board–shareholder relations in the UK 'were almost more dedicated to the pursuit of shareholder value than the fund managers they were meeting'. Managers used compliance with shareholder value benchmarks to augment their internal authority: 'having fashioned themselves in the image of the demand for shareholder value and been acquitted of guilt in their encounter with the shareholder, they thereby achieve the capacity to speak for the investor within the business, and can add the weight of investor power to their own hierarchical authority' (Roberts, Sanderson, Barker, and Hendry, 2006: 288). Thus shareholder value did not just take the form of pressure on managers and board coming from the investment community. This research found that while some managers drew a distinction between creating long-term shareholder value and satisfying the short-term demands of the market, in practice the borderline between these two conceptions of value was blurred (Hendry, Sanderson, Barker, and Roberts, 2006, 2007).

Dore noted the consequences of this shift for corporate strategy in this account of the changing attitudes of managers in US companies:

They operate under the close surveillance of a board of directors who represent exclusively the interests of shareholders and may frequently include a dominant shareholder. In the mixture of motivations that drive their work, notions of doing a socially useful job or building an organization which will last and will honour their memory are likely to be overshadowed by the carrots and sticks of stock options, bonus systems and the overhanging threat of instant dismissal – all carefully designed, and specific in hard-bargained employment contracts, to induce them to meet those shareholders' expectations. And those expectations are now much more likely to be a steadily rising, rather than a stable, return on equity. (Dore, 2008: 1103)

British managers, similarly, had 'come to transform themselves, their understanding and actions, in the image of investors' desires' (Roberts *et al.*, 2006: 287).

4.6 The reaction to shareholder primacy

The rise of shareholder primacy was not uncontested. A first critique was associated with stakeholder theory, the body of ideas associated with the work of the Stanford Research Institute from the 1960s onwards (Freeman and McVea, 2001: 190). Stakeholder theory argued for the importance of an approach to managerial strategy that took the multiple perspectives of the firm's different constituencies into account. In itself, this did not amount to a core challenge to shareholder primacy, since the advocates of the shareholder value norm could readily accept the idea that management should consider the interests of employees, creditors, and others: 'To the extent that stakeholder theory says that firms should pay attention to all their constituencies, the theory is unassailable' (Jensen, 2001: 9). A more radical critique, at least from the point of view of corporate governance regulation and practice, was that the shareholder primacy approach did not provide an adequate account of the role of the board, or of the managerial function more generally. In this respect, 'team production theory' emphasised the sense in which the business firm was 'a "nexus of firm-specific investments" in which several different groups contribute unique and essential resources to the corporate enterprise, and who each find it difficult to protect their contribution through explicit contracts' (Blair and Stout, 1999: 275). Each stakeholder group, it was argued, agreed within the terms of the corporate contract 'to give up control rights over the outputs from the enterprise and over their firm-specific inputs', deferring to the board as 'mediating hierarchs' to run the company for the benefit of all (Blair and Stout, 1999: 291, 296). For shareholder value advocates, this view was defective in allowing managers excessive discretion to run the business as they saw fit (Jensen, 2001). In the course of the 1990s and 2000s these differing views of the firm were increasingly put to the test by reference to empirical evidence of their apparent economic effects.

In 1992 Porter published an analysis of the American system of capital investment in which he noted, among other things, that 'the US system first and foremost advances the goals of shareholders interested in the near-term appreciation of their shares – even at the expense of the long-term performance of American companies'. He conceded the advantages of flexibility that were conferred by this system but questioned whether it was encouraging healthy long-term investment behaviour by corporate management, particularly in comparison with the German or Japanese models (Porter, 1992: 67, 74). Kennedy (2000) argued on the basis of corporate case studies that a focus on shareholder value at the expense of long-term planning and investment was leading outwardly successful companies into a situation where they had 'mortgaged their futures in return for payback now' (Kennedy, 2000: 69). Lazonick and O'Sullivan extended this critique to a more far-ranging examination of the impact of shareholder-value orientated corporate governance on firm-level innovation (Lazonick and O'Sullivan, 2000). As O'Sullivan observed elsewhere:

The Anglo-American debates on corporate governance that have taken place over the last two decades have been largely confined to shareholder theory, the dominant perspective, and stakeholder theory, its main challenger. Both theories of corporate governance recognize the fact that, in practice, 'residual returns' that cannot be attributed to the productivity of any individual factor are generated by business enterprises and persist for sustained periods of time. Indeed, it is with the allocation of these residual returns that they are centrally concerned. The focus of these theories is on the recipients of the residual, and how this affects corporate performance, rather than on how these residuals are generated through the development and utilization of resources. (O'Sullivan, 2000: 41)

In similar terms, Yoshimori argued that the focus of governance research had been misplaced: 'so far most researchers have been dealing with corporate governance issues without relating them to the interwoven areas of corporate mission, corporate culture, corporate ethics and strategy' (Yoshimori, 2005: 456).

These arguments had little resonance as long as the American economy, in particular, maintained outward signs of success. Throughout the 1990s, as 'US investors were intoxicated by what the shareholder value model apparently had wrought', they 'concluded that changes in corporate governance had produced the US boom' (Jacoby, 2005b: 80). Summers, responding directly to the investment-based critique of shareholder value, argued in 2001 that it was 'impatient, value focused shareholders who did America a great favor by forcing capital out of its traditional companies, and thereby making it available to fund the venture capitals and the Ciscos and the Microsofts that are now in a position to propel our economy very rapidly forward' (Summers, 2001).

The crisis triggered by the collapse of Enron in the same year gave momentary pause for thought, as Enron was a company which had very publicly articulated the virtues of a shareholder-value-based approach to management and of related accounting and human resource practices. The 'dark side' of shareholder value (Bratton, 2002) provided evidence from inquiries into Enron's bankruptcy of the 'possible perverse incentives the shareholder principle exerts on management' identified shortly before by critics of the mainstream approach (Koslowski, 2000: 138). The original proponents of agency theory were now among those who argued that the overvaluation of shareholder equity in the period of the 'dotcom bubble' between 1998 and 2001 had led to investment in non-productive activities and in the destruction of wealth through speculative takeover bids (Jensen, 2005). However, the policy response to the crisis in governance triggered by the bursting of the bubble and the collapse of Enron was to reinforce the prevailing model (Deakin and Konzelmann, 2004). In the USA, the Sarbanes Oxley Act of 2002 reinforced the principle of management accountability to shareholders by imposing for the first time minimum statutory requirements for independent director membership of board sub-committees. The Act also put in place an extensive statutory regime governing internal audit procedures and tightened corporate disclosure requirements. In the UK a parallel reform of the Combined Code on Corporate Governance (now the UK Corporate Governance Code) was conducted in the same spirit, resulting in new standards intended to emphasise the autonomy of independent directors from the company's management and from the executive members of the board.

During the 2000s, far from declining in importance, the shareholder value model which was widely associated with both the British and American economies, notwithstanding certain differences in law and practice between the two countries (Armour and Gordon, 2008), attained wider influence as a template for reforms to law and practice in other countries (Armour, Deakin, Lele and Siems, 2009a). For a time, at least, it could still confidently be asserted that 'the triumph of the shareholder-oriented model of the corporation over its principal competitors is now ensured' (Hansmann and Kraakman, 2001: 468). The financial crisis which began in 2007 led to a serious rethink. A higher failure rate of banks and other financial sector companies with a substantial independent director presence and strong external shareholder influence has been identified in several empirical studies (Adams, 2009; Beltratti and Stulz, 2010; Erkens, Hung, and Matos, 2009; Fahlenbrach and Stulz, 2010; Ferreira, Kirchmaier, and Metzger, 2010), confirming worries over the moral hazard implications of excessive shareholder protection at the cost of diluting boards' executive expertise (Strine, 2008). Yet while there has been a tangible loss of influence of the Anglo-American model in other countries, including Japan (Nakatani, 2008), this has not yet led to the abandonment of the model in its 'home' jurisdictions (Deakin, 2011b).

4.7 Conclusion

In this chapter we have examined the rise of the idea and practice of shareholder primacy in the British and American economies. We saw that, from a theoretical perspective, the roots of shareholder primacy lie in agency theory and the related aspects of the theory of finance which came to the fore from the 1970s. In contrast to earlier accounts of the separation of ownership and control in the widely held joint stock company, these theories did not begin from the premise of shareholder ownership of the firm. Instead, the principle of managerial accountability to shareholders was advanced as the basis for the maximisation of firm value and for the optimal allocation of societal resources. This necessitated the activation of capital market mechanisms for ensuring effective control of managerial discretion, in particular over the distribution of the free cash flow generated from corporate earnings. Agency theory and finance theory intersected with developments in corporate and financial practice which assisted the spread of these ideas. The rise of institutional shareholders as an influential constituency able to put direct pressure on corporate managers and to lobby for corporate governance standards reflecting their interests advanced this agenda. It was then manifested in developments in securities law, principally in the form of the protection of minority shareholder interests in the context of takeover bids, and in the emergence of corporate governance codes and, in some contexts, legal changes setting out standards for the independence of boards. Over time, the principle of shareholder primacy has been very largely internalised by the senior managers and boards of large American and British companies, and reflected in corporate strategy and practice. This remains the case notwithstanding some questioning of the now dominant model in the face of the corporate scandals of the early 2000s and the global financial crisis which began in 2007.

The theory and practice of shareholder primacy provide essential context for understanding the phenomenon of hedge fund activism. We now turn to an analysis of the links between them.

5 | *The emergence of activist hedge funds*

5.1 Introduction

In this chapter we chart the rise of hedge funds in general and of hedge fund activism in particular as a type of investment strategy. Hedge fund activism is intimately bound up with the idea and practice of shareholder primacy, according to which the principal purpose of the company, and the overarching goal of corporate management, is to return value to its shareholders (see Chapter 4 above). However, the immediate purpose of hedge fund activism is not to improve corporate governance practices. This may be one of its consequences, but it is an indirect effect of the hedge fund managers' goal of providing absolute or real returns for their investors which outstrip the market norm.

Hedge funds in general are a response to the demands of certain types of investors for above-average returns, for which they are prepared to forego some of the protections available to investors in more cautiously managed asset classes. More conventional institutional investors, such as pension funds or mutual vehicles such as unit trusts, which handle the savings or insurance monies of the general public, are restricted in the risks they can take by regulation and by the expectations of their investors for stable returns with minimal danger of capital loss. As long-term custodians of the funds at their disposal, they tend to prefer limited-risk, limited-return strategies, many of which are based on index-linked instruments that track share price movements in the market as a whole. Hedge funds, by contrast, offer the possibility of above-average investment performance, together with the related risk of greater losses should these strategies fail; in this respect they are similar to other specialist investment funds focused on particular asset classes such as property, commodities, or private equity opportunities. What is loosely termed the 'hedge fund sector' covers a wide range of funds with often disparate strategies and also includes the so-called 'activist hedge funds'.

In charting the emergence and development of hedge fund activism, we first examine the growth of hedge funds in general as a type of investment vehicle, before defining the core features of activist hedge funds as a distinct subset of the wider hedge fund category. We then look in more detail at the operations of activist hedge funds in their main markets, namely the USA (where they originated), the UK, and mainland Europe.

5.2 The hedge fund sector and activist hedge funds

The nature of hedge funds and hedge fund activism

'Hedge fund' is a generic term that has come to include a variety of very different investment vehicles. Although some definitions of the term 'hedge fund' exist, they are not very informative. For example, the draft EU Directive on Alternative Investment Fund Management includes hedge funds in a category of 'alternative' funds which also covers private equity funds and specialist investment vehicles focused on certain asset classes, such as property or commodities. This classification defines hedge funds negatively, by reference to their exclusion from the categories of pension funds or unit trusts which are subject to specific regulations, rather than by reference to what they actually do (Ferran, 2011). The US Dodd-Frank Act of 2010 takes a similar approach (Skeel, 2010).

The origins of hedge funds are usually traced to developments in the USA such as the 'investment trusts' of the 1920s, which imported the concept of pooled investment from Britain and exploited the multiplier effects of leverage (Galbraith, 1954: 52–65). Alfred Winslow Jones' private investment partnership, founded in 1949, had much in common with modern hedge funds. Jones avoided regulatory supervision by virtue of the limited and closed nature of his partnership, used shorted shareholdings to hedge his portfolio, borrowed to gear his capital, and took compensation as 20 per cent of profits (Partnoy and Thomas, 2007: 115). The firm that Jones founded, A. W. Jones, still exists. It describes itself as 'the first hedge fund' but has developed into a fund of funds which selects from a range of hedge funds on behalf of its own investors. A *Fortune* article in 1966 entitled 'The Jones that nobody keeps up with' described Jones' investment strategy and observed that his accomplishments had spawned a number of other 'hedge funds', some run by former associates (Loomis, 1966: 237). By this time, the expression 'hedge fund' was becoming current but was still evidently somewhat unfamiliar and novel.

In an interview given in 2007, Henry Blackie, Chairman of the UK investment management firm Arlington Capital Investors, commented that he no longer knew what a hedge fund was, but that the true definition was probably that of a fund which hedged, or took a position in an instrument which acted contrary to the main investment (ECGI, 2007). However, some funds now generally considered to fall within the hedge fund category do not engage in hedging strategies at all, and the expression 'hedge fund' is arguably misleading in this context. The investments of modern hedge funds may include almost any kind of negotiable security, and the rapid development of the derivatives market during the past 20 years, coupled with the expansion of automated trading, has opened up a potentially vast field of activity for them. Many funds now operate partially or even fully computerised trading strategies that react to arbitrage opportunities identified from electronic data inputs.

An IMF report by Eichengreen and Mathieson published in 1999 identified three major categories of hedge fund: 'macro funds', which take directional unhedged positions in national markets based on top-down analysis of macroeconomic and financial conditions; 'global funds', which take worldwide positions based on analysis of individual companies; and 'relative value funds', which arbitrage between closely related securities. There is further diversity within these categories: activist hedge funds, for example, could be located within 'global funds' and many 'fund of funds' investment firms have emerged which act as intermediaries to select a spread of specialised hedge funds for their clients. The IMF report summarises the resulting problems of definition: 'Any attempt to generalize further about the features of hedge funds immediately confronts two problems: first, their investment and funding techniques vary enormously, and second, other individual and institutional investors engage in many of the same activities as hedge funds' (Eichengreen and Mathieson, 1999: 3). In practice, 'hedge fund', for many observers, has now come to mean any opaque investment vehicle that is not run according to the normal procedures of the institutional fund management industry.

A number of more functional or analytical definitions of hedge funds have emerged. Partnoy and Thomas proposed the following:

'Hedge funds generally have four characteristics: (1) they are pooled, privately organized investment vehicles; (2) they are administered by professional investment managers; (3) they are not widely available to the public; and (4) they operate outside of securities regulation and registration requirements' (Partnoy and Thomas, 2007: 115).

Connor and Woo effectively qualified point (4): 'many people think that hedge funds are completely unregulated, but it is more accurate to say that hedge funds are structured to take advantage of exemptions in regulation'. They noted that hedge funds measure their performance in absolute return units (as opposed to seeking to match or surpass a market index) and commonly borrow to increase leverage, magnifying the effects of both success and failure. They also pointed to the distinctive remuneration pattern of hedge fund managers, typically 1–2 per cent of assets under management and 15–20 per cent of the return achieved in excess of the fund's agreed benchmark.[1] A further feature of nearly all hedge funds, distinguishing them from most other kinds of non-banking investment vehicle, is that they control withdrawals by their investors through notice requirements and initial 'lock-up' periods. Moreover, they are not restricted by regulators in their use of leverage, short positions, or derivative products (Connor and Woo, 2004: 1–14).

Drawing these elements together, we see the distinguishing features of a hedge fund as being the ability to provide a more labour-intensive fund management service to sophisticated clients who have sufficient resources to contemplate high risk by using more incentivised, expensive, and skilled staff who are able to operate outside the restrictions that regulators impose on more conventional investment management firms for the protection of their numerous clients of limited means whose impoverishment could easily become a major social and political issue. On this basis, we offer our own definition of a hedge fund for the purposes of this study:

A hedge fund is an investment club governed by private contract, and therefore beyond the scope of many regulatory requirements, in which investors who accept increased market risk and usually an initial restriction on early withdrawal, mandate fund managers whose remuneration is weighted to

---

[1] This fee structure came under pressure after 2008 and was rumoured to have been relaxed at many funds (Walker, 2008).

performance through bonuses to exploit any legitimate opportunities for exceptional gains over an agreed benchmark, usually through a pre-advised investment strategy which may include borrowing or use of derivative instruments.

Because hedge funds usually require minimum investment stakes out of the reach of most individuals and because they sometimes produce remarkably high returns, there is a tendency to see them as a unique and mysterious phenomenon. In practice, they are simply a particular manifestation of the long-standing desire of wealthy individuals or institutions to increase their wealth faster than the market would normally permit by employing skilled investment managers. Exactly like any other fund managers, hedge funds offer a basic service whereby capital is received from investors and applied by salaried managers to securities or other assets in order to produce a profit. In principle, any institutional investor, such as a pension fund manager or an insurer, could do just the same, but in practice they do not. Clifford noted that mutual funds in the USA are subject to a variety of prudential fiduciary requirements concerning diversity and liquidity, and that US pension and mutual funds are typically barred by their charters from using leverage or derivatives. Moreover their fund managers' remuneration is much less dependent on performance-related bonuses than is the case with hedge funds (Clifford, 2008: 325). A study published in 2006 by Chen, Yao, and Yu on the performance of US mutual funds managed by insurers concluded that 'mutual funds managed by insurers or their investment subsidiaries underperform non-insurance peer funds' and attributed this to a general lack of alertness to the market and a lack of pressure from either their mostly unsophisticated investors or their supervisory boards (Chen, Yao, and Yu, 2007: 202). By contrast, hedge funds combine the desire of relatively more sophisticated investors to see improved returns with the desire of specialist managers to earn fees that reflect their ability to generate superior performance; this has produced a new market segment with an effectively distinct model.

The size of the hedge fund market, both in terms of assets managed and in terms of the number and location of funds, is difficult to estimate because hedge funds have few disclosure requirements, and generally prefer to avoid publicity. The situation has not changed much since the IMF's report observed in 1999 that 'a variety of commercial services report on hedge funds, but they are given information

voluntarily, and no authoritative estimates exist either of the number of such funds or of the value of their capital' (Eichengreen and
Mathieson, 1999: 5). The same report quoted data from Managed
Account Reports Inc., which it considered to represent a low end estimate, placing the extent of total hedge fund capital at the end of 1998
at approximately US$110,000 million. A study by the Alternative
Investment Management Association nearly ten years later estimated
that total assets under management by hedge funds had reached
approximately US$2,500,000 million as at June 2008 (AIMA, 2008).
This figure is believed to have decreased from the latter half of 2008 as
the effects of the global financial crisis took hold but – bearing in mind
that accurate data are scarce – appeared to have recovered to its earlier
level by late 2010 (FT, 2009b, 2010a). This is equivalent to just over
7 per cent of the total assets estimated by the OECD to be controlled
by institutional investors such as pension funds and insurers at around
that time in only 28 of its 34 member countries,[2] although leverage at
hedge funds would have a multiplier effect and their portfolio turnover was likely to have been more frequent than that of many investors. The greatest concentrations of hedge funds are in the USA and
the UK: a report from IFSL[3] entitled *Hedge Funds 2010* (using 2009
data) estimated that there were approximately 9,400 hedge funds at
the end of 2009, of which 68% were managed from the USA and
23% from European countries. The predominant centres were New
York (41%) and London (20%). The report noted that about 60%
of registered domiciles were offshore, notably in the Cayman Islands,
although management was usually carried out from onshore locations
(IFSL, 2010).

Activist hedge funds have emerged as a distinct subset within this
wider hedge fund sector, of which they comprise only a relatively small
proportion. A study by J.P. Morgan, cited by Kahan and Rock in 2007,
estimated that only about 5 per cent of total hedge fund assets were

---

[2] OECD Annual Statistics on Institutional Investors' Assets (www.oecd.org): this
source is designed to give country data for all of the 34 OECD member states
except for New Zealand but at time of access showed no figures for Finland,
Germany, Ireland, Norway, or Switzerland. Most of the data used were for
2009 but in five cases were from 2008 and in two cases from 2007. Totals were
converted to US$ at the appropriate calendar year-end middle rates. The fact
that many mainstream institutional investors also invest through hedge funds
creates further imprecision in these data.

[3] International Financial Services London.

currently available for shareholder activism (Kahan and Rock, 2007: 1046), which implies a total of around US$125,000 million when calculated on the 2008 AIMA estimate for the whole market and less than 0.4 per cent of the OECD's 28-country figure for institutional investors' assets. However, these funds attract a disproportionate degree of attention from the financial press, corporate management, and other investors precisely because they are activist.

Activist hedge funds share the same client base as other hedge funds, namely wealthy individuals or institutions willing to accept high risk in exchange for the possibility of high return, with long lock-up periods of at least six months and possibly several years, and employ well-regarded managers incentivised by performance-linked remuneration. Activist hedge funds may be leveraged but in many ways they operate very differently from 'macro funds' and 'relative value funds'. They do not use automated systems for rapid arbitrage like so many of the mainstream hedge funds. Instead, they research individual companies carefully to locate targets that appear to have the characteristics of the latent value they seek and then undertake controlled investments, which tend to be few in number because this process requires intensive use of both their capital and their fund managers' time and energy. Where a 'conventional' hedge fund manager might be, by training, a mathematician, a trader, or even a computer specialist, activist hedge fund managers tend to have backgrounds in financial analysis.

A further key element is that activist hedge funds acquire their shareholdings specifically in order to create a foothold as shareholders from which they can exert pressure, as opposed to other investors who might become shareholders initially with no intention to influence management but subsequently decide that this is the only way to protect their investment: activist hedge funds see activism as a profit-making strategy and they do not buy shares in the first place unless they intend to promote a premeditated agenda (Kahan and Rock, 2007: 1091).

On the basis of the above, we offer our own definitions of an activist hedge fund and of an activist hedge fund 'intervention', as follows:

An activist hedge fund is a hedge fund that carries out proprietary research on individual companies to identify potential for improved returns and uses shareholder activism to agitate for changes which will realise those returns. In an intervention by an activist hedge fund, the fund acquires shares in a company and uses its position as a shareholder, either unilaterally or in

cooperation with other shareholders, to influence the strategic or financial
policies of that company's management, in order to extract higher value in
some form for all the shareholders, but ultimately for the benefit of its own
investment clients in a timeframe acceptable to those clients, which usually
would be no more than a few years.

Hedge fund activism distinguished from other forms of shareholder engagement

Just as 'hedge fund' itself is a vague term, there are many fund management firms that resist categorisation as 'activist hedge funds'. The
expression 'value fund' has been used for some time to describe funds
that seek opportunities to invest in companies that they consider to be
undervalued by the market and whose fundamentals should deliver
a future improvement in the share price. Such investors are in principle patient and not confrontational, but many have limits to their
patience and are capable of expressing opinions to management or
even of taking more public action to secure a favourable outcome
for their investment. Consequently it can often be difficult to decide
exactly which funds are 'activists' and which are not. In theory, any
shareholder that seeks to influence management in any way could
be described as an 'activist', but for the purposes of this study we
focus on activists who intend to impose their opinions on management from the start and generally use publicity as a tactic in their
interventions. For this purpose, rather than enter a debate over which
funds are true activists and which are in fact value funds, we prefer
to divide them into those which consciously seek publicity (which we
shall call confrontational or 'noisy' activists) and those which generally do not (which we shall call 'quiet' activists). Inevitably, some
value funds which eschew any sort of activism may be included in our
'quiet' category. This distinction becomes important when we examine the behaviour of activist hedge funds in Japan because in that
market, more than anywhere else, the noisy activists crystallised what
was effectively a public debate on the ownership of the company and
the purpose of the firm, while the quiet activists tended to remain
unnoticed.

Activist hedge funds can also be distinguished from 'corporate raiders', high-profile activist investors who were active from the 1980s,
such as Sir James Goldsmith in the UK and the USA, or T. Boone

Pickens in the USA and Japan. Hedge fund activism is driven by professional managers who invest on behalf of a wider set of institutional and personal clients, rather than investing capital that they beneficially control, as the corporate raiders classically did. Activist hedge funds can be thought of as hybrids which share features of the approach of delegated portfolio managers, such as those managing the assets of pension funds and mutual funds, and those of the corporate raiders (Clifford, 2008: 325). Like corporate raiders, they seek target companies in which the current yield to shareholders is considered to be less than optimal, where value is considered to have been stockpiled unnecessarily, or where other opportunities are waiting to be exploited. Unlike raiders, they are acting for their clients and present themselves to corporate management as minority shareholders who seek to improve returns for the benefit of the entire shareholder body. They are integrated into the wider fund management system and usually need the goodwill of other investors in order to achieve their objectives because they prefer not to seek full control of their targets. Their reluctance to acquire companies is largely dictated by limits on the resources available to them, but may also be attributed to a fund management perspective which sees the role of the asset manager as investing in companies but not buying them outright. However, they are not averse to triggering situations where targets are subsequently acquired by third parties, as we discuss later in the context of the US market. This reliance on influence rather than absolute majority positions further distinguishes activist hedge funds from the earlier generation of corporate raiders who would normally have needed to obtain control of companies in order to realise their goals. Colin Kingsnorth, one of the founding partners of the UK activist hedge fund Laxey Partners, said in 2007: 'Laxey often has only a minority stake in a company and consequently will need to persuade, cajole and influence the other investors of the wisdom of its proposed course of action' (ECGI, 2007: 10).

In addition to drawing a distinction between 'noisy' and 'quiet' activists, it is possible to divide activist hedge funds further into two strategic groups, although it is conceivable that a single fund might exhibit both strategies: 'small-cap strategists' and 'large-cap strategists'. As an example of a small-cap strategist, the UK fund Arlington Capital Investors (which appears to have adopted new strategies from 2010) stated on its website in July 2009:

In making investments, Arlington primarily focuses on companies with: low absolute valuations; ownership of a product or franchise which is capable of generating higher returns; a robust balance sheet and net debt which is appropriate for both the cash generation profile of the business and the economic environment; and capacity for change ... These companies tend to be concentrated in the small and mid cap segments and are often misunderstood or overlooked by the market. However, they offer great potential for improvement and share price appreciation. (Arlington, 2009)

By contrast, the US activist hedge fund Knight Vinke Asset Management, which was established in 2003 with seed capital from CalPERS and focuses on western European situations, described itself on its website in July 2009 as 'an institutional asset management firm that specializes in identifying and unlocking unsuspected value in large and super-large cap public companies' (Knight Vinke, 2009). Funds of this kind are relatively rare. Another example is The Children's Investment Fund Ltd ('TCI'), which practised this approach until 2009 in Europe, the USA, and Japan. The approach of the large-cap fund is based on the idea that the size and complexity of the target's operations may have concealed complacent management or structural weaknesses which the intervention of the fund can address.

In principle, there is no reason why investors of all types should not become activists. From the 1990s, some pension funds in the USA have taken overtly activist stances with regard to their investments. Until the emergence of activist hedge funds, public-sector pension funds and union-influenced funds were seen as the most assertive investors in the USA. One of the most active, the teachers' pension fund TIAA-CREF, is reported to have reached private agreements with the majority of 45 companies it contacted between 1992 and 1996 to request corporate governance changes, without putting proposals to a shareholder vote (Carlton, Nelson, and Weisbach, 1998; Gillan and Starks, 2007: 57, 63). In the UK, direct engagement of this kind is unusual, with most institutional investors preferring to engage with their investee companies through informal dialogue (Black and Coffee, 1994). A more recent British development is the model of the focus fund, pioneered by the investment manager Hermes, through which the fund engages with its investee companies by offering expertise and advice in a manner which combines financial investment with a form of management consultancy. The Hermes UK Focus Fund appeared to have achieved success with essentially activist investments of this kind in 41 companies from October 1998 until December 2004, mainly by means of direct engagement with management and without significant publicity (Becht, Franks, Mayer, and Rossi, 2009).

In general, however, evidence suggests that institutional investors are not successful activists. Various reasons have been suggested for this lack of enthusiasm for activism among institutional shareholders. Kahan and Rock noted that most of the pressure known to have been exerted on boards in the USA by pension funds and other mainstream institutional investors in recent years has been focused on changes in corporate governance rules within those companies rather than on specific aspects such as share buy-backs, spin-offs, or mergers. Moreover whole groups of portfolio companies' boards tend to be approached at the same time, rather than individual targets being singled out for special attention. As they put it: 'Viewed charitably, this mode of activism is designed to achieve small changes in multiple companies at little expense, but it is unlikely to result in big changes at specific companies' (Kahan and Rock, 2007: 1043–4). Bratton observed a systemic pattern of disincentives to activism among these investors:

The requisite financial incentives never have fallen into place. Collective action problems, conflicts of interest, and investment duration all stand in the way. The free rider problem discourages investment managers from incurring the costs of challenges – gains must be shared with competitors who do not share costs. At the same time, many fund managers sell services to managers, importing an independent business reason to stay cooperative. (Bratton, 2007: 1384)

The view that institutional investors have effective conflicts of interest has been expressed by others too. Bainbridge noted that because of these relationships 'corporate managers are well-positioned to buy off most institutional investors that attempt to act as monitors' (Bainbridge, 2010: 229). This has created a communality of interest among investors and corporate management: a UK activist hedge fund director observed to us in 2009 that when UK institutional investors find themselves as fellow-shareholders with an aggressive activist demanding change 'they'll blatantly use you as a stalking horse but at the end of the day the big institutions are not really going to sack a FTSE[4] chairman'. By contrast, activist hedge funds can mitigate the free rider problem by holding a greater percentage of the target's shares than the average pension fund or insurer would wish to hold and, because their managers' remuneration comes mainly from a percentage of the fund's profits, they have a clear incentive to identify and exploit opportunities for successful activism. Moreover, they will not be swayed by the possibility of ancillary business links with their target companies.

Activist hedge funds as agents of change in corporate governance

From the mid-2000s, activist hedge funds were increasingly seen as a distinct phenomenon in the investment world. Moreover they were believed to have the potential to reshape corporate governance in a manner more conducive to the needs of shareholder value. As Klein and Zur observed in a working paper publicised in 2006: 'the main debate surrounding hedge fund activism is whether it represents a new paradigm in the role that institutional shareholders play in corporate governance' (Klein and Zur, 2006: 1). As we have seen, free rider problems and the constraints of prudential regulation made it unlikely that pension funds and other institutions would be able to press for better accountability of managers to shareholders or, more generally, to enhance shareholder returns. In this 'bleak landscape', the rise of hedge fund activism was 'the great, shining beacon of hope' (Macey, 2008: 272). Activist hedge funds would be able to act more freely in their search for superior returns and their managers would be appropriately incentivised to do so.

Activist hedge fund managers do not generally see themselves first and foremost as agents of change. As an activist fund manager in Japan observed to us in 2004: 'The primary objective for the investors is to make money, so I think corporate governance is just a tool ... as long as I am gathering other people's money together, my first objective is to increase that money.' A similar observation was made also in the US market by Bratton in 2007: 'hedge fund activism is about value;

---

[4] Financial Times Stock Exchange indices: this conventionally refers to the FTSE 100 index of the hundred largest UK listed companies by market capital.

governance and the process of capital market discipline take second place on the agenda' (Bratton, 2007: 1397).

At the same time, the practice of hedge fund activism is also underpinned by a philosophy which is entirely consistent with the agenda of pro-shareholder corporate governance reformers. Their approach can be summarised as: *the company belongs to its shareholders who as principals have appointed management to be their agents in order that they should maximise shareholder value.* Suggestions that shareholders should see themselves as anything less than the owners of the company or that they should oblige management by holding shares for longer than dictated by their own financial advantage are vigorously opposed. Moreover, at the same time as they seek to maximise returns in any legal way that they can, most activist fund managers probably believe quite sincerely in the force of these ideas. Barry Rosenstein, managing partner of Jana Partners, a US activist hedge fund, expressed what was probably a widely held view among practitioners when, in the course of responding to criticism of hedge fund activism in an article in the *Financial Times* in 2006, he wrote that 'the portrayal of management as "defenders" of the corporation versus "attackers" fundamentally misrepresents the nature of these contests, which are not played out solely between management and activists but, rather, are campaigns between them for the support of the company's true owners, its shareholders' (Rosenstein, 2006).

We consider in the following sections what activist hedge funds have achieved and how they are perceived in the USA, the UK, and Continental Europe. The USA is the market where they began to attract attention and in which they remain most engaged; the UK and Continental Europe were the first areas to which their business model was first exported.

5.3 Activist hedge funds in the USA

Hedge fund activism began in the USA and the US market currently has the greatest concentrations of both activist funds and interventions. A commentary in FINalternatives, an online hedge fund and private equity news service, identified 500 activist hedge fund interventions in the USA during 2007 and a further 80 during the first seven weeks of 2008 (Park, 2008). The market probably peaked at the end of 2008, when many funds reported losses, but commentators have suggested that a recovery is in progress (Market Watch, 2010). The most comprehensive investigation of activist hedge funds has taken place in the USA and a body of particularly detailed studies has emerged during the past five years. Brav, Jiang, Partnoy, and Thomas looked at a sample of 1,059 activist interventions by 236 funds in the USA between 2001 and 2006; Klein and Zur examined 155 schedule 13D regulatory filings[5] linked to hedge fund activism between 1 January 2003 and 31 December 2005; and Bratton studied interventions at 130 companies (114 in the main sample) between 1 January 2002 and 30 June 2006. In addition to these specific surveys, Kahan and Rock published an examination of the dynamics and importance of hedge fund activism, Greenwood and Schor investigated the takeover bias in US hedge fund activism, and Klein and Zur compared activist hedge funds with other activist investors and subsequently considered the impact of activism on the targets' bondholders. Several valuable working papers have also been publicised by, among others, Klein and Zur, Partnoy and Thomas, and Xu and Li, whose investigation of the impact on targets' banking arrangements complements Klein and Zur's work on bondholders (Bratton, 2007; Brav, Jiang, Partnoy, and Thomas, 2008a, 2008b; Greenwood and Schor, 2009; Kahan and Rock, 2007; Klein and Zur, 2006, 2009, 2011; Partnoy and Thomas, 2007; Xu and Li, 2010).

A composite picture of the sort of companies that attracted activist hedge funds in the USA between 2001 and 2006 emerges from these studies. Typically, targets were profitable and financially healthy, with strong cash flow and low levels of debt but undervalued by the market, leading to low market capitalisation relative to book assets. They also tended to have high institutional shareholding ratios and good liquidity, rather than dominant or controlling shareholders. Klein and Zur and Bratton noted that they tended to be cash-rich, which is commensurate with their low debt, and Bratton and Brav *et al.* observed a preponderance of relatively small targets: in Bratton's group of companies 61 per cent had market capitalisation of less than US$1,000 million, with a mean of US$281 million and a median of US$172 million (Bratton, 2007: 1387).

---

[5] The return submitted to the US Securities and Exchange Commission ('SEC') when a shareholding in a listed company exceeds 5 per cent.

Most of these surveys focus on events where a shareholding of 5 per cent or more was taken by a fund, requiring the submission of a Schedule 13D under US regulations. Brav *et al.* (2008a) pointed out that this does not capture all the activist hedge fund investments because it is possible to exert pressure on a board while still owning less than 5 per cent, and they give examples of this at major companies where larger shareholdings would have been expensive. However, even in Brav *et al.*'s sample, the emphasis is still on shareholdings in excess of 5 per cent and, as Becht *et al.* observed in their 2010 paper, which we cite later in the context of the European market, it is possible to overlook a lot of less public activism by concentrating on investments that require official notification.

These studies are generally in agreement on the issue of the activist hedge funds' preference for cooperation with other shareholders rather than seeking outright control. Brav *et al.* summarised their own findings as follows: 'Despite their frequently aggressive behavior, activist hedge funds do not typically seek control in target companies. The median maximum ownership stake for the entire sample is about 9.1% ... Activists rely on cooperation from management or, in its absence, on support from fellow shareholders to implement their value-improving agendas.' Brav *et al.* found that boards quickly accepted the activists' demands 29.7% of the time, negotiated with them 29.1% of the time, and opposed them 41.3% of the time. Klein and Zur found a complementary result in that 40% of their sample featured an actual or threatened proxy solicitation when boards did not cooperate (Brav *et al.*, 2008a: 1732 and 1746; Klein and Zur, 2009: 215). However, Cheffins and Armour noted a widely reported increase in aggressive tactics by activist hedge funds in the US market from the early 2000s (Cheffins and Armour, 2011: 53–4).

Bratton and Brav *et al.* analysed the nature of the demands made by the activist hedge funds in their samples to the boards of their targets. Brav *et al.* found that in 48.3% of the cases the funds made an initial public announcement that they planned to communicate with the board in order to enhance shareholder value. Such an announcement does not immediately imply a confrontational approach and appears to be a tactic to alert the market and encourage boards to cooperate, as Brav *et al.*'s findings suggested that they often do. In 32% of the cases the funds submitted formal proposals or openly criticised the board's conduct and demanded changes. In 13.2% of the cases the funds solicited the support of the whole shareholder body to replace the board but the incidence of legal action against boards (5.4%) and attempts to acquire companies outright (4.2%) were relatively few. Bratton noted that 32% of his sample announced from the very outset that their targets should sell or spin off assets. Interestingly, Kahan and Rock, in their general review of the dynamics of US hedge fund activism, found no evidence of greenmailing: targets did not appear simply to be paying activist hedge funds to go away (Bratton, 2007: 1393; Brav *et al.*, 2008a: 1743; Kahan and Rock, 2007: 1082).

Although, as we have seen, the activist hedge funds in these studies seldom sought absolute control of their targets, there are indicators that exchanges of control frequently follow their interventions: since it is customary for acquirers of companies to pay a control premium above the market price, this is an attractive outcome for the funds. Brav *et al.* noted the highest abnormal returns in their sample where the activism focused on sale of the target and Greenwood and Schor found that targeted companies were much more likely to be acquired within 18 months of the intervention than similar companies. As they put it: 'Hedge funds invest in small, undervalued companies with the ultimate goal of seeing those targets bought out.' Using a sample of 980 activist events (784 initiated by hedge funds and 196 by activists classed as 'non-hedge funds') they found that for the hedge fund activist cases 22.8% of targets were delisted within 12 months of the first 13D filing, of which 18.6% were acquired, and that within 18 months 27.4% were delisted, of which 21.9% were acquired. Although it appears that the majority of targeted companies retain their independence, acquisition by a third party is clearly part of the funds' repertoire of realising value from their targets (Brav *et al.*, 2008a: 1759; Greenwood and Schor, 2009: 372–4).

The hedge fund market as a whole is generally perceived to be one of fast arbitrage but Brav *et al.* rejected the claim that US activist hedge funds are exclusively or excessively short-term investors: they found that the median holding period for their sample was about one year after submission of a 13D, or closer to two years if the funds' own share turnover data were used. Bratton noted that although 'short term' is often assumed to be a bad thing, the whole point of stock markets is to provide liquidity. Moreover, in his sample, which covers companies where the first recorded interventions spanned the period 2002–6, 44 per cent of those that began before June 2005 and

54 per cent of the whole sample were still in place in some form at the end of 2006. From the point of view of the US capital markets, this is not particularly short term, but in our view it tends to obscure the fact that the boards of most companies would normally prefer investors to retain their shares for as long as possible (Bratton, 2007: 1410–12; Brav *et al.*, 2008a: 1731–2).

The outcomes from hedge fund activism in the USA have been viewed from the various perspectives of profit to the funds, success in achieving their stated objectives, effects on the financial state of their targets, and contributions to corporate governance in general. We consider these four aspects in turn below.

Brav *et al.* observed abnormal turnover of targets' shares in their sample around the date of the first 13D filings, which in these cases would normally imply a rise in the share price. Looking at the share prices over a longer period they concluded that although typical deals did not earn more than investments in untargeted benchmark companies, the upper 25 per cent of their sample produced good results. As we have seen, activism aimed at sale of the target earned the best abnormal returns of all. Bratton noted that activist hedge funds press boards to recommend higher dividends or to buy back their own companies' shares and found 41 companies, corresponding to 31.5 per cent of his full sample, where payouts exceeded prior levels. Although this does not suggest consistently exciting returns for investors in all activist hedge funds it does suggest that the most astute funds may be performing well (Bratton, 2007: 1415; Brav *et al.*, 2008a: 1755–60).

In terms of achieving their objectives, activist hedge funds in the USA seem to be generally successful. The consensus from the surveys we have cited was that they succeeded in achieving their stated objectives either wholly or partially in 60–70 per cent of cases. Brav *et al.* provided an analysis from their sample broken down by the funds' main objectives and distinguishing between outwardly hostile and non-hostile events: the incidence of some degree of success is high in most cases for both sorts of intervention but slightly more so for the hostile interventions except for oppositions to offers made for the target by third-party acquirers, where non-hostile approaches delivered more examples of complete success (Brav *et al.*, 2008a: 1742).

In terms of US activist hedge funds' effect on their targets' financial well-being there are differing opinions. Brav *et al.* found that the companies in their sample experienced a deterioration in return on assets

('RoA') and operating profit margins during the year of the intervention but had recovered to their former levels one year later and even showed improvement in the year after that, implying that an activist hedge fund intervention generally improves the target's financial state. Although they conceded that wealth was being redistributed from managers to shareholders, they stated that 'we find no evidence that activist hedge funds redistribute wealth from creditors to shareholders' (Brav *et al.*, 2008a: 1767 and 1771). However, Klein and Zur (2011) reported declining earnings and cash flows at the target companies in their sample in the year following the initial 13D submission, and no recovery in the following year for a reduced group of companies that they observed further. More worryingly, Xu and Li examined the impact of activist interventions on the terms and conditions of banking facilities at 2,626 companies targeted by 505 activist hedge funds in 3,686 interventions between 1994 and 2008 and discovered that loan margins rose both in absolute terms and in relation to market benchmarks. As they observed: 'hedge fund activism increases credit risk and banks respond with active measures to mitigate the impact' (Xu and Li, 2010: 5). Klein and Zur (2011) carried out an examination of the impact of hedge fund activism on the target companies' bondholders. Looking at a sample of 193 companies where there had been activist interventions between 1994 and 2006, they discovered that in the majority of cases bond returns (which they defined as change in price plus accrued interest) fell and ratings declined. As they pointed out:

In the year subsequent to the initial 13D filing date, target firms, on average, significantly decrease their cash on hand, double their dividends to common shareholders, and increase their debt-to-asset ratios. While these actions may be beneficial to shareholders, they amount to a reduction in cash available for future interest and principal repayments to existing bondholders ... more creditors are competing for a smaller amount of cash on hand. (Klein and Zur, 2011: 1737)

In spite of these issues regarding the effect on target companies' financial situations, the contribution of hedge fund activism to corporate governance is normally considered to be positive because of the US market's strong focus on shareholders' interests and on agency theory ideas implying that managers must be constrained to return value to their principals. Brav *et al.* described activist hedge funds as 'informed monitors' of management and saw their activism as 'a new middle ground between internal monitoring by large shareholders and external monitoring by corporate raiders' (Brav *et al.*, 2008a: 1730 and 1774). Moreover they did not hesitate to imply that this activism created 'value' which, by definition, was 'shareholder value'. But this view has been questioned. As Kahan and Rock expressed the key issue: 'Are hedge funds the "Holy Grail" of corporate governance – the long sought-after shareholder champion with the incentive and expertise to protect shareholder interests in publicly held firms? Or do they represent darker forces, in search of quick profit opportunities at the expense of other shareholders and the long-term health of the economy?' (Kahan and Rock, 2007: 1026). As we have seen, only 41.3 per cent of targeted boards among Brav *et al.*'s sample initially opposed the activists, so there is clearly a widespread acceptance of hedge fund activism in the USA. Both Xu and Li, and Klein and Zur, have noted important issues regarding the financial effects on the businesses targeted but there has been no general reaction against activist hedge funds in the market. At least within the US financial and investment sectors, many people still appear to believe that hedge funds 'actually deliver on their promise to provide more disciplined monitoring of management, to reduce the incidence of fraud on investors, and to improve actual operational performance' and consider them a fundamentally beneficial phenomenon (Macey, 2008: 272).

5.4 Activist hedge funds in the UK

The UK is generally considered to have the second largest concentration of activist funds and interventions after the USA. However, the British market is less well researched and there is little information readily available to support this belief beyond press reports of certain well-documented interventions. Despite the existence of a more stringent reporting regime for major shareholdings since 2007, there is no body of research on UK interventions comparable to the US studies cited above.

In principle, the UK offers ideal conditions for the emergence of hedge fund activism. There is a large population of widely held listed companies, while institutional investors whose support can be solicited by activists dominate the share registers of leading companies. Non-residents, who are likely to view their British investments more objectively than local investors, have progressively been increasing their share of the total UK market for many years, reaching 41.5 per cent in 2008 (ONS, 2010). A partner at a British activist fund commented to us in 2009 that US institutional investors, in particular, tended to be more receptive to his firm's initiatives: 'most of the US institutions – even their big institutions – will be supportive because they're much more numerate'.

The UK has its own tradition of shareholder activism, predating the rise of activist hedge funds along US lines. The UK's earlier activists were not categorised as hedge funds, but the term would probably have been applied to at least some of them had it been used then as it is now. Investors such as the UK Active Value Fund attracted attention in the mid-1990s by buying large minority stakes in companies and agitating for changes intended to improve the share price. In the late 1990s, Phillips and Drew's fund managers frequently adopted an activist approach, although the purpose of their activism was to improve share values rather than to transform their targets' structures in any major way. As we have seen, Hermes, the pension fund manager owned by the BT Pension Scheme, launched the Hermes UK Focus Fund in 1998 in order to develop profitable returns through active involvement with management of underperforming companies.[6] It is unusual in being a major institutional investor that has sponsored an activist fund. However, in keeping with its institutional approach, Hermes tries not to use the media to apply pressure; its activism is handled mostly through private discussion, with the board and other shareholders.

In general, the UK seems to lack the more confrontational types of intervention associated with the US market, where activist hedge funds have clashed more publicly with targets' boards and appear to have been more successful in redirecting corporate strategies. There have been some publicised interventions: in 2002–3 Laxey Partners

---

6 The UK Focus Fund is part of a group of focus funds specialising in various geographical areas, run directly or in partnership by Hermes. In January 2009 Hermes described them as holding 'concentrated portfolios of fundamentally sound but underperforming companies' and stated that 'the funds seek to improve the long-term performance of those companies through tailored relational shareholder engagement programmes' (Hermes, 2009). In early 2011 it continued to run these funds under the generic name of Hermes Focus Asset Management.

demanded management changes and share buy-backs at British Land, achieving partial success and a reportedly good return, and in 2005 it brought about the resignation of the chairman of Wyevale Garden Centres but was unable to impose its preferred alternative candidate; more recently, in 2010–11 Laxey engaged in a public disagreement with the board of Alliance Trust over the level of its share buy-backs and its CEO's remuneration, and concurrently the US fund Elliott Advisors attempted to force board changes and impose a new strategy at National Express, with apparently minimal success as of May 2011, but these are exceptions (FT, 2002, 2003, 2005c, 2006e, 2011a, 2011b). When a fund controlled by the American activist shareholder Nelson Peltz took a 3 per cent shareholding in Cadbury Schweppes[7] in March 2007 and was widely credited with stimulating management to begin the process of selling off the US beverages business, this attracted a great deal of attention. A respected UK fund manager, who found Cadbury Schweppes' statement that it had already been planning such a move unconvincing, wrote of this development: 'A world where a 3 per cent activist shareholder could have this degree of influence on the board of a listed UK business is a different one from the one I have known for the past 35 years. I do not think that the relationship between UK companies and their shareholders will ever be quite the same again' (Bolton, 2007). As the Alliance Trust and National Express interventions show, there have been further high-profile interventions since that date, but they have been few in number, suggesting that the relationship between UK companies and their shareholders has not changed irrevocably yet.

The senior managers of UK-listed companies seem to be prepared to meet hedge fund investors on a regular basis. A survey by Lintstock of investor relations officers at 20 major UK companies, published in 2005, found that more than 20 per cent of all their investor meetings were conducted with hedge funds.[8] This study suggested that companies

---

[7] Renamed Cadbury plc in May 2008 and acquired by Kraft in February 2010; this is an example of an activist hedge fund's intervention ultimately triggering a third party tender offer, in line with the observations by Greenwood and Schor (2009) quoted above.

[8] Lintstock's survey treats hedge funds as a single sector, whereas we consider activist hedge funds to be distinct. However, the survey contains input from at least one activist hedge fund and we assume that most of the funds involved were activists because it seems unlikely that non-activist hedge funds would even wish to meet their targets' management.

distinguished between 'thought leaders' – who offered strategic opinions – and speculative short-term position holders in determining whom they were willing to meet. 'Thought leaders' were regarded as a valuable source of ideas. Concern was expressed not about potential activism so much as the difficulty of knowing how much of the companies' equity these funds really controlled once all their interests were taken into account. Few of the managers interviewed expressed concern over the ability of hedge funds to interfere in governance aspects, and most commented that funds showed little interest in exercising voting rights (Lintstock, 2005: 15–21). Nevertheless, around this time Laxey Partners was doing precisely this with respect to its holdings in British Land and Wyevale Garden Centres.

One way to view the UK market for hedge fund activism is as a pallid reflection of that in the USA, one in which confrontational activism is less advanced, but where it will eventually develop along similar lines. But there is a belief in the UK, at least among certain institutional investors, that the relationship between shareholders and management is fundamentally different to that in the USA. Those holding this belief tend to think that matters can be settled without public confrontation. In 2007, Michael McKersie, manager of investment affairs for the Association of British Insurers, was reported as saying:

Dialogue between shareholders and companies in the UK is well-ordered and responsible, and is often kept low-profile … In the US you see relatively little shareholder engagement with companies; they go through the SEC or wage proxy fights, and it is a confrontational exercise. We don't think it is necessarily going to help the company to have shareholders speaking negatively about it in public. (Freudmann, 2007)

Hermes' chief executive, despite the existence of his own firm's focus fund, spoke in a similar vein when he reportedly said in 2007 that activist hedge funds pressing for corporate change tended to create more noise than value and could make it harder for companies to work out what shareholders were telling them, and that activist hedge funds' short-term approach could conflict with the interests of longer-term investors pushing for corporate change (Reuters, 2007a).

Other UK institutional investors to whom we spoke in the course of our interviews emphasised the fundamental difference between their position as continuing shareholders and that of activist funds. One observed in 2009:

We are very much longer term in our horizon and we do want a governance structure and a strategic direction which is going to generate sustainable long-term earnings. We are looking beyond the horizon almost in that regard. Clearly the objectives of the hedge fund may be quite useful to move on a situation which is a bit stuck but they're not the same objectives as ours.

This aspect of using activist hedge funds to move situations that are 'a bit stuck' was noted by others too. A UK institutional investor remarked to us in 2007 that, at least in one recent intervention, it had suited his firm to support an activist hedge fund: 'it can be a very useful lever'. However, this respondent was also careful not to identify his fund with activists' demands for short-run shareholder value. An activist hedge fund director confirmed this situation from the funds' viewpoint in 2009, pointing out that major institutional investors often preferred to use activists' presence as leverage as they pursued their own agendas through private discussions: 'The City sees activists as someone suggesting the ugly truth occasionally, with which they can sit down and say "Look here, a bit of merit in what they're going on about here but we don't need to go down that [road] … how about we just sort things out like this?"' This interviewee also made the point that the degree of cooperation from institutional investors in activist interventions depended very much on whether the same issues had already been raised by those investors in the recent past: 'You have to kind of look at what the situation was at any particular company you're taking action against, and whether the institutions suggested things and they've just ignored [them] for the last two or three years'. This point was substantiated by an institutional investor who expressed the view to us that, although Cadbury Schweppes had appeared to react to pressure from Nelson Peltz in 2007, it was more likely that a majority of its institutional investors had already made it clear in private, either before or after the move by Peltz's fund was made public, that they shared the same opinion. In his view, this – rather than Peltz's intervention – had been the decisive influence.

The UK market for activist hedge funds thus appears to function differently from that of the USA. Although there are occasional cases of well-publicised 'noisy' and even antagonistic interventions, these are rare. The institutional investors whose support would be needed for confrontational interventions to succeed seem less willing in the UK to see the activists as fellow-seekers after shareholder value. On the contrary, they tend to emphasise differences in the investment objectives of the institutions and hedge funds, and the different time horizons on which they operate. The institutions are willing to make use of the activists when it suits them to do so but generally prefer to solve problems by talking directly with companies' boards.

Both the institutional investors and the activist hedge fund managers whom we spoke to pointed to fundamental differences in the corporate governance environments of the UK and the USA that influenced styles of activism in the two countries. The first difference lies in the degree of effective power that shareholders possess in each market. As an officer at an institutional investor put it, in the USA it is because:

Shareholders don't have access to boards of directors, they aren't able to vote against directors' re-elections there, they aren't able to really engage easily with boards of directors, that you need that activism as this other exercise ... Whereas in the UK there isn't probably much observed activist activity precisely because we have a much more engaged process by which shareholders and directors are able to dialogue with each other.

A UK activist hedge fund director put his view bluntly as to why activism tends to be so different in the USA: 'As a shareholder you have absolutely no shareholder rights in the US ... So the US tends to be loud noise, you know; tends to be 13D filings, open letters.' Another activist hedge fund director made this comment, placing the publicity-seeking stance of US funds in a wider context:

In the US, where the power of individual shareholders is very limited, having an impact almost always requires a very public approach – either to try to catalyze massive support from other shareholders, or, more often, to embarrass the company into submission by shining a spotlight on its underperformance. In the UK and Europe, if you are a big shareholder, you essentially have a seat at the table, which normally makes the public approach unnecessary.

Another element that differentiates the UK from the USA relates to the nature of its regime for takeover bids. Two relevant aspects of the regulatory framework established by the Takeover Code are the so-called mandatory bid rule and the rules on concert parties. Under Rule 9.1 of the Code, a mandatory offer is triggered primarily when an investor acquires 30 per cent or more of a listed company. However, 'persons acting in concert' are included in this total. These persons can even include advisers to the acquirers of shares. The Takeover Panel has the power to decide whether parties are acting in concert during a bid and requires clear evidence that a concert party situation no longer obtains once a ruling of this kind has been made (Takeover Panel, 2010, Definitions C2, Rule 9.1). The director of a hedge fund explained that this situation effectively made any sort of collaboration between funds or other investors in advance of an intervention difficult. Hedge funds and their sympathisers faced the danger of being declared part of a concert party at a stage in the intervention where tactics were still undecided and the parties concerned were not ready to bid: 'You can't really coordinate. You can't pre-coordinate things. You used to be able to but the concert party rules now mean that you can't pre-coordinate things. Which is terrible: you have to take the action, then go round and talk to the institutions.'

A further difference between the UK and the USA is that many British activist interventions are believed to take place around smaller listed companies or listed vehicles like closed-end funds, often listed on the AIM exchange rather than the London Stock Exchange, where the financial press tends to show limited interest. A director of an activist hedge fund pointed to this situation in 2009 in response to the suggestion that the UK had less activism than would be expected from its market structure:

You talk about less activism in the UK: that is true but only with two caveats: first, there is less visible activism, though much happens without public disclosure, and second, that's true primarily for the large cap companies. If you go trawling through the sort of stuff that happens on AIM for instance, and increasingly in mid-cap UK companies, there's a lot of activism of different types, primarily because many of the big shareholders are not classic institutions.

Essentially, the community of institutional investors whose cautious attitude to activists of any sort makes it difficult to gather allies among fellow-shareholders at larger companies in the UK is simply not present at these smaller companies, creating a different environment where activist hedge funds can operate with less restraint. A director at another activist hedge fund explained his firm's preference for property companies and closed-end funds rather than the largest UK companies on these grounds. As he explained it: 'Everything is driven by the share register. You can't push something that doesn't want to go in that direction. That's why activism in big companies never works. You don't get activism in the FTSE companies, because the institutional dead wood [isn't] going to support it'.

Thus the UK is a market where activist hedge funds are present and where they intervene in listed companies. However, the interview evidence we have reviewed suggests that, at least from the point of view of those engaged in hedge fund activism or observing it as institutional investors, the UK activist hedge fund market is not just a smaller version of the US one. It has its own dynamics and is driven by a different set of behavioural norms and expectations. The power of major institutional shareholders to influence boards is stronger in the UK and there is less need for the noisy public confrontations often seen in the USA. The greater influence over investee companies of institutional shareholders in the UK makes it easier for them to take an assertive stance. While this might have been expected to encourage activist hedge fund interventions, in practice it has led institutional investors to crowd out the specialist activists from larger targets. The institutional investors are seldom sufficiently frustrated to countenance collaborating with a group of investors whose aims they often consider to be excessively short term and hence at odds with their own.

5.5 Hedge fund activism in Continental Europe

Continental Europe is often seen as a region whose corporate governance systems and managers reject the concepts of shareholder primacy and shareholder value. In 1997 an article in the *McKinsey Quarterly* commented: 'In Britain and the United States, maximizing shareholder value is universally accepted as management's paramount goal. While some Continental Europeans share this point of view, most continue to believe that shareholder value comes only at the expense of other stakeholders, leaving in its wake diminished job security, higher unemployment, poorer products and services, and weaker overall economic performance' (Bughin and Copeland, 1997).

The three largest Continental European economies, Germany, France, and Italy, while exhibiting differences among themselves, all differ from the USA or the UK in that companies there are less likely to be widely held and more likely to be controlled by families or pyramid voting structures. Consequently, as Enriques and Volpin observed in a study published in 2007, dominant shareholders experience much less of the classic agency problem in enjoining management to deliver value. Conversely there is a sharper divergence of interests between majority and minority shareholders and many recent corporate governance changes in these countries have been inspired by the idea of protecting minority shareholders (Armour *et al.*, 2009a). With encouragement from the company law harmonisation programme of the European Union, legal efforts to enhance the voting, voice, and income rights of minority shareholders, support the principle of independent boards, and to improve disclosure in capital markets have been widely adopted (Enriques and Volpin, 2007: 117–19 and 137–8). There is also evidence of a shift in the attitudes of managers. Lane noted in 2003 that in Germany, although foreign institutional investors had still made only limited inroads as shareholders of large companies, among many managers, 'perceptions, interests and motivations are increasingly being shaped by the ideology of shareholder value' (Lane, 2003: 94). More recent studies suggest that this trend continues. Bauer, Braun, and Clark, in an examination of the relationship between shareholder value and capital investment in corporate governance across a wide sample of European companies during the period 1997–2005, noted that: 'Managers are adopting practices consistent with the interests of global investors even if convergence in the formal models of corporate governance is less systematic than expected by global portfolio investors. Even managers domiciled in countries with less well established governance codes and limited takeover markets appear to be adjusting to Anglo-American expectations regarding shareholder value' (Bauer, Braun, and Clark, 2008: 443).

Thus although shareholder value and all that it has come to imply in the USA or the UK may not be universally accepted in Continental European markets, the concept is increasingly perceived to have validity and is in keeping with legal and regulatory efforts to strengthen the rights of non-controlling shareholders and to improve transparency at listed companies. Activist hedge funds have moved to exploit this shift in sentiment but not exactly in the same ways as in the USA or the UK. Becht, Franks, and Grant, in a working paper first made available in May 2010, reported the findings of an empirical study of 362 interventions by activist shareholders of various kinds including activist hedge funds, focus funds, and other activists in 15 European countries (including the UK) between 2000 and 2008. Included in this total are 57 interventions researched from proprietary data provided to them by five focus and hedge funds. They divided both samples between interventions which they described as 'public' in the sense that they involved open engagement with the targets, and 'private' in the sense that the interventions involved private engagement only. The fact that there were so many private interventions made by only this small number of funds implies that they may account for a greater proportion of the market than hitherto suspected. They found evidence of positive abnormal returns to activism in both cases. The returns they identified were higher in the case of public interventions but they noted that the costs for the private interventions were generally much lower. They observed no evidence of returns varying by jurisdiction. One important finding was that a relatively high proportion of these interventions involved negotiation with holders of large shareholding blocks, something that appears to be much rarer in the USA where activist hedge funds consciously target companies with good liquidity: in the public sample this amounted to 24 per cent of interventions but in the private sample it accounted for 58 per cent, suggesting a market with some fundamentally different characteristics (Becht *et al.*, 2010).

Nevertheless, there has been activism by hedge funds in Continental Europe more reminiscent of the US style, involving public confrontation. From 2005 two British activist hedge funds carried out interventions in Continental European companies in the style that we have categorised as 'noisy' activism. One fund, The Children's Investment Fund ('TCI'), followed a 'large cap' strategy of locating hitherto unnoticed situations at large companies, while the other, Laxey Partners, followed more of a 'small cap' strategy by intervening in relatively smaller companies where it was possible to accumulate larger positions.

TCI's European interventions attracted attention worldwide because they involved a number of high-profile institutions and large corporate targets, in such a way as to suggest that the concept of shareholder value could successfully be exported. Its first target was Deutsche Börse, originally the Frankfurt Stock Exchange and the principal stock exchange in Germany, which was then hoping to acquire the

London Stock Exchange ('LSE'). After earlier approaches had been rebuffed, Deutsche Börse had made an 'informal' bid to the LSE on 16 December 2004, planning to finance the acquisition partly from its cash holdings of over €600 million. The LSE's board rejected this proposal. On 16 January 2005 TCI proposed that the bid be abandoned because it would be 'value destructive' and that the cash instead be returned to Deutsche Börse's shareholders through share buy-backs, a programme for which had already been implemented. Although Deutsche Börse's articles permitted it to make acquisitions without shareholder approval, a majority of shareholders was entitled to dismiss supervisory board members at an extraordinary general meeting ('EGM'). As the holder of just over 5 per cent of Deutsche Börse's shares, TCI had the right to propose an EGM, and threatened to use such a meeting to call for the dismissal of Deutsche Börse's supervisory board. Deutsche Börse's management initially refused to withdraw the bid, but TCI was soon backed publicly by another hedge fund, Atticus Capital, and by the end of January 2005 it was clear that other shareholders, such as Harris Trust, with about 3.4%, and Standard Life, with about 1%, supported its stance. Moreover, Deutsche Börse had an unusually international and institutional shareholder base: as of 31 December 2004, 50% of its equity was believed to be held by US and UK shareholders. Subsequently, the proportion in US or UK hands increased further, to around 70%. Deutsche Börse's share price strengthened when the degree of this opposition became clear, suggesting that other investors in the market saw merit in abandoning its proposed bid for the LSE. TCI continued to apply pressure on Deutsche Börse's executive management and supervisory board, calling in February 2005 for the chairman of the supervisory board to consult the exchange's largest investors as a matter of urgency, and querying the state of the exchange's corporate governance. The bid for the LSE was abandoned in March and the chief executive, Werner Seifert, resigned on 9 May. At the annual general meeting ('AGM') on 25 May, it was announced that share buy-backs would continue. Although TCI's call for the immediate resignation of Rolf Breuer as chairman of the supervisory board was resisted at the AGM, it was announced in September that he would leave his post in October of that year (BBC, 2005; Deutsche Börse, 2005a, 2005b, 2008; FT, 2005a, 2005b, 2005d, 2005e; Guardian, 2005; IHT, 2005). It is not known exactly when TCI bought its shares or sold them but, as an indication of the potential return, Deutsche Börse's share price in December 2004 was around €45 and in December 2005 it was approaching €90 and still rising.

The following year, TCI and Atticus Capital attracted attention again in a European context, this time in support of an acquisitive move. In May 2006 they urged the management of Euronext[9] to merge with either the NYSE or Deutsche Börse, both of which were potential merger partners or acquirers. Both funds had various holdings in both Euronext and one or both of the potential acquirers. Atticus Capital warned that it would seek dismissal of Euronext's top management if a suitable proposal were not put to its shareholders. As of 15 February 2006, shareholders domiciled outside Belgium, France, and the Netherlands held 75.16 per cent of the capital and 75.98 per cent of the voting rights. Since the beginning of 2006 a series of filings with the French financial regulator, the AMF,[10] had revealed new holdings by various activist hedge funds and banks. In the event, Euronext merged with the NYSE on 4 April 2007 (BBC, 2006; Businessweek, 2006). It is difficult to tell how successful this exercise proved for the funds involved because, although the NYSE offered a premium, its offer was partly in shares and its share price generally declined thereafter, with a temporary recovery in autumn 2007.

The next significant impact on European corporate governance from hedge fund activism came in February 2007 when TCI, as a 1 per cent shareholder in the Dutch banking group ABN AMRO, wrote to its chairman urging ABN AMRO to withdraw from acquisitive activity, particularly the possible acquisition of Capitalia in Italy then under study, and to consider either the sale or demerger of some of its own businesses, in order to return funds to shareholders, or sale of the entire bank. ABN AMRO had produced disappointing performance for several years and its share price rose 6.1% on the news of this approach. TCI responded to what it evidently considered an inadequate response to its proposals by demanding the dismissal of ABN AMRO's chief executive, Rijkman Groenink, in May 2007. As of 31 December 2006, some 60% of ABN AMRO's shares were held by institutional investors, and US and UK investors within this body of shareholders held approximately

---

[9] The Euronext exchange group was formed from the merger of the Amsterdam, Brussels, and Paris stock exchanges in September 2000. It subsequently acquired the London International Financial Futures Exchange ('LIFFE') in 2001 and the Bolsa de Valores de Lisboa e Porto ('BVLP') in 2002.

[10] Autorité des Marchés Financiers.

24.6%. As the affair proceeded, the press reported that about 40% of all ABN AMRO's shares were believed to be held by hedge funds of some kind. Faced with increasing shareholder pressure and apparently accepting that their recovery plan would not succeed in time to save their position, ABN AMRO's board entered into merger discussions with Barclays Bank. However, a competing approach was received from a consortium of Royal Bank of Scotland, Banco Santander, and Fortis which proposed to divide ABN AMRO's assets between them. Subsequently, Barclays withdrew and the consortium acquired ABN AMRO for €71,000 million in October 2007 in what was to prove a fatally over-geared investment for Royal Bank of Scotland and Fortis when the global financial crisis erupted soon after (FT, 2007a, 2007d; Guardian, 2007; Independent, 2007). The consortium paid €35.6 in cash and 0.296 Royal Bank of Scotland shares for each ABN AMRO share, amounting to over €38 per share. ABN AMRO's share price in mid-February 2007, just before TCI first wrote to its management, had been around €25 per share. The share price had risen progressively from that point (ABN AMRO, 2008; Eurex, 2007).

During the same period that TCI made these interventions, Laxey Partners ('Laxey'), the UK activist hedge fund that had confronted British Land's board in 2002–3, was pursuing its own style of 'small cap' activism in Switzerland. The first intervention began in late 2005 when Laxey bought 15% of Saurer, an engineering company where 31.56% of the shares were described as 'in the process of transfer' as at 31 December 2004; one year later the percentage shown in this category had risen to 61.78%. In August 2006 Laxey questioned the compatibility of Saurer's two core businesses of textile machinery and transmissions and called for the resignation of most of the board of directors, having increased its stake to a level variously reported as 24% and 26%. Before matters could proceed further, another Swiss company, Oerlikon, made an offer to buy Saurer, and Laxey made its exit by selling to Oerlikon (FT, 2006a, 2006b, 2006d).

In April 2006 Laxey was reported to have bought more than 20% of a Swiss building group, Implenia. The board of Implenia stated that it considered this a hostile act. In November 2007 Laxey raised its holding to 33.4%, thereby triggering a requirement for a mandatory bid. Matters were complicated by the board's refusal to register more than a parcel of Laxey's shares equivalent to 4.9% of the total equity, and a threat by the Swiss Federal Banking Commission in March 2008 that it would recommend criminal action against Laxey for allegedly breaching disclosure rules by concealing parts of its initial shareholding through intermediaries (FT, 2007b, 2007c, 2008i; Reuters, 2007b). There matters rested during a period when the press appeared to lose interest in the whole affair. However, Implenia's corporate website on 29 October 2009 showed Laxey and related funds as holding 50% of the company's shares. Subsequently, by November 2009, Laxey had sold its shares to existing and new shareholders, apparently to the satisfaction of Implenia and without taking a loss (Implenia, 2009a, 2009b; MarketWatch, 2009).

No further successful examples of highly publicised major interventions by activist hedge funds in mainland Europe have been reported to date since TCI's confrontation with ABN AMRO's management in 2007. There has been no appearance of a flood of 'noisy' activist interventions developing in the region. The financial crisis that developed from 2007 is one reason for this. Activist hedge funds' own investors found themselves short of cash, bank credit became more difficult to obtain, and market sentiment became less supportive of the idea of releasing short-term value from companies while the future remained uncertain. Another factor may be that there are only a limited number of mainland European companies where there are sufficient institutional shareholders without commercial or political commitments to the companies in which they are investing to permit the sort of confrontational interventions that TCI was able to carry out at Deutsche Börse and ABN AMRO.

The case of Generali is instructive in this regard. In 2007 Algebris, a UK activist hedge fund, invested in Generali, the Italian insurance company, and launched a series of public attacks on Generali's management and practices; US hedge funds added their support (FT, 2008b). However, after Generali's board had largely ignored the funds' demands, Algebris was reported to have sold its stake in April 2009 (Reuters, 2009a). Generali's shareholder structure suggests why its management could resist the funds' demands. As of 17 January 2008, while Algebris was publicising its demands, nearly 32% of Generali's shareholders were Italian banks or other investors who are assumed to be closely identified with the board's strategy. A more detailed shareholder breakdown, as at 14 July 2009, showed that those classed as 'main shareholders' held 31.42%, other institutions held 31.21%, and retail investors, who seldom identify with activist hedge funds, held 37.37%. Overall, Italian shareholders held 69.48%, against foreigners with 30.52% (Generali, 2009). From these data it is possible to infer that while Algebris was encouraged by the presence of foreign institutional shareholders, it was ultimately blocked by the predominance of local Italian investors comprising 'main shareholders' and retail investors.

While every intervention by an activist hedge fund is likely to have its own distinctive features, the cases described above indicate some general features of hedge fund activism on the European mainland. The three investments by TCI show an activist hedge fund applying what we have called a 'large-cap' strategy in a 'noisy' manner: these interventions all involved large or complex targets in respect of which TCI was able to identify opportunities to extract shareholder value that other investors appeared not to have noticed. TCI's targets all exhibited an element of instability which was then exploited as an arbitrage opportunity. TCI's strategy involved a public assertion that shareholder value of one kind or another was hidden or in danger of being squandered. Pressure was then put on the boards to release this value and a decisive majority of shareholders was convinced to join TCI's campaign. The matter in each case was decided by shareholder votes, or the threat of a vote; there were no tender offers and TCI did not become engaged in litigation. The key in all these cases seems to have been the preponderance of foreign institutional shareholders willing to support a strategy of value extraction. TCI could not have acted if there had not been underlying discontent with corporate performance and strategy in each case. Algebris' experience at Generali suggests a similar strategy that failed for lack of a critical mass of foreign institutional investors interested in releasing free cash flow. Laxey's approach was different. Its Swiss strategy relied less on gathering allies and more on selecting targets where its own resources were sufficient to amass shares. At Saurer it appears to have succeeded in its aims while at Implenia it appeared to meet a more implacable response, although apparently without losing money on its investment.

These cases do not demonstrate that a majority of companies in mainland European countries were ripe for investment by activist hedge funds in the period just prior to the onset of the global financial crisis. They show that overseas institutional investors, predominantly from the USA and the UK, had become sufficiently influential at certain European companies to impose their standards of shareholder value. The three TCI interventions demonstrated how institutional investors who had previously been relatively quiescent could, more-over, be stirred into action by an activist hedge fund intervention. The other side of Continental European hedge fund activism is indicated by the findings of Becht *et al.*'s study, summarised above. Together with these limited opportunities to execute very public confrontations that would not be out of place in the US market, there appears to be a much more numerous core of often privately negotiated interventions, sometimes cooperating with the major block shareholders who are common at many Continental European companies, where confronta-tion is much rarer and the whole style of intervention is distinct.

5.6 Conclusion

We have reviewed the emergence of hedge fund activism in the USA, Britain, and Continental Europe. We have seen that hedge fund activ-ism, and 'noisy' activism in particular, became a widespread phe-nomenon in the USA from the late 1990s and has come to enjoy considerable legitimacy there. Provided that funds choose their tar-gets well and offer convincing arguments in support of organisational change or higher returns to shareholders, there is a good chance that they will be perceived to have at least some positive aspects and that other shareholders will support them. While equally dedicated in prin-ciple to the search for 'shareholder value', the UK has followed a dif-ferent path to the USA, involving less open confrontation. Whereas in the USA the major institutional investors often appear to share a commonality of interest with well-informed activist hedge funds, their British equivalents focus instead on the funds' desire for short-term gain and tend to remain aloof, cooperating only when it suits them and to a very limited degree. Continental Europe exhibits still differ-ent characteristics, despite signs of greater acceptance of shareholder primacy ideas in recent years. Although US-style confrontational activ-ism was shown to be effective in a limited number of situations where sufficient support was available from US or UK institutional investors, there is evidence that the wider market for hedge fund activism in Continental Europe operates less publicly, with more negotiation and less confrontation. Thus where hedge fund activism has spread from the USA to other markets, it has not emerged as a duplicate of US practice but has followed a path dictated by local conditions. In subse-quent chapters we will see how it fared in Japan.

6 | Firm-centric corporate governance: the evolution of the Japanese model

6.1 Introduction

In this chapter we review the development of Japanese company law and corporate governance practice from their beginnings in the final decades of the nineteenth century, when the model of the joint stock company was consciously imported with the aim of promoting economic development, to the early years of the twenty-first century, when activist hedge funds began to take an interest in the Japanese market. As we shall see, Japan has followed a path of institutional development which is similar in many respects to that of other market economies. Japan adopted the legal and organisational forms associated with the business enterprise very quickly in the period from 1893 to 1899 when it was also undergoing rapid industrialisation. Successive company law reforms modelled on aspects of initially German and subsequently American legal systems privileged the position of shareholders, both in relation to other stakeholders, and in terms of their power to hold managers to account. Although the pace of Japan's industrialisation to some degree set it apart from other countries, its corporate governance arrangements were largely indistinguishable from those in America and Europe for the first decades of the twentieth century. By the 1940s this had changed. The model of the business enterprise which emerged in the post-1945 period was one in which shareholder voice was marginalised and the powers of management strengthened. Both in managerial rhetoric and in practice, the interests of the firm, and by extension those of the employees and customers who sustained it, were given priority over those of outside investors. The firm was seen as a community of interests that deserved to be preserved for the benefit of all its active stakeholders.

The co-existence of this 'community firm' model with a legal structure that recognised the rights of shareholders requires explanation. We shall offer an account based on the particular evolutionary path taken by the Japanese economy and polity since industrialisation. This evolutionary process exhibits two main features: on the one hand, the alignment of laws and institutions to accommodate a market economy dominated by firms organised along capitalist lines; on the other, the embedding of that market economy in institutions reflecting Japan's own experience of industrial development.

6.2 The legal structure of Japanese joint stock companies

The legal structure of the Japanese joint stock company of the early twenty-first century exhibits many points of resemblance to similar legal forms in other economically developed countries. The legal rules and principles that define the structure and conduct of Japanese companies were drawn together in the Company Law (*Kaisha Hō*) of 2006 (for a summary see, for example, DIR, 2006). Companies may establish rules for their own governance through their articles of association, within the framework set by the national law. The Company Law continues most of the underlying corporate structures and protocols of its predecessor elements in the Commercial Code which dates back to the late nineteenth century. The shareholders' meeting is the ultimate governing body of the company, whether as an AGM or EGM. Differences in the extent of shareholders' powers arise depending on whether the company is a company with corporate auditors, as the majority are, or a company with committees, a distinction we explore in more detail below (see Section 6.5), but in both cases the shareholders' meeting elects the board of directors. All shareholders are entitled to attend general meetings, ask questions, present opinions, and vote. Any shareholder who has held more than 1 per cent of the issued shares of a listed company continuously for six months may propose agenda items for consideration at a shareholders' meeting. Any shareholder who has held more than 3 per cent of the issued shares of a listed company continuously for six months may require the directors to convene a general meeting. In most cases, resolutions at general meetings are adopted if supported by a simple majority, with a quorum of at least half of issued shares taking part; shareholders who control more than 50 per cent of the shares in a listed Japanese company can normally dictate dividend levels and the composition of the board. Certain major decisions such as amendment of the articles and disposal of major assets require a two-thirds majority from the same quorum. Although different classes of shares are now permitted, the vast majority of companies still issue only one class of share, combined in trading units determined by the company, each with a single vote and the right to receive whatever dividends the company pays. The amount of the dividend is approved by the AGM at most companies but, in the case of the minority that are companies with committees, dividends are approved by the board of directors.

This basic legal structure applies to all companies limited by share capital. Companies with a stock market listing are subject to securities legislation and stock exchange listing rules which also largely mirror those found in other industrialised economies. Thus listed joint stock companies in Japan possess a legal structure which is essentially the same as that of similar companies in the USA or West European countries. Within this structure, there would seem to be no formal impediments to shareholder activism, of the kind which has been practised elsewhere.

However, the embedding of formally similar legal structures in distinctive national practices means that the written law is only a limited guide to how corporate governance works on the ground (Jacoby, 2005a). In Japan, the adjustment of the legal model to local conditions goes back to the beginnings of modern economic development. Writing of the organisational structures adopted in the police force, the postal system, and the press in late nineteenth century Japan, Westney observed that 'Western models provided both inspiration and legitimation; later they continued to supply inspiration, but the grounds for legitimation were increasingly sought in the Japanese tradition and environment' (Westney, 2000: 220). Her observations have wider resonance. Iwai, for example, argued that treatment of employees at merchant houses in the later Tokugawa Period[1] foreshadowed corporate practices that emerged in the latter half of the twentieth century, including long-term employment and the linking of wage increases to seniority in the firm (Iwai, 2008: 191–3). This is just one of the respects in which the Japanese company, rather than being simply a clone of Western models, developed its own path. We now consider this historical process of development in more detail.

---

[1] The Tokugawa family's military government ruled Japan (though nominally on behalf of the Emperor) from 1603 until 1868.

6.3 The advent of joint stock companies in Japan

The institution of the joint stock company was imported into Japan during the latter half of the nineteenth century in conscious imitation of European and US models. From the beginning of the seventeenth century, while the economies of Europe were starting to expand and formalise their commercial systems, in Japan the Tokugawa regime had sought to sustain an agrarian-based military society in which industry and commerce were tolerated only to the extent that they appeared to support this structure. A merchant class had evolved and prospered mainly by default, as an unforeseen but essential intermediary to provide liquidity in an economy otherwise focused on barter. The progressive transfer of national wealth to this class over a period of some two and a half centuries was an important factor in the economic collapse which left the regime so poorly equipped to resist foreign pressure for commercial access in the 1850s (Sheldon, 1958). Against this background, joint stock companies and the laws that sustained them in Japan began as imports of foreign models, which were expected to deliver similar outcomes to those that they delivered in their home countries.

In the second half of the nineteenth century a systematic effort was made, led by the state, to codify and clarify Japan's commercial and corporate laws (see Röhl, 2005; Tokuda, 2002; and West, 2001). With the decline and eventual collapse of the Tokugawa government, industrial and commercial expansion, spurred on by the opening of the economy to foreign trade, had created a growing practical need for clearer commercial legislation. Partnership-style structures had emerged since the 1850s. These forms were based on contract and the drafting of bespoke articles of association, and did not confer limited liability. But in 1876 a National Banking Decree defined national banks as joint stock companies with limited liability. Vagueness regarding the degree of limited liability enjoyed by shareholders in other kinds of company became an increasingly prominent issue during the 1880s as deflationary policies triggered a spate of bankruptcies, and the situation was recognised as an impediment to economic development; clarity with regard to the legal nature of business associations and the obligations of their shareholders and officers was seen as a priority.

There was also growing political pressure for commercial legislation. The rulers of nineteenth century Japan had been impressed by the military and industrial power of the USA and the leading European countries, and they wished to stimulate similar economic growth in their own country, with all the benefits it promised. The concept of *fukoku kyōhei* ('a prosperous country and a strong military'), drawn from Chinese sources of the Warring States Period, was frequently invoked during the Meiji Period[2] as a national goal. The Japanese government was also keen to dismantle the unequal treaties imposed upon the Tokugawa regime by the USA and European powers at the time of the opening of the country in the 1850s and one precondition for this move, proposed by Britain and Germany in 1868, was the creation of a system of commercial law.

Japan enacted parts of its first set of commercial and corporate laws (latterly known as the *Kyū Shōhō* or 'Old Commercial Code') in 1893, implementing it fully in 1898 and then revising it in important respects in 1899 as the definitive Commercial Code (*Shōhō*). The Old Commercial Code was based on the work of a German scholar, Hermann Roesler, who had undertaken a commission from the Japanese government in 1881 to carry out research into suitable foreign laws and to produce a draft law. His work was criticised by the business community as paying too little attention to traditional practices. It did however encourage enterprises to adopt specified corporate forms whose structure was defined by law. The Japanese legal experts who dominated the drafting committee for the revised Commercial Code sought to eliminate certain perceived weaknesses of the first version: limited liability joint stock companies could henceforth be established without prior official permission, internal auditors could not act as directors, and a merger mechanism was established. At this stage all directors were required to be shareholders.

This extended legislative exercise established the legal foundations for joint stock companies and put in place the institution of limited liability for shareholders. The process up to this point offers few pointers as to how the Japanese system would evolve in the course of the twentieth century. The legislation of the 1890s was a conscious imitation of systems in North America and Western Europe. But it was also a response to internal pressures for organisational change; commercial dynamics were at work in the Japanese economy alongside the desire to mimic foreign ways. What made the subsequent Japanese experience

[2] 1868–1912.

distinctive was the way that the demands of a wartime economy, and then the necessity for reconstruction, created an environment in which capitalist ideas were adjusted to the needs of the moment, with only minor modification of the legal structures underlying them.

By 1905, encouraged by tax incentives during the Russo-Japanese War, joint stock companies accounted for well over 80 per cent of the Japanese corporate sector's paid-up capital, though less than half the total number of companies as such. Companies with liquid share-holdings – whether formally listed or merely traded on an informal basis – were also becoming more common, and from the late 1880s onwards the business of the Tokyo and Osaka Stock Exchanges had begun to shift from government bond trading to the trading of cor-porate shares, to the point where the latter soon became their main activity (Tokuda, 2002). Shareholders played an active role in the gov-ernance of these early companies. Tōyō Keizai and TSE data quoted by Okazaki (Okazaki, 1999: 98–110) show that in 1935 65.9% of the share capital of *zaibatsu*[3] firms was held by their top ten sharehold-ers, while the equivalent at non-*zaibatsu* firms was 32.1%, with hold-ing companies playing a major role in both cases. The *zaibatsu* firms tended to employ a greater number of professional managers, in the sense of salaried specialists rather than shareholders participating dir-ectly in management. It is estimated that in 1935 more than 20 per cent of directors at non-*zaibatsu* firms were concurrently major sharehold-ers. Although efforts were made by many companies to retain valued employees during the 1920s and 1930s, the rate of employee turnover was still more than double the low levels that would become accepted as normal from the 1950s. As Okazaki noted, the sharp break in prac-tice after 1945 is captured in the observations of the businessman Takasaki Tatsunosuke, firstly on his return to Japan in 1916, and then on his return in 1947. In 1916 Takasaki observed:

---

[3] Morikawa, in his detailed study of the *zaibatsu*, defined them as 'A group of diversified businesses owned exclusively by a single family or an extended family' (Morikawa, 1992). As he makes clear, one of their characteristics was the employment of skilled professional management as they expanded during the Japanese industrial revolution of the late nineteenth and early twentieth centuries. They were dissolved as groups after the Second World War although former member companies subsequently sustained a loose connection through interlinked minority shareholdings; these links weakened at the end of the twentieth century as cooperation between unaffiliated companies increased.

The first thing I found unacceptable was that large blocks of a firm's stock could be transferred from A to B without the knowledge of the employees. Whenever this happened the top management would change and so there was never any consistency in company policy. Second, instead of working to improve the corporate base, directors opted to pay high dividends to curry favour with shareholders. They also aimed to boost the stock price. The management thus appeared to be more concerned with the ups and downs of the stock price than the overall performance of the firm or, to put it another way, the shareholders had enormous power while the wishes of the employees went unheard.

In 1947, when he returned once more from overseas, Takasaki discovered that the situation had apparently become inverted:

When I think of it now, it was a scandalous situation. The interests of shareholders were dismissed entirely and business was run at the behest of the workers. It was the exact opposite of the situation I found in 1916 when I returned to Japan the first time. Shareholders' dividends, the stock price and the like were all given low priority, while workers' pay and conditions were of paramount concern, and not a single person thought about strengthening the corporate base or building up capital. This state of affairs subsequently improved to some degree when the need for capital was felt, but there has been no significant major change right up to the present. (Okazaki, 1999: 99)

During Takasaki's absence, Japan had moved from a system prioritising the rights of providers of capital, to one in which those who contributed their labour to the firm formed its principal constituency. Various threads of development can be traced to account for this change.

The shareholder-focused corporate system that had developed in Japan from the late nineteenth century came under pressure during a period of economic and political turbulence in the early decades of the twentieth century. Labour disputes escalated in the period of economic downturn following the First World War. The Japanese economy was shaken by a general fall in global demand in the 1920s, by the natural disaster of the Great Kantō Earthquake in 1923, and then by the global Great Depression of the 1930s. A rural crisis developed from late 1929 with a sharp decline in the silk price, followed by fluctuating rice harvest yields which brought market prices below production costs and culminated in widespread famine in northern

Japan from 1931. In 1929 only 30 per cent of new graduates from the prestigious Imperial Universities succeeded in finding jobs on graduation (Fairbank, Reischauer, and Craig, 1965: 579–97; Okazaki and Okuno-Fujiwara, 1999: 3).

At the same time that the Japanese economy was being buffeted by these developments, military and right-wing pressures were beginning to destabilise society. Throughout the 1930s the military became increasingly assertive and from 1937 the onset of war, first with China and then from 1941 also with the Allied Powers, required the redirection of the economy to concentrate on production of munitions. From this situation emerged interrelated pressures that diminished the standing of shareholders and gave increased autonomy to management, while at the same time raising the status of the workforce. As the shift to a wartime economy took hold, Japan's planners were influenced by the perceived success of the command economy in Soviet Russia. Central control of key industries was instituted and the Planning Board (*Kikakuin*) viewed shareholders and their pursuit of profit as an impediment that needed to be constrained in order to promote the war effort. Measures to separate ownership and control were considered. In 1940 the Planning Board published proposals for its Outline of the Establishment of a New Economic System (*Keizai Shintaisei Kakuritsu Yōkō*) in which it stated that 'the firm is an organic body composed of capital, management and labour'. Despite opposition from business circles, this was approved by the Cabinet in December of that year (Okazaki, 1996: 367).

This set the scene for a number of changes as the war progressed. Although the Commercial Code was not amended, other laws introduced at this time had a significant impact on the way companies were governed and managed. Radical change began with the Munitions Corporations Law (*Gunju Kaisha Hō*) of October 1943, which established a 'responsible person' – usually the CEO – for each company in the designated munitions-related sector, who was granted executive powers to run the company without any formal approval by shareholders. By 1945, shareholders had virtually no say in the running of listed companies, dividends were controlled, and shares had become tantamount to fixed interest securities (Okazaki, 1996: 373).

In parallel to these developments there was a campaign to raise workforce morale and stimulate labour input in the national interest. From the late 1930s, labour was portrayed as a patriotic duty, and arguments were put forward that pay should be adjusted to households' consumption needs rather than being based on labour's contribution to enterprise performance. Although productivity-linked elements in wages did not disappear entirely, during the course of the Second World War a system of fixed pay with annual increases for all employees became standard. Meanwhile, a shortage of labour reduced the gap between clerical and labouring pay and, in some cases, reversed it. In a relatively short space of years, a capitalist system in which the owners of capital ran industry for their own benefit and treated labour as an input to production was tilted towards a system in which the state dealt directly with management and labour to further the national interest, in the form of the war effort, almost to the exclusion of shareholders. These developments were not unique to Japan. Alfred P. Sloan Jr described how at General Motors, 'the War Administration Committee practically ran the organization. This was because our wartime policy was set and nearly all the corporation's work was war production' (Sloan, 1965: 185–6). Yet, for a number of related reasons, the wartime experience was to shape post-war developments in Japan to a greater degree than in the USA and other industrialised countries (Okazaki and Okuno-Fujiwara, 1999: 30).

The priority immediately after the Second World War was to rebuild the Japanese economy as quickly as possible. The two directing forces in Japan in the early post-war years were the Japanese government and the Allied Powers' GHQ[4] which was effectively under American control. The Japanese government was subject to pressure from GHQ, in the form of directives aimed at promoting demilitarisation and democratisation (Röhl, 2005: 383). Much of the country's manufacturing plant had been destroyed by military action, food shortages were acute, and the industrial workforce was determined to defend its interests. GHQ's initial encouragement of the labour movement served to stimulate a union militancy which managers found hard to resist (Odaka, 1999: 163–4, 168). Management re-established control of industry during the 1950s, sustained by GHQ's decision to withdraw its support for union activism in 1947, the Japanese government's determination to oppose workforce unrest, and the imposition in 1949 of the so-called

---

[4] The General Headquarters of the US occupying forces, known also as Supreme Commander for the Allied Powers ('SCAP').

Dodge Plan of economic reforms[5] which ended the soft loan regime that had encouraged inflationary wage settlements. Out of this period there gradually emerged a consensus that management and labour should cooperate for the sake of the industrial enterprise in which they had a shared interest. The principle of managerial control was largely accepted, in return for a commitment to inform and consult labour on matters of corporate organisation and strategy. In this emerging consensus, 'The good of the company was the good of all its members and of society at large. The interests of workers and managers, of labor and capital, were in basic accord' (Gordon, 1998: 201).

After being marginalised during the wartime years, shareholders played little or no part in the post-war struggles between management and labour. Initially, neither the Japanese government nor GHQ saw any need to reassert the capitalist orientation of the pre-War economy or to safeguard shareholders' rights. With the approval of GHQ, labour unions were legalised in December 1945 and encouragement was given to the establishment of management councils designed to promote cooperation between management and labour, and to give labour a voice in decision-making. A report by a Keizai Dōyūkai[6] study group in 1947 summarised the prevalent atmosphere when it recommended that ownership and management of companies should be clearly separated and that management should act in the public interest. Its call for harmonious industrial relations echoed the wartime Planning Board in describing firms as communities of management, capital, and labour (Inagami, 2009: 165). Meanwhile, confiscations of the property of previously dominant families and the 1946 property tax which was designed to redistribute the nation's wealth – for which it is estimated that 29 per cent of payments were made in stocks and shares – had concentrated the share capital of major companies in government hands. Between 1947 and 1949, these shares were sold off, with preference given to employees of the companies concerned, resulting in about 43 per cent of the total being held by employees and some 70 per cent being held by individuals. This sell-off led to a stock market boom which was halted by the

---

[5] This package of reforms was named after Joseph Dodge, chairman of the Detroit Bank, who served as economic adviser to the GHQ.
[6] The Keizai Dōyūkai (Japan Association of Corporate Executives) was founded in 1946 to promote reconstruction of the Japanese economy. In 2010 it had approximately 1,400 members from some 900 companies (www.doyukai.or.jp).

economic reforms of the Dodge Plan in 1949. A problem was now apparent: industrial revival was needed, but capital was no longer available from official credits. The capital markets which had funded Japanese industrial expansion in the 1920s, despite their brief post-war revival, had effectively been stifled as a source of fresh funding by many years of anti-shareholder policies (Okazaki, 1999: 120–32). Another source of funding was required.

Instead of seeking ways to rebuild the capital markets, the Japanese government turned to banks and other financial institutions both to provide the necessary finance and to underpin stock prices by purchasing shares and other securities. The banks, in particular, found themselves in a favoured and powerful position, and often took it upon themselves to force their commercial customers to reorganise; they became in effect a counterweight to the strength of organised labour, able to impose conditions for staff reduction and other measures that management had hesitated to propose. Shareholders played no part in this process and an environment developed where the interests of management, employees, and banks drove corporate strategy. Against the background of the national consensus on the need to revive industry and rebuild the economy, this structure proved resilient: 'by the early 1950s, a pro-growth corporate governance structure had been formed, its major players being growth-oriented lifetime employees and a similarly growth-oriented financing body of investors centred round a main bank' (Okazaki, 1999: 132–8).

Concurrently with these changes in the Japanese economy, the GHQ instigated a number of amendments to Japan's commercial law. In 1948 a Securities and Exchange Law had been passed to regulate capital market activity, and in 1950 a comprehensive revision of the Commercial Code was enacted. As West observed, the impetus for this revision appears to have come completely from GHQ, which seems to have viewed commercial reform as an integral part of the democratic impetus it wanted to give to Japan. The objectives were to redistribute the balance of power within the corporate structure, strengthen shareholders' rights, and encourage capital investment. The form of the new legislation was substantially similar to the American Illinois Business Corporation Act of 1933, apparently because several of the GHQ legal staff involved in the revision exercise were Illinois lawyers. West noted 11 subsequent revisions between 1950 and 2000 to address specific issues, but, despite the initial lack of enthusiasm from the Japanese side, only three of the core features of the 1950 Act were later reversed: mandatory cumulative voting, prohibitions on share transfer restrictions, and the inclusion of pre-emption rights in corporate articles (West, 2001: 538–46 and 558). To begin with, the powers of the board of internal auditors to monitor and supervise management were restricted, but subsequently revised in several stages when it became evident that shareholder derivative suits of the kind that functioned as a monitoring device in the USA were not working in the same way in Japan. At the same time, the revised Commercial Code reduced the powers of the shareholders' meeting to control the company directly, making it clear instead that the responsibility for the management of the company vested in the board of directors, as in the USA (Röhl, 2005: 393). Most of the individuals and employees to whom shares had been distributed in the sell-off of 1947–9 sold their holdings to corporate buyers as soon as they could profitably do so (Aronson, 2010: 61). All these factors tended to secure the autonomy of management from shareholder pressure, formal legal protection for shareholder rights notwithstanding.

Thus, in the course of a few decades, Japan had implemented a legal structure for joint stock companies with limited liability, drawing largely on foreign models, and seen its corporate sector develop through this structure at a pace far in advance of anything experienced by the economies it had imitated. After experiencing a period of shareholder-dominated capitalism until the 1930s, it had emerged from the Second World War with management effectively unrestrained by shareholders and primarily focused on its relations with an assertive workforce. By the 1950s, an understanding between managers and the managed was in the process of emerging. This was based on the importance of the long-term growth of the firm as the best means of combining their interests. Industry's demands for capital and working funds were met by bank funding, a solution that appealed to the interventionist tendencies of a civil service that could exercise influence over the principal banking groups more easily than it could hope to control the capital markets. These were the conditions under which industrial regeneration began. The revised Commercial Code of 1950 accelerated these trends in its attempt to reduce the power of the shareholders' meeting and to support the board's freedom to run the business free of interference from investors. Takasaki had been shocked by the situation in 1947 in which the workforces claimed the attention of management and no heed was paid to shareholders' interests, long-term planning, or the financial needs of the firm. Now that workforces had been co-opted successfully into the corporate consensus and a more stable system for corporate finance through the banks had been put in place, management could turn its attention again to the long term. Shareholders were largely irrelevant to this process.

6.4 The rise of the community firm

The model of the firm that later came to be regarded by many, in and beyond Japan, as 'traditional', was a phenomenon of the post-1945 period. It applied to large, listed companies which were relatively few in number but disproportionately important to the economy. Okuno-Fujiwara summarises its main features as the following:

... the characteristic features of labour-management relations in Japan, such as long-term fixed employment, pay by seniority, and internal promotion; the features of the financial markets such as the preference for indirect funding and the main bank system; the characteristics of relations among firms, such as subcontracting and *keiretsu*[7] alignments; the weakness of small shareholders, their power undermined by the practice of crossholdings of shares as well as boards comprised almost exclusively of internally promoted directors; government-enterprise relations, such as the liberal use of administrative guidance and the unique status of industrial associations run by ex-Ministry officials – these are frequently described as the special characteristics of the Japanese economic model, and are rarely seen in other countries. (Okuno-Fujiwara, 1999: 266)

As we have seen, this model was contingent on a certain configuration of institutional and economic forces, and it was not static even in the period of the 1950s and 1960s when it seemed to enjoy its greatest stability. By the 1970s the ability of government ministries to influence industry directly had already begun to decline and companies were turning increasingly to the capital markets for external funding.

---

[7] The word *keiretsu* is often used to refer to corporate groups in Japan; but *keiretsu* sometimes means a series of subcontractors organised under a principal manufacturer (vertical *keiretsu*), and at other times refers to a group of large firms in diverse industries (horizontal *keiretsu*) (Hoshi, 1994: 287). For a critical view of the concept of the *keiretsu*, suggesting that its importance to the Japanese economy has been exaggerated, see Miwa and Ramseyer (2006).

This process led to a related loss of influence on the part of the banks, which gradually ceased to supply firms' core financing needs directly, becoming instead purveyors of commoditised bridging loans, with little scope to influence their corporate clients (Hoshi, 1994: 299–300). On the other hand, the role of employees within the firm continued to grow. This view of the company as consisting first and foremost of its workforce, up to and including those responsible for its management at board level, rather than as a collection of assets ultimately owned by its shareholders, became the principal distinguishing feature of Japan's post-1945 corporate governance. As Matsumoto was later to put it: 'a new economic system has developed and been nurtured in Japan inside the shell of capitalism' (Matsumoto, 1983: viii).

Alongside this development, there was a growing legal debate about the nature of the corporate enterprise. Japanese scholarship of the 1960s and 1970s had little in common with the notion of the company as a 'nexus of contracts' which began to influence the US debate at this time. While US scholars were criticising the error of 'thinking about organizations as if they were persons with motivations and intentions' (Jensen and Meckling, 1976: 310–11), Japanese commentators were debating the difference between two contrasting views of the joint stock company as *hōjin meimoku setsu* ('the theory of the nominal legal person') and *hōjin jitsuzai setsu* ('the theory of the legal person as a real entity'). The predominance of the idea that the firm was an entity in its own right (Iwai, 2008: 117–18) was an echo of early twentieth century debates on the nature of the corporation in Germany (see Gelter, 2010).

The idea of the 'community firm' which entered social science discourse on Japan in the same period bears a family resemblance to the legal theory of *hōjin jitsuzai setsu*. The concept of the firm as a community, as Inagami and Whittaker recognised, 'eludes neat definition, and easy quantification' (Inagami and Whittaker, 2005: 3). At one level, the community firm can be thought of as an organisation in which all employees feel a strong vested interest, and with whose continuity and success they strongly identify. But the significance of the community firm goes further: it implies a conception of the business enterprise as a stable social system which instantiates certain values concerning the way that companies are seen by their employees and the way in which managers, up to and including board directors, interpret their duties as owed to the organisation: 'The community nature of a Japanese firm – partly predicated on the fact that it is not run primarily for the benefit of shareholders – imposes peer-group moral constraints on those who are selected, as the culmination of their lifelong membership, to be its "elders" – much like the constraints on permanent secretaries of British ministries' (Dore, 2000: 79).

Effectively this means that management will consider its obligation to the company as a continuing entity to be more important than any duty it may feel towards any single stakeholder group, including the shareholders. The identification by employees at all levels with the firm and its interests produces a strongly 'internalist' orientation to management practice. In his study of unionism and labour relations in the post-war Japanese steel industry, Gordon emphasised the initial similarity of Japan's historical labour relations experience with that of other industrialised countries. The significant exception he observed was the 'corporate hegemony' whereby large companies have established themselves as the long-term focus of their employees' lives, offering security and internal advancement in return for loyalty and subordination of personal interest to the needs of the company: 'corporate hegemony has been stronger and more enduring in Japan since the early 1960s than anywhere in the world' (Gordon, 1998: 196). In 2006 Mitarai Fujio and Niwa Uichirō, then chairmen of Canon and Itochū respectively, published a book of commentaries on the purpose of the company entitled *Kaisha wa dare no tame ni* ('Who is the company for?'). Mitarai wrote: 'When one talks about things like a "spirit of love for one's company" it may be dismissed by many people as old-fashioned but it is something that I personally want to emphasise at this time particularly. I want management, for a start, and every single employee to have this feeling of love for the company' (Mitarai and Niwa, 2006: 100).

Promotion at every level of the community level is overwhelmingly internal. Managers who are both able and fortunate can hope to reach the very highest levels of the predominantly executive board. Thus Japanese senior managers have been described as the winners of a fierce competition for internal promotion who run the business for the sake of the whole body of employees (Tachibanaki, 1998: 249). This environment creates boards that see themselves as integral with the whole body of management and indeed of employees in general. As a senior director at a large manufacturer described his company's situation to us in 2004: 'We don't have an American-style board, you see.

We have our CEO and everyone forming our board but they are not a board designed to control the actions of executive officers. From the CEO down, they are an executive officers' meeting.'

The integrity of the community firm is under increasing pressure. Even at the largest companies, the concept of job security has been eroded progressively since the 1970s as the practice of transferring surplus labour out of parent companies has developed. The growing importance of contract labour also poses a threat to stability of employment (Sako, 2005: 591). According to official figures, 15 per cent of the total labour force was employed on short-term contracts of various kinds in 1984; by 2009 this had risen to 29 per cent (MIC, 2010). If this trend persists, increasing mobility of labour and the emergence of an inter-company management labour pool in the future could potentially undermine the cohesive internal personnel structure on which the edifice of the community firm rests. Inagami and Whittaker nevertheless concluded in their 2005 study that the community firm will persist, although the traditional model may be giving way to a reformed version – 'the community firm is being modified or reformed but not abandoned' (Inagami and Whittaker, 2005: 241).

6.5 The community firm's internal focus

The community firm is an organisation designed to be enduring and self-supporting. It relies on outsiders as customers and suppliers but the attention of those who spend their entire working lives within it tends to be focused inward. Because of this internal focus, the community firm is predisposed to absorb or seek understandings with influences that it considers useful or indispensible and to shut out anything else. To illustrate this point we offer three examples: the situation regarding corporate auditors, developments regarding the optional 'company with committees' system introduced in 2003, and attitudes towards external directors.[8]

---

[8] The normal Japanese terms *gaibu torishimariyaku* or *shagai torishimariyaku* stress externality but do not touch on independence. They may have been influenced by the American expression 'outside directors' but the unspoken implication in the USA that such people will also be independent of the company's insiders is often lacking in Japan. We therefore refer to them here as 'external directors' to emphasise this distinction.

Corporate auditors

Japan's nineteenth century Commercial Code relied on internal *kansa-yaku* or corporate auditors (also translated as 'statutory auditors') to monitor the board's business decisions and accounting practices. As Dore observed, this was an element adopted from the German concept of the supervisory board or *Aufsichtsrat* (Dore, 2000: 101). This system is not used in the companies with committees described below but it is still the standard pattern at most Japanese companies. These corporate auditors are officers of their companies and distinct from the company's outside auditors who would normally be a firm of independent accountants. Their powers were limited to accounting matters by the US-influenced 1950 revision but they were not abolished. Subsequently, various legal amendments were enacted to define and strengthen their authority, often in response to corporate scandals that suggested inadequate supervision (Shishidō, 2001: 666). In 1975 their responsibility for business supervision was restored at 'large companies'[9] and in 1993 the concept of the board of corporate auditors was introduced to focus their authority more effectively.

In spite of these efforts, they are generally considered to have become co-opted into the corporate structure. A senior director at a very large company whom we interviewed in 2004 admitted that they were not an effective check on management: 'Our corporate auditors are legally obliged to supervise the directors but in practice they are tied up with lower level stuff, what you might call operational matters, and they are busy checking fine details of daily business.' Moreover, the status of most internal corporate auditors within the firm is not sufficiently high to challenge senior management easily. As one corporate auditor observed to us in 2004 regarding the process of selecting the internally appointed members of the board of corporate auditors: 'Procedurally, the approval of a majority at the AGM, preceded by agreement of the board of corporate auditors is needed. In practice, just like the most ordinary personnel transfer, appointments are made by the top management.'

Under an amendment to the Commercial Code approved in 2001 and implemented in 2002, the corporate auditors' position was further

---

[9] Officially defined for this purpose as those with capital of more than ¥500 million or total liabilities of more than ¥20,000 million.

strengthened in various ways, and large companies, as defined, were required to have at least three corporate auditors, of whom half had to be persons who had not been either directors or employees of the company or of its subsidiaries. This has introduced an explicit require-ment for externality. Some corporate auditors reported to us that they are now able to bring matters to management's attention through their externally appointed colleagues in a way that would not have been possible before but it is hard to tell how much the situation has really changed overall. Perhaps the most telling example of how corporate auditors are still effectively subordinate to the board of directors came from a conversation in 2004, over two years after the implementation of the 2002 reform, when we asked about their ability to compel discus-sion of topics that the board or internal planning meetings might prefer to ignore. A corporate auditor (who was internally appointed) told us: 'The chairman of the meeting always calls for the corporate auditors' opinion. On such occasions there are instances where we express opin-ions and also those where we do not. Our policy is where possible to state our opinions on management matters.' What seems implicit to us from this comment is that the corporate auditors as a whole are often seen more as a resource available to senior management rather than as a group of fully independent monitors. Another corporate auditor at the same company emphasised at a separate meeting that his colleague's view represented the older, internalised viewpoint and that it no longer reflected accurately the current policy of his company. He conceded that the resource represented by the corporate auditors was not always uti-lised fully by executive management, even when the corporate auditors clearly had relevant experience. However, he pointed out that corporate auditors are legally obliged to take a more assertive attitude to their monitoring duties and that many are increasingly doing so.

There are also some corporate auditors who, by force of person-ality, may overcome these problems. One such person, an internally appointed officer who enjoyed a formidable reputation within his company, when asked in 2004 what he would do if a senior director were suspected of misconduct, replied confidently: 'I would go and have it out with them.' He conceded that he would normally report his concerns initially to the president but stressed that if the presi-dent were himself suspect, he could take the issue to the full board and, failing that, directly to the courts, following the procedures of the Commercial Code. However, we believe that most internally appointed corporate auditors are less assertive, especially when dealing with issues that are not obvious instances of gross malpractice. The community firm embraces all its participants but one condition of this embrace is an acceptance of its hierarchy, making it difficult for insiders to question their superiors' decisions, even if they are specifically appointed to monitor their behaviour. The perceived need for external appointees to supplement the efforts of their internal colleagues is a further indication that most observers in Japan believe that corporate auditors who were formerly executives are more likely to identify with their companies' management than to act as true monitors.

The company with committees system

The company with committees (originally *iinkaitōsetchikaisha*, but subsequently *iinkaisetchikaisha*) was introduced as an optional corporate structure from April 2003, together with a little-used variant, the company with committee for important assets (*jūyōzaisaniinkai*). The two main features of the company with committees were that it had no corporate auditors and that three committees were selected from the board of directors to handle nomination, remuneration, and audit, all of which had to comprise at least three directors, of whom a majority had to be external directors (defined as persons who were non-executive directors, who had not been executive directors or employees of the company or of its subsidiaries and who currently held no executive appointments in the company or its subsidiaries). The intention was that the board of directors would concern itself with strategy and with supervision of the executive members of the company, while a new class of executive officers (*shikkōyaku*) was created to manage the business. This aspect closely resembled informal changes implemented by Sony in 1997 and widely copied elsewhere in Japan. The underlying principle was that a totally internal corporate governance system would be replaced by one where key board functions were dominated by external appointees and in which the board would cease to operate as an executive committee, becoming instead a supervisory body for the executive. In this way the hitherto unbroken line of promotion from the most junior executive to the highest board appointments was theoretically interrupted or at least restricted. The Japanese press hailed the new system as 'US corporate governance' and Miyauchi Yoshihiko, chairman and CEO of ORIX, observed in an interview in June 2003: 'The opportunity of this amendment to the Commercial Code has created a distinction for the moment between firms that take corporate governance seriously and those that do not' (Nikkei, 2003b; Nikkei Sangyō, 2003b).

The public debate that accompanied the process of consultation between the ministries concerned and the Keidanren gives an indication of the strength of opposition within the business community to the whole concept of external supervision. The then chairman of the Keidanren, Imai Takashi, said in a public speech at the Imperial Hotel on 20 June 2001:

> However one recent development that causes us some concern is the issue of corporate governance. A little while ago the Ministry of Justice published a summary of legislation to make external directors compulsory and invited comment; we find it difficult to agree with this particular element concerning external directors. We feel that the issue of how supervision of management is carried out is something where every company will have its own different approach that works best for it. Of course I am sure that there are plenty of companies where external directors will work well. But if this is made compulsory, it becomes a different matter. I am conscious that the flow of Japan's corporate governance to date has focused on strengthening the corporate auditors. External directors should never be more than one of the options available. We have commented on these lines. (Imai, 2001)

Ultimately, pressure from the Keidanren and the business community in general appears to have persuaded the Ministry of Justice to retreat from its initial stance and accept that the new system had to be optional (Gilson and Milhaupt, 2005: 354).

Moreover, the response from Japanese companies was muted. As of June 2003, when most companies' AGMs for that year had been held, the *Nikkei* article cited above noted only 36 adopting companies, of which 19 belonged to the Hitachi group. In the same article *Nikkei* reported the results of a survey carried out in February 2003. The response from 111 company presidents, chairmen, and other senior directors was that 60 per cent firmly intended not to transfer, implying no intention even to study the matter, although there was also an impression that some would wait to see how the first adopting companies fared. The Japan Corporate Auditors' Association 'JCAA' has monitored the number of transferring companies since the system began. After a gradual increase to 111 companies in November 2009 (of which 28% were Hitachi or Nomura affiliates) the total for October 2010 fell back to 102 companies (of which 25% were Hitachi or Nomura affiliates). This is equivalent to just under 2.8% of the 3,647 companies listed on all markets in Japan at the end of 2010 (JCAA, 2009, 2010; TSE, 2010).

This reaction can be attributed to various causes. The initial doubts expressed during the consultation exercise had revealed a general wariness within the Japanese business community and the Enron scandal, revealed in October 2001, had further diluted enthusiasm for what was perceived to be US corporate governance. Perhaps more importantly, several respected companies such as Toyota and Canon decided not to adopt the new system. Mitarai Fujio, then president of Canon, publicly expressed his doubts about the new system on a number of occasions. Quite apart from his company's high standing, the fact that he had been resident in the USA for many years and was credited with the successful expansion of Canon's subsidiary there made him almost unassailable in this debate. In a press interview in June 2003, reported in the same *Nikkei Sangyō* article cited above, he commented:

I don't dismiss the company with committees system out of hand. Intellectually I can understand it. But it is questionable whether it can work in practice. At the great majority of American companies, in fact, the external directors just end up listening to the explanations of the executives because, being non-executive, they don't understand the company well. I suspect their supervision is really rather precarious … Firms cannot escape from their countries' culture and practices. I am certainly not in pursuit of a 'Japanese style'. All I seek is the most appropriate system for modern Japanese companies that do not have the [staff] turnover that characterises America.

As Mitarai noted, there was something in the new system that did not fit well with the Japanese view of how a company should be run and the main manifestation of this appeared to be its emphasis on external directors. We examine this particular aspect in more detail below.

Attitudes towards external directors

Activist hedge funds have on several occasions demanded that Japanese companies in which they are investing should appoint external directors. This kind of demand is in keeping with agency theory; if vigilance is needed in case management is not working in the best interests of shareholders, external supervision of their activities should be advantageous. These demands, in Japan as in other markets, are often a reaction to initial refusal by management to increase payout to shareholders, and the assumption that has emerged largely unquestioned in the US and UK markets is that directors who take a more objective view of the company's position will be more inclined to respect shareholders' rights. The funds usually suggest suitable directors, which naturally implies that their candidates may be biased towards the funds' interests, but in the USA or the UK even genuinely independent directors might be expected to support reasonable demands for higher shareholder remuneration.

In other markets where activist hedge funds operate, the concept of appointing external and ideally independent directors is now well established. In the USA, there has been a progressive shift for many years towards greater numbers of 'outside directors' on boards. This was further encouraged by the Sarbanes Oxley Act's requirements for greater independence in audit committees, leading in turn to pressure from the SEC, and both the NYSE and Nasdaq have required since late 2003 that listed companies have a majority of independent directors on their boards. In the UK, the process has been more subdued but the Combined Code now states as a major principle: 'The board should include an appropriate combination of executive and non-executive directors (and, in particular, independent non-executive directors) such that no individual or small group of individuals can dominate the board's decision taking' (UKCGC, 2010: B1).

Japan lacks an effective tradition of external monitoring through the board. In theory this role should be fulfilled by the corporate auditors whose perceived weakness as monitors we have discussed. Nevertheless, many Japanese companies have a long history of appointing external directors and their number has increased since implementation of the company with committees system, but it is often unclear whether many of them are genuinely independent. Even taking the most lenient criteria for externality and independence, they are heavily outnumbered at large companies by executive directors who are predominantly internally appointed (Abe and Jung, 2004: 9–10; Miwa and Ramseyer, 2005; Miwa and Ramseyer, 2006: ch. 5). This preponderance of internal directors has been criticised as a weakness of

Japanese board structures that needs to be remedied (JCGF, 2001: 5), but many Japanese managers would disagree and feel that experience of the business is essential in order to be effective (Learmount, 2002: 136). On this subject, Mitarai observed in his book with Niwa, cited earlier: 'I have never felt any need whatsoever for external directors. I really cannot believe that Canon would develop better than it is doing already just by virtue of introducing people from outside who don't know anything' (Mitarai and Niwa, 2006: 94).

A distinction exists between external directors at companies that are not companies with committees, where they have no legally defined role beyond their directorships, and those at companies with committees, where the law gives them powers, at least in theory, over nomination, remuneration, and audit by virtue of their majority presence on the three committees that decide these matters. But although the majority executive board members at some companies with committees may listen seriously to their external director colleagues, there is a widespread and deeply entrenched view that all such people lack real power. Yano Tomomi, executive managing director of the Pension Fund Association ('PFA') observed to us in 2004: 'in Japan companies have lifetime employment so people work for decades in the same company right from graduating from school or university and all the directors are internal appointees. So they don't like outsiders at all, you see, and external directors are outsiders, aren't they?' He continued: 'External directors are there to check the management of the firm with external eyes but they hardly ever carry out that function. In Japan, they are advisers.'

Also speaking in 2004, one senior director at a large company, while broadly supportive of the need to maintain an external presence on his company's board and claiming to appreciate its benefits, was explicit about the limitations of external directors. They were not expected to participate directly in running the business: 'The function of external directors should be valued for their ability to give objective opinions and comments from outside the company, rather than make forceful comments about specific matters when they have not grasped the actual situation properly. They should be more concerned with social and objective observations.'

Even at companies with committees we felt unsure whether the external directors were really integrated with their boards. Speaking to the executive chairman of one such company in 2006 we asked whether the external members took a strong role in the decision-making process. He replied:

> They come up with opinions all the time at board meetings and you see we on the board pay a great deal of respect to the opinions of these external directors ... Sometimes they express opinions where we have our doubts, on various subjects. So, because we try to respect their opinions, we try to do things that way. We really do respect their opinions very much and they have influence.

Despite this reassurance we received the impression that 'we on the board' were really only the executive members and that the external directors were seen as distinct; their role appeared closer to that of respected advisers.

In much the same way, people who are not an accepted part of the community firm are not welcome if they try to tell management how to run it. When T. Boone Pickens proposed to nominate his representatives to Koito Seisakusho's board in 1989 (this case is described below in Section 6.7), the company's president, Matsuura Takao, commented at a press conference that although Pickens might know about the oil industry and takeovers, he had no experience of the manufacturing industry and thus could have no suitable candidates to send to Koito Seisakusho as directors (Yomiuri, 1989b). There was no suggestion that as a major shareholder he had an unquestioned right to nominate whomsoever he chose or that outsiders would by definition bring valuable objectivity.

In terms of the perceptions of its management, the community firm is a business before it is a joint stock company. Its board is traditionally an executive committee of insiders rather than a monitoring mechanism or an agent to protect shareholders' interests. The company with committees system gives external directors specific duties but, as we have seen, only a few companies have adopted it and it is unclear how much influence even these empowered external directors wield in practice. The community firm does not have natural channels for outside intervention and external directors tend either to be rejected or treated as advisors to the executive core of the board.

6.6 The role of shareholders in the community firm

One would expect shareholders to show interest in shareholder value, and most listed Japanese companies are widely held by both institutional and retail shareholders. As Miyauchi of ORIX said to a US audience in April 2004[10] when changes appeared to be imminent in Japanese corporate governance: 'At the end of the day it is investors, in particular institutional investors, that will dictate the pace and direction of corporate governance reform in Japan.' Activist hedge funds usually claim that their activism is not purely selfish but helps the entire shareholder body to obtain a fairer share of the company's wealth. Yet this formula does not appear to have operated smoothly in Japan.

Although, as we have seen, shareholders as a class were mostly ignored in the post-war reconstruction of the Japanese economy, and although the community firm tends to function without any major governance contribution from them, many shareholders' rights are established by law. However, in practice, these rights do not translate automatically into an atmosphere of commensurate shareholder empowerment. The Nomura Research Institute ('NRI'), began its online definition of 'corporate governance' (last updated in April 2008) with the explanation: 'Although at law the shareholders own the company, in most Japanese companies there was a deep-rooted feeling that "the company belongs to the management and employees"' (NRI, 2008). The definition continued with an explanation that the intervention of more vocal foreign and institutional shareholders has led to a questioning of this situation and an awareness of corporate governance issues. Nevertheless, at many Japanese companies the power of shareholders is still not evident because the community firm allows little scope for it: Learmount found that most senior managers whom he interviewed at Japanese companies in 1998–9 had difficulty reconciling the notion of accountability to shareholders with their sense of responsibility to the company and all its constituents. They saw their company as a social organisation whose purpose was more than just maximisation of profits (Learmount, 2002: 136–7).

To many foreign observers, the often perfunctory nature of most Japanese companies' AGMs for much of the latter half of the twentieth century exemplified the nature of the relationship between the company and its shareholders. As Gerlach observed, writing in 1992:

---

[10] Address given at the Corporate Governance Forum organised by the Committee for Economic Development and Keizai Dōyūkai in Washington, DC on 13 April 2004.

The reality ... is that it is a legal formality – a ceremony, the significance of which lies not in what gets communicated between shareholders and managers but in what it indicates about control over the firm and in the ways it satisfies demands for legitimacy in the larger business community. Large, stable shareholders do not typically bother to show up. In nearly 80 percent of the firms, those attending meetings account for less than 20 per cent of the company's shares. (Gerlach, 1992: 234–5)

A corporate auditor at a bank, speaking some 12 years later about his own organisation in 2004, still considered that AGMs remained a formality: 'It's something one does. So rather than the shareholders exercising power in managing the business, it's an information meeting.'

That big gatherings of shareholders such as AGMs lack dynamism is hardly surprising; this is not a situation unique to Japan, although the traditional bunching of AGMs on a few days in June every year in the past by major listed companies to protect themselves against *sōkaiya*[11] has probably exacerbated the problem. Similar concerns about the effectiveness of AGMs have been expressed in other markets, such as the UK: 'The usefulness of the AGM has arguably diminished in recent years as they have progressively become opportunities for private shareholders, pressure groups and environmental lobbyists to generate publicity' (London Stock Exchange, 2003). What is perhaps most important here is that, as Gerlach observed, 'large, stable shareholders do not typically bother to show up'.

One aspect of the relative unassertiveness of shareholders in Japan is the widespread assumption of the value of managerial autonomy. Most Japanese boards are not accustomed to taking instructions from shareholders. A journalist summarised his view of the general position in Japan in the course of a discussion with us in 2008 on the likelihood of boards being willing to entrust the question of implementing anti-takeover measures to a shareholders' vote:

I believe the management takes pride in being professional, you see. So they don't know how to react when external pressures appear. And the idea of convening a shareholders' meeting and requesting a decision on every little matter that arises is tantamount to saying that they themselves are stupid. So, to answer your question, I don't expect them to entrust matters

---

[11] Extortionist activists who typically demand money not to disrupt AGMs (discussed further in Chapter 7).

completely to the wishes of the shareholders. Then, additionally, there's the added incentive of self-preservation, so if you ask whether they will entrust things entirely to the shareholders, the answer is 'no'.

A foreign investor gave his view of how this situation can manifest itself in extreme cases: 'There are some Japanese, particularly old guard types, who are just not interested in talking to shareholders at all. So the shareholders are all tarred with the same brush whether they are foreign or Japanese as far as they are concerned. Their general attitude is "get lost, we are running this show"'.

The contrast between attitudes to shareholders at Japanese and 'Anglo-Saxon' firms has been summarised by Dore as 'the employee-favouring firm versus the shareholder-favouring firm' (Dore, 2000: 26) and this is still a succinct description of the general situation. However, there are nuances within this. The important shareholders who do not bother to attend AGMs evidently obtain satisfaction in ways other than speaking publicly. Learmount noted, in particular, that shareholders who were active contributors to companies were accorded different treatment: 'In the case of shareholders who were also long-term business partners, the sense of responsibility and obligation appeared in many cases to be especially strong' (Learmount, 2002: 145). Moreover, as Miyauchi observed, institutional shareholders, irrespective of any business links with companies, seem best positioned to drive corporate governance change. One pension fund, the PFA, attracted attention for much of the first decade of the twenty-first century by doing exactly this in a methodical and publicised way but it remains exceptional (Jacoby, 2009: 109–13). The issue that arises from this is why major shareholders in Japan have not chosen to ask for higher returns. The institutional investors among them are precisely the kind of investors who might be seen as the logical allies of activist hedge funds, who might be interested in aligning themselves with the activists once the issues had been defined, as seems to have been the case in TCI's European interventions. Hitherto this has not happened in Japan and it is relevant to consider why the situation there should be different.

According to share ownership data on the five largest Japanese stock exchanges (Tokyo, Osaka, Nagoya, Fukuoka, and Sapporo) as at the end of March 2011, published in June 2011 (National Stock Exchanges, 2011), the four largest groups of shareholders in Japan's listed companies, accounting for approximately 98% of the total, were: financial institutions (comprising commercial banks, trust banks, insurers, and pension funds[12]) 29.7%; non-residents (who are mostly institutions) 26.7%; corporate shareholders 21.2%; and retail investors[13] 20.3%.

Any one of these groups, even in isolation, is sufficiently large theoretically to exert influence on governance issues should they decide to vote on shareholder resolutions in a concerted manner. However, we discount two of these groups from our present discussion. Non-residents and their importance are discussed in Chapter 7. Their shareholdings fluctuated during the post-war period at a low level until the late 1980s when they began to rise from around 4 per cent to reach their present level. They are an important factor now, as we shall discuss later, but until the 1990s they played only a minimal role. Retail investors' holdings have decreased since the 1970s but appear to have stabilised at around the 20 per cent level for some time now (TSE, 2011b). In particular situations, such as the Tokyo Kohtetsu intervention discussed in Chapter 8, they play important roles but generally they do not act in a coordinated manner. Pressure groups such as the Kabunushi Ombudsman, founded in 1996 to promote a stronger voice for private individuals, have begun to ask questions at major companies' AGMs and may succeed in focusing attention on specific issues. It is also evident that the total of non-resident and retail shareholders across the Japanese stock markets is now approaching that of so-called stable shareholders. However, we do not think that most activist hedge funds are currently motivated to appeal to retail shareholders when they can hope to find a more concentrated and powerful audience among the institutional investors. Our discussion below therefore focuses on two of these shareholder categories: financial institutions and corporate shareholders. We look first at financial institutions, with a combined 29.7 per cent of the total, considering in turn the slightly

---

[12] No subtotal for 'pensions' is available as such. Private pension assets are understood to be included within 'trust banks' and public pension assets are understood to be spread between 'trust banks' and 'insurers' but no estimate of size is available.

[13] Strictly speaking this category includes private individuals and all other shareholders not already defined. Since 2010 it has included non-resident private individuals.

different circumstances of each sub-group: commercial banks, trust banks, insurers, and pension funds.

Commercial banks

Commercial banks, with 4.1 per cent, are now a relatively small subgroup, holding far fewer shares than they did until the 1990s. They are in the business of taking deposits, lending money, and providing various financial services. Additionally, in Japan, they followed the common commercial practice of the post-war period in cementing their relationships with customers through shareholdings, often in the form of cross-shareholdings, which we discuss below. However, as an officer at a market infrastructure body pointed out in 2008, they remain focused on banking:

… for a shareholder it is eminently reasonable to demand that shareholder value be maximised … from the point of view of someone making a bank loan, the greatest shareholder value is paying the money back so, rather than issue dividends, it's better to hold the money in the company – the attitude is that if there's money enough to pour it out in dividends or whatever, then pay back the loan. So since their shareholder value is being maximised they have no complaints and, in that sense, from the viewpoint of these shareholders, 'maximising shareholder value' is the wrong way to manage things.

Banking income now depends increasingly on services rather than loans but the same logic applies; Japanese banks still invest in many of their customers to sustain business relationships and the rents from those relationships are more important to them than dividend income or potential capital gains on disposals – which, in any case, are usually not an option if the relationship is to be sustained.

Trust banks

Trust banks, with 18.2 per cent, are a much bigger constituent. They are both trustees and banks. As lenders, their interests are similar to those of commercial banks and, since their loans tend to be long term, their preference for borrowers who continue to service their loans over long periods, rather than choosing to pay out dividends, is perhaps even more acute. As trustees, the trust banks handle stock transfer, fund management, and many related services, extending to a complete actuarial, administrative, and investment service for pension funds. Until the 1980s, nearly all pension fund management was restricted to trust banks and insurers, but specialist asset managers, including foreign firms, have established an increasingly strong position since then (EIU, 2009). Trust banks retain a pivotal administrative role but most of the shares recorded under their names and nominally votable by them are held on behalf of others; in some cases they are simultaneously managers of the assets concerned, but often they are not. Traditionally, trust banks have been seen as unassertive custodians and managers but this may be changing. As a pension fund officer explained to us in 2006, there is a growing tendency for at least some of the trust banks to exercise voting rights at corporate AGMs, either as fund managers in their own right or under instruction from asset management companies. However, the fundamental situation is still that the outwardly large domestic equity holdings of the trust banks have disparate beneficial owners, may not even be managed by the trust banks, and do not represent unified blocks of shares that are easy to mobilise in a particular cause.

Insurers

Insurance companies held 7.4 per cent in March 2011, which is an important but not massive percentage. Life insurers have been under pressure since the 1990s to fund guaranteed yields to subscribers that often tend now to be above normal market levels and they might be expected to take more interest in dividend income and capital gains. But many of the shares registered in their names, as with the trust banks, are in fact pension fund assets. Moreover, as well as reducing their equity portfolios in recent years, all the insurers also have other lines of business to consider. In addition to pure insurance business, they also extend loans on the wholesale market, giving them the same motivation as banks to see the ultimate borrowing customers able to service their debt. Where insurers hold shares for their own account or as managers of pension fund assets, their motive to seek higher returns seems clearer. However, there is a widespread belief that insurers tend to underpin insurance underwriting relationships with major customers by holding their shares. When a senior board member of a life insurance company was asked in 2004 whether his firm, acting as a portfolio investor, might sell shares in a company because it disapproved of its corporate governance, even though the company was a good customer for insurance products, he chose to interpret this as an accusation that his company might be holding shares for other than pure investment reasons and reacted with evident irritation: 'The best way to put it is the other way around: we don't buy shares because we owe firms something on the business front.' The chairman of a competitor, speaking at about the same time, conceded that this sort of situation could indeed be problematical but stressed that his asset managers theoretically acted as pure investors:

It's not entirely without foundation. I think virtually all Japanese life insurance companies have this link whereby they hold shares so they receive insurance business: they have insurance business so they hold shares. But, even though when it comes to exercise of voting rights – as I said earlier, they mostly approve and send proxies – when there are serious problems I think they judge them on an individual basis as investors.

Pension funds

Pension funds, whose shareholding percentages are included in the trust bank and insurer totals, have a clearer motive to raise yields on their investments and would seem much less constrained by other considerations than either banks or insurers. However, apart from the PFA, no Japanese pension funds have taken a strong stance in this regard. This is largely because they have mostly reduced their equity holdings since the depressed markets of the 1990s (and additionally the process whereby many companies have exercised the option to return onerous corporate pension assets and liabilities to the state, known as *daikō henjō*, resulted in a big reduction in overall pension equity holdings because the state pension fund has a much higher fixed interest weighting) and because few pension funds are sufficiently large to make it worthwhile to be other than passive investors. A senior director of a pension fund explained in 2004 why so few Japanese company pension funds showed the same sort of interest in corporate governance as the PFA, citing their reliance on external managers, whom they tend not to control closely, and their lack of scale: 'You see, most of the pension funds don't do in-house management, so generally their position is different. Then there's the aspect of the amount of money involved: as I said, the PFA has ¥8,000,000 million,[14] while the ordinary small pension funds might have ¥10,000 or ¥20,000 million – that accounts for three quarters of them.'

In contrast to these corporate funds, Japan's state pension fund, the Government Pension Investment Fund (*Nenkin Tsumitatekin Kanri Unyō Dokuritsu Gyōsei Hōjin*) or 'GPIF', is the largest in the world, with total invested assets of approximately ¥113,746,900 million as at 30 June 2011 (GPIF, 2011). Assertive action by this fund, despite its relatively low 11.6 per cent domestic equity ratio (equivalent to around 4.5 per cent of the total capitalisation of the TSE at that date), could exert a major influence on the behaviour of Japanese listed companies, but up to now it has shown little interest in activism. In an interview with Global Pensions in August 2006, following a major reorganisation of the GPIF's structure, the Director General of the GPIF's Investment Management Department stated that although activism was not totally impossible, the objectives set by the government effectively made it difficult. He observed that the GPIF sought average 'beta' market returns rather than the extraordinary levels known as 'alpha': 'We are a beta investor and we are not seeking alpha. We considered the size of the assets we are managing and concluded that obtaining alpha would be difficult for us' (Global Pensions, 2006). Nevertheless, shortly after declaring major investment losses for the year to March 2009 (with a negative overall return of more than minus 10 per cent), the GPIF announced in July 2009 that it would appoint 14 external asset managers to manage its foreign holdings actively (Reuters, 2009c, 2009d). It is conceivable that this policy may gradually begin to influence the GPIF's domestic portfolio at some stage in the future.

Corporate shareholders

We now consider corporate shareholders, amounting to 21.2 per cent of the total in June 2011. That they should be as large as they are – despite reductions during past years – is a distinctive feature of the post-war Japanese economy and is mainly the result of the stable shareholding patterns that evolved. These are essentially the same phenomenon as

---

[14] This refers to total funds under management at that time, rather than domestic shares, and is an under-estimation.

the shareholdings maintained by banks and insurance companies in their corporate customers, which the banks openly acknowledge to be supports for their business relationships but, as we have seen, some insurers deny. These shareholdings, whether in the form of unilateral investments or cross-holdings, have attracted the attention of foreign commentators for many years. A 'stable shareholder' in the Japanese context is defined by Sheard as one who:

holds the shares as a friendly insider sympathetic to incumbent management; agrees not to sell the shares to third parties unsympathetic to incumbent management, particularly hostile take-over bidders or bidders trying to accumulate strategic parcels of shares; agrees, in the event that disposal of shares is necessary, to consult the firm or at least to give notice of its intention to sell … (Sheard, 1994: 314, 318)

Such shareholdings developed mainly in two phases after the Second World War, in 1950–5 and in 1965–74. At their height, in 1974, they were estimated to account for 62.2% of the entire market (Miyajima and Kuroki, 2007: 85) but by 2003 this had fallen to around 24.3%, of which cross-held shares were estimated to be 7.6% of the market. Nevertheless, it was estimated then that over 83% of 2,690 listed companies studied at about that time had some kind of cross-shareholding in place (NLI Research, 2004). There has been a minor resurgence in recent years driven by concerns about hostile takeover – similarly to the situation in 1965–74 – but they still remain low in comparison with the 1970s. From the viewpoint of shareholder rights, stable shareholdings and cross-holdings may be considered pernicious because they often permit boards to run publicly listed companies without concern for minority shareholders, sustained by strategic minority share blocks that will always support their proposals. However, until very recently, few Japanese directors or managers are likely to have seen them in this way. They would see these shares not just as financial instruments but as 'important symbolic tokens, that by being exchanged with another company served to embody a relationship or affiliation'. Moreover, such shareholdings would be booked separately from portfolio investments and their market value was not generally considered to be important (Learmount, 2002: 56–7). Probably the last thing on the mind of the holder of a stable or cross-shareholding would be dividends; the real objective was to sustain a valued commercial relationship. The holders of this kind of shareholding are unlikely to be interested in maximising short-term returns or in anything that seems likely to weaken the continuing ability of the company in question to be a strong and reliable business partner.

The salient point from this examination of the various sub-groups is that most of them derive benefit, in whole or in part, from the companies in which they invest other than through payouts, while even those who have a stronger motive to value shareholder returns are either compromised by other interests or ill-equipped to undertake an active role. Nearly 51 per cent of the Japanese shareholder universe in 2011 tended to have other concerns than just shareholder value and some players were unlikely to show any interest at all. In 2000, at the start of the activist hedge fund interventions in Japan, this percentage was just under 61 per cent.

6.7 T. Boone Pickens and Koito Seisakusho

An illustration of how this situation could operate in practice was provided by T. Boone Pickens' investment in Koito Seisakusho. During 1989 and 1990 the US investor T. Boone Pickens assumed ownership of a parcel of shares in a medium-sized Japanese listed manufacturer of automotive lighting equipment called Koito Seisakusho, initially of 20.2 per cent and subsequently increased to 26.4 per cent of the issued equity, and attempted to obtain board representation for his nominees and access to company records in line with the treatment that appeared to be extended – though by practice rather than by regulation or company articles – to at least one other large minority shareholder, Toyota. A majority of shareholders did not support his proposals in general meeting and ultimately he withdrew after an unsuccessful lawsuit (Yomiuri, 1989a, 1991). Despite its essentially mundane nature, this incident attracted great attention in Japan and is still remembered by many people. Several factors contributed to its notoriety.

T. Boone Pickens himself was controversial in his own country[15] and the descent on the relatively grey world of Japanese business of

---

[15] According to the T. Boone Pickens website (www.boonepickens.com) in June 2011: 'During the 1980s, T. Boone Pickens and his young band of hungry Mesa Petroleum managers grabbed hold of a monster and shook it like it'd never been jostled before. They rode that monster, and got thrown some, but Big Oil was never the same again.'

a Texan oilman who had made his fortune buying and selling US oil and gas businesses caused a sensation in Japan. He made his approach to Koito Seisakusho's board very public and gave widely reported speeches when he was rebuffed. Koito Seisakusho's board appears to have added to the publicised nature of the case by its own comments to the press in which it refuted his arguments for higher dividends and board representation. Further interest was aroused because Pickens had acquired or borrowed his shareholding from the Japanese investor Watanabe Kitarō, who had already made approaches suggestive of greenmail to Koito Seisakusho's board to encourage it to arrange a buyer for his shareholding. Watanabe was considered by many people to be a player in Japan's extortionist tradition and, by extension, T. Boone Pickens became equally suspect, although he consistently denied these allegations (Nikkei, 1989; Yomiuri, 1989b). This encouraged the board of Koito Seisakusho not to accede to his requests. What makes this case interesting is that it demonstrated a lack of deference to an important minority shareholder by the directors of a listed company who plainly saw their duty to the firm as paramount.

It is significant that Pickens' proposal to Koito Seisakusho's AGM in June 1989 was rejected by a properly constituted quorum of shareholders; despite the uncompromising attitude of the directors, due form was observed. Although Pickens was not reported to have asked anyone to buy his shareholding, a spokesman for Toyota, the next largest shareholder in Koito Seisakusho, was quoted as saying that Toyota had no intention of buying Pickens' shares and that purchasing shares at more than their true value would be a betrayal of his own company's shareholders; Tricker pointed to the fact that the Toyota group had been the victim of an expensive greenmailing raid on Toyoda Automatic Loom[16] in 1987 as a likely explanation of this determined attitude (Tricker, 1994: 32).

The reaction of Koito Seisakusho's board to T. Boone Pickens' requests and its consistently close relationship with the next largest shareholder, Toyota, illustrate a crucial point regarding shareholders and their treatment in Japan. The great distinction between a minority shareholder like Pickens and one like Toyota lies in their relevance to the community firm. Rightly or wrongly, Pickens was assumed to

---

[16] Now known in English as 'Toyota Industries Corporation', although the Japanese name is unchanged.

have acquired his shareholding in order to make a speculative profit as a portfolio investor; his suspected association with Japanese green-mailing made him seem even more mercenary (NYT, 1990). By contrast, Toyota was an important customer of Koito Seisakusho whose involvement as a shareholder had a lot to do with an enduring commercial relationship and very little to do with investment returns. It was clear that there were effectively two classes of shareholder at Koito Seisakusho and that portfolio shareholders were not welcome to contribute their ideas on corporate structure or strategy. The conclusion of many foreign observers was probably that Japan was an opaque and devious market. In a speech to the Chicago World Trades Association in May 1989, T. Boone Pickens had portrayed himself as struggling to persuade a closed and inefficient Japanese establishment to accept the obvious justice of shareholder rights; he further implied that Japanese industry was gaining an unfair trading advantage against the USA through its failure to do this (Pickens, 1989). After reading of his notable lack of progress, which was widely reported both in Japan and elsewhere, few US or European investors in 1990 are likely to have considered Japan to be an attractive market for shareholder activism. Among amendments to the Securities and Exchange Law implemented in December 1990 was a set of regulations requiring disclosure of shareholdings of 5 per cent or more in any listed company, as well as a revision of the takeover rules. It appears that both of these amendments were prepared by the Ministry of Finance in late November 1990 (Ishiguro, 1991). Coming so soon after the Koito Seisakusho affair, there is at least a possibility that they were the result of official concerns regarding such situations.

6.8 Conclusion

In this chapter we have reviewed the evolution of companies in Japan, from their origins as foreign implants to becoming totally Japanese organisations, and noted the marginalisation of shareholders within the practice of corporate governance, in contrast to the provisions of Japan's formal law and regulation, where shareholder rights are clearly articulated. We suggest that the community firm is not deeply rooted in Japan's traditional societal practices. It is a relatively recent phenomenon which grew out of a certain configuration of economic and institutional forces in the immediate post-1945 period. Shareholders had been consciously excluded from influence under wartime conditions, and this exclusion continued thereafter as part of the post-war reconstruction.

For most of the post-war period, Japanese shareholders, both institutional and retail, have appeared generally unwilling to assert their legal rights to hold boards to account. Key corporate governance actors seemed to be indifferent to what agency theory suggests should be a rational assessment of their own best interest. We have argued that Japanese institutional investors, including corporate shareholders, usually have overriding interests other than portfolio return at stake, making them disinclined to challenge boards while the company's business appears viable. This, in turn, complements the operation of the community firm, where management autonomy is taken for granted. Challengers of the system, such as T. Boone Pickens at Koito Seisakusho, met with determined opposition from management and local investors alike.

Given all these factors, there seemed to be few opportunities for any kind of shareholder activism in Japan at the start of the 1990s. How this situation changed thereafter and why the Japanese market became attractive to activist hedge funds, notwithstanding the continued dominance of the community firm, is the focus of our next chapter.

7 | *Japan's unexpected credentials as a target for hedge fund activism*

7.1 Introduction

The development of Japan's corporate practices and attitudes to governance had thus created an environment that prioritised the social and economic importance of the firm over its function as the shareholders' property. Where the USA and the UK had both seen reassertion of shareholder primacy from the 1970s after periods of corporatist autonomy, Japan had not deviated significantly from the direction chosen in the late 1940s when the combination of factors in its postwar situation led to the emergence of the community firm, together with the increasingly institutionalised practices that surrounded and sustained it. Outwardly, there seemed to be little hope of acceptance for ideas like agency theory and shareholder value.

However, even T. Boone Pickens' disappointments at Koito Seisakusho provided clues that activism was not impossible. The requirements of company law and Koito Seisakusho's own corporate articles of association had been fulfilled throughout; Japan was clearly a market where the rule of law was observed and where shareholders' voting rights were upheld. As an activist hedge fund partner observed to us in 2008: 'Activism only works when you have pressure from shareholders, so in Japan that is the number one thing; you have enough shareholder votes and you win. There is sufficiently good company law and voting rights that you can get things through.'

In this chapter we consider various other factors that were changing the investment environment in Japan and potentially offered encouragement to activist hedge funds. Beneath the surface of Japanese corporate governance there was already a persistent undercurrent of activism that was more disruptive than anything that most American hedge fund managers would contemplate, in the form of a long tradition of corporate extortion. We review this tradition below. We then consider how Japan's whole corporate governance environment began to change during the 1990s, first on an intellectual level as observers began to question how companies should be run, and second on a practical level as economic pressures caused a decline in stable shareholdings which coincided with an increase in purchases by non-resident investors. A parallel and complementary factor was the growing attention paid by the largest companies to institutional portfolio investors who provided finance as bondholders and shareholders. Finally, we consider the underlying financial attractions of the Japanese market at the end of the 1990s.

7.2 A vulnerability of the community firm: corporate extortion in Japan

As we have seen from Chapter 6, the community firm is an outwardly robust organisation which generally pays little attention to outsiders, including its own portfolio shareholders. However, it has an innate weakness to shareholder pressure should its shareholders exercise their rights to challenge the board through the formal channels established by company law and by corporate articles of association. This weakness was exploited by extortionists from as early as the nineteenth century, when joint stock companies began to proliferate, not usually by exercising their rights as such but by threatening to do so in a disruptive way.

Japanese corporate extortion takes advantage of the fact that where the community firm is a listed company, it is simultaneously both an internally focused organisation which seeks to perpetuate itself and also a legally defined joint stock company in which shares can freely be traded and voted. This situation creates a contradiction in that shareholders have clear rights at law which define their status as the 'members of the company' and which can impede the working of the community firm if they are exercised without restraint. An obvious opportunity for disruption would be to demand high dividends but this seems to have been rare until the present century; most instances of shareholder extortion appear to involve manipulation of the community firm's desire to keep its affairs private and to be left in peace to carry out its business. Extortionists have been able to exploit this situation by becoming shareholders and threatening the smooth running of the organisation, either by the mere fact of their unwelcome presence or by explicitly disruptive behaviour at shareholders' meetings. Criminal gangs have often become involved in this process.

These activities tend to fall into two main categories: *shite* ('greenmailers') who generally take fairly large shareholdings in listed companies in the expectation of being bought out by concerned stable shareholders, and *sōkaiya* ('AGM-operators'), who tend to hold fewer shares and extract blackmail payments directly from the company in return for not disrupting and prolonging AGMs with embarrassing questions. A variant of this approach is for *sōkaiya* to receive payments in order to ensure that other shareholders do not ask such questions: Chisso, which was facing disruption from civil rights activists in the 1970s in connection with allegations of mass mercury poisoning linked to its chemical factory in Kyūshū in the 1950s, is a well-known instance of an ostensibly reputable firm allegedly recruiting gangsters to suppress dissent at its shareholder meetings (Szymkowiak, 2002: 68–72).

The activities of *shite* are not generally illegal, since their method of operation is to acquire freely traded shares and then accept attractive offers from willing buyers, in a manner similar to that of US greenmailers. In his 1991 study of the Japanese takeover market, Kester quoted a published source from 1988 which listed 120 investors considered to be *shite*, with positions in 156 different listed companies. He made the point that targets tend not to be companies with a large free float of shares but rather those where there are large block shareholders willing to buy out unwelcome outsiders: 'the *shite* groups are actually turning the close, stable ownership of targets to their advantage'. This kind of situation, particularly in cases where it has links to criminal gangs, has undoubtedly coloured the Japanese perception of corporate takeovers: 'To the extent the public confuses them with genuine contests for corporate control, it will be much harder for the Japanese business community to accept such future contests as legitimate shareholder responses to breakdowns in the traditional Japanese corporate governance system' (Kester, 1991: 246–54).

The *sōkaiya* problem is more fragmented but more pervasive. It also tends to be more closely associated with criminal gangs and has been linked to general violence and several murders. Its origins are traced to the late nineteenth century when Japan's rapid industrial revolution offered opportunities to those interested in manipulating shareholders' meetings to their own advantage, but the early *sōkaiya* tended to act behind the scenes. Their noisier tactics and their increasing association with criminal gangs developed in the post-war period (Szymkowiak, 2002: 34–66). Milhaupt and West noted from data publicised by Mainichi Shimbun in 1997 on a selection of large Japanese firms that nearly 90 per cent said they had been approached by *sōkaiya* with demands for money. They quote another survey in *Nikkei Business* from the same year which found that, of 1,200 responding firms, 77 per cent admitted having made payments to *sōkaiya*. Milhaupt and West saw the roots of this situation in traditionally low levels of corporate transparency and a tendency for share prices to fall on news of protracted shareholders' meetings. They made the point that relatively opaque corporate governance in Japan, at least until the 1990s, created a rich stock of secrets that management might wish to conceal, enabling *sōkaiya* to blackmail boards with threats to cause personal embarrassment to senior directors at shareholders' meetings if payment were not forthcoming (Milhaupt and West, 2004: 109–39).

Unlike the greenmailing of the *shite*, key aspects of the activities of *sōkaiya* are illegal, primarily through duties imposed on management. Payments to suppress shareholder rights were forbidden in the Commercial Code from 1950 and a revision in 1981 (effective from 1982) forbade the offering of benefits to shareholders regarding the exercise of their rights. Restrictions and penalties were made more severe in 1997. However, it is not easy to eliminate extortion without the full cooperation of the victims and there is a general suspicion that *sōkaiya* still exist. As Milhaupt and West observed in 2004: 'a better way to proceed might be to employ mechanisms to increase the flow of information from companies to the market' (Milhaupt and West, 2004: 139).

The systemic weakness of the community firm to pressure from *shite* and *sōkaiya*, and the success of often criminal groups in exploiting it for so many years, has created suspicion of shareholders who acquire shares rapidly and challenge boards: when Livedoor began its attempt to take control of Nippon Broadcasting System and effectively the whole Fuji Sankei group in 2005 (an affair with many ramifications, to which we refer again later), the then Keidanren chairman, Okuda Hiroshi, who was also chairman of Toyota, immediately drew a parallel with T. Boone Pickens' attempt on Koito Seisakusho. He is reported to have said that Livedoor's president should clarify whether he was seeking to restructure Fuji Sankei group or was simply trying to make a speculative profit, like T. Boone Pickens – the implication being that, in the latter case, society should close ranks against him (Nikkei, 2005b). In one sense this kind of perception is a negative factor for activist hedge funds: although they are distinct from the Japanese tradition of extortion, the public nature of their interventions has encouraged confusion among the general public and probably hindered their attempts to raise support from Japanese institutional investors. But in another sense, the existence of this tradition demonstrates clearly that the community firm is vulnerable to shareholder pressure.

7.3 Shocks to the 'traditional' system of governance

Corporate extortion is an irritation to the boards of Japanese companies but it does not challenge their fundamental authority. But during the 1990s economic problems triggered a series of scandals at Japanese companies which began to call into question the whole approach to corporate governance that had broadly been accepted hitherto. The consensus among the Japanese business community that board autonomy should be respected, so clearly demonstrated at Koito Seisakusho in 1989–90, rested in large part on a belief that Japanese companies were efficiently run. From its economic recovery that began in the late 1940s until the end of the 1980s, Japan had enjoyed an almost uninterrupted period of growth during which the corporate governance practices of the community firm developed largely unquestioned. Their evident success was accepted as proof of their validity both within and beyond Japan: in the early 1980s Matsumoto wrote, 'The mechanism that moves Japanese industry today is powerful almost beyond comparison' (Matsumoto, 1983: ix) and, even before that, Vogel had talked in the late 1970s of the 'Japanese miracle' and enumerated the social strengths that seemed to underpin it (Vogel, 1979: 9–23). But after the collapse of Japan's economic 'bubble', usually dated from the peak of the stock market boom at the end of 1989, there began a period of over ten years when economic problems and corporate scandals seemed endemic, calling into question the fundamental nature of the way that Japanese companies were run. The 1990s in Japan have been described as a 'lost decade' of economic stagnation (Callen and Ostry, 2003: 1; Hayashi and Prescott, 2002: 206) and the contrast with the confidence of the bubble years is very marked. One result of this was a focus on corporate governance in the latter half of the 1990s as a likely cause of the corporate failures so evident from the succession of scandals and bankruptcies. As one company president observed to us in late 2003, corporate governance had become a convenient scapegoat for fundamental economic weakness caused by poor planning at governmental and corporate levels. Pressure groups, the media, and even some corporate executives urged that Japanese firms should adopt a 'global standard' of governance in order to compete successfully in the global economy. 'One of the most striking aspects of corporate governance reform during this period was the widespread acceptance, at least in rhetoric, that Japanese firms needed to adopt a global standard of corporate governance.' Moreover, this 'global standard' often seemed to reflect US practice (Ahmadjian, 2003: 221–2).

The problems of the 1990s influenced the thinking of politicians, bureaucrats, academics, and many senior managers. As a result, during the period from 1997 to the present, there have been numerous changes to the format of Japanese corporate governance, some taking place within existing legal structures and some specifically legislated. The institution of the corporate executive officer (or 'executive officer' within the company with committees system), ostensibly with full executive powers yet below the board, has become widespread; the statutory powers of corporate auditors have been reinforced; and the option for companies to become companies with committees, described in Chapter 6, theoretically imposing a degree of external supervision and isolating the board, responsible for strategic and supervisory matters, from the purely executive officers of the firm, has created a legally sanctioned route for companies to adopt what in Japan is often called 'US-style' corporate governance. Taking all these formal and informal changes together, Japan introduced a considerable number of amendments and new structures to its corporate scene in the short space of years between 1997 and 2003. When one investigates what actually happens at most Japanese companies, the impression is that surprisingly little has really changed; most of the former practices and attitudes of Japanese corporate governance appear to be surviving well and have not been swept away by a 'global standard'. The system has absorbed new elements to amend the details, though not the core, of its structure (Buchanan and Deakin, 2008: 81). However, at least from the outside, Japanese corporate structures and practices seem to have undergone a massive transformation since T. Boone Pickens confronted the board of Koito Seisakusho.

One aspect of this wave of reform was a re-evaluation of the position of shareholders. This was an extension of the feelings noted by Ahmadjian that Japan should adopt the 'global standard' for its corporate governance. Although concepts like shareholder primacy and the agency theory belief that there is a need to control potential excesses by management have not explicitly been part of Japan's postwar corporate culture, they gained a degree of acceptance during the 1990s, at least at a theoretical level. In May 1996 the Keizai Dōyūkai commented: 'Hitherto it has been the view that "companies owe their existence to the continued support of a variety of stakeholders" and a corporate governance stance has been adopted that gives too much weight to employees; it is necessary to take a new look at this situation' (Dōyūkai, 1996, section 2 (1)).

Even more explicitly, in the introduction to its Interim Report on corporate governance principles, published in October 1997, the Japan Corporate Governance Forum, which was then a new organisation attracting attention as a promoter of fresh governance ideas that might reinvigorate the faltering Japanese economy, stated:

But shareholders in particular are given a special position. As owners of the company, they are the last risk-takers who are entitled to claim the residual profits of the company. Under the system of private ownership, shareholders are granted the right of governance over the company for the benefit of their own interests. This idea forms the foundation for the corporate governance concept ... Therefore, the executives must be responsible for pursuing the shareholders' profit with the most prudent fiduciary duty. Moreover, management executives, as the shareholders' trustees, must be fully accountable to the shareholders for their actions. (JCGF, 1997)

This movement to reform Japanese corporate governance on a 'global' or more specifically US pattern lost some of its impetus following the discovery of scandals in the USA such as those at Enron in 2001 and at WorldCom in 2002, which demonstrated that not everything in US corporate governance was perfect. Subsequently the consistently strong performance of several leading Japanese companies, such as Toyota and Canon, whose managements were seen by the public as being opposed to wholesale adoption of US-style reforms and which had elected not to become companies with committees, helped to restore confidence in more familiar styles of governance. As we have seen, the number of companies adopting the company with committees system was small and is currently in decline. However, many of the new corporate governance ideas that entered Japan in the late 1990s remained as intellectual concepts and the unquestioning attitude to existing corporate governance practices that prevailed in Japan until the 1990s has faded. Although, as stated above, the current state of Japanese corporate governance is one of surprisingly solid continuity in many respects, the turmoil of the 1990s has produced what Teubner, writing in the context of corporate law, called 'irritants' which may exert little immediate influence but remain in circulation, ready to inspire unexpected changes in the future (Teubner, 2001: 418). Two particularly important irritants were the changing mix of institutional shareholders, as stable shareholding patterns declined and non-residents became a force in the market, and the increasing attention paid to shareholders in general through investor relations, which was already being stimulated by market trends before the 1990s.

7.4 The decline of stable shareholdings and the rise of non-resident investors

One important feature of post-war Japanese corporate governance that underpinned the community firm was, as we have seen, the development of stable shareholdings, including cross-holdings, which were predicated by commercial relationships rather than any quest for portfolio income. These shareholdings gave boards confidence that, as long as their actions were acceptable to a majority of their company's contributing stakeholders, they were unlikely to face effective opposition from shareholders. Banks participated widely in these cross-shareholding arrangements but their importance began to decline as early as the 1970s as the strongest companies came to rely less on bank finance, undermining the close ties between banks and their best customers, and weakening the rationale for cross-shareholdings between them (Aoki, 1994: 135). Then, from the 1990s, further factors came into play that caused a major reduction in all stable shareholdings.

The exuberance of Japan's so-called bubble economy during the late 1980s had led many Japanese companies to invest unwisely in securities and real estate, often sustained by finance from banks which were eager to replace the loan volumes lost as their better customers migrated to the capital markets and whose lending officers were convinced that the value of real estate security would never decline. As Hanazaki and Horiuchi summarised the problem:

The weakness had been there for many years but had been hidden by the banks' tendency to lend to successful manufacturing companies who were forced to have efficient management practices by the competitive markets in which they operated. The flight of these customers to the capital markets left their bankers with cash to lend but credit skills blunted by years of protection. (Hanazaki and Horiuchi, 2004: 26–9)

After the collapse of the 'bubble', during the decade of the 1990s, financial pain among borrowers developed over several years into a banking and securities industry crisis. In 1997 Yamaichi Securities, Hokkaidō Takushoku Bank, and Sanyō Securities collapsed, followed in 1998 by two of the three long-term banks, Long Term Credit Bank of Japan and Nippon Credit Bank. Despite injections of public funds, banks in Japan faced problems with effective bad debts, frequently secured by real estate assets whose market value was severely impaired. Their holdings of customers' shares, whose value had fallen with the general market decline, had become a problem not just because of the resources these were absorbing but also because under Bank of International Settlements rules banks were obliged to include unrealised capital gains and losses from shareholdings in their Tier 1 capital. In recognition of this situation, the Bank Shareholding Restriction Law (*Ginkōtō no Kabushikitō no Hoyū no Seigentō ni kansuru Hōritsu*) was passed in November 2001 requiring banks to reduce holdings of shares to the level of Tier 1 capital by 2004 (subsequently extended to 2006) and establishing the Banks' Shareholdings Purchase Corporation (*Ginkōtō Hoyū Kabushiki Shutoku Kikō*) in January 2002 to facilitate the selling process. Throughout the 1990s, because of these linked pressures, there had been a progressive decline in both banks' holdings of corporate shares and companies' holdings of bank shares but this accelerated after 1996, with bank sales of corporate shares accelerating even faster after 1999 and gaining further impetus thereafter with enactment of the Bank Shareholding Restriction Law in 2001. Both banks and companies thus had strong motivation to reduce their crossholdings and any move by one side generally encouraged the other to move too (Miyajima and Kuroki, 2007: 88–91). Independently of this process, many manufacturing companies in Japan were re-examining the need to tie up capital in stable shareholdings with their suppliers. The most striking reduction was that carried out by Nissan as part of its recovery plan after 1999 which entailed reductions in its holdings of almost all its suppliers' shares (Ikeda and Nakagawa, 2002).

What this process of reduction in stable and cross-held shareholdings meant in practical terms is illustrated by a comment made to the authors in 2004 by a senior director at a medium-sized listed company, who saw his company's willingness to engage with shareholders as directly linked to this process:

Well, with regard to institutional investors, one element is that our cross-shareholdings are decreasing so all sorts of shareholders are there and ... we shall have to start listening progressively more to the opinions of institutional shareholders, in particular.

He stressed the contrast with the situation he remembered in the past:

Apart from the banks ... the stably held proportion of our shares ... used to be as much as 70 per cent – 30 per cent was held by all sorts of retail shareholders and so on. So, no matter what sort of criticisms people might make, we had that 70 per cent. Nowadays it's under 60 per cent, progressively going down towards 50 per cent. With that kind of 70 per cent, you're not afraid of anything. You don't care who says what – that's how it used to be.

The decline in stable shareholdings has roughly been compensated by an almost uninterrupted rise in purchases by non-resident investors who increased their purchases of Japanese shares in the 1990s when prices fell from the previously high levels of the 1980s and there was potential to benefit from recovery situations. At the end of March 1995, foreigners held 8.1% of shares listed on the five major markets in Japan; in March 2011, as shown in Figure 7.1, they held 26.7%, partially reversing a decline from their high point of nearly 28% in March 2007 (National Stock Exchanges, 2004, 2011). Most of these shareholders were internationally active institutional investors whose main interest was to obtain the best possible return on their investments. Ahmadjian noted that their importance in the Japanese market was generally greater even than their high aggregate shareholdings would

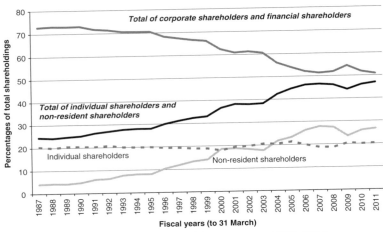

Figure 7.1 Trends in Japanese shareholding patterns 1987–2011
(*Source:* National Stock Exchanges Shareholder Distribution Survey)

suggest because surviving stable shareholdings effectively removed liquidity from circulation and foreign shareholders tended to trade more actively, accounting for a disproportionate level of market movement. In 2002 and 2003, when their aggregate holdings were still below 22%, they were estimated to have accounted for more than 30% of all sales and purchases of Japanese shares. While it is not possible to say what the ultimate effect of these non-resident shareholders on Japanese corporate practices will be, many of them are fund managers from markets where fiduciary duty is emphasised, who tend not to be conflicted by other business interests in Japan (Ahmadjian, 2007: 131–3).

   These non-resident investors represent a new phenomenon within the Japanese shareholder body. They are mostly the same sort of investors who can often be persuaded to support activist initiatives in the USA or Europe, who understand the financial concepts that justify activist interventions. However, the same reasons why they are not naturally activists themselves apply just as much in Japan as they do in the US or European markets. It is important not to exaggerate their influence or their willingness to take confrontational positions: their support for activist hedge funds cannot be taken for granted. CalPERS, the US pension fund, provides an illustration of the limitations facing even the strongest foreign investors in Japan (see Jacoby, 2009). From the 1980s CalPERS had pursued an increasingly activist stance in the USA and began to apply this to its Japanese investments from the 1990s, cultivating links with like-minded Japanese organisations such as the Japan Corporate Governance Forum and the PFA, and pressing for improved governance at the companies in which it held shares. Any disapproval from CalPERS concerning Japanese companies' behaviour was assiduously reported in the Japanese press and there was a feeling that not only CalPERS but the entire international investment community was focusing on the shortcomings of Japanese corporate governance. But by 2003 this campaign had lost impetus and CalPERS changed from a stance of direct activist pressure in Japan to a policy of investing either passively in its own name or through third-party fund managers such as Sparx and Taiyo Pacific Partners who had developed a reputation for delivering consistent returns through a degree of activism without open conflict. Despite creating a lot of noise, CalPERS' efforts do not seem to have produced much increment in its investment results in the face of widespread indifference from the Japanese investment community. Matters might have been different if every non-Japanese institutional investor had cooperated closely with CalPERS in its campaign, but there was little sign of this kind of solidarity.

7.5 Increasing attention paid to shareholders

As we have seen, the questioning of post-war governance structures in Japan that arose in the 1990s extended also to the status of shareholders, at least at a theoretical level. The opinions about over-emphasis on employees and the importance of shareholders quoted earlier from the Keizai Dōyūkai and Japan Corporate Governance Forum were precisely the kind of sentiment that any activist investor would like to hear and implied an increased tolerance of shareholder voice. To some extent it reflected genuine underlying trends within the corporate sector. In conversations at Japanese companies in 2003–4 we observed that there had been a big increase in investor relations ('IR') activities in recent years at nearly all of the companies visited. A few could trace their IR back in some form as far as the 1960s but most had begun to organise their contacts with investors and their style of disclosure systematically in the late 1990s or early 2000s. All of the larger companies among them had dedicated IR departments which were distinct from the public relations and finance departments that once acted as the main sources of information for investors. The smaller companies

generally committed fewer resources, although they all showed awareness of the IR concept.

There was commonly an underlying situation of some kind at the
companies visited that had stimulated investment in IR resources.
With the larger companies, this tended to be linked initially to capital markets fund-raising and subsequently to the desire to cultivate
their new shareholders, especially among foreign investors. One senior
manager in charge of IR activities at a very large company summarised
the situation there:

The reason it began as it did is because in the 1980s our finance was centred
on the issue of convertible bonds to foreign investors. So there was a period
when we were raising funds in that fashion and we developed from overseas
fund-raising to the need to have foreign investors buy our shares. Then, after
they buy, there has to be a follow-up, so we started IR.

Japanese management has been criticised at various times by foreign
investors for lack of transparency and, as we have seen, Milhaupt and
West linked this tendency to its vulnerability to extortion. But, at least
at the larger companies we visited, there appeared to be a genuine
resolve to tell investors the facts. Several heads of IR at such companies emphasised the need to communicate: 'The first objective is to let
investors know the true situation about our company's current state';
'One objective is to get people outside the company to understand us
correctly and adequately'; and 'My idea of the objectives of IR is that
it should create an accurate understanding of the company's situation'.
Officers at one very large company drew attention in 2004 to the way
that their willingness to divulge information had increased in recent
years:

The quality of what we give out, in particular, and also the quantity of stuff,
has changed too. Previously we would reply that we couldn't disclose things
when we were asked slightly delicate questions. We have opened up the
range of our disclosure quite a bit to date and we feel that the content of
what we say and the quality of the information have improved.

Several heads of IR also emphasised the need to engage in a dialogue
with investors, to discover how their company was perceived and to
benefit from objective opinions.

This interest in shareholders and willingness to tell them more about corporate affairs that has emerged at many Japanese companies are often driven by the fact that foreign institutional shareholders have become more numerous and consequently more influential. These shareholders tend to be more demanding and more accustomed to receiving detailed information than most Japanese institutions. Ahmadjian saw the increase in foreign ownership at Japanese companies as something closely linked to changes in their corporate governance practices since the early 1990s (Ahmadjian, 2007: 144–7). We are doubtful as to the extent to which the various outward changes have penetrated to the inner core of real practice at these companies but there is clearly a connection. Some of this effect appears to be transferring to Japanese investors too. An officer in the IR department of a very large company commented in 2004 on the changing style of domestic investors: 'When you compare them to European and US investors, they are pretty mild. But, even so, I think the Japanese [investment] firms are making progress within industrial sectors and there is an increasing number of clarifying questions regarding the industry. In that sense, every year they seem to be growing naturally more assertive.'

This trend has gained further momentum over the past few years and Japanese institutional shareholders and fund managers have become more vocal. Although, as we have noted, the PFA's efforts did not attract a wide following among other institutional investors, there has developed a general awareness of benchmarks for the sort of corporate governance practices that shareholders are entitled to expect. At a meeting with a medium-sized listed company in July 2004, the following comment was made – rather sourly – by the head of IR in connection with the changing tone of his company's AGMs: 'In Japan an organisation called the PFA has made American institutional investors' question lists into a manual and nearly all the investors in Japan are putting out questionnaires to every firm following those topics ... Now everyone who comes is the same – they're all based on the PFA. It all comes from opinions collected from American investors.'

This trend has persisted and AGMs are becoming more serious affairs. The idea that any shareholder who asks a question is a troublemaker appears to be fading and one senior officer in charge of IR at a major Japanese company confirmed that his company, at least, has come to take these questions seriously, in spite of a wide range in their quality: 'There are some knowledgeable people, who ask very high quality questions, and also, although it's rude to say this, there are some questions that really make you wonder. Well, it's the shareholders' privilege.' But whatever managers may think privately about shareholders' opinions and their right to express them, it is no longer acceptable to ignore them. Quite apart from the illegality of such practices, it would now be a serious moral embarrassment if any company were discovered to be paying *sōkaiya* to suppress shareholders' complaints. It has become commonplace to describe corporate policy in Japan in terms of its value to the shareholders; in 2004, when the president of a large company explained his decision not to appoint external directors to his board, he said: 'Our decision is that in order for us to manage responsibly with regard to our shareholders, the most important thing is to have managers taking responsibility who are specialists and really understand the detail of the business.' To anyone accustomed to US or UK ideas that external directors are beneficial to shareholders' interests, this may seem paradoxical but it illustrates the growing consciousness of shareholders among Japanese management. All of this creates an environment where shareholder activism by persons who can offer logical arguments in support of their demands and can demonstrate that they are not extortionists is becoming increasingly hard to dismiss out of hand. The focus has moved inexorably from whether shareholders even have a right to speak at all to a discussion of whether their demands are reasonable.

7.6 The financial attraction of the Japanese market

In addition to these changes in the general environment, there needs also to be a financial attraction to make activist interventions worthwhile. Activist hedge funds invest in specific companies rather than whole markets, but the basic effort required to start looking at companies in any particular country implies that there will need to be at least some general market attraction before funds begin their research. Comparison in Figures 7.2 and 7.3 of *Nikkei* 225 data for the period 2000 to 2007 to similar indices in other markets where activist hedge funds were then making investments (S&P 500 for the USA; FTSE 100 for the UK; DAX for Germany; CAC 40 for France; and Hangseng for Hong Kong) shows Japan to have generally the lowest return on equity

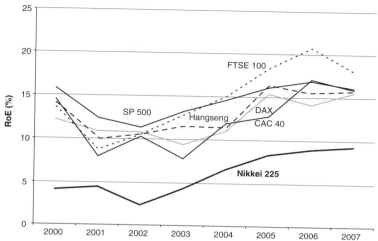

Figure 7.2 RoE data 2000–7 for selected stock markets
(*Source:* Thomson Reuters Worldscope)

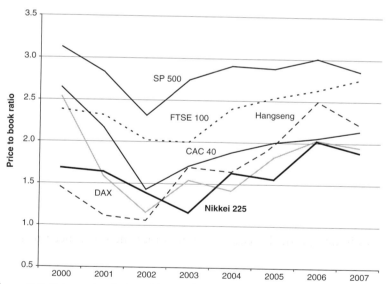

Figure 7.3 Price to book data 2000–7 for selected stock markets
(*Source:* Thomson Reuters Worldscope)

('RoE') and price to book value of all. Low RoE at a specific company would generally imply that corporate capital was not being exploited sufficiently and that there might be ways to improve profitability. Low price to book value would imply both that it would be cheap to acquire shares in comparison with the value of the underlying assets and also that some deficiency in the company might have caused the market to rate its shares lowly, creating opportunities to reverse the situation and raise the share price rapidly if the deficiency could be identified and remedied.

The individual national indices quoted here are not all strictly comparable because they cover populations of companies of different size and market weighting. Moreover, the *Nikkei 225* used here covers only the largest Japanese listed companies and the majority of the targets that we have seen in Japan were relatively small. However, these comparative data do at least give some indication of what general market characteristics might have encouraged activist hedge funds to investigate Japanese opportunities further. A study reported by Bloomberg in July 2007 concluded that 22 per cent or approximately 380 of all first section companies on the Tokyo Stock Exchange covered by the wider Topix index were then trading below book value (Bloomberg, 2007).

A further attraction of the Japanese market is its population of companies with cash reserves but relatively low dividends. Michael Lindsell, an investment adviser posting comments on the Internet in early 2007, described the portfolio of Japanese companies whose shares his fund had bought because of their perceived undervaluation: 'These firms all have one key characteristic: they should all be able to pay steadily growing dividends ... Of the 24 shares in the portfolio, 22 have excess net cash, which, on average, equates to as much as 22% of their market capitalisation, based on estimates for this financial year.' Lindsell considered that dividends in Japan were bound to rise and that these companies had sufficient excess cash flow to fund them. He described the way that the majority of the companies in the portfolio had raised dividends hitherto and still seemed to have capacity for more:

They have responded to shareholder pressure, collectively raising dividends by 27% over the last three years, but even so, their dividend payout ratios were just 37% last year. With payouts forecast to rise to 46% this year as dividends rise further, these firms still retain more cash than they disperse and, as a result, cash reserves are increasing all the time. (Lindsell, 2007)

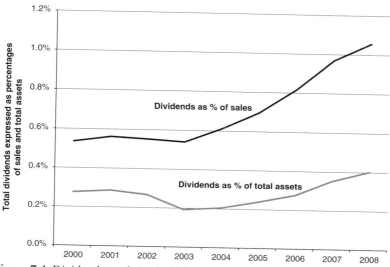

Figure 7.4 Dividend trends in the Tokyo and Osaka markets 2000–8. (Tokyo 1st section, 2nd section, and Mothers; Osaka including JASDAQ) (*Source:* Thomson Reuters)

Dividend payout ratios, although of interest to investors, do not necessarily show that the amounts paid out are rising. For example, if net profits decline, a dividend maintained at the same level as in previous years or even slightly reduced would produce an improved payout ratio. However, there are indications that the amounts paid out were increasing too. As Figure 7.4 shows, aggregate dividend payments by the companies listed on all the Tokyo and Osaka markets (TSE Sections 1 and 2, Mothers, Osaka, and JASDAQ) rose progressively from 2003 to 2008 as percentages of both sales and total assets. Thereafter they declined in 2010 as the influence of weaker corporate performance in 2009 made itself felt.

To some extent this trend may well have been encouraged, at least among smaller listed companies, by the activist hedge funds' interventions which were gathering pace and attracting increasing attention from around 2003. However, it is relevant to consider how major companies in Japan too were increasing their payouts at this time. Comparable data for the period 2000–8 for Canon, one of the most prestigious and emulated companies in Japan at that time, often cited by smaller companies' officers as a benchmark, shows an even faster and steeper increase, as shown in Figure 7.5, suggesting that the most

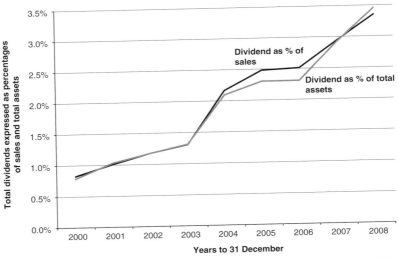

Figure 7.5 Canon's dividend as percentage of sales and total assets 2000–8
(*Source:* Company accounts)

profitable companies had adopted a definite policy of increasing payouts to their shareholders.

Commentators, corporate managers, and hedge fund officers to
whom we spoke all confirmed this impression that activist hedge funds
saw Japan as a market with potential ready to be exploited. In autumn
2007 a market commentator observed to us:

> I think that it is evidenced that many companies in Japan are even today
> chronically undervalued and therefore targets for hedge fund activism or
> they are seen as targets for opportunity. There are still companies who are
> trading below book value or barely at book value – companies with lots of
> cash on the balance sheet and without clear plans for using that cash.

A foreign investor interested in corporate turnaround situations, speaking at about the same time, put this even more succinctly: 'Broadly
speaking it is a target-rich environment in that 60 per cent of Japanese
companies are destroying shareholder value in some way or other.'

The activist hedge funds themselves, at least when dealing with
managers who understood their financial arguments, tended to declare
their interests openly. Directors to whom we spoke at companies that

had been targeted by foreign activist hedge funds reported a fairly consistent response when they asked the funds why they had been chosen. One said: 'When we asked [the fund] what had most attracted them to [our company] and led them to become shareholders, they told us that [our] share price was fundamentally discounted and not correctly valued.' An officer at another company recalled:

They explained their reasons for being interested in us: it was mostly to do with free cash flow ... It was that and also the fact that our own funds ratio was as high as it was in comparison to other companies ... I think it was those sorts of things, and the idea that we should distribute more of it, that triggered their interest.

Sometimes the reasons for the approach were couched in less explicit terms, which could lead to misunderstandings. One director reported a fund's explanation of its interest as follows: 'because [our company] was such an attractive company they wanted to cooperate with the management in raising the value of the company; they showed us their own valuation data'. To the board of a company that considers itself to be a community firm, increasing value is an attractive goal that sits well with the idea of promoting the company as an enduring community. Unfortunately, to an activist hedge fund manager 'the value of the company' does not normally mean anything as difficult to quantify as the intrinsic strengths of the firm and benefits to all stakeholders. It means specifically the potential future share price, augmented by the market's realisation that the company is committed to increasing dividend payments and adopting a leaner financial structure. It is possible that many foreign activist fund managers genuinely did not understand that there was any other way to define 'value', setting the scene for conversations at complete cross-purposes to one another.

A partner of a foreign activist fund conceded that Japan was not an easy market but thought that the same fundamental logic should work there as elsewhere. He estimated that, in general, most of the companies approached by his fund – presumably after careful selection – did ultimately raise their dividends. Another fund's partner drew attention to the availability of data to support financial analyses in the Japanese market. He saw Japan as an interesting challenge to unlock potential but was aware of the cultural barriers:

Western countries have a more advanced state of accepting shareholders exercising their rights than in Japan … But the other way to look at it is that nobody has tried it and so to the extent that it can be successful, it becomes a test case: it becomes an event where you think maybe you can do this, to unlock value in Japan.

The combination of high cash reserves and low market valuations is attractive to professional investors of any kind because it suggests a situation where the market has undervalued financially sound businesses with the ability to disburse cash. Foreign activist hedge funds, which had made it their speciality to extract payments in one form or another from unwilling boards in the USA and Europe, would consider this an especially good opportunity. By the end of the 1990s there were evidently sound financial reasons to consider activist interventions in Japan.

7.7 Conclusion

We have considered certain aspects of the Japanese market that made it more welcoming by the end of the 1990s than first impressions might suggest. We have looked at the community firm's chronic vulnerability to extortion; the underlying regulatory transparency of the confrontation at Koito Seisakusho which demonstrated that the market abided by its own rules; the shocks that had subsequently called into question hitherto accepted ideas of corporate governance in Japan; shifts in the composition of corporate shareholders away from the protective format of stable shareholdings towards a higher ratio of more dispassionate non-resident investors; and an apparent improvement in the willingness of boards to disseminate information and communicate with shareholders, perhaps driven by the demands of their non-resident shareholders. All of this created a background that was much more favourable than the initial impression of the community firm suggested. In addition, the Japanese market appeared to have an unusually large population of companies whose low share prices and accumulated cash made them interesting targets for activism, precisely at a time when sentiment in Japan was already moving towards more generous dividends. Opportunity for determined activists was clearly present. What was still unknown was whether it would be possible in practice to take advantage of these favourable trends and how robust the resistance of the community firm might prove.

8 | *Hedge fund activism in Japan: funds, targets, and outcomes*

8.1 Introduction

In this chapter we provide an overview of the wave of hedge fund activism in Japan which began in January 2000 when M&A Consulting, one of several investment vehicles collectively known as the 'Murakami Fund', made a hostile bid for the industrial and real estate company Shōei. Thereafter, a succession of Japanese listed companies was targeted by hedge funds from both Japan and overseas which acquired minority shareholdings and engaged with boards on matters of corporate strategy and financial structure, especially the issue of payouts to shareholders. Among the wide range of investors operating in the Japanese market, it is often difficult to identify specific strategies or to even to say definitively that any investor is a 'hedge fund' or an 'activist'. Tactics varied not only between funds but even at different interventions by the same funds. However, the US fund Steel Partners, in particular, soon established a reputation for taking uncompromising positions and being willing to provoke public confrontation, fostering the image in Japan of aggressive foreign activists targeting Japanese companies.

We first look at the rise and fall of the Murakami Fund, which was in many ways a precursor to the others. By the time it was wound up in 2006 in controversial circumstances, other funds had begun to apply a broadly similar approach in the Japanese market, using the arguments of financial capitalism to call for greater financial efficiency and higher returns to shareholders. We then focus on the situation at the end of 2007 which we consider to be the high point of hedge fund activism in Japan in terms of its public impact. We examine the background and orientation of the funds which had investments in Japanese companies at that point, focusing particularly on those which attracted public attention for various reasons and those whose strategies of engagement can be characterised as more confrontational. We look at the methods they used, the companies they targeted, and the results of their interventions. Our emphasis in this chapter is on general trends; in Chapter 9 we will analyse in more detail the tactics employed on both sides when two of the more confrontational funds, Steel Partners and TCI, made especially high-profile interventions at Bull-Dog Sauce and J-Power.

8.2 'A plant flowering out of season': the Murakami Fund

The first investors to use activist tactics to challenge the autonomy enjoyed by management in listed companies in Japan were themselves Japanese. From the late 1980s, a number of funds began to take stakes in underperforming or undervalued companies with a view to profiting from subsequent improvements in their performance. These included Sparx Asset Management, founded in 1989 (see Jacoby, 2009: 114–15), and Tower Investment Management (*Tower Tōshi Komon*), founded in 1998, both of which have gone on to become prolific investors in a range of Japanese listed companies, generally without becoming involved in publicly confrontational situations. M&A Consulting, founded by Murakami Yoshiaki in 1999, was the first fund to use public confrontation as part of a strategy of engagement with management. Murakami had previously been a civil servant with the trade and industry ministry, MITI (now METI). His status as a former official who had become a professional investor, together with his rigorous style, made him the focus of public attention to the point where his firm and the funds it managed became widely known as the 'Murakami Fund'. Although there was no fund bearing this precise name, we use it here as a convenient abbreviation for the various funds linked to Murakami.

The trajectory of the Murakami Fund

The Murakami Fund's first major transaction was a hostile tender offer launched on 24 January 2000 for Shōei, a former silk spinning company then listed on the Second Section of the Tokyo Stock Exchange that had transformed itself since the 1970s into a real estate and general investor with electronic parts manufacturing operations. The value of the bid was estimated to be approximately ¥14,100 million. Murakami told the press that Shōei was a 'classic case of inefficient management'. The condenser operations of its electronics parts business were consistently unprofitable, and much of its real estate business was, he argued, excess to requirements. The company had over ¥5,100 million of financial debt. It also had an unusually large board, with approximately one director for every six employees. Murakami revealed that his attempts to discuss Shōei's performance with its management had been rebuffed.

To target Shōei, notwithstanding the scope it had to increase returns to shareholders, was audacious. Shōei was the former parent of one of the two companies that had merged in 1944 to form Canon, regarded as one of Japan's most successful and prestigious companies. When the bid was announced, Mitarai Fujio, then Canon's president, observed: 'we have no intention of releasing the shares we hold, not only because of [Shōei's] historical links to the circumstances of our founding but also because it does business with our electronics operations'. Moreover Shōei was closely associated with the Fuji Bank,[1] which had seconded its employees to run the company for a number of years, and also made its opposition to the bid clear. The bid was unsuccessful and the Murakami Fund's final shareholding was only 6.5 per cent, but Murakami used Shōei's AGM to call for higher shareholder returns and greater transparency. Subsequently, in February 2007, Shōei disposed of its electronics business to Taiyō Yūden, a move that implicitly vindicated Murakami's arguments (Nikkei, 2005a; Nikkei Sangyō, 2000, 2007j).

Concurrently with its investment in Shōei, the Murakami Fund had bought shares from January 2000 in Tokyo Style, a clothing company with an unimpressive performance but strong reserves.[2] From early 2002 until mid-2004 it pressed Tokyo Style's board to raise dividends and accept external directors, resorting to legal action that alleged improper internal procedures when the board did not accede to these demands. Under threat from a derivative suit, Tokyo Style's president ultimately paid ¥100 million of compensation to his company in 2005 for apparent irregularities. As Murakami pointed out, this did not profit the Murakami Fund. However, the Tokyo Style affair served to

[1] Part of Mizuho Bank from 1 April 2000.
[2] Tokyo Style's accounts show that when the Murakami Fund made its approach in 2000, the company's profitability had been in almost uninterrupted decline for ten years.

draw attention to Murakami as a 'standard bearer of corporate governance' and is thought to have attracted new investors to his funds (Kawakita and Miyano, 2007; Nikkei Sangyō, 2005).

In April 2004 we were told unofficially that its main fund, the MAC Active Shareholder Fund, was managing some ¥100,000 million, from an initial capital of about ¥70,000 million, but the press reported the aggregate assets of all the related funds to have reached around ¥400,000 million at their highest point (Nikkei, 2006h). In 2004 the Murakami Fund also included two smaller, similar funds, and had recently established a strategic acquisition fund. Funds were also registered at that point in the Cayman Islands and in Singapore. Its website described its objective as the promotion of *motazaru keiei*, which literally translates as 'management that does not hold things' and implies efficient use of capital without tying up resources in unproductive assets. About 60 per cent of its investors were then resident in Japan but these included some foreign-owned firms; the major Japanese institutional investors are believed to have stayed aloof.

A study by the Japan Center for Economic Research (JCER) estimated that the Murakami Fund held positions in 52 companies by late 2005 and defined its investment priorities as seeking targets that were cash-rich, with accumulated surpluses, low dependence on bank loans, and no apparent plans to apply their reserves. This study also observed that the Murakami Fund tended to favour companies with relatively high foreign shareholder ratios and suggested that foreign shareholders were more likely than domestic ones to support Murakami's style of activism. A subsequent and more detailed study by Kawakita and Miyano, published by NLI Research in 2007, found 135 companies in which the Murakami Fund had intervened, but observed that there were probably many more, evidence for which was available from internet searches, in which the Fund had taken shareholdings below 5 per cent without triggering disclosure requirements. These researchers confirmed the same target characteristics found by the JCER study and further divided the targets into two categories: what they called '*meimon kigyō*' or established businesses where there were accumulated reserves and possibly a lack of energy in applying them, and recent start-up companies. They suggested that as Murakami's capital under management grew, he had moved from an early emphasis on corporate governance concerns to a more pragmatic investment stance. This policy was confirmed to us in a separate conversation with a related party and is supported by the fact that over half of the 135 interventions noted by Kawakita and Miyano involved investments of apparently less than one year. This tendency accelerated after 2004 (JCER, 2005; Kawakita and Miyano, 2007).

The Murakami Fund seems to have used tender offers on only two occasions: at Shōei in 2000 and at New Japan Radio ('NJR') in 2005. The NJR tender offer was an attempt to exploit a situation in which an agreed intergroup takeover appeared to undervalue the target. Nisshinbō had offered to take control of NJR in a bid agreed with the target's board and its controlling shareholder Japan Radio by buying up most of Japan Radio's roughly 50% shareholding for ¥840 per share. Nisshinbō was simultaneously a major shareholder in Japan Radio, with over 19% of its equity. This gave the impression that the transaction was being arranged for the benefit of the major shareholders. Murakami countered with an offer for about 47% of NJR priced at ¥900 per share on 21 November 2005. Nisshinbō's bid was subsequently accepted by Japan Radio at the increased level of ¥880 per share on the grounds that Nisshinbō offered synergies to NJR that Murakami could not match (Nikkei-BP, 2005; Reuters, 2005; Yomiuri, 2005a).

The Murakami Fund's largest and most publicised investment was its intervention in Hanshin Electric Railway, which began in September 2005 and ended in July 2006 when MAC Singapore, Murakami's Singapore fund, sold its outstanding shares to Hankyū Holdings. In the Hanshin intervention the Murakami Fund confronted a large target and demanded redeployment of its assets in a very public way, building up its shareholding until it held nearly 46 per cent as of 22 February 2006. Protracted discussions of strategy with the target's board produced no results amid accusations from Hanshin's executives that Murakami did not understand the railway sector or 'corporate value', whatever he might know about shareholder value. Finally, faced with the imminent possibility that the Murakami Fund might accumulate more than 50 per cent of Hanshin's equity, Hankyū Holdings were persuaded to make an agreed bid in May 2006 after only three weeks of negotiation by Hanshin's president, Nishikawa Kyōji, who had apparently already approached other potential bidders unsuccessfully. This was reported as a profitable outcome for the Murakami Fund (Yomiuri, 2005b, 2006).

In the midst of the Hanshin intervention, most of the funds that comprised the Murakami Fund sold off their positions and were wound up in June 2006 following admission by Murakami himself of insider trading in connection with Livedoor's attempt to win control of Nippon Broadcasting System and the Fuji Sankei group in 2005 (see Chapter 7 above). MAC Asset Management Pte in Singapore was still operating in July 2006 but closed later that year. Murakami was reported to have been considering the transfer of all of his funds and his personal residence to Singapore in 2006. Miyake's account of the events of June 2006 in his book *Shijō to Hō* (Miyake, 2007: 15–17) suggests that Murakami vacillated over whether to challenge the insider trading accusation or whether to protect his colleagues by admitting personal guilt; a transfer to Singapore would probably have been an important element of the former strategy. Subsequently, some of his colleagues began to operate from Singapore under the name of Effissimo Capital Management Pte Ltd. This fund can be seen from EDINET submissions to have made numerous interventions in Japanese companies after 2006 and was still operating in 2011. It has been seen as the successor to the Murakami Fund and has been prepared to confront uncooperative boards on several occasions, notably in 2008 at Gakken, where it demanded the resignation of the CEO; at Daiwabō Information Systems, where it challenged defence measures during 2008 and ultimately provoked a bid from the company's parent, Daiwabō, which allowed it to sell its shareholding; and at Nissan Shatai where it took legal action in July 2009 (Nikkei, 2008y, 2008z, 2009a). However, it has maintained a consistently lower profile than the Murakami Fund and has attracted less publicity.

Indicative returns from the Murakami Fund's interventions

It is difficult to trace all of the Murakami Fund's interventions from publicly available sources and the points of the Fund's entry and exit into particular companies cannot always be located precisely because shareholdings may have been maintained for some time below the 5 per cent threshold for disclosure. As we have seen, other studies noted between 52 and 135 interventions. We have identified 44 interventions at or above the 5 per cent level, as shown in Figure 8.1.

Figure 8.1 shows the chronological progress of these interventions, noting developments such as tender offers ('B'), known extraordinary payouts ('¥') and exits ('E'). For the purpose of this exercise we define the benchmark for 'success' as an annualised return of 5% or more, from a combination of capital gains, specific payouts, or dividend income up to the point of exit. Depending on whether it reached this 5% benchmark or not, each intervention is marked with upward or downward arrows as either 'successful' (⇧) or not (↘). A 5% benchmark is a low hurdle for this purpose. The annualised yield on ten-year US Treasury bonds for 2000–8 was 4.59% and the average return of funds in the Dow Jones Credit Suisse Event Driven Hedge Fund Index 2000–8 was 7.37%.

Our estimates of returns will not reflect the exact prices paid for the shares, and our dividend yield figures are derived from year end share prices rather than the true aggregate cost of the shareholdings acquired. However, we believe that these estimates are a reasonable proxy for actual returns. Precise data on the Murakami Fund's performance, as in the case of similar activist funds, are not publicly available. Another limitation of this style of analysis is that it does not consider the size of each investment. In principle, a single, huge intervention that delivered good returns could compensate for all the interventions that failed to deliver: for example, the Hanshin intervention, where the Murakami Fund ultimately held 46 per cent of the target's shares, tied up at least ¥90,000 million of the fund's capital, calculated at our estimated entry price of ¥461 per share, and generated a receipt of around ¥180,000 million at the tender offer price of ¥930 per share.

We have not considered currency movements in our analysis. There are several reasons for this. First, we are presenting only a rough picture here, based on estimated data, where added layers of analysis could create a spurious sense of precision. Second, although hedge funds' clients will be sensitive to exchange losses they will generally not choose their funds on the basis of whether they expect them to be lucky with currency movements: they seek managers who can create wealth from their investment skills, with currency movements as an important but still secondary concern. Finally, in the case of the Murakami Fund, while many of its clients were ultimately non-resident, it was still a Japanese fund which served some Japanese investors. However, currency movements could become an important factor, as we discuss later in this chapter and in Chapter 9.

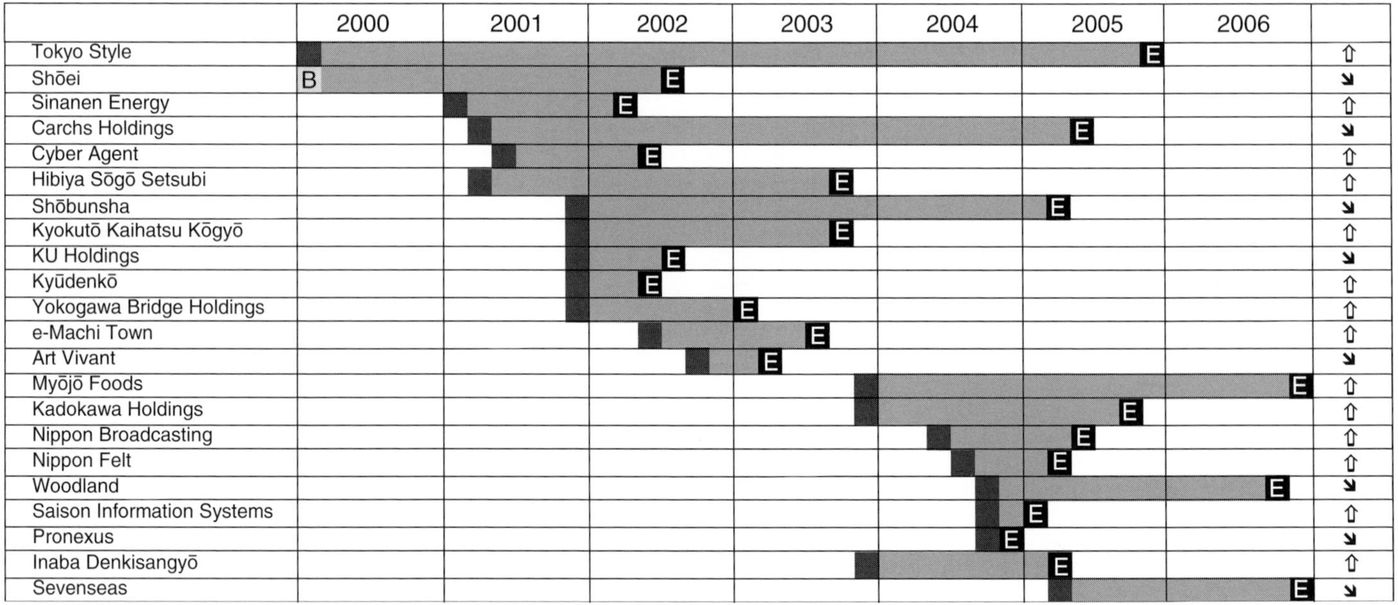

Figure 8.1 Chart of 44 interventions by the Murakami Fund

(*Sources*: EDINET, Thomson Reuters, company accounts, press reports)

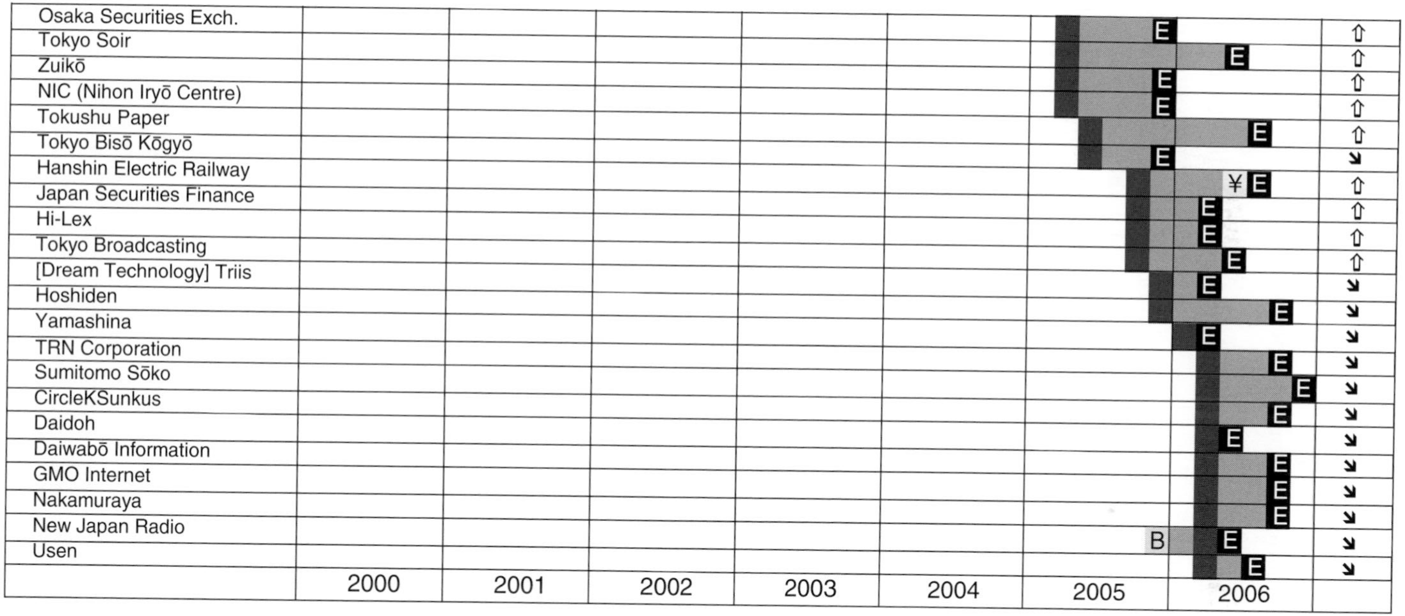

Company	2000	2001	2002	2003	2004	2005	2006	
Osaka Securities Exch.								←
Tokyo Soir						E		←
Zuikō						E	E	←
NIC (Nihon Iryō Centre)						E		←
Tokushu Paper								←
Tokyo Bisō Kōgyō						E	E	←
Hanshin Electric Railway						E	E 木	↗
Japan Securities Finance								←
Hi-Lex							E	←
Tokyo Broadcasting							E	←
[Dream Technology] Triis							E	←
Hoshiden						E	E	↗
Yamashina							E	↗
TRN Corporation								↗
Sumitomo Sōko							E	↗
CircleKSunkus							E	↗
Daidoh							E	↗
Daiwabō Information							E	↗
GMO Internet							E	↗
Nakamuraya							E	↗
New Japan Radio						B	E	↗
Usen							E	↗

Figure 8.1 (*cont.*)

With these caveats, Figure 8.1 indicates that most of the Murakami Fund's interventions in our sample were successful. Several remunerative investments were closed fairly quickly, in contrast to the slower progress in the cases of Tokyo Style and Shōei, where discussions with the targets' boards were particularly confrontational and protracted. Nine of the apparently unprofitable interventions shown here were liquidated when the Murakami Fund was withdrawing from the market in the latter half of 2006, essentially as a forced seller.

Murakami's philosophy and the reactions to it

In a press interview in 2003 with *Nikkei Sangyō Shimbun*, while he was still engaged in litigation against Tokyo Style's management, Murakami explained his philosophy in the following terms:

The real job of shareholders is to seek fairness. What I have been demanding of my investment targets, put in simple terms, is that they apply their cash in the most appropriate manner – that they concentrate economic resources in their core business. If they have no projects that they need to invest in, they should implement share buy-backs. If their share price has reached a reasonable level, they should make return to shareholders through dividends. It's all incredibly simple. At US companies they do this as a normal and obvious thing.

In the same interview he focused on cross-shareholdings as the most pernicious element of the Japanese corporate governance scene, and foretold damage to the whole economy if this situation were not ameliorated in some way. He described himself as *adabana* – a plant flowering out of season – which proved prescient in the light of subsequent events (Nikkei Sangyō, 2003a).

Although Murakami was on the fringe of the Japanese business establishment, he was not a complete outsider; he appeared to enjoy good relations with the Governor of the Bank of Japan, Fukui Toshihiko, who was an investor in the Murakami Fund on a personal basis from 1999 until Murakami's arrest in 2006, and Miyauchi Yoshihiko, chairman and CEO of the financial services company ORIX. When the Shōei bid was launched in 2000, *Nikkei Sangyō Shimbun* had commented that apart from his MITI background, Murakami was virtually unknown and very much dependent on Miyauchi's support. The same article further suggested that Miyauchi had a strong personal interest in this kind of activism but was constrained by his public position from promoting it directly (Bloomberg, 2006a; Nikkei Sangyō, 2000).

Murakami's approach was not to everyone's taste. Ōsaki Sadakazu, writing in *Nomura Capital Market Review*, observed:

> Although I have never been confronted by Murakami and been subject to his demands, like the executives of many listed companies, I did have the opportunity to hear his opinions as a member of the cash management committee of the Osaka Securities Exchange [in which the Murakami Fund took a shareholding at one stage]. My experience at that time lent further credence to the negative opinion of Murakami's words and conduct that many have expressed. (Ōsaki, 2006: 15)

However, condemnation of Murakami was not universal. The president of a company in which the Murakami Fund had earlier held a shareholding told us in 2004:

> In fact, he's come to the company many times and made lots of suggestions – we've exchanged all sorts of ideas – and we've played golf together; we get on very well. But, he says all sorts of weird things. For example, he says things like 'If I were you, I would buy out all your own shares in a self-TOB and de-list.' Or, 'Without going that far with the shares, why not make around half the issued shares that you hold all into stock options?' and things like that. Well, that's the sort of thing he says. But we're always telling him that we don't want to do anything drastic like that – that we want long-term shareholders who will develop along with us, taking a long-term view. And when we explain that we want to proceed with that sort of shareholder relationship, that we want to take that sort of stance towards our shareholders and that the sort of thing we want to do is to move along gradually, he just says 'Oh, really' and there is no quarrel. Well, during that time we've issued some stock options, we've bought up some of our own shares and we've gathered some treasury shares, you see. He's very satisfied.

The activities of the Murakami Fund also stimulated considerable press comment, but this was by no means all hostile. As Figure 8.2 shows, the Murakami Fund was more frequently reported in *Nikkei* during the period 2006–8 than either of the two most prominent overseas funds, Steel Partners and TCI, whose coverage we discuss later. However, *Nikkei*'s interest was relatively muted until 2005 when it hit a sudden peak: in 2006 *Nikkei* (morning and evening editions) carried 718 articles referring to the 'Murakami Fund', often in conjunction with Murakami Yoshiaki's own name. Examination of the headlines indicates that 356 (49.6%) of these articles related either to Murakami's arrest for alleged insider trading, to commentaries on the background to this case and its links to Livedoor, or to the uproar that greeted the news that the Governor of the Bank of Japan had invested personally in some of Murakami's funds; 146 (20.3%) related solely to the Murakami Fund's intervention in Hanshin Electric Railway; and only 216 (30.1%) related to different matters, including other interventions. Many of these articles are general commentaries on Murakami's investment model and behaviour, and seem to have been stimulated more by his arrest than by his investment activities.

It did not escape the attention of observers that while Murakami was sentenced to prison for two years in July 2007 (this was reduced to a suspended sentence on appeal in 2009) and heavily fined,[3] Tsutsumi Yoshiaki, former chairman of Seibu Railway, had received a 30-month deferred sentence and a relatively small fine of ¥5 million for insider trading and falsifying of shareholder records only a year earlier. Murakami was seen as having annoyed powerful figures in business and official circles who had been determined to pursue any errors he might make to the maximum possible degree (Bloomberg, 2006b; Japan Times, 2009). As the CEO of a Japanese company described it to us later: 'just as the saying goes "the nail that sticks up will be hammered down", he was put away by the establishment'.

More generally, Murakami was seen as having demonstrated that an activist investment fund which justified its position in the name of shareholder returns could operate successfully in Japan. According to Kawakita and Miyano, writing in 2007: 'the single greatest

---

[3] The judgment by the Tokyo District Court on 19 July 2007 sentenced Murakami to two years in prison and fined him ¥3 million with an additional penalty of ¥1,149 million, with further penalties for his firm. On appeal to the Tokyo High Court, his conditions were reduced to a deferred three-year sentence on 3 February 2009 but the financial penalties were unchanged (Nikkei, 2009c; Yomiuri, 2007).

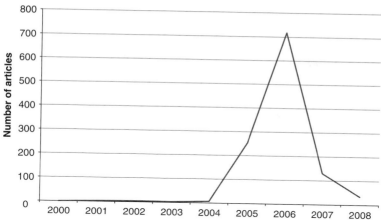

Figure 8.2 Incidence of *Nikkei* articles on the Murakami Fund, 2000–8 (*Source:* Nihon Keizai Shimbun)

achievement of the Murakami Fund [was] that it put pressure on listed companies to ensure that their profitability was in line with their cost of capital' (Kawakita and Miyano, 2007: 1). In 2006 Ōsaki had summarised Murakami's contribution to changing the general attitudes of Japanese management as follows: 'The Murakami Fund has done much to impress upon the management of Japanese corporations the need to raise shareholder value, an area that had received very little attention until then, and to encourage a change in management's attitude. At the very least, Murakami's success in this regard should be remembered' (Ōsaki, 2006: 14).

8.3 After Murakami: the spread of public and confrontational activist strategies

The Murakami Fund had demonstrated that a public and even confrontational style of activism, grounded in the arguments of financial capitalism, could deliver returns in Japan. It was not unreasonable to suppose that the era of T. Boone Pickens and Koito Seisakusho was over, even though some boards were still hostile to assertive shareholders. Other funds, broadly characterised as 'activist' but embracing a wide variety of strategies, had entered the market. Some of the foreign funds among them attracted more sustained attention than the Murakami Fund itself, partly just by virtue of being foreign and partly because some of them showed less awareness of the niceties of doing business in Japan and tended to take more intransigent positions. Whereas Murakami had latterly shunned the press, funds like Steel Partners, which entered the market in 2002, and TCI, from 2006, often distributed releases of communications with their targets on their websites and stimulated a public debate with targets' boards through the medium of the press, effectively crystallising the opposing views of each side. We now consider the spread of hedge fund activism in Japan beyond Murakami, first at its high point in late 2007 and then more generally across the extended period of 2002–8, focusing on funds that engaged in public and confrontational engagement and thereby played a specific role as catalysts for debate within the corporate governance system.

December 2007 represents the high point of hedge fund activism in Japan. Interventions by funds that had developed into public confrontations were being widely reported and the full impact of the global financial crisis had not yet affected the funds' investors. Despite their high profile, those forms of activism which caught the attention of the press and the general public were just one part of a wider phenomenon of shareholder engagement with the boards of listed companies in Japan at this time, much of which went on behind the scenes. In order to analyse the specific role of the more public and confrontational funds, it is necessary to separate out their activities from those of the larger group of investment funds which had sizable holdings in Japanese companies during the 2000s.

For the purposes of our study, we have defined 'activist hedge funds' as funds which, among other things, seek to influence the strategic or financial policies of their targets (see Chapter 5 above). The term 'activist hedge fund', used in this sense, is not a legal term of art, and there is some disagreement, among both researchers and practitioners, as to which funds it should be applied to. There is a multitude of ways by which shareholders may try to exert influence on the companies in which they invest, and some funds described as 'activist' by the press would define themselves differently.

In this context we emphasise again the point made in Section 5.3 regarding the implications of relying mainly on formally notified shareholding data. In Japan, as in the USA, the threshold for obligatory formal notification is 5 per cent but it is possible to exert influence at listed companies through shareholdings below this level that need not attract public attention unless either the investor or the target chooses to publicise them. Within our database we have included one investment (by TCI at Chūbu Electric) where the fund's investment remained well below 5 per cent throughout. Since our main interest is in the degree of friction resulting from activist hedge funds' interventions, concentration on investments in excess of 5 per cent is not generally a problem. However, we stress that the data we are studying do not represent the entire universe of activist involvement in Japan, even for the funds on which we are concentrating.

The starting point in our analysis is to look at the categorisations made by the widely used and publicly available Thomson Reuters' database of companies. This provides details of shareholdings held in a number of countries, including Japan, by investment entities which are described as 'hedge funds' with 'active orientation'. According to Thomson Reuters, activist hedge funds, so defined, had shareholdings of 1 per cent or more in 145 non-financial companies listed on the various markets in Tokyo or Osaka as of 31 December 2007. We exclude financial companies, such as insurance companies or asset management companies, which are investment vehicles in their own right, since in these cases it is unlikely there was any engagement by activist funds with management over issues of corporate strategy or financial structure. Then we remove several companies which were delisted after December 2007, for which full data are unavailable, and several which were not listed in 2006, the date from which we source our data on the financial structure and performance of targets (see further below). Then we further exclude those companies where the hedge fund shareholding in question fell below 5 per cent more than three months before 31 December 2007.[4] Since official data sources in Japan (available through EDINET) do not track shareholdings below 5 per cent, there is no certainty regarding the progress of shareholdings when they go below that level, unless they attract publicity in some other way. We observe a three-month cut-off on the assumption that it would be common practice, where an activist hedge fund's holding went below the 5 per cent

---

[4] Shareholdings in the Thomson Reuters database below 5 per cent mostly appear to relate to investments which had been at or above the 5 per cent level, and were reduced subsequently, leaving the official record of their final reduction from above 5 per cent to a named percentage below it as the only verifiable data from that point.

disclosure threshold, for it progressively to reduce its investment rather than maintain a small shareholding without publicity. Additionally, we exclude companies where we were unable to confirm a hedge fund shareholding on EDINET as at 31 December 2007. Finally, we add three companies whose status as hedge fund targets we were able to confirm independently through EDINET and our own research. This produces a list of 119 target companies in which a total of 19 activist hedge funds were present. The full list of targets and funds is shown in the Data Appendix as Table A.3. This table shows that numerous foreign funds were prominent in the activist hedge fund market in Japan in late 2007, but that several Japanese funds continued to operate after the withdrawal of the Murakami Fund.

Even with this series of qualifications, the group of 119 targets may overstate the activist hedge fund presence in the Japanese market. The Thomson Reuters category of hedge funds with 'active orientation' is broad, and we know from discussion with practitioners in the course of our interviews that it includes some funds which reject the description 'activist'. Some of our interviewees queried Thomson Reuters' selection of activist funds, and informed us that certain funds listed there from time to time have taken steps to have their names removed from that category. Our understanding, based on our interviews, is that the Thomson Reuters category includes both activist hedge funds which engage publicly with the management of companies in which they invest, and also funds that would more usually be classed as 'value funds', and which, on the whole, eschew public activism.

In order to get a clearer picture of the extent of hedge fund activism in Japan and of the relative importance of public versus non-public engagement, the next step is to look more closely at the 19 funds that we have just identified as potentially engaged in activism, but with the provisos we have discussed above. Figures 8.3 and 8.4 present data on them by the number of their investments and by the estimated capital outlays implied by those investments. Our capital outlay estimates are not the actual amounts invested progressively by the funds to accumulate their shareholdings, but rather the market values as at 31 December 2007 of each fund's total stake in each target company.

Figure 8.3 shows that the most prolific investor was Tower Investment Management ('Tower'), the Japanese fund founded just before Murakami's M&A Consulting. Tower accounts for 29 per cent of the total number of investments in our list of targets. Market

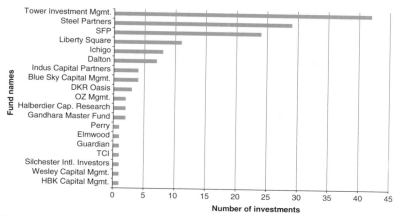

Figure 8.3 Number of investments at 31 December 2007 by funds categorised as 'active orientation' by Thomson Reuters
(*Source:* Thomson Reuters)

practitioners speaking in early 2011 told us that Tower was a value fund which generally relied on the market to deliver an upturn, without engaging in overt activism. Tower's large number of generally small holdings reinforces this impression of its strategy; it would have been difficult for such a fund to conduct activist campaigns simultaneously at so many companies. After Tower, foreign – or at least foreign-owned funds – predominate, led by Steel Partners with 20 per cent. However the presence of Tower as the biggest investor of all, in terms of the number of its investments, shows that at least one local fund was a major force in the market as an investor, although its credentials as an activist are unclear.

Figure 8.4 shows the same funds ranked by estimated capital outlays. Steel Partners account for over 51 per cent of the total and foreign funds again predominate. Tower is again prominent but much less so (with under 4 per cent) than in the comparison by number of investments in Figure 8.3, because of its smaller units.

Since our sample includes funds with a variety of strategies, we now seek to distinguish between them more precisely. We first divide our sample of 19 funds between those that attracted sustained attention in the Japanese financial press and those that did not. We characterise the former as 'public' funds and the latter as 'non-public' funds. Two important caveats are, first, that we make no distinction here between

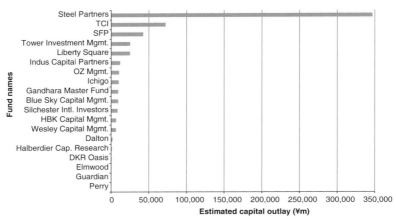

Figure 8.4 Capital outlays at 31 December 2007 by funds categorised as 'active orientation' by Thomson Reuters
(*Source:* Thomson Reuters)

funds which intentionally sought public attention, of which there were several, and those who merely received it because their strategy, their particular tactics, or the reaction of the targeted board generated interest, and, second, that once we have categorised a fund as 'public' we do not distinguish 'non-public' approaches by the same fund at different target companies. Ichigo, for example, appears to have attracted extensive press attention only in one instance (at Tokyo Kohtetsu) but still appears throughout in the 'public' category. In order to place funds in one category or the other, we analyse the coverage given by *Nikkei* during 2007 and also, by way of confirmation, throughout 2001–8. We choose *Nikkei*'s coverage as the proxy for publicity because it is the most widely read financial newspaper in Japan, seen or discussed by most senior managers on a daily basis. We show the citation data for 2007 in Figure 8.5.

Steel Partners, the second most prolific and the most committed in invested capital terms of the funds in the Thomson Reuters end-2007 data, dominates the *Nikkei* 2007 data with 339 articles (roughly 70% of the total for all funds). Tower Investment Management, despite being the most prolific fund at the end of 2007 according to Thomson Reuters, received no mention at all in *Nikkei* in this year. TCI, which had only one investment outstanding in 2007, is in equal second place with Ichigo, which had five investments in progress (35 articles or 7%

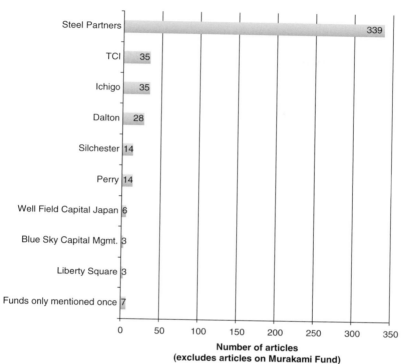

Figure 8.5 Articles on activist hedge funds in *Nikkei* during 2007
(*Source:* Nihon Keizai Shimbun)

each). Then comes Dalton, which had three investments in progress
(28 articles or 6%), followed by Perry and Silchester, both of which
had one investment in progress (14 articles or 3% each). Symphony
Financial Partners ('SFP'), the third most prolific fund in the Thomson
Reuters' data in terms both of capital outlay and number of investments, receives no mention.

The same pattern emerges from our broader chronological search
of *Nikkei* on the same basis for the period 2001–8, shown in
Figure 8.6, suggesting that the interest shown by the financial press
was sustained and not limited to 2007. Steel Partners still dominates with 662 articles (64%), then TCI with 144 articles (14%),
Dalton with 68 articles (7%), Ichigo with 46 articles (5%), and
Perry with 26 articles (3%). Not all of these funds were operating
in Japan throughout the whole period: TCI, Ichigo, and Perry only

began their Japanese investments part way through, implying a bias towards Dalton and Steel Partners, which were present in the market from an earlier stage. The Murakami Fund, which would have been prominent here, is omitted because it was no longer operating at the end of 2007.

In our final selection of the 'public' funds we choose the top five names: Steel Partners, TCI, Dalton, Ichigo, and Perry. We omit Silchester, despite its sustained programme of investment in Japanese companies and its equal position with Perry in 2007, because we believe that its prominence can be attributed mainly to its legal action against Autobacs Seven in November 2007 and because we consider the circumstances of Perry's sole investment in Japan to reveal more about Japanese corporate governance. Although they shared a common feature in attracting the attention of the press when they proposed strategic changes at their investment targets, these five funds all adopted different strategies in Japan and do not comprise a homogenous group. TCI was a 'large-cap' investor in Japan, and Steel Partners began to move in that direction latterly, though never to the same extent. The other three funds were 'small-cap' investors. In terms of investment style, Steel Partners and TCI both took aggressive and publicly confrontational stances with the boards of their targets during the period of our study. The other three funds did not do so, with Ichigo and Perry, in particular, presenting arguments that gained approval from other shareholders and the general public. Our justification for combining these funds into a single category is that the publicity they attracted during the period of our study brought their strategic agendas to public attention and generated precisely the kind of debate over corporate governance in which we are interested.

We will now take a closer look at the strategies of these five 'public' funds.

8.4 The five 'public' funds and their Japanese strategies

Of the five funds which we have characterised as engaged in 'public' activism in 2007, four were established funds which brought with them experience of activism from their home markets in the USA and Europe. Ichigo, which was a newer asset manager operating only in Japan, was run by a former academic and officer of a US investment

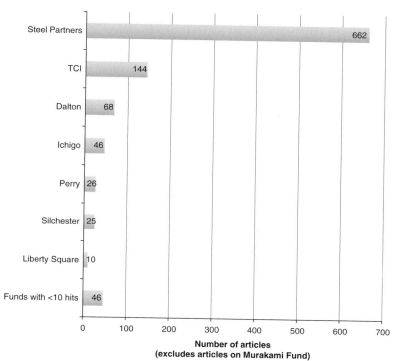

Figure 8.6 Articles on activist hedge funds in *Nikkei* 2001–8
(*Source:* Nihon Keizai Shimbun)

bank. As we have observed, their strategies were not uniform. Our account of them, set out below, draws on our data set of hedge fund interventions, based on press reports and the EDINET database, and our interview material.

1. Steel Partners

Description
Steel Partners (Steel Partners LLC) was founded in 1990 by Warren Lichtenstein and Lawrence Butler. In 2010 Lichtenstein was described as the head of the firm. In the US context, he has been described as 'a demanding investor [who] exercises shareholder rights whenever he feels necessary' (Chatterjee, 2007; Hedgetracker, 2011; Lichtenstein, 2007). Steel Partners restrict access to their website but public

information from *Bloomberg Businessweek* accessed in June 2011 showed that they were based in New York with additional offices in Tokyo and East Brunswick, New Jersey. Thomson Reuters reported Steel Partners' equity assets to be US$1,147 million in August 2010 but did not indicate whether this figure included debt as well as equity. Their main Japanese operation was Steel Partners Japan Strategic Fund (Offshore) LP, owned jointly with Liberty Square Asset Management LP, but evidently managed by Lichtenstein.

Lichtenstein and Steel Partners had already established a reputation in the USA. Kruse and Suzuki noted that between July 1995 and October 2009 Steel Partners filed 63 initial Schedule 13D forms notifying holdings of 5 per cent or more in US companies. A prospectus issued for one of these interventions summarises their objectives as follows:

We will seek to acquire established businesses that are easy to understand. Additionally, we will target businesses that we believe are fundamentally sound but potentially in need of certain financial, operational, strategic, or managerial redirection to maximize value. We do not intend to acquire start-up companies, companies with speculative business plans or companies that are excessively leveraged.

Kruse and Suzuki also noted press reports that the fund had made an impressive annual return of 25 per cent from its founding until 2003 inclusive and had achieved even better results thereafter. Initially the fund had targeted companies capitalised at around US$100 million each but more recently had invested in larger companies, with up to US$10,000 million capitalisation (Kruse and Suzuki, 2011: 8–9).

Steel Partners in Japan

Steel Partners made their first investment in Japan in late 2002. In early 2005, the Japanese financial press counted 30 Japanese companies in which Steel Partners held or had recently held shareholdings (Nikkei Kinyū, 2005). Their first interventions showed the same pattern of an initial investment followed by a tender offer, followed by a payout. In three 2003 interventions – in the condiment manufacturer, Bull-Dog Sauce, the fabric dyer, Sotoh, and the instant noodle manufacturer, Myōjō Foods – exit followed soon after the payout, but Steel Partners only sold their holding in one of the first companies they invested in, the chemicals company Yushiro, in December 2008, despite an apparently large payout in early 2004.

Steel Partners' confrontational style delivered high returns, at least in the beginning. Their intervention in Sotoh was typical of their early approach. Sotoh was a small company with consolidated turnover for the year to 31 March 2003 of ¥9,466 million. Sotoh's March 2003 consolidated accounts showed shareholders' equity of ¥24,076 million, but its market capitalisation in September 2003, when Steel Partners' initial purchases are thought to have been made, was less than ¥14,000 million. Sotoh was profitable, had no net financial debt and held ¥23,039 million of cash or similar assets, equivalent to 73 per cent of its total balance sheet. It would have been a prime hedge fund target in more or less any setting; in Japan, it did not stand out among many listed companies which were trading below book value.

Steel Partners appear to have begun purchasing Sotoh's shares from September 2003 and as of 14 October 2003 they and associates had accumulated 12.2 per cent, or as much as 12.4 per cent according to one press report. They announced a tender offer in December 2003. The stated objective of the tender offer, which ran from 19 December 2003 until 26 January 2004, was to increase Steel Partners' shareholding to 33.3 per cent, paying ¥1,150 per share. This would not have created a controlling position as such but it would have enabled Steel Partners to block any special resolutions at Sotoh and made them the company's most powerful shareholder. Demand for Sotoh's shares intensified and trading ceased on the day of the announcement as the share price hit the exchange's limits.[5] Takaoka Sachirō, a director of Sotoh, commented to the press that this was quite sudden and unexpected, and that he had no idea how to respond (Nikkei, 2003a).

Sotoh's board decided to launch a management buyout ('MBO'), backed by NIF Ventures,[6] the venture capital unit of Daiwa Securities, Sotoh's principal broker. On 15 January 2004 the MBO offered

---

[5] The TSE sets trading limits to restrict volatility in the form of a maximum daily price fluctuation band permitted for each stock which is calculated on a sliding scale from the level of the previous day's closing price or any special quote. Once a share price reaches its relevant limit for fluctuation, either upwards or downwards, its trading is suspended for all trades outside that band during that business day.

[6] Now 'NIF SMBC Ventures'.

¥1,250 per share. In response, on 26 January, Steel Partners offered to purchase all the outstanding shares of Sotoh at an increased offer price of ¥1,400 per share and extended the offer period to 16 February. On 5 February, the offer price for the MBO was raised to ¥1,470, but on 12 February, Steel Partners again raised their offer price, to ¥1,550 (Nikkei, 2004a). On 16 February Mabuchi Yoshiaki, Sotoh's president, announced a radical change of plan: NIF's MBO proposal was to be abandoned in favour of a massive increase in the dividend for the year to March 2004, from the previous year's ¥13 to ¥200 per share. Steel Partners welcomed this decision and their bid lapsed when less than 1 per cent of shares was tendered, the price in the market having exceeded their offer price following the announcement of the dividend. The press did not seem to notice that this was probably Steel Partners' preferred outcome (Nikkei, 2004b; Nikkei Sangyō, 2004). Sotoh had effectively raised its annual payout to shareholders from around ¥200 million to around ¥3,000 million, equivalent to about 10 per cent of its entire balance sheet. Mabuchi's explanation that there had been no plans to utilise these funds only served to emphasise the board's lack of strategic thought.

During March 2004 Steel Partners sold down their shareholding in Sotoh, taking advantage of their target's improved share price, and reduced it to 3.7 per cent on 17 March. On an annualised basis they would have almost doubled their investment in this intervention. Subsequently, Sotoh paid high dividends of ¥150 per share for the next two years and then reduced the amount to ¥54 per share for the year to March 2007, at which level it has remained to date. While this level of payout maintained Sotoh's share price at a level well above that prior to Steel Partners' intervention, it exceeded Sotoh's consolidated net profit for several years in a row. In 2010 Sotoh appeared still to be paying out its reserves to its shareholders.

Myōjō Foods ('Myōjō') was another relatively small company. It reported consolidated turnover in the year to 30 September 2003 of ¥75,622 million. It had a market capitalisation of under ¥12,000 million in August 2003 – which had risen to around ¥16,600 million by December of that year, probably in response to Steel Partners' purchases – compared with shareholders' equity of ¥25,781 million. A further attraction was that over 20 per cent of its entire balance sheet was net cash or cash equivalents. The company responded to

Steel Partners' approach by increasing its dividend and accepting the appointment of a Steel Partners nominee as one of its directors. In October 2006 Steel Partners issued a tender offer in response to which Myōjō approached a competitor, Nissin Foods, which then acted as a 'white knight', mounting an offer of its own at a premium to the pre-bid three-month-average share price of 31.4 per cent and undertaking to maintain Myōjō's operational autonomy. The press estimated that this bid offered Steel Partners the opportunity to double the value of their investment in Myōjō. Steel Partners did not raise their bid, allowing it to lapse, and the merger went ahead. It soon became known that they had tendered their entire shareholding to Nissin (Flexnews, 2006; Nikkei, 2006f, 2006g).

The management of Myōjō were reported in the press to have regretted that their company would be taken over by a long-standing rival, but saw this as a lesser evil. Concern was expressed that Steel Partners had not made clear their post-takeover strategy, that they could not manage an instant noodle business in the long term, and that they might simply be in search of capital gains. In contrast, Myōjō could expect to reap business advantages through association with a company from the same sector as a long-term shareholder (Nikkei, 2006f). Steel Partners had profited from the dividend increases paid by Myōjō and by the premium offered by Nissin to take control. They had executed a classic activist hedge fund manoeuvre by stimulating a counter-bid and had achieved a profitable exit

The case of Bull-Dog Sauce, another tender offer by Steel Partners, which we examine in detail in Chapter 9, led to a payout which was directed exclusively to the fund, effectively at the expense of the other shareholders. This was the price which the board was prepared to pay to preserve its autonomy. When Steel Partners initiated litigation to challenge the board's defence plan, which involved the issue of dilutive share warrants, the fund was labelled an 'abusive acquirer' in a judgment by the Tokyo High Court. Although financially rewarding, Steel Partners' intervention in Bull-Dog Sauce harmed their reputation in Japan and encouraged other companies' boards to resist all hedge fund activism.

Steel Partners' early interventions generated some favourable press comment but there were also some hostile reactions to what was seen as the firm's single-minded pursuit of gain. The press reported negatively on Lichtenstein's public statements on visits to Japan. He was seen as projecting an attitude of uncompromising focus on financial considerations to the exclusion of the operational and social aspects of corporate performance. In May 2007, Lichtenstein expressed in the course of a newspaper interview a desire to 'enlighten' Japanese firms about shareholder value[7] (Nikkei Business, 2007), a remark that he subsequently repeated at a public conference in Tokyo the same year. From the autumn of 2008, however, he appeared to be taking a different line. In an interview reported in the *Nikkei Weekly* in September 2008, he said that his firm had begun to communicate more with the Japanese companies in which it was investing, following the contentious Bull-Dog Sauce intervention and the litigation surrounding it. He contrasted Steel Partners' stress on dialogue with management elsewhere in the world to their initial approach to Japan: 'in Japan, we did not do that, and it was a mistake' (Nikkei Weekly, 2008). Steel Partners' early confrontational strategy appears to have given rise to internal disagreements within their Japanese operation. In June 2006 the press reported that several of Steel Partners' Japanese managers had resigned following differences of opinion about strategy (FT, 2006c) and at least one more senior Japanese manager resigned subsequently to this.

In their first four Japanese interventions, Steel Partners demonstrated a variety of timings within their basic approach. The Sotoh intervention progressed rapidly from the initial investment to tender offer and payout, but in the case of Yushiro a year passed before the tender offer was made. With Myōjō Foods there was a gap of over two years between the first investment and the tender offer, and in the case of Bull-Dog Sauce, an interval of more than three years. Steel Partners appear to have followed a strategy of making an initial investment and opening up a dialogue, followed by a tender offer to put pressure on the board if it did not agree to their suggestions. This kind of gradual pressure was applied in the beginning at Myōjō Foods, where the board accepted Steel Partners' nominee as an external director for a while. Steel Partners appear to have become frustrated with the slow responses of target boards, whose members may have been uncertain

---

[7] Lichtenstein's comment, presumably translated by his interviewer from the English, was given in the context of his observation that Japanese companies generally were increasing their dividend payouts but still falling short of his expectations and was reported in this article as '*kono ten wa chōkiteki ni nihon kigyō o keimō shite ikitai*' ('in this regard, looking to the long term, I want to enlighten Japanese firms').

with regard to the fund's objectives (Uchida and Xu, 2008: 9): tender offers for Yushiro and Sotoh were registered on the same day, 19 December 2003.

Although Lichtenstein only commented publicly in 2008 about taking a less confrontational approach to Japanese interventions, changes were evident earlier. Two of Steel Partners' 2004 interventions, at the brewer Sapporo and the wig-maker Aderans, involved extensive public discussion and the presentation of proposals to the board. Although the Sapporo intervention involved the threat of a tender offer, it was ostensibly a friendly approach, seeking board support, and was abandoned when this was not forthcoming. Steel Partners maintained their holding for an extended period during which Sapporo's management responded in a manner which could only be construed as obstructionist. No tender offer was made at Aderans, but Steel Partners succeeded in harnessing the support of other shareholders – though this proved only barely adequate to achieve a majority – to remove an incumbent board which was seen as having produced consistently weak performance (Nikkei Kinyū, 2007a; Nikkei Sangyō, 2008d, 2008g).

In their interventions at relatively larger companies after 2004, Steel Partners encountered management teams which were more determined in resisting pressure and more sophisticated in their ability to communicate with shareholders than had been the case at some of the earlier, smaller targets. At Aderans, Steel Partners achieved changes in board membership, but were not subsequently able to reorganise the business as they had intended. At Sapporo and at the water heater manufacturer Nōritz, Steel Partners were effectively blocked by a strategy of playing for time, supplemented by the use of anti-takeover defences. At Kikkōman, a soy sauce manufacturer, and Nisshinbō, a textiles manufacturer, despite share buy-backs in which Steel Partners do not appear to have participated, they seemed to make no progress in changing the boards' strategies. At the engineering and electronics company Brother and the watch manufacturer Citizen, the targets' boards opposed Steel Partners' proposals until the fund sold out, reportedly at a loss in each case (EDINET data and Nikkei, 2007g, 2007i, 2007an, 2008j; Nikkei Sangyō, 2008d, 2008e, 2008g).

In January 2009 it was reported that Steel Partners had reduced their shareholdings in 13 Japanese companies, falling below the 5 per cent level in seven of these cases. Analysts speculated that the fund's customers were short of liquidity and were withdrawing cash, but it was also suggested that Steel Partners had invested too heavily in Japan and needed to reorganise their portfolio (Reuters, 2009e). The global financial crisis was probably a major factor in their retrenchment. The crisis affected hedge funds worldwide after 2007 as clients withdrew cash where they were able to do so and called for more immediate returns on committed resources where they were not. After many years of consistently high returns, 2008 was Steel Partners' first loss-making year (Bloomberg, 2009b). Subsequently they appear to have come under pressure to meet investors' demands for withdrawals, apparently facing requests equivalent to 38 per cent of their capital under management. Steel Partners responded by converting their main fund into a publicly traded company, allowing the fund to make payouts in the form of partnership units which would reflect the fund's fluctuating value, rather than paying out cash. In January 2009 this process was challenged in the courts by Carl Icahn, an activist investor previously closely associated with Lichtenstein, who was presumably one of the affected clients of the fund. Steel Partners subsequently obtained dismissal of this suit and a further, related petition at the Delaware Supreme Court, in July 2009, and at the Cayman Islands Grand Court, in November 2009, and it was reported in March 2010 that Icahn and Lichtenstein had reached agreement (Bloomberg, 2009e; Hedgetracker, 2010; Reuters, 2009b). Meanwhile, in Japan, only the Aderans intervention still continued at the end of 2010, with a shareholding of nearly 28 per cent, then entering its seventh year with no immediate sign of a clear resolution in terms of a profitable exit. EDINET filings showed no new Japanese interventions by Steel Partners during 2010.

2. TCI

Description

TCI (The Children's Investment Fund Management (UK) LLP) was established in London in 2003 by Chris Hohn, formerly a fund manager at Perry Capital. Until at least 2009, TCI also had an office in Hong Kong. TCI derives its name from the contributions it makes to a charity, The Children's Investment Fund Foundation (CIFF), run by Hohn's wife (www.ciff.org), which 'funds projects to improve the lives of children living in poverty in developing countries'. According to an article published in the *Economist* in 2007, 'charity and rapacity sit surprisingly comfortably together' in TCI, while its founder 'is driven less by greed than by a desire to be proved right' (Economist, 2007). TCI is authorised and regulated in the United Kingdom by the Financial Services Authority, but most of its interventions and general investments hitherto appear to have been outside the UK.

In 2007 TCI was reported by Thomson Reuters to have equity assets of approximately US$5,500 million, with a bias towards larger targets and very little exposure to smaller companies. The same source reported that TCI's portfolio was located approximately 40% each in Asia and North America, with about 8% each in Latin America and Europe, and comprised approximately 40% railways, 20% electrical utilities, 19% real estate, and 7% steel. If the railway investment was that in CSX (the US railway company where TCI intervened from 2006 until 2009) and the electrical utility investment was that in J-Power, 60% of TCI's total assets were deployed in only two interventions. TCI attracted attention worldwide from its interventions in Continental Europe (see Chapter 5 above), most notably in Deutsche Börse and ABN AMRO, where it had demonstrated an ability to extract shareholder value by confronting the boards of high-profile businesses.

Bloomberg reported that TCI had achieved returns of some 42 per cent from 2003 to 2007. However, the same source reported a loss of 43 per cent in 2008. In June 2009 it was reported that TCI intended to reduce fees and ease withdrawal limits to retain clients and that it was scaling back its activist investments after disappointing outcomes at J-Power in Japan and CSX in the USA, where a protracted and increasingly bitter confrontation with the board had ended with TCI's withdrawal in April 2009. According to a report by Bloomberg, Hohn had told *Alpha* magazine in September 2008: 'we are going to be more cautious about it when we look at making new investments, because quite frankly activism is hard' (Bloomberg, 2009c, 2009d; FT, 2009d; Hedgetracker, 2009). In November 2010, the hedge fund bulletin *FINalternatives* reported:

It has been clear for some time that the last few years have been hard on The Children's Investment Fund Management. Now, it is clear just how hard ... The hedge fund's fee income has fallen precipitously over the past several years. The charity from which it gets its name reported this summer that it had received just £19 million from the hedge fund in 2009, down from £486 million in 2008. (FINalternatives, 2010)

Nevertheless, as we note in Chapter 11, TCI did return to the Japanese market with a new intervention in June 2011.

TCI in Japan

TCI made two interventions in Japan during the period of our study, both in electrical utility companies. The first of these was the Nagoya-based electrical utility Chūbu Electric from late 2005 until September 2007. TCI took only a small percentage shareholding that is believed not to have exceeded 1.4 per cent, and restricted itself to applying pressure to management and soliciting support for its dividend increase proposal with relatively little publicity. The press subsequently reported information obtained from Chūbu Electric's management that TCI had begun to purchase shares in autumn 2005 but, since the shareholding remained below the obligatory disclosure level, it appears to have been generally unnoticed and overshadowed by the subsequent accumulation of shares in J-Power by TCI, which had exceeded 5 per cent in October 2006. It was only in March 2007 that the Japanese press, followed by foreign news services, reported that TCI had acquired 'around 1%' of Chūbu Electric's shares and had already met the company's senior management on several occasions to propose dividend increases, share buy-backs, and more efficient use of capital. The catalyst for this publicity appears to have been a letter from TCI to Chūbu Electric's board dated 16 March 2007 in which it notified its intention to submit a shareholder proposal for an increased dividend, which the board dismissed in a website posting of 27 March, observing that 'the Company believes that TCI's proposal differs from the Company's policy on shareholder return'. At the AGM on 27 June, TCI's proposal was defeated and the board's proposed level of dividend was accepted. However, TCI's proposal was supported by about 10 per cent of the votes, which the press noted as an unexpectedly large percentage, suggesting that some private shareholders gave their support. Mita Toshio, president of Chūbu Electric, spoke at a press conference on 27 June 2007 where he said remarkably little about TCI and the issues it had raised. He expressed his belief that most shareholders understood the management's position and supported its aim to provide a stable supply of electricity to customers. He commented that management should not be distracted by short-term profit considerations because stability was needed for the longer term. TCI sold its shares in September

2007, probably achieving a neutral exit in the opinion of sources close to the target. This sale was not reported in the Japanese press until November and Chūbu Electric's management would not confirm any details beyond the fact that TCI was no longer one of its top ten shareholders. Although sources close to the company implied that TCI took an uncompromising position at several private meetings, it did not use extensive publicity (Chūbu Electric, 2007; Nikkei, 2007z, 2007aa; Nikkei Kinyū, 2007c).

In 2006, TCI began its second intervention, in J-Power. This investment, which we examine in detail in Chapter 9, attracted more attention and developed into a more contentious and publicised intervention. J-Power, like Chūbu Electric, was an electrical utility designated of importance to the national interest, with a potential cap on any single foreign shareholding at the 10 per cent level. The small size of TCI's shareholding in percentage terms had prevented this from becoming an issue at Chūbu Electric. J-Power's management responded confidently and assertively; in October 2008, after increasingly acrimonious exchanges with all concerned, TCI sold its shares back to J-Power at a loss estimated to have been about ¥12,500 million before any effect of exchange rate movements.

TCI appears to have adopted an uncompromising tone in its dealings with both of its Japanese targets, insisting on the importance of viewing corporate strategy from a financial perspective. However, the quieter approach used at Chūbu Electric contrasts with the way in which the discussion at J-Power ultimately developed into a highly publicised contest. TCI's principal spokesman in Japan was the head of its Hong Kong office, John Ho, who used TCI's Japanese website and communication with the press to promote the agendas he was proposing at J-Power. Ho was interviewed extensively in the Japanese press and, at least until the later stages of the J-Power intervention, received favourable comment from some mainstream newspapers and specialist publications for his stress on the financial case for reorganisation.

3. Dalton

Description
Dalton (Dalton Investments LLC) maintains a detailed website open to the public (www.daltoninvestments.com). According to information

on this website (accessed on 30 June 2011) Dalton is a US fund management company founded by three partners – James Rosenwald, Steve Persky, and Gifford Combs – in 1998 and established in its present form in 1999. Its head office is in Los Angeles and it has further offices in Tokyo, Shanghai, and London. In May 2011 it reported total funds under management of approximately US$1,300 million. The company categorised itself as a value investor and as a 'global investment management firm committed to capital preservation and long-term growth' and described its business as 'focused on global equities, Asian equities and distressed investing since inception'. Its Tokyo office's business was not described in detail, but in late 2009 its Japanese management buyout strategy was said to be 'designed to achieve returns by taking strategic stakes in undervalued Japanese public companies, whereby we may unlock value through restructuring balance sheets and placing majority control into the hands of management and friendly investors'. However, changes to its structure, described below, had been implemented soon after this. Dalton's website stated that Sano Junichirō, formerly an officer of Nikkō Securities, became a senior adviser to Dalton in 2006 and he appears to have run its Japanese operations from that time.

Dalton in Japan

Dalton did not attract the same level of attention from the press in Japan as Steel Partners and TCI. In the beginning, at least, it appears to have progressed its interventions with minimal publicity. Subsequently, two of its MBO proposals, in particular, seem to have attracted greater public attention, although this may also be the result of generally heightened sensitivity to foreign activists with the advent of Steel Partners in Japan.

The earliest major intervention by a foreign activist hedge fund in Japan that we can identify was that of Dalton in Sun Telephone, which began in 2001 but only attracted wide attention from May 2006, when Dalton's funds already held over 30 per cent of the company.[8] Sun Telephone was a wholesaler, importer, and exporter of telecommunications equipment, then listed on the first sections of the Tokyo and Osaka stock exchanges. Its board was evidently uncomfortable

---

[8] Press reports are sometimes unclear because they tend to confuse Dalton's purchases with those of Dalton's JMBO fund but we have assumed that the combined holding was just over 30 per cent by May 2006.

with Dalton's presence because it sought to issue potentially dilutive warrants to Mitsubishi UFJ Securities, only to be halted when
Dalton obtained an interim injunction from the Tokyo District Court
on 30 June 2006. Dalton then launched a tender offer for up to 9%
of Sun Telephone's outstanding shares with the stated objective of
reaching around 40% in order to be able to block any extraordinary
motions (which would require a two-thirds majority). Sano, who now
appeared to be in charge of Dalton's intervention, emphasised that this
was not a hostile bid, and explained that management intransigence
had made it necessary to seek a major shareholding in this way. Nearly
9% of Dalton's issued share capital was tendered, and Dalton's shareholding rose to 39.6% in November 2006. Dalton proposed that Sun
Telephone should be delisted through an MBO but the board opposed
this idea, citing Dalton's lack of experience in Japanese MBOs and
accusing it generally of being coercive. Sun Telephone's president,
Yamagishi Keiji, expressed his unhappiness with the presence of any
shareholder in such a dominant position. Subsequently the board
arranged an MBO through Japan Industrial Partners and Bain Capital
in December 2006, into which Dalton sold its shareholding in early
2007, reportedly gaining a profit of approximately ¥3,000 million on
its investment (Nikkei, 2006a, 2006b, 2006c, 2006d; Nikkei Kinyū,
2006a; Sun Telephone, 2006).

This intervention shows a foreign fund proceeding with a degree of
caution, without seeking much publicity, but willing to protect its interests through the courts. The investment lasted for over five years and
there seems to have been a gradual build-up to the decisive events of
the latter half of 2006 and early 2007. The length of time elapsed suggests that Dalton pressed Sun Telephone's board to implement changes
for a long time through private meetings and only decided to increase
its shareholding in the way it did when it failed to achieve success by
other means. It is not known whether Dalton planned the MBO from
the start, but by proceeding in this way it was able to deflect accusations of predatory takeover. Sun Telephone's board reacted defensively
to Dalton's involvement and did not see the outcome as beneficial to
the company. The president, at a press conference following the MBO,
regretted delisting the company, since he saw its listing as the fruit of
his father's labours to build the business before him (Nikkei, 2007ab).

Dalton made no further major interventions of which we are aware
until three in early 2005, while events at Sun Telephone were still

not attracting attention. Two of these, at the manufacturer of base materials for pharmaceuticals, cosmetics, and other chemical products Nippon Fine Chemical and the lift manufacturer Fujitec, follow a common pattern of taking shareholdings in conservatively run companies which either had underperforming operations or businesses under their control which were unrelated to their core activities. Both attracted attention in the press. In each case, Dalton argued that a major reappraisal of the companies' structures, coupled with delisting through a management and employee buyout ('MEBO'), offered better prospects than current strategies. Both boards rejected the proposals, with Nippon Fine Chemical's board maintaining a muted response and Fujitec's board reacting more strongly. Fujitec's US and European operations had made an operating loss of ¥70 million in the year to 31 March 2007 and Dalton proposed that it should concentrate its resources in Asian markets where there was currently a construction boom. It conceded that this move might temporarily affect performance and the share price and therefore, to avoid damaging shareholders' interests, proposed the MEBO. The ratio of operating profit in South Asia was said to be 10 per cent and in East Asia 8 per cent. Uchiyama Takakazu, Fujitec's president, opposed Dalton's idea publicly on the grounds that the USA and Europe were showcases for Fujitec's world-scale business strategy and that Fujitec's performance in orders received from European customers would help it to obtain orders from customers in other parts of the world. Moreover he considered that this strategy was necessary to overcome Fujitec's lack of market visibility compared with other manufacturers. However, the press noted that Fujitec had accepted many unprofitable US and European orders over the years in its pursuit of growth. When neither board showed willingness to cooperate, Dalton proceeded to obtain exits for the bulk of these shareholdings, through a share buy-back scheme in the case of Nippon Fine Chemical and through a trade sale to a competitor in the case of Fujitec (Nikkei, 2007ac, 2007am, 2008o; Nikkei Sangyō, 2007c, 2007d, 2007k, 2008f). In this sense, neither intervention followed the normal pattern of an MBO which would have generated returns for investors through an eventual re-listing or sale to a trade buyer. However, both investments appear to have generated gains for the fund, and Dalton, with its MBO-based approach, does not appear to have been accused openly of being a greenmailer or 'abusive acquirer'.

In October 2009 Bloomberg reported that Dalton planned to merge its Japanese operation with the real estate specialist Lexington Corporation, a Japanese-registered company that was created in 2002 from the former Commerzbank Special Products Group. Dalton had apparently reduced its Tokyo staff numbers from 15 to 6 in preparation for this reorganisation. Sano was reported as commenting, 'as part of our scrap and build effort, this is what we came up with in the wake of Lehman's collapse that changed the world'. Whether intentionally or not, this gave the impression that Dalton's Japanese business was in difficulties. Sano also explained that Dalton was seeking to acquire further businesses in Japan which held asset-management licences to complement those of Lexington. Although this implied refocusing Dalton's approach away from MBOs in the Japanese market, Sano told Bloomberg in the same interview that 'while the portion of Japan assets at Dalton have declined along with the benchmark *Nikkei 225* Stock Average's 42 percent slide, the company has been able to raise money for its existing distressed fund and slightly increase its total assets' (Bloomberg, 2009a). The Thomson Reuters database showed six investments by Dalton outstanding in Japan at the end of 2009 but an EDINET search on 30 June 2011 showed that all of these had been reduced to below the 5 per cent level by August 2010. However, one new investment had just been instigated in June 2011, demonstrating that Dalton had not withdrawn from the Japanese market. The latest reference to Dalton in *Nikkei* since 2008 that we could trace as of July 2011 was an article on 20 January 2009 about its recent investments in some 20 real estate investment trusts ('REITs').

4. Ichigo

Description

Ichigo (including Ichigo Asset Management K.K. or Ichigo Asset Management, Ltd and Ichigo Asset Management International Pte Ltd) is a Japanese fund management company founded and controlled by Scott Callon, a former Stanford University academic and investment banker. In July 2011 (according to information we received from the fund) all of Ichigo's assets were held by Ichigo Trust, a unit trust investing primarily for US and UK endowments and foundations. Ichigo also ran a JASDAQ-listed operating company with over 20,000 Japanese shareholders, engaged in management of Japanese real estate investment funds, Ichigo Group Holdings. We refer to all of Ichigo's companies and funds hereafter simply as 'Ichigo'. According to Ichigo's website (www.ichigoasset.com), its name is derived from the saying *ichigo ichie*, a phrase that enjoins the listener to focus keenly on every moment because it will not come again. In July 2011 Ichigo's website described it as 'an independent investment manager specializing in Japanese equities' and stated: 'we believe good corporate governance lies at the heart of strong company performance, and are seeking a new model for Japanese corporate governance that includes active, committed, and responsible shareholders'. Ichigo confirmed its approach to us in July 2011 as follows: 'We are not activists or a hedge fund. We are a traditional long-only asset manager that is dedicated to Japan and invests in companies and management teams that we respect and believe in. We do not short, we do not deal in complex financial instruments, and we invest for the long term.' Ichigo's reported funds under management as at the end of 2010 were US$1,058 million equivalent.

Ichigo in Japan

Ichigo made several investments in generally small Japanese companies during the period we are studying, beginning in 2006 and extending until early 2008. The most publicised of these was in the steel products maker Tokyo Kohtetsu, at the end of 2006. This was distinct from most other interventions by activist funds in Japan (although, as we noted above, Ichigo rejects the description 'activist') because it was widely seen as having helped minority shareholders overcome the interests of an obstructive majority share block and an uncommunicative management. By questioning as a shareholder Tokyo Kohtetsu's proposed merger on possibly unfavourable terms with a competitor, Osaka Steel, and gathering sufficient support from fellow-shareholders to block the required extraordinary resolution on the grounds that the terms proposed did not reflect the company's true value, while still supporting the strategic logic, Ichigo appeared as a champion of shareholders' rights. However, the boards of Tokyo Kohtetsu and Osaka Steel closed ranks and refused to consider any adjustment to the terms of the merger, preferring to abandon it altogether rather than grant concessions (Ichigo, 2007; Nikkei, 2007v, 2007w, 2007x; Nikkei Sangyō, 2007l; Tokyo Kohtetsu, 2007).

A distinctive feature of the Tokyo Kohtetsu intervention was that Ichigo solicited the support of retail investors through an extensive mailing exercise. An announcement on Ichigo's website on 16 February 2007 of the number of proxy votes received prior to Tokyo Kohtetsu's crucial shareholders' meeting included the statement: 'Scott Callon, Partner and Chief Executive of Ichigo, comments: "Ichigo sincerely thanks the many individual shareholders of Tokyo Kohtetsu who have responded to our proxy solicitation. This proxy solicitation has reaffirmed our belief in the power of Japan's individual shareholders to make a positive difference ...".' One month before that Callon had told the press: 'One force that sustained me here was that so many individuals were annoyed by the smallness of the premium and had made an issue of this over the internet' (Nikkei Kinyū, 2007). This reporter, as did others, remarked on Callon's excellent command of Japanese and his enthusiasm for Japan. In a posting on the website of the Japan Society (an American organisation dedicated to promoting US–Japanese understanding) in May 2007, Callon explained why Ichigo had chosen to question the Tokyo Kohtetsu merger terms: 'We didn't think this was right ... At the end of the day, we wanted to stand up for shareholders. And if we walked away from this, who was going to do it?' (Callon, 2007).

The Tokyo Kohtetsu affair presented Ichigo as a defender of shareholders' rights, rather than as an activist demanding higher payouts to shareholders. The widespread publicity that it attracted reflected public interest in a situation where board autonomy had successfully been challenged, essentially in a reaffirmation of the rights of the retail investors who had traditionally been ignored in Japan since the 1940s. Ichigo does not appear to have become involved in further transactions thereafter involving the sort of publicity that the Tokyo Kohtetsu affair generated. Thomson Reuters' database showed that Ichigo had 16 investments in Japan pending at the end of 2009. EDINET data viewed on 30 June 2011 showed it taking shareholdings in excess of 5 per cent at a small but steady number of Japanese companies, with the last increased investment noted in May 2011. There was a growing number of real estate-related holdings by 2011, whether in the form of specialist funds or real estate companies. The Tokyo Kohtetsu shareholding was still in place in July 2011 and Ichigo confirmed to us then its satisfaction with this situation, in line with its policy of long-term investment.

5. Perry

Description

Perry (Perry Corporation, mostly operating as 'Perry Capital, LLC', although apparently not in the case of the Japanese market) restricts access to its website but according to information available in June 2011 on *Bloomberg Businessweek* was founded in 1988, had its head office in New York, and also had offices in London and Hong Kong. According to data from Thomson Reuters accessed in late 2010, Perry Japan Investment LLC, which does not appear to be operating now, was a private company based in Japan with all of its investments in Asia. Its equity investments were reported to be approximately US$169 million in 2007, with its entire portfolio comprising shares in NEC Electronics. On the other hand, EDINET data show Perry's investment vehicle for its investments in NEC Electronics throughout to have been 'Perry Corporation' with the firm's New York address. Perry Capital itself was reported by Thomson Financial to have equity assets of US$1,326 million in August 2010.

In 2008 Perry was reported to have recorded its first annual loss in 20 years of operations. A letter sent to its investors was circulated on the Internet. The *New York Times* reported in February 2009 that Perry Partners International, the firm's main fund, had declined in value by 27 per cent over the whole of 2008 after a promising start, principally because of a 20 per cent fall in the fourth quarter. Earlier, in October 2008, the *Wall Street Journal* had reported departures from among the fund's managers, a general reduction in staff, and a refocus of strategy away from equities (NYT, 2009; WSJ, 2008a). Informal market bulletins circulating on the Internet in June 2011 suggested that performance has improved since then.

Perry in Japan

In early 2007 Perry bought shares in NEC Electronics, a loss-making manufacturer of specialist semiconductors for the automotive and telecommunications industries with consolidated sales for the year to March 2006 of ¥645,963 million. It had been established as a separate company from part of NEC's semiconductor operations and listed on the first section of the Tokyo Stock Exchange in November 2002. NEC continued to control a shareholding of 70 per cent (65 per cent held directly) in NEC Electronics.

Perry initially invested alongside other funds but soon emerged as the main proponent for change. It appears to have identified NEC Electronics as a potentially successful company handicapped by its unprofitable supply of certain products to NEC, arguing that elimination of this business and other improvements would restore profitability and raise the share price. Perry did not achieve its objective because the relationship between NEC and NEC Electronics proved too robust. Despite exchanging letters with both companies' boards and asking questions at their AGMs, Perry's requests for meetings were refused and it reduced its shareholding in NEC Electronics below 5 per cent in December 2008. Perry's intervention in NEC Electronics coincided with criticism from the Tokyo Stock Exchange of situations in which subsidiaries were listed as independent companies while continuing to serve only the parents' business objectives (Nikkei, 2007e; Nikkei Kinyū, 2007d; Nikkei Sangyō, 2008c; TSE, 2007b: 5). In April 2010, NEC Electronics merged with Renesas (itself formed in 2003 from the semiconductor businesses of Hitachi and Mitsubishi Electric) to create a three-way joint venture called Renesas Electronics (Renesas, 2009). Although NEC's board had rejected Perry's arguments, it had apparently accepted that a resolution of some kind was needed to address the issues that Perry had identified.

Perry presented itself throughout its investment in NEC Electronics as a serious investor requesting a considered response to its proposals from the boards of its target and its target's parent, NEC. It did not launch personal attacks on the directors of the two companies, but it did encourage media coverage to publicise the merits of its case. Its principal representative in Japan, Alp Ercil, spoke on several occasions to the financial press, where his insistence that Perry hoped to meet NEC's directors for a constructive discussion contrasted favourably with terse responses from NEC, in particular. Ercil explicitly associated Perry's intervention in NEC Electronics with the wider question of subsidiary listings as a potential abuse of minority shareholders' rights, on one occasion presenting his view at Tokyo University to academics interested in this question (Nikkei Kinyū, 2007d, 2007e; Nikkei Veritas, 2008).

In a more favourable environment Perry might have built on the goodwill that Ercil had created and persisted with its Japanese interventions, but the global financial crisis intervened. As we have seen,

Perry was facing problems at its main funds and an EDINET search in June 2011 showed no further Japanese investments in its name since the final NEC Electronics filing in December 2008.

Assessing hedge fund strategies: distinguishing between 'confrontational' and 'non-confrontational' activism

The review of the strategies of the five 'public' funds that we have just presented suggests that in Japan, as in the USA, activist hedge funds engaged with management at their target companies with a view to bringing about changes in corporate strategy and financial structure which were intended to enhance returns to shareholders, both in the short run in the form of increased payouts, and in the longer term as a result of improved capital efficiency and, ultimately, enhanced operating performance. Among these five 'public' funds, however, there were significant differences of approach. Steel Partners and TCI can be characterised as engaging with companies in an openly confrontational way: they challenged the strategic direction and financial stewardship of their target firms and employed bids, litigation, and general publicity when they encountered resistance. The cases of public engagement that we have considered by the other three funds are less clear-cut in this respect. These funds described themselves as value investors rather than as activists, and, although Dalton had recourse to litigation in one instance, tended to use less adversarial methods, often presenting themselves as responding to particular policies which threatened to undermine shareholder value.

On this basis, we can further refine our analysis of the 119 interventions identified from the Thomson Reuters database and other sources into a subset of 30 targets of *confrontational* activism (the companies targeted by Steel Partners and TCI) and 89 targets of activism which, whether public or not, can be characterised as *non-confrontational*. We use the distinction between confrontational and non-confrontational funds as the basis for the analysis, which follows below, of the characteristics of target firms and of the impact of activist interventions, because the focus on confrontation most clearly captures the clash between the financial perspective of the activist funds and the communitarian orientation of most listed Japanese companies, which is the focus of our study.

8.5 Characteristics of companies targeted by activist hedge funds

In undertaking a more systematic, statistical analysis of the phenomenon of hedge fund activism in Japan in the period we are studying, the first step is to examine the characteristics of the companies targeted by activist hedge funds, first in respect of the group of 119 targets, and then by reference to the two sub-categories of confrontational and non-confrontational activism (30 and 89 targets respectively) that we have just identified. To do this, we compare the properties of the targets with those of a sample of similar companies in the Japanese market. We follow here the methods used by Brav *et al.* (2008a, 2008b) and Klein and Zur (2009) to study targeting by hedge funds of US companies.

The financial data we use for our analysis are derived from the Thomson Reuters and Tōyō Keizai data sets for the nearest financial year of each company ending in calendar year 2006 (mostly, but not always, 31 March 2006). In some cases the investments we are analysing began several years before 2006, but we choose 2006 data as the basis for analysing the characteristics of firms targeted in 2007 as the best proxy for the financial information available to the funds, either as forecasts or final figures, in advance of making their investments. Choosing this single date for our analysis also simplifies the process of comparing the target firms with a sample of matched companies.

We match each target company with a group of other companies which were comparable to it by reference to industry, total asset book value, and book-to-market ratio (that is, the ratio between the book value of the company's net assets and the stock market value of the company's issued share capital). More precisely, we employ a matching algorithm according to which, for each target company, we first choose the ten closest companies in total assets from all companies with the same two-digit industry classification, using the US Standard Industry Classification or 'SIC' coding. From these ten possible matches, we then choose the five companies with the closest book-to-market ratio (the 'matched samples').

The results of our analysis are shown in Table 8.1. This sets out summary statistics on the characteristics of the target companies, and reports the results of univariate analyses of the differences between the targets and the matched samples. Panel A presents the summary statistics and analysis for the group of target companies as a whole. Panel B reports those for the 30 companies targeted by the funds we have categorised as involving confrontational activism, and Panel C those for the 89 companies where activism took a non-confrontational form.

In our analysis, we use two tests of difference. In each Panel, column 5 shows the *t*-statistics, which measure differences in means, while column 6 reports *z*-statistics for differences in medians, using a Wilcoxon signed rank test. The Wilcoxon test is less influenced by extreme observations and is included here as a robustness check, given that the skewness of the variables included in the analysis can be expected to affect the analysis of the means. In presenting our results we assume that a difference between the target company and its peers is statistically significant if both the *t*-statistic and the Wilcoxon test indicate a two-tail significance of at least 5 per cent.

For the group of targets as a whole, Panel A of Table 8.1 shows that target companies had a higher Tobin's Q, meaning that their stock market value was higher, on average, in relation to their asset base, than that of comparable firms. This result is significant using only one of the two statistical tests we are employing, so must be treated with caution. The analysis more clearly shows that target companies were more profitable on average than their counterparts. The return on assets (RoA) is about 1.8 percentage points higher than for the matched peers. This result is statistically significant using both tests.

A second set of variables relates to capital structure. We can see from Panel A of Table 8.1 that target companies had lower leverage than the matched samples; the average book value of total debt to total assets is around 9.9 percentage points lower for the targets. Second, as might be expected for companies with low leverage, target companies were more cash-rich: their average cash-to-assets ratio is about 5 percentage points higher than that of the matched samples. Target firms also paid out higher dividends (defined here in terms of the ratio of dividends to total assets) than their peers.

Finally, Panel A of Table 8.1 reports on the relationship of insider ownership to targeting. Target companies had slightly lower inside ownership than their peers, although this result is not statistically significant. Insider ownership is defined by the Tōyō Keizai data set in terms of the extent of holdings by the top ten shareholders plus

Table 8.1 Characteristics of target companies

Panel A. All hedge fund activism (119 targets)

Firm characteristics	Summary statistics			Difference with matched firms		
	Mean (1)	Median (2)	SD (3)	Avg. diff. (4)	t-stat of diff. (5)	Wilcoxon (6)
Market capitalisation	69.256	25.073	109.948	13.528	1.218	2.283**
Tobin's Q	1.280	1.137	0.482	0.093	2.678**	0.960
Sales growth (%)	5.182	4.700	9.490	-0.749	-0.994	-0.458
RoA	0.035	0.036	0.038	0.018	4.748***	5.264***
Leverage	0.166	0.067	0.205	-0.099	-7.260***	-7.836***
Cash/assets	0.168	0.138	0.134	0.050	6.061***	3.084***
Dividend/assets	0.010	0.008	0.007	0.003	7.119***	3.927***
Insider ownership (%)	51.931	49.700	12.792	-0.762	-0.541	-0.547

Panel B. Confrontational activism (30 targets)

Market capitalisation	137.401	81.798	154.565	81.673	3.871***	4.680***
Tobin's Q	1.229	1.123	0.338	0.038	0.650	0.884
Sales growth (%)	5.230	5.220	12.446	-0.700	-0.507	-0.326
RoA	0.027	0.031	0.035	0.010	1.393	2.074**
Leverage	0.120	0.043	0.199	-0.155	-6.308***	-6.428***
Cash/assets	0.144	0.131	0.090	0.026	2.086**	1.722*
Dividend/assets	0.014	0.012	0.008	0.006	10.639***	5.418***
Insider ownership (%)	45.487	45.000	7.729	-7.177	-4.579***	-4.562***

Table 8.1 (*cont.*)

Panel C. Non-confrontational activism (89 targets)

Firm characteristics	Summary statistics			Difference with matched firms		
	Mean (1)	Median (2)	SD (3)	Avg. diff. (4)	t-stat of diff. (5)	Wilcoxon (6)
Market capitalisation	46.025	18.945	78.400	−9.704	−0.796	−0.088
Tobin's Q	1.303	1.149	0.523	0.112	2.839***	0.643
Sales growth (%)	5.165	4.700	8.350	−0.765	−0.932	−0.722
RoA	0.037	0.037	0.038	0.021	4.831***	5.068***
Leverage	0.181	0.096	0.205	−0.084	−5.573***	−5.691***
Cash/assets	0.175	0.144	0.146	0.058	6.241***	2.689***
Dividend/assets	0.009	0.008	0.005	0.001	3.663***	1.633
Insider ownership (%)	54.103	52.800	13.446	1.440	1.375	0.554

This table reports the characteristics of target companies and comparisons with a set of matched companies. Panel A summarises all hedge fund activism samples. Panel B summarises the confrontational activism samples. Panel C summarises the non-confrontational activism subsamples. The first three columns report the mean, median, and standard deviation of the characteristics for the target companies. Columns 4 through 6 report the average difference between the sample firms and the industry/size/book-to-market matched firms, the t-statistics for the average differences, and the Wilcoxon signed rank statistics, which is asymptotically normal, for the median differences. All variables are retrieved from the year 2006. *Market capitalisation* is market capitalisation in American billions of yen; *Tobin's Q* is defined as (equity market value + book value of total liabilities excluding shareholders' equity)/(equity book value + book value of total liabilities excluding shareholders' equity); *Sales growth* (%) is the percentage growth rate of sales over the previous year; *RoA* is return on assets, defined as net income/assets; *Leverage* is the debt to capital ratio (where 'capital' is the sum of debt and equity) defined as debt/(debt + book value of equity); *Cash/assets* is defined as (cash + cash equivalents)/assets; *Dividend/assets* is total dividend payments divided by total assets; *Insider ownership* (%) is the percentage of shares held by the top ten shareholders plus directors' holdings and treasury stocks.

*** significant at the 0.01 level; ** significant at the 0.05 level; * significant at the 0.10 level.

directors' holdings (including those held as trusts) and treasury stock (that is, shares issued and held by the company itself). These can be assumed to be solid share blocks whose holders will generally back the board (although they could, of course, include holdings by funds).

When we break down the analysis by reference to whether the companies were targeted by confrontational or non-confrontational funds, a number of further features emerge. The confrontational funds targeted companies with a higher market capitalisation than their peers, less leverage, higher dividend payouts, and less inside ownership (Table 8.1, Panel B). In the case of non-confrontational funds, on the other hand, the high cash-to-asset ratio of the targets stands out, although high profitability (as measured by return on assets) and low or negative leverage are also significant using both statistical tests (Table 8.1, Panel C).

We expand on the univariate analyses by using conditional fixed logistic models to identify the partial effects of all covariates. We fit the models separately for the all hedge fund activism samples, confrontational fund samples, and non-confrontational fund samples. The results, presented in Table 8.2, are broadly consistent with the univariate tests presented above. They show that lower leverage, a high cash-to-asset ratio, high dividends compared with assets, and low insider ownership were the most important factors attracting investments across the group of targets as a whole. In the case of the confrontational funds, high dividend payouts was the most important factor driving targeting, while for non-confrontational funds the most significant characteristic was again a high cash-to-asset ratio.

Our results echo those for the USA, which show that activist hedge funds tend to target profitable and financially healthy firms which are rich in cash (Klein and Zur, 2009: 189) and whose shareholders may accept financial arguments rather than support management unquestioningly (Brav *et al.*, 2008a: 1753). The combination of lower leverage, low insider ownership, and high dividend yield which characterises the targets of the 'confrontational' funds suggests that they were following the same logic of selection as applied in the USA. Our findings on the importance of insider ownership are also consistent with the observations of the JCER on Murakami's targeting criteria that we cited earlier (see Section 8.2 above).

Table 8.2 *Logistic models predicting targeting*

Dependent variable:	All hedge fund activism=1		Confrontational activism=1		Non-confrontational activism=1	
	(1) Coefficient	(2) z-statistics	(3) Coefficient	(4) z-statistics	(5) Coefficient	(6) z-statistics
Size	-0.001	-0.86	0.001	0.16	-0.002	-1.26
Tobin's Q	0.252	0.69	0.017	0.01	0.348	0.91
Sales growth (%)	-0.005	-0.65	-0.012	-0.08	-0.010	-1.11
RoA	2.712	1.02	-12.836**	-2.07	8.500**	2.19
Leverage	-1.572**	-2.35	-3.242	-1.61	-1.291*	-1.73
Cash/assets	2.639**	2.94	5.325*	1.70	2.617***	2.59
Dividend/assets	38.988*	1.93	147.328***	2.81	-18.773	-0.70
Insider ownership (%)	-0.015*	-1.66	-0.037	-1.41	-0.009	-0.95
Number of targets	119		30		89	
Log likelihood ratio	43.170***		39.690***		28.480***	
McFadden's R-squared	0.103		0.371		0.091	

This table reports the results of logistic regressions of the firms that are targeted by activist hedge funds. The dependent variable is a dummy variable equal to one if there is hedge fund activism targeting the company in the year 2007 (that is, all covariates are lagged values from 2006). All independent variables are as defined in Table 8.1. Columns 1 and 2 report coefficients and z-statistics for all activist hedge fund samples. Columns 3 and 4 report coefficients and z-statistics for firms targeted by confrontational activists. Columns 5 and 6 report coefficients and z-statistics for firms targeted by non-confrontational activists. *** significant at the 0.01 level; ** significant at the 0.05 level; * significant at the 0.10 level.

8.6 The impact of interventions on target firms and returns from activism

We now consider the impact of hedge fund interventions on target firms and the returns to the funds themselves. We look first at the impact on target companies one and two years on from December 2007, returning to the full list of 119 companies and the two sub-categories of 30 investments by confrontational funds and 89 investments by non-confrontational funds. We then take a look at broadly indicative evidence, based on share price movements, of returns made from 34 investments by the two more confrontational funds across the whole period 2001–8.

The impact of interventions on target firms

In order to analyse the impact of hedge fund interventions on performance and capital structure we compare outcomes at the target companies with those at a sample of comparable companies in 2008 and 2009, one year and two years on from the high point of hedge fund interventions in 2007 that we have used as the baseline for our earlier analysis (see Section 8.3). The results are reported in Tables 8.3 and 8.4.

Across the group of targets as a whole, there is no clear impact on managerial effectiveness. The effects on return on assets and return on equity are negative a year on, but not significantly so. Two years on, there is weak evidence of an increase in return on assets compared with similar companies. When the sample is broken down according to the nature of the intervention, this finding is retained in the case of confrontational activism, but not for non-confrontational activism, where the impact of activism on return on assets is negative. For the sample as a whole, there is evidence two years on of a better than average performance for both sets of targets in terms of return on equity. This finding is statistically significant on both tests, and is significant for each of the two sub-samples on the basis of the test of medians, but not that of means.

We next look at the impact on key measures of firm performance and capital structure. Target companies across both categories saw sizable and statistically significant declines in Tobin's Q compared with similarly situated companies, both one and two years on. This implies a negative market valuation of companies targeted by hedge

Table 8.3 *One-year changes in target firm performance*

Panel A: All hedge fund activism (N=119)

	Summary statistics $(t+1)-(t)$			Difference with matched firms		
	Mean	Median	SD	Avg. diff.	t-stat of diff.	Wilcoxon
Firm characteristics	(1)	(2)	(3)	(4)	(5)	(6)
Management effectiveness						
ΔReturn on assets	-0.012	-0.005	0.033	-0.005	-1.604	-1.249
ΔReturn on equity	-0.023	-0.011	0.114	-0.002	-0.090	-0.145
Key indicators						
ΔLn(Total assets)	-0.035	-0.034	0.091	0.000	-0.109	-0.615
ΔLn(Market cap.)	-0.386	-0.364	0.283	0.008	0.465	1.295
ΔTobin's Q	-0.212	-0.183	0.194	-0.047	-3.618***	-2.018**
ΔDividend/assets	0.002	0.001	0.004	0.001	3.666***	2.581***
ΔLeverage	0.006	0.000	0.045	0.008	2.120**	0.218
ΔCash/assets	0.005	0.000	0.044	0.004	1.535	0.839
ΔCapital expenditure/assets	-0.001	0.001	0.026	-0.001	-0.532	0.162

Panel B: Confrontational activism (N=30)

	Mean	Median	SD	Avg. diff.	t-stat of diff.	Wilcoxon
Management effectiveness						
ΔReturn on assets	-0.007	-0.003	0.028	-0.001	-0.159	0.456
ΔReturn on equity	-0.007	-0.005	0.046	0.014	0.266	1.146
Key indicators						
ΔLn(Total assets)	-0.051	-0.048	0.069	-0.017	-1.391	-1.539
ΔLn(Market cap.)	-0.328	-0.297	0.187	0.066	2.295**	1.730*

ΔTobin's Q	-0.201	-0.208	0.134	-0.036	-1.720*	-1.627*
ΔDividend/assets	0.003	0.002	0.004	0.002	6.450***	3.601***
ΔLeverage	0.008	0.000	0.035	0.010	1.530	0.502
ΔCash/assets	-0.005	-0.000	0.035	-0.006	-1.589	-0.556
ΔCapital expenditure/assets	0.006	0.001	0.017	0.006	2.071**	1.658*

Panel C: Non-confrontational activism (N=89)

Management effectiveness						
ΔReturn on assets	-0.013	-0.007	0.034	-0.006	-1.800*	-1.728*
ΔReturn on equity	-0.028	-0.013	0.129	-0.007	-0.256	-0.808
Key indicators						
ΔLn(total assets)	-0.029	-0.031	0.097	0.005	0.588	0.128
ΔLn(market cap.)	-0.405	-0.371	0.307	-0.110	-0.539	0.570
ΔTobin's Q	-0.215	-0.175	0.211	-0.050	-3.446***	-1.481
ΔDividend/assets	0.001	0.001	0.003	0.000	1.393	1.051
ΔLeverage	0.006	0.000	0.048	0.007	1.694*	-0.021
ΔCash/assets	0.008	0.001	0.047	0.007	2.585***	1.300
ΔCapital expenditure/assets	-0.003	0.001	0.028	-0.003	-1.657*	-0.729

This table summarises changes (Δ) in firm characteristics between the years 2008 and 2007 for firms targeted by all activist hedge funds (Panel A), confrontational activists (Panel B), and non-confrontational activists (Panel C). The first three columns report the mean, median, and standard deviation of the one-year characteristics changes for the target companies. Columns 4 through 6 report the average difference of one-year changes between the sample firms and the industry/size/book-to-market matched firms, the t-statistics for the average differences, and the Wilcoxon signed rank statistics, which is asymptotically normal, for the median differences. Difference is taken between the target company and the average of the matching firms and then averaged over all companies. In addition to the variables defined in Table 8.1, *Return on equity* is defined as net income/shareholders' equity; *Ln(total assets)* is the natural logarithm of total assets; *Ln(market cap)* is the natural logarithm of market capitalisation; *Capital expenditure/ assets* is defined as total capital expenditure spending divided by total assets. *** significant at the 0.01 level; ** significant at the 0.05 level; * significant at the 0.10 level.

Table 8.4 *Two-year changes in target firm performance*

Panel A: All hedge fund activism (N=119)

Firm characteristics	Summary statistics $(t+2)-(t)$			Difference with matched firms		
	Mean (1)	Median (2)	SD (3)	Avg. diff. (4)	t-stat of diff. (5)	Wilcoxon (6)
Management effectiveness						
ΔReturn on assets	-0.025	-0.014	0.039	0.001	1.748*	1.631
ΔReturn on equity	-0.050	-0.031	0.104	0.100	1.792*	3.969***
Key indicators						
ΔLn(total assets)	-0.096	-0.096	0.136	0.011	1.011	0.846
ΔLn(market cap.)	-0.713	-0.658	0.387	0.004	0.148	1.283
ΔTobin's Q	-0.350	-0.310	0.260	-0.114	-6.071***	-4.112***
ΔDividend/assets	0.002	0.002	0.004	0.001	2.502*	2.011**
ΔLeverage	0.030	0.001	0.075	0.003	0.462	-1.574
ΔCash/assets	0.008	0.000	0.053	-0.008	-2.427**	-2.458**
ΔCapital expenditure/assets	0.000	0.000	0.036	0.001	0.272	0.626
Panel B: Confrontational activism (N=30)						
Management effectiveness						
ΔReturn on assets	-0.016	-0.013	0.032	0.018	1.838*	2.051**
ΔReturn on equity	-0.024	-0.023	0.053	0.126	1.133	3.409***
Key indicators						
ΔLn(total assets)	-0.107	-0.101	0.096	0.001	0.034	-0.177

ΔLn(market cap.)	-0.729	-0.669	0.295	0.012	0.233	0.130
ΔTobin's Q	-0.390	-0.352	0.216	-0.154	-4.799***	-4.048***
ΔDividend/assets	0.003	0.002	0.004	0.001	2.732***	2.214**
ΔLeverage	0.038	0.015	0.075	0.010	1.086	0.050
ΔCash/assets	0.001	0.000	0.048	-0.015	-2.601***	-1.895*
ΔCapital expenditure/assets	0.003	0.005	0.017	0.005	1.250	1.610

Panel C: Non-confrontational activism (N=89)

Management effectiveness						
ΔReturn on assets	-0.028	-0.015	0.041	0.006	1.005	0.788
ΔReturn on equity	-0.059	-0.034	0.115	0.091	1.416	2.798***
Key indicators						
ΔLn(total assets)	-0.093	-0.086	0.148	0.015	1.169	1.097
ΔLn(market cap.)	-0.707	-0.658	0.415	0.010	0.295	1.443
ΔTobin's Q	-0.336	-0.286	0.273	-0.101	-4.770***	-2.612***
ΔDividend/assets	0.002	0.001	0.004	0.000	1.645*	1.143
ΔLeverage	0.028	0.000	0.076	-0.000	-0.017	-1.888*
ΔCash/assets	0.010	0.000	0.055	-0.006	-1.625	-1.852*
ΔCapital expenditure/assets	-0.001	-0.000	0.041	-0.001	-0.230	-0.153

This table summarises changes (Δ) in firm characteristics between the years 2009 and 2007 for firms targeted by all activist hedge funds (Panel A), confrontational activists (Panel B), and non-confrontational activists (Panel C). The first three columns report the mean, median, and standard deviation of the two-year changes for the target companies. Columns 4 through 6 report the average difference of two-year changes between the sample firms and the industry/size/book-to-market matched firms, the *t*-statistics for the average differences, and the Wilcoxon signed rank statistics, which is asymptotically normal, for the median differences. Difference is taken between the target company and the average of the matching firms and then averaged over all companies. All variables are defined in Tables 8.1 and 8.3. *** significant at the 0.01 level; ** significant at the 0.05 level; * significant at the 0.10 level.

fund activism in comparison with their peers. On the other hand, we see a clear increase in dividend payouts both one and two years on in the companies targeted by the confrontational funds. These companies had also decreased their holdings of cash in relation to assets two years on.

The picture here is of companies that were subject to confrontational activism paying out higher dividends in response to hedge fund pressure, in the process using up part of their cash reserves. There was no significant change either one or two years on in the leverage taken on by targets of confrontational activism, or in their capital expenditures. The evidence points to companies which were not making any major strategic or structural changes, other than paying out more money to shareholders. Despite some evidence of an improvement in profitability two years on, the fall in the value of Tobin's Q of target firms by comparison to their peers suggests that the stock market responded negatively to confrontational hedge fund interventions.

In the case of non-confrontational activism, there are weaker signs of an increase in dividend payouts; there is a significant rise in dividend payments for only one of the two statistical tests, and only after two years. For these targets, cash holdings increased relative to comparable companies in the first year but fell in the second. There is weak evidence (significant, in each case, for only one of the two statistical tests) of leverage increasing after one year and rising again after the second year. Again, the result which stands out in the case of non-confrontational activism is the fall in Tobin's Q.

These results can be contrasted with those found for the impacts of hedge fund activism in the US context. Brav *et al.*, whose analysis included both confrontational and non-confrontational funds, reported an increase in payouts at target firms and an improvement in profitability, as measured by return on assets, after an initial dip following the intervention (Brav *et al.*, 2008a: 1770–3). Klein and Zur, whose analysis was specific to interventions made by confrontational funds, reported an increase in dividends at hedge fund targets, but a fall in the profitability of firms. They also found evidence that target companies were selling off assets and taking on increased debt following hedge fund interventions (Klein and Zur, 2009: 222–5).

Our results suggest that in the Japanese case, dividend payments increased as a result of interventions, with the increase being more marked in the case of confrontational interventions. This mirrors the US experience. However, there is little evidence of Japanese targets of activism, whether confrontational or otherwise, changing their capital structure in the face of hedge fund intervention by taking on increased debt, as US firms did. Consistently with the story emerging from our case studies of interventions, this suggests that in the Japanese case, hedge fund activism, notwithstanding some success in generating higher payouts, met resistance on issues of managerial strategy.

Indicative returns from investments by confrontational funds

We now refine our analysis of the impact of interventions in the case of confrontational activism. Using data collected from EDINET (supplemented by historical EDINET data obtained from commercial websites), press reports, and postings on companies' and funds' websites we show 34 interventions by the 2 funds which most clearly pursued confrontational strategies, Steel Partners (32 interventions) and TCI (2 interventions, including the less publicly confrontational Chūbu Electric intervention). Figure 8.7 shows the chronological progress of these interventions over the period 2002–8, on the same basis as our account of the Murakami Fund interventions in Section 8.2 above. We note tender offers ('B'), extraordinary payouts ('¥'), and exits ('E') against the progress of each intervention. The timing of any anti-takeover measures implemented by target companies is indicated ('D'). Interventions continuing beyond 2008 are marked (▶).

As with our analysis of the Murakami Fund, we define the benchmark for 'success' as an annualised return of 5 per cent or more, from a combination of capital gains, specific payouts, or dividend income up to either the point of exit or to the initial cut-off point of 31 December 2008. We use this date initially to provide an indication of where the investments stood then, approximately at the point when the global financial crisis had reached Japan. Depending on whether each intervention reached the 5 per cent benchmark or not, it is marked with upward or downward arrows as either 'successful' (⇧) or not (↘). As before, we have not taken currency movements into account. Since we assume that both Steel Partners and TCI

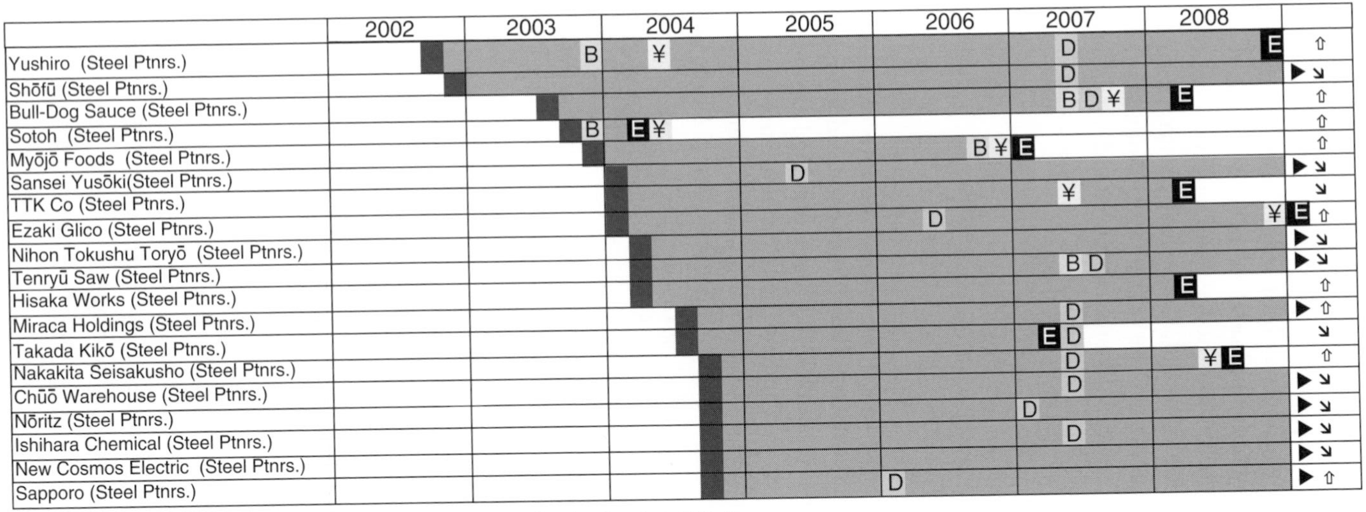

Figure 8.7 Interventions by confrontational activist hedge funds 2002–8 (*Sources*: EDINET, Thomson Reuters, company accounts, press reports)

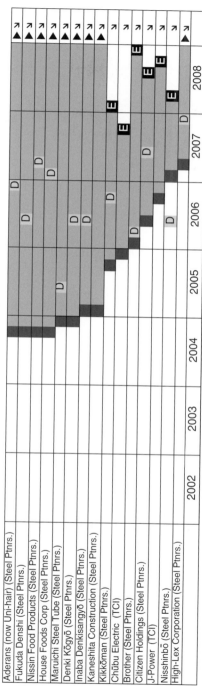

	2002	2003	2004	2005	2006	2007	2008	
Aderans (now Uni-hair) (Steel Ptnrs.)						D		▲ ↗
Fukuda Denshi (Steel Ptnrs.)					D			▲ ↗
Nissin Food Products (Steel Ptnrs.)						D		▲ ↗
House Foods Corp (Steel Ptnrs.)						D		▲ ↗
Maruichi Steel Tube (Steel Ptnrs.)				D				▲ ↗
Denki Kōgyō (Steel Ptnrs.)					D			▲ ↗
Inaba Denkisangyō (Steel Ptnrs.)					D			▲ ↗
Kaneshita Construction (Steel Ptnrs.)					D			▲ ↗
Kikkōman (Steel Ptnrs.)						E	E	▲ ↗
Chūbu Electric (TCI)					D			↗
Brother (Steel Ptnrs.)						D	E	↗
Citizen Holdings (Steel Ptnrs.)							E	↗
J-Power (TCI)								↗
Nisshinbō (Steel Ptnrs.)					D		E	↗
High-Lex Corporation (Steel Ptnrs.)						D		▲ ↗

Figure 8.7 (*cont.*)

Figure 8.8 US$ against Yen (closing rates) 2001–8
(*Source:* Global Financial Data – closing rates are the final rates irrespective of buy/sell)

denominate their funds in US dollars, movements in the US$–Yen exchange rate have an impact on these investments. Figure 8.8 shows the movement of the US$–Yen rate between 2001 and 2008 inclusive.[9] Apart from the fluctuations that characterise the whole eight-year period, the sharp decline in the value of the US$ against the Yen in the latter half of 2008 created an opportunity for exchange profit in US$ terms for any Yen investment made from a US$ base between early 2001 and early 2008, assuming that positions had been left open. However, our purpose here is to present a rough estimate of these investments' success in purely strategic terms, without considering the ancillary effect of exchange. Moreover, we expect that many funds would close their currency positions through forward contracts. In Chapter 9 we consider in more detail the specific case of

---

[9] Our data use daily final trade prices irrespective of buy or sell and are therefore only indicative. We start in 2001 to allow for gradual acquisition of shares.

TCI's investment in J-Power, where the US$–Yen exchange rate may have assumed greater importance.

Some clear patterns emerge from Figure 8.7. First, these interventions were not based on short-term trading positions. Most of them extended beyond one year and many continued for four or more years. Second, while the majority of the interventions initiated from 2002 until early 2004 were successful (as defined above), those initiated thereafter were generally not. The middle of 2004 seems to have marked a turning point. Extension of the data to the end of 2010 shows a fall-off in the number of investments, and no signs of an upturn in performance. Of the 19 interventions pending as of 31 December 2008, only 1 (in Aderans, now known as Uni-hair) remained pending on 31 December 2010. Of the 18 investments that had been liquidated during 2009–10, none had produced better results that had been implied by their status at the end of 2008, and the return on the Sapporo intervention appeared to have deteriorated. Third, as a symptom of the strengthening opposition to the funds, we can see a concentration of new defensive measures during 2006 and 2007. No fewer than 23 companies, or nearly 67 per cent of the sample, introduced such measures during this two-year period alone, in addition to several companies that had already done so earlier. Funds that hold their investments for the long term are not necessarily inconvenienced by lack of immediate returns if their intention is to hold the shares in the expectation that planned improvements in the targets' performance will eventually be realised. However, in these interventions, liquidations took place in all but one case before the end of 2010, crystallising any losses.

8.7 Conclusion

In this chapter we have provided an overview of the main trends in hedge fund activism in Japan in the period from the first activist interventions in the early 2000s to the arrival in Japan of the global financial crisis in 2008. We have charted the ups and downs of particular funds, the extent of their investments, the nature of their target companies, and the impact of their interventions on those targets. As in other countries, hedge fund activism in Japan was not a uniform phenomenon. The sector contained investors with a variety of strategies, ranging from a small number of confrontational funds which used public engagement with target companies to press for changes in corporate strategy aimed at enhancing shareholder returns, to a less confrontational group which eschewed publicity and relied to a greater extent on behind-the-scenes dialogue with firms. Our focus in this chapter has been on the more confrontational funds, and on contrasting their experience to funds which, whether or not they engaged in public engagement, took a less confrontational approach. It was the interventions by confrontational funds which implied the greatest disturbance to the autonomy previously enjoyed by management within the Japanese community firm; they were the most vocal in pressing for a realignment of Japanese managerial practice in line with the dictates of the shareholder primacy norm and they generated the greatest public debate.

The targeting strategy that emerges from our study of the 119 companies selected by activist funds listed in our revised Thomson Reuters data is similar to that already identified in the case of the USA. With some differences between confrontational and non-confrontational funds, the key attractions of targets appeared to be low leverage, high cash ratios, and a practice of already paying relatively high dividends, as well as slightly higher market valuation and RoA than comparable companies. The more confrontational funds favoured companies with low insider ownership. In terms of the impact of interventions on targets over one and two years, although there is evidence of higher dividend payouts, there are also declines in stock market valuations by comparison with target companies' assets (as defined by Tobin's Q). This is the opposite result to what we would have found if investors had seen activism in a positive light. There are few signs of companies undergoing the kind of capital restructuring that was implied by the hedge funds' arguments for the efficiency effects of higher leverage.

When we considered the two funds among the 'public' funds whose strategy involved a greater use of public confrontation, Steel Partners and TCI, we found a pattern of initially good returns (as defined by our criteria) which deteriorated in interventions initiated after mid-2004 to produce mostly disappointing results thereafter. Since TCI entered the market later, these good returns relate to Steel Partners' interventions. The robust and public style of intervention that had served these funds well in the USA and Europe did not appear to deliver the same results in Japan. We will now explore the reasons for this lack of success, beginning with a closer look at two important turning points, both involving these funds: Steel Partners' intervention in Bull-Dog Sauce, and TCI's intervention in J-Power.

9 | *Two turning points: Bull-Dog Sauce and J-Power*

9.1 Introduction

In the last chapter we saw how the confrontational activism pioneered in Japan by the Murakami Fund from the early 2000s and later taken up by a number of foreign funds enjoyed considerable initial success, at least in terms of the payouts generated by early interventions. Through a combination of public pressure on boards, hostile tender offers, and a willingness to engage in litigation to secure their position, activist funds were able to access the accumulated reserves of the companies they targeted. Steel Partners appeared particularly adept, forcing an increase in dividends at companies such as Sotoh and Yushiro, obtaining a takeover premium at Myōjō Foods, and receiving an extraordinary payment at Bull-Dog Sauce. But, notwithstanding their success in terms of generating some high payouts, these activist funds were less successful in bringing about changes of strategy at the companies they approached or in gaining acceptance for the financial arguments that they promoted. Where payouts were forthcoming, as at Sotoh, Yushiro, and Bull-Dog Sauce, they had the appearance of payments to buy off an unwelcome shareholder, while the board of Myōjō Foods preferred to negotiate a merger with a competitor which preserved the company's operational independence rather than accept the possibility of control by Steel Partners. Dalton's calls for MBOs at Nippon Fine Chemical and Fujitec were rejected, and Ichigo's intervention in Tokyo Kohtetsu, despite gaining widespread support for the way it championed minority shareholder rights by preventing an allegedly unsatisfactory merger, did not persuade the board to review the terms. As we also saw, from mid-2004 the funds' interventions were less successful from the perspective of payouts. From this point on, resistance from target managements became both more determined and more sophisticated.

To see how the tactics of both sides in these disputes developed, we look at two pivotal events: Steel Partners' intervention in Bull-Dog Sauce and TCI's intervention in J-Power. These two cases are important not just because of the immediate outcomes for the actors involved but because of the way they shaped wider attitudes towards the phenomenon of hedge fund activism in Japan and altered its course over the longer term. The Bull-Dog Sauce case, while in financial terms a success for Steel Partners, cast the fund in a negative light which affected its subsequent dealings with Japanese companies. TCI's intervention in J-Power not only failed to bring about the changes that the fund had argued for, but left it with a large nominal loss on its shareholding after an increasingly acrimonious series of exchanges with the target's board and the government's bureaucracy. In their different ways, both these cases were turning points.

9.2 'Enlightening Japanese firms': Steel Partners and Bull-Dog Sauce

Steel Partners' approach to Bull-Dog Sauce

Bull-Dog Sauce (hereafter 'Bull-Dog') is a manufacturer of Worcester sauce products and a household name in Japan. It was formed in 1926 from a merger of two companies dating, respectively, from 1902 and 1905, and is listed on the second section of the Tokyo Stock Exchange. It had been discussed occasionally by bankers since the early 1990s as a potential takeover target for larger groups but had retained its independence. Its unconsolidated turnover in the year to 31 March 2003 was ¥14,168 million (we use 31 March 2003 figures as a general indication although Steel Partners' first purchases appear to have predated these). Throughout 2001 and 2002 its share price had generally fluctuated within the ¥600–700 range, although it started to rise in 2003, at the same time as Steel Partners made its initial purchases. At the end of March 2003 its market capitalisation was below 14,000 million, compared with shareholders' equity of ¥16,383 million. More than 47 per cent of the balance sheet was in cash or cash equivalents.

Steel Partners, acting with associates, appear to have begun to accumulate Bull-Dog's shares from as early as the end of 2002 (as explained in Steel Partners' press release of their tender offer for Bull-Dog, issued 16 May 2007). We assume that they were the beneficial owners of the

5.2 per cent holding recorded on Bull-Dog's share register in the name of Morgan Stanley in March 2003 which appears to transform into Steel Partners' subsequent shareholding. This shareholding was gradually increased during 2004 and 2005, with no purchases recorded during 2006, until Steel Partners formally held 10.15 per cent on 1 January 2007. Bull-Dog's president, Ikeda Shōko, talking about the intervention to *Nikkei* afterwards, in November 2007, said that Steel Partners had first contacted her through their lawyers in late 2002 to advise that they held in excess of 5 per cent of Bull-Dog's issued shares. Ikeda immediately made enquiries to brokers as to what sort of investor Steel Partners might be, but apparently felt little the wiser from their replies. The first direct communication seems to have taken place in October 2005 when representatives of Steel Partners from the USA and Japan contacted Bull-Dog to request efforts to improve operating efficiency and to raise the share price, as well as suggesting that senior management take shareholdings in the company. The subsequent Tokyo High Court judgment in June 2007 stated, presumably based on information from the company's lawyers, that Steel Partners suggested an MBO to Bull-Dog's board on 19 October 2005 (Nikkei, 2007ad). However, it is unclear what responses were made to these requests or what happened thereafter during 2006 and early 2007.

On 16 May 2007, Steel Partners, whose shareholding still stood at 10.15 per cent, announced an intention to make a tender offer for all the shares they did not already hold in Bull-Dog, offering ¥1,584 per share, a premium of 20 per cent over the closing price on 14 May. Bull-Dog's board responded on 16 May by saying that it would consider the takeover proposal carefully, but was concerned because the fund lacked experience of managing listed companies, particularly food companies. The offer was made on 18 May, by which time Steel Partners' shareholding had increased to 10.52 per cent, with closing on 28 June. The press estimated the implied cost of the bid at around ¥27,000 million. Steel Partners stressed that they had no intention to interfere in the running of Bull-Dog. On the same day, Bull-Dog's board announced that it had appointed Nomura Securities as its financial adviser and Nishimura Tokiwa Law Office as its legal adviser (Nikkei, 2007y, 2007ae, 2007af; Nikkei Sangyō, 2007f).

Tamiya Masaomi, a Senior Managing Director of Bull-Dog, commented at the publication of his company's results on 18 May 2007: 'I wonder why our company became a target and would like to know the real intention behind this tender offer.' Tamiya also expressed his mortification and confusion at seeing his company, with its hundred-year history, suddenly in play (Nikkei Sangyō, 2007g).

At this point, financial markets legislation (the Financial Instruments and Exchange Act 2006, previously the Securities and Exchange Law) required the target company's board to express its opinion on whether to accept the takeover within ten working days after the announcement of a tender offer. However, on 28 May 2007, Bull-Dog's board announced that it would postpone its decision on whether to accept the proposed tender offer; it had sent a letter to Steel Partners enquiring about their purpose in seeking to purchase the company and their experience of management in the food industry, requesting an answer by 1 June. Bull-Dog's board said that on receipt of a response from Steel Partners, it would form an opinion on the merits of the takeover proposal. The board said that it was concerned to establish whether the takeover would increase 'corporate value'. On 1 June Steel Partners replied to this letter stating that they had no intention of becoming involved in the management of the company, and that they had no plan to sell their holdings in Bull-Dog (Nikkei, 2007q; Ryūtsū Shimbun, 2007b).

Bull-Dog's defence

On 7 June 2007, Bull-Dog's board announced that it would oppose Steel Partners' takeover in the interests of 'corporate value' and 'benefit to shareholders'. The board proposed to seek approval of a takeover defence plan from shareholders at the next AGM, brought forward from 28 to 24 June. This defence plan would allow the company to allocate warrants conferring options to receive three new shares without payment for each existing one held to all its shareholders (previously stock options had to be attached to convertible bonds but since 2002 a company could issue stock options in isolation). Steel Partners alone would not be allowed to convert their options into new shares. Instead, Bull-Dog would buy Steel Partners' options for ¥396 each, a quarter of the tender offer price, thereby producing the same financial outcome for Steel Partners as they were offering to other shareholders in their bid. At the same time, this would dilute the fund's stake from 10.52 per cent to around 3 per cent. A special resolution of two-thirds of the voting rights was required to approve this defence measure.

In a press conference held on the same day, Ikeda was asked why her board had responded negatively to the proposed takeover. She answered that Steel Partners had failed to present a post-acquisition plan with their proposal to acquire a large number of voting rights, and that therefore the takeover would not lead to enhancement of corporate value. When asked whether the offer price was appropriate, Ikeda said that she believed that the value of the company was higher. Ikeda was also asked whether the proposed takeover had been a trigger for the board to consider the company's business development more seriously. She answered that the company had always endeavoured to increase corporate value. On 8 June, Bull-Dog's board announced that it had received written confirmation that the company's employees opposed the tender offer. The employees' letter stated that they supported the board's decision to oppose the takeover on the grounds that it would threaten the company's relationship with its customers. On 11 June, the board announced that it had received a similar document from employees at Bull-Dog's subsidiary, Ikari Sauce (Nikkei, 2007f, 2007j, 2007l; Ryūtsū Shimbun, 2007a).

On 13 June 2007, Ikeda and Lichtenstein met for an hour, but no agreement was reached. Ikeda is reported to have again asked Lichtenstein about his purpose in seeking to acquire Bull-Dog and his post-acquisition business plan. Lichtenstein apparently did not respond to Ikeda's question and asked her what sort of offer price she could agree to, in an attempt to reach a compromise (Nikkei, 2007k; Nikkei Sangyō, 2007h). There seems to have been a lack of understanding between the two sides. The impressions of Bull-Dog's lawyer from this meeting were recounted in the Japanese press some ten months later:

A discussion was held between Bull-Dog Sauce's president Ikeda Shōko (64) and Steel Partners' chief executive Warren Lichtenstein (42) in Ōtemachi, Tokyo. Bull-Dog's adviser [the lawyer] Iwakura attended and heard Lichtenstein comment as follows: 'I hate sauces' and '30 days is plenty for the tender offer. I like the number 30.' That was enough for Iwakura. This man was not out to improve Bull-Dog; he was just a predator. (Asahi Shimbun, 2008)

On the same day, Steel Partners announced that they planned to challenge the actions of Bull-Dog's board through litigation and had applied to the Tokyo District Court. Subsequently, on 15 June, Steel Partners announced that they had increased their offer price to ¥1,700 per share and had extended the duration of the tender offer to 10 August 2007 (the maximum permissible). In response to this announcement, Bull-Dog's share price temporarily increased to ¥1,750, a gain of ¥160 over the previous day. However, Bull-Dog's board commented on the same day that the offer price still did not reflect the true value of the company (Nikkei, 2007h, 2007p).

At the AGM held on 24 June 2007, the proposal to establish a defence strategy was approved by more than 80 per cent of the shareholders. At the meeting, Steel Partners' lawyer commented that all shareholders should be allowed to choose either cash or new shares, and asked how much the company was spending on legal and financial advice. Ikeda said that this expense was whatever was necessary to protect the firm's value and that it could not be disclosed because of confidentiality agreements. The lawyer responded that Bull-Dog should spend money on its business rather than for defence measures as the cost of paying cash to Steel Partners and paying for advice was likely to exceed ¥3,000 million. Ikeda said that although there might be a deficit for the year ending March 2008, it was necessary to protect corporate value and the interests of shareholders (Nikkei, 2007s).

Ikeda gave a press interview on the same day. When asked why she thought that 80 per cent of shareholders had approved the defence strategy, she said that the shareholders had recognised the value of a company with more than a hundred years of history. When asked whether the company should have adopted its defence strategy earlier, Ikeda said that the company had judged that defence was necessary in the face of Steel Partners' sudden tender offer. Asked why she felt that the takeover would harm corporate value, Ikeda said that because manufacturing industry sought profit in the long term, there would inevitably be a clash with Steel Partners' desire for short-term profit. By this stage, the affair was engendering considerable discussion. A number of commentators questioned the propriety of a defence measure that would lead to the exclusion of particular shareholders. The former head of Sony's investor relations division observed that the concept of management choosing its shareholders contradicted the principle of the market, and that widespread adoption of such structures would risk damaging the international credibility of Japan's capital markets (Nikkei Kinyū, 2007b, 2007f; Nikkei Sangyō, 2007e).

The Bull-Dog Sauce litigation

On 28 June 2007, the Tokyo District Court rejected Steel Partners' request for an interim injunction to prevent Bull-Dog from exercising its defence measure. The judge concluded that issuing these share options would not violate the principle of shareholder equality because it did not involve any allotment to third parties and was purely a bonus issue to existing shareholders. He further considered that the proposed redemption of ¥396 per warrant offered to Steel Partners, although causing dilution of their shareholding, appeared to be an appropriate price since it protected their economic interest. The judge took the view that the decision on whether a takeover harmed corporate value should be left to shareholders in a shareholders' meeting; here, the shareholders had debated the issues and arrived at a clearly expressed decision. This decision was that a defence measure was needed because the fund had launched the tender offer without negotiating with the company's board and without allowing it time to consider any alternative plan; moreover Steel Partners had failed to explain their post-acquisition business plan or their future intentions as investors. In this situation, the proposal to introduce a defence measure and the subsequent approval of the measure could not have been avoided (Nikkei, 2007n; Tokyo District Court, 2007).

Subsequently Steel Partners appealed to the Tokyo High Court but, on 9 July 2007, the court dismissed this appeal. Steel Partners claimed that the defence measure violated the principle of shareholder equality, that the dilution of their shareholding was unfair, and that the AGM's decision regarding the warrants issue and related change to the company articles should be overturned. In response the judge stated that the Company Law did not forbid discriminatory treatment of some shareholders in terms of economic benefit and voting rights, and that a defence measure did not violate shareholder equality if it was a rational response to prevent damage to corporate value. This judgment went beyond the decision of the earlier court to characterise Steel Partners as an 'abusive acquirer'. This terminology referred to an earlier decision of the Tokyo High Court, in the successful case brought by Livedoor against Nippon Broadcasting System at the time of its takeover bid for the company, which we discuss further in Chapter 10 (Hayakawa and Whittaker, 2009: 78–80; Milhaupt and Pistor, 2008: ch. 5). In that judgment, which had confirmed an earlier judgment by the Tokyo District Court, the court had ruled that although equity warrants issued simply to sustain the position of the board were unacceptable, takeover defences could be invoked in a case where an acquirer had 'predatory and abusive intentions'. A non-exhaustive list of four examples had been proposed: greenmail; 'scorched earth', where the acquirer's objective was to transfer intellectual property, know-how, commercial secrets, or customers to itself at the expense of the target's business; loading the target with excessive debt; and selling off the target's core assets in order to raise a high dividend. The Tokyo High Court's ruling on the Bull-Dog case did not say into which of these four categories Steel Partners might fall but it expressed its view clearly that a company was more than shareholders' property and linked Steel Partners repeatedly, by strong implication, to the expression 'abusive acquirer' (Tokyo High Court, 2007):

A joint-stock company is in theory a for-profit organisation that maximises its corporate value and pays it out as dividends to shareholders. But, at the same time, a company cannot earn its profit without associating with employees, suppliers and consumers. Thus, it can be said that a company is a social entity. Therefore, it must consider its relationships with stakeholders to enhance its corporate value. The idea that it is enough for a company exclusively to consider shareholder value is too limited. When a so-called abusive acquirer, of the sort that shows no serious interest to participate in the running of the company and embarks on acquisitions in order to raise the share price of the target company and cause parties associated with the company to buy its shares at a high price, governs and operates the company abusively as the majority shareholder with a view only to its own profit, then the company is not being run in a healthy manner and therefore its corporate value will be harmed and this will lead to damage to the collective interest of all the shareholders. Therefore there is no alternative but to treat such an abusive acquirer as a shareholder in a discriminatory fashion.

The judgment then stated that Steel Partners, as a fund, was by definition an unsuitable shareholder for any company since it was predisposed to prioritise short-term gain over the company's interest:

The plaintiff, by its nature as an investment fund, has obviously undertaken a responsibility to prioritise the profit of its customers and, being sustained by the incentive of performance fees, is incentivised as a firm to prioritise that profit. Since it has not shown particular interest in the running of the business for which it has bid, nor involved itself generally, and since after acquiring its shares in the company it has entertained various strategies such as first demanding that management purchase the company and then embarking on this sudden public tender offer, it is clear that it might attempt to realise an exit profit in the short or medium term by selling on these shares to the target company itself or to third parties and would pursue solely its own profit, ultimately even contemplating disposal of the target company's assets.

On 10 July 2007, Steel Partners announced on their website that they had submitted an appeal to the Supreme Court of Japan against the ruling by the Tokyo High Court, requesting an injunction barring Bull-Dog from executing its defence measure. Without awaiting the outcome of this appeal, Bull-Dog exercised its takeover defence measure on 11 July. Since Steel Partners were compensated for being unable to obtain new shares, they received a payment of ¥2,300 million and their shareholding was reduced to roughly 3 per cent. A favourable decision from the Supreme Court could still have reversed this situation (Nikkei Sangyō, 2007i). However, on 7 August 2007, the Supreme Court rejected Steel Partners' appeal.

The Supreme Court's judgment explicitly avoided calling Steel Partners 'abusive', observing that its decision was justified irrespective of whether the plaintiff might be the sort of 'abusive acquirer cited in the earlier judgment'. The essence of its position was that discriminatory treatment of shareholders could be justified by the defence of corporate value. This was for the shareholders, not the courts, to define, and in this case 83.4 per cent of them had voted in support of the company's defence plan at the AGM. The judgment focused on Steel Partners' lack of interest in involvement in the company as a business and found no fault in the AGM's decision for that reason (Nikkei, 2007r; Supreme Court, 2007):

Moreover, since it is believed that this decision [by the AGM] was taken in the light of a situation where the plaintiff, although attempting to acquire all the issued shares, had no plans for the running of the business and had not made clear its intended management strategy subsequent to acquiring control, nor addressed aspects such as how it planned to recoup its investment, no defects are observed in this decision that might make it unjustified.

The reaction

Steel Partners had continued with their bid while legal action proceeded. When, as expected, it failed, they gradually sold down their shareholding. They announced on 8 August 2007 that they would reduce their bid price from ¥1,700 to ¥425 in anticipation of the fourfold increase in the number of outstanding shares and that they would extend the duration of the tender offer by 13 days (10 working days) to 23 August 2007. Bull-Dog's board confirmed its continued opposition at a meeting on 9 August (Nikkei, 2007m). On 24 August 2007 Steel Partners announced that only 1.89 per cent of Bull-Dog's shares had been tendered. As the fund had undertaken to buy all shares tendered, its stake increased to 4.44 per cent. Steel Partners began to sell their Bull-Dog shares from October 2007 and had disposed of them all by the end of March 2008. Bull-Dog's share price had declined gradually after August 2007, with a closing price on 1 April 2008 of ¥248 but Steel Partners had already received a good return on their total investment. In the meantime, Bull-Dog had announced on 30 August 2007 that it would adopt an advance warning defence measure, to be approved at its 2008 AGM. In the event of an acquirer attempting to buy more than 20 per cent of the equity, an independent committee would decide whether to implement defence measures (Nikkei, 2007o, 2007u, 2008ac).

The responses to this affair fell into four categories: the immediate public relations response of the wider public to the idea of an established company defending itself successfully from a speculative investor; a debate among members of the government and bureaucracy and the business community over the implications of the court judgments; practical reactions that emerged in the form of new official guidance and countermeasures adopted at companies; and the impact on Steel Partners' reputation and their ability to influence boards at target companies in Japan.

In terms of public relations, Bull-Dog's board appeared to have won decisively. In addition to the expressions of support from Bull-Dog's employees which we have noted, consumers of the company's products had written to Ikeda while Steel Partners' intervention was in progress to express their affection for the brand: 'From being no age, sauce has always meant "Bull-Dog" for me; please don't give up' (Nikkei, 2007ag). The unassuming image that Ikeda projected to the

press and her status as a loyal employee of Bull-Dog who had reached
the presidency after many years of selfless effort was contrasted with
Lichtenstein's views: it was precisely in May 2007, just before this tender offer, that he had made his comment to *Nikkei Business* about his
desire to enlighten Japanese boards about shareholder value.

Politicians, bureaucrats, and the business community were more
concerned with the governance implications of the Bull-Dog affair
and its impact on perceptions of Japan as an investment market. Dore
noted two critical commentaries on the Tokyo High Court judgment,
one from a politician and one from an investor. The Liberal Democrat
member of the Diet Tamura Kōtarō wrote in his blog that this judgment would 'kill our efforts to globalise the Tokyo stock market' and
that the judge did 'not understand the first thing about why the Tokyo
Stock Exchange exists'. If Steel was an abusive acquirer, 'there's no
scope for any fund to be active in Japan'. Yano Tomomi, the head of
the Pension Fund Association, pointed out that as a result of the payout
to Steel Partners, 'Bull-Dog Sauce went into the red; its share price collapsed, and its shareholders have been denied the right to respond to a
high-premium offer'. The various courts' rulings were 'tantamount to
sending the message that Japan is a country where capitalism and the
rules of the market are not understood, which is not unrelated to the
large fall in Japanese share prices' (Dore, 2009: 143–4). As a Japanese
journalist put it to us during a discussion in January 2008: 'Just as you
have asked this sort of question, when that judgment came out the *FT*
and the *Wall Street Journal* both carried articles saying "This kind of
judgment has been issued in Japan." This news spread worldwide, to
the effect that Japan's courts are strange. It gave the impression that
Japan is not a capitalist country.'

Most officials commenting on the case took pains not to criticise
the judgments directly and maintained the position that no damage
had been done to Japan's international standing. Yamamoto Yūji,
the Minister for Financial Services, speaking at a press conference on
10 July 2007, while litigation was still in progress, said that he totally
disagreed with the view that the decision of the Tokyo High Court
would deter foreign investment in Japan (Nikkei, 2007ao). Kitabata
Takao, Administrative Vice Minister of METI, said in a press conference on 9 August 2007 that the Supreme Court's denial of Steel
Partners' appeal against the defence measure should be seen as significant, and criticised Steel Partners for causing chaos in the market; in

his opinion, a foreign fund such as that did not need to come to Japan (Nikkei, 2007ah). However, there was clearly official concern at the issues raised by the Bull-Dog affair: although he welcomed the Supreme Court's decision, Kitabata of METI subsequently questioned the strategy of Bull-Dog's board in making the payment to Steel Partners when he addressed a press conference on 3 September 2007, arguing that such defence measures would unnecessarily encourage hostile acquirers. The press reported on 27 October that the Corporate Value Study Group (originally reporting jointly to the Ministry of Justice ('MOJ') and METI, but now organised by METI) would now be looking into post-offer defences (Nikkei, 2007ai, 2007aj).

As METI's reaction showed, the blurred line between greenmail payments and justifiable defence of the firm that Bull-Dog's board had exposed was the greatest concern. A senior director at a company then targeted by another activist hedge fund said to us in September 2007,

My own personal opinion is that Bull-Dog did not do this very well. What I mean is that Bull-Dog already had over 80% of what are traditionally called 'stable shareholders' who would support them. But in spite of that they activated defensive measures and tried to maintain a sort of parity by paying out money to Steel Partners ... I really feel that it would be much better if people did not think of this widely as an appropriate way of handling those sorts of defensive measures.

A civil servant, speaking in early 2008, accepted that Bull-Dog Sauce's board should have resisted Steel Partners but found its tactics morally unacceptable: 'My feeling is that, as a matter of principle, paying money to someone trying to buy you is to sanction greenmailing. So while saying that they were opposed to it, Bull-Dog Sauce effectively sanctioned greenmailing, you see.' Ikeda herself appeared to have mixed feelings over what she had achieved. She said in a press interview in November 2007 that she had concerns about her company's defence measures for two reasons: she was worried that other companies might copy Bull-Dog in offering cash to dilute acquirers, and executing such plans in the form of a special resolution requiring a two-thirds majority was a challenging task (Nikkei, 2007ad). In March 2008 the PFA announced that it would generally oppose any resolutions at AGMs held that year to introduce defence measures permitting payments to acquirers. This was in response to rumours that a number of companies were considering copying Bull-Dog's tactics (Nikkei, 2008ab). It was precisely these concerns that the Corporate Value Study Group would ultimately address, as we describe in Chapter 10.

Inevitably many people in Japan saw Steel Partners' intervention in Bull-Dog purely as a takeover attempt. The results of a survey conducted in 2007 by the Japan Management Association (*Nihon Nōritsu Kyōkai*) among 2,013 newly appointed directors of listed companies (of whom 298 responded) had been announced on 2 August 2007. When asked what concerned them most, the percentage of those who named takeover (either in that form or as an acquisitive merger) was 23.6 per cent, a more than twofold increase over the previous year and the highest in the survey's history since its inception in 1998. *Nikkei* attributed this concern directly to hostile takeover incidents such as Steel Partners' Bull-Dog intervention (Nikkei, 2007ak).

The Bull-Dog Sauce affair had been beneficial to Steel Partners in financial terms: they had received a payout considerably greater than the value of their initial investment, and had effectively forced the board to release the company's accumulated cash surpluses as a condition of retaining its independence. In the longer term, the implications were less advantageous. The Tokyo High Court's characterisation of Steel Partners as an 'abusive acquirer' catalysed a negative reaction to them in Japan. The court judgments had made clear that not only their tactics in the Bull-Dog intervention but their fundamental attitude to investment was basically unacceptable, and prompted a negative response to their whole strategy of confrontation. Steel's interventions in individual companies were less successful from this point on, and the corporate governance environment became less accommodating to activist engagement. Meanwhile, concern among the business community about the possibility of hostile takeover was raised to a higher pitch. However critical commentators might be about the quality of the court judgments in the Bull-Dog case, few questioned their underlying message that a company was a community that needed to be defended from abusive forces. Bull-Dog's board had demonstrated here that, however clumsily it was done, rejection of activist hedge funds would generally be accepted as the correct reaction.

9.3 'A desire to be proved right': TCI and J-Power

Targeting larger companies: TCI's arrival in Japan

By 2007, Steel Partners' struggle with the board of Bull-Dog Sauce, as well as their other interventions and those by other funds, had ensured widespread and often unfavourable publicity in Japan both for activist hedge funds in general and for foreign funds in particular. Steel Partners had begun in Japan by targeting smaller companies whose boards were unaccustomed to discussing shareholder value with assertive investors. These targets typically traded at a discount to book value and held accumulated reserves. The financial logic that demanded that these reserves be disbursed rather than hoarded was a relatively simple one: if the boards could not find a profitable use for their reserves, they should return them to their ultimate owners, the shareholders. But from about 2004, Steel had started to target larger companies, such as Nōritz, Sapporo, and Aderans, where they began to address strategic aspects: it was no longer a case of pointing to reserves that boards seemed incapable of exploiting. This was the context in which TCI entered Japan. Its predominant mode of operation in Europe had been to select larger targets where it had succeeded by cutting through the complexities of corporate structures to reveal points of strategic and financial weakness. It now applied this approach in Japan.

As we have seen, TCI made only two interventions in Japan during the period of our study: at Chūbu Electric from autumn 2005 until September 2007, and at J-Power from October 2006 until October 2008. The Chūbu Electric intervention, although involving a large target, was handled relatively discreetly and, with hindsight, has the appearance of a pilot exercise. By contrast, the J-Power intervention involved a bigger investment and ultimately a more confrontational approach. We estimate, using values at 31 March 2006 for Chūbu Electric and values at 31 March 2007 for J-Power, that the Chūbu Electric intervention at 1.4 per cent required some ¥32,000 million of investment, whereas the J-Power intervention at nearly 10 per cent would have required approximately ¥98,000 million. It also attracted vastly more public attention. It was at J-Power that TCI gave a definitive demonstration of how its brand of analytical activism could be applied in Japan.

J-Power (originally called Dengen Kaihatsu or the Electric Power Development Company) is a company that was established in 1952 for the purpose of developing electrical power generation capacity in locations where the privately owned utility companies would not wish to invest. Initially it was owned 66.69 per cent by the Japanese state, through the Ministry of Finance, and the remainder by the major utility companies. It was fully privatised and became a first section listed company in October 2004, when its former shareholders sold out. During the year to March 2008, while TCI's intervention was gathering momentum, it accounted for approximately 7 per cent of Japanese installed electrical power generation capacity, and produced the same proportion of national output. Just over half of its facilities were hydroelectric and just under half were thermal, including geothermal plants (J-Power, 2008). It had no nuclear capacity at that stage but, on 23 April 2008, METI authorised J-Power to operate the world's first mixed uranium-plutonium oxide fuel nuclear power plant, in Ōma (Aomori Prefecture), and construction was scheduled to begin in May 2008 after submitting the final construction plan. This schedule was subsequently postponed to allow redesign for better earthquake resistance but, at the time of TCI's investment, construction was expected to begin very soon (Bloomberg, 2008; Nikkei, 2008p).

The latest full year accounts available to TCI when it began to purchase J-Power's shares in late 2006 were those for the year to March 2006. J-Power's consolidated turnover for the year to 31 March 2006 was ¥621,933 million and its market capitalisation was then in the region of ¥620,000 million, rising to about ¥800,000 million by October of that year. This compared with book value of shareholders' total equity in the 31 March 2006 consolidated balance sheet of ¥433,028 million. Unlike most of the Japanese companies targeted by other activist hedge funds in this period, J-Power was not trading at a discount to book value. It was profitable, but had relatively high borrowing by the conservative standards of its sector with gearing of over three times; subsequently, in 2008, it was announced that further borrowing was planned to finance the Ōma reactor project.

In some respects, J-Power was an unexpected target for an activist hedge fund to select. The company was not obviously undervalued and was not holding excessive reserves. It had recently paid a dividend equivalent to over 21% of net profits, which was relatively generous by contemporary Japanese standards, which subsequently rose to 28% in the year to March 2007. The 2004 listing exercise had provided detailed corporate information to international investors who had responded favourably: over 35% of total equity had been held by foreign institutional investors since the initial public offering. More than any other electrical utility board in Japan, J-Power's senior directors had been exposed to the thinking of the international investment community. This had occurred during the preparations for the company's listing, through the initial public offering (IPO), and then through annual international investor relations exercises thereafter. If these investors supported the board against TCI, the alternative tactic of buying a controlling stake in the market would be expensive. It could also be blocked by the Japanese authorities. Holdings by any single non-resident investor in power companies, considered of national strategic importance, were limited to 10% without explicit permission. Nevertheless, four factors appear to have encouraged TCI.

First, similar concentrations of foreign shareholders had been persuaded to support TCI at Deutsche Börse in 2005 and were soon to be solicited again successfully at ABN AMRO in early 2007. Second, J-Power's profitability was declining as it continued its investment programme in Japan and overseas following a reduction in wholesale electricity tariffs from October 2005, suggesting that the board might be vulnerable to accusations of empire-building at the expense of shareholder returns. Third, J-Power's strong free cash flow, roughly equivalent to its annual operating income, may have suggested that there was room for higher gearing (a point already noted in a Japanese equity analyst's report), although, at about three times net assets, J-Power's net debt in March 2006 was already relatively high. Fourth, the view on Japan in 2006 among activist hedge fund managers, despite Murakami's problems, was that this was a market ready for change. The reaction against Steel Partners which followed the litigation in the Bull-Dog Sauce affair lay in the future.

TCI's engagement with J-Power: arguments over cash flow

TCI began buying J-Power's shares in 2006 and reached 5.07% on 12 October. It continued to buy shares during October and November 2006 and had reached 9.4% by 24 November. On 7 March 2007 it raised its shareholding further, to 9.9%, just short of the 10% limit beyond which, as a non-resident investor, it would need ministerial clearance to hold further shares in an energy-related Japanese business. Throughout this intervention TCI publicised its letters to J-Power's board on its Japanese website, in Japanese and English. J-Power's board generally reciprocated using J-Power's website, making this a very public exchange of views. Both sides also gave frequent press interviews to explain their positions.

On 9 March 2007, TCI proposed to J-Power's board that the company should raise its annual dividend from ¥60 to ¥130 per share. The board's response was negative and, in a press interview with *Nikkei* on 2 April, J-Power's president, Nakagaki Yoshihiko, commented that more time was needed, until profits had risen, before dividends could be raised. In a further interview, published on 15 May, the interviewer questioned Nakagaki about several points raised by TCI. Nakagaki said that it was inappropriate for J-Power to increase its dividend every year because the company was being run as a public utility. He said that the board intended to consider increasing the dividend in the light of prospects for the next 5–10 years, but that it was also necessary to maintain a balance between shareholders, customers, and retained earnings when deciding how to apply profits. TCI had drawn attention to the risks of foreign investments being undertaken by J-Power but Nakagaki commented that J-Power's board adhered to strict standards of internal rate of return, supervised by an independent committee, when evaluating foreign projects. TCI had argued for greater use of debt, but Nakagaki said that although the board aimed to rely primarily on debt for the estimated ¥300,000–400,000 million cost of the nuclear power project in Ōma, he wished to maintain a 23 per cent element of the company's own funds within total liabilities (our estimate from the 31 March 2006 figures is 22 per cent) (Nikkei, 2007c, 2007d).

From May 2007, John Ho, the head of TCI's Hong Kong office, who was the public face of TCI throughout this intervention, delivered a series of arguments for better financial economy within J-Power as a means to fund a higher dividend. On 29 May 2007, Ho told the press that there was room for improvement in J-Power's cost of funds, and argued that the company would be able to raise the dividend if it improved the efficiency of its fund-raising by assuming more debt and relying less on equity finance. He also observed that pressure to pay interest and increase dividends gave a company an incentive to care about its earnings, and thereby brought discipline (Nikkei Sangyō, 2007b).

On 8 June 2007, TCI revealed that it would submit a formal proposal for a total annual dividend of ¥130 per share (up from ¥60) at J-Power's AGM, scheduled for 27 June 2007, and began to send letters to J-Power's shareholders asking for their support. This document stated that the current dividend was low and that retained earnings would still remain for reinvestment even if J-Power raised its dividend to the level requested. J-Power's board planned to send letters to shareholders from 11 June encouraging them to support its original proposal for a total annual dividend of ¥60 (Nikkei, 2007ap).

At its AGM on 27 June 2007, the majority of J-Power's shareholders rejected TCI's proposal to raise the dividend, although more than 30 per cent voted for it. The outcome was that the dividend remained unchanged. In a press conference given after the AGM, Nakagaki said that he would bear shareholders' wishes in mind and, should it prove possible to do so, would seriously consider dividend increases in the future. However, he also mentioned his interest in ensuring a 'stable' shareholder base. J-Power's board subsequently began to try to increase the number of retail shareholders, who were believed to comprise 8.2 per cent of the total as of September 2007, holding a presentation especially designed for them for the first time at the end of November 2007 and organising a tour of a thermal power station in Isogo (Yokohama) in February 2008. There was speculation in the press that this interest in investments from retail shareholders was stimulated by J-Power's troubles with TCI, especially since the 30 per cent of votes in support of TCI's dividend increase proposal may have been greater than the board expected (Nikkei, 2007a; Nikkei Sangyō, 2007a).

TCI's engagement with J-Power: arguments over strategy

From November 2007 TCI shifted its emphasis. Hitherto it had proposed financial restructuring and argued that potential for higher dividends was being overlooked. Now it began to focus on issues of policy, moving closer to direct criticism of the incumbent board and its judgment. On 22 November, TCI sent a letter to Nakagaki expressing concern about 'the continuing decline in the Company's corporate value over the past six years' and noting particularly declines in return on both equity (RoE) and assets (RoA), lack of a plan to address these, a recent reduction in electrical tariffs (which had reduced income), lack of incentive elements in directors' remuneration, and recently increased cross-shareholdings. In the same letter, TCI asked J-Power's board to appoint TCI's nominees Ho and Philip Green – both of whom worked for TCI – as external directors, to sell cross-held shareholdings and to freeze directors' remuneration. J-Power's board responded by dismissing these arguments in a formal reply on 7 December, posted on its website. It argued that TCI had not considered the whole situation, that consolidated ordinary profit was increasing, and that efforts were already in hand – attested by specific website submissions – to address the other points, and specifically justified J-Power's cross-shareholdings with Nippon Steel Corporation and Mitsubishi Heavy Industries as being in the interests of its business. Moreover J-Power's board argued that the decrease in electricity charges was justified by a corresponding decline in the company's financial expenses. The press observed that there appeared to be a fundamental discrepancy between J-Power's board and TCI: on the one hand, TCI saw J-Power's declining RoE and RoA as problematic, while on the other hand, J-Power's board believed that the business was being run satisfactorily because income was rising and it was meeting its RoE target. In January 2008 J-Power's board formally rejected the idea of accepting TCI's nominees but the press reported that on 22 February 2008 TCI had sent a further document to J-Power recommending instead that three external directors independent of both the company and TCI should be appointed (Nikkei, 2007b, 2008s).

By early 2008 TCI seemed to have resolved to unblock what it evidently saw as a stalled situation. Support from other institutional investors had proved insufficient at the June 2007 AGM – although the size of the vote in favour of TCI's resolutions may still have caused concern to J-Power's board – and the obvious alternative was to seek a stronger shareholding position, much as the Murakami Fund had chosen to do at Hanshin Electric Railway in 2006. In this process, TCI's intervention was transformed from a disagreement between the shareholders of a listed company and its board into a matter which was ostensibly one of national security. On 15 January 2008, TCI announced that it planned to increase its shareholding in J-Power from 9.9% to 20%. On the same day, the fund duly submitted a request for permission to do this. A non-resident investor attempting to buy more than 10% of a Japanese company designated to be relevant to national security was obliged to make an advanced report under the Foreign Exchange and

Foreign Trade Control Law (*Gaikoku Kawase oyobi Gaikoku Bōeki Hō*) so that the ministry which oversaw the industrial sector concerned and the Ministry of Finance could block the investment plan if they considered it prejudicial to the national interest. The designated industrial sectors were the electricity, munitions, aviation, nuclear, communications, and machine tool industries, making J-Power relevant on two separate counts. In this case, METI was the responsible ministry. On 15 January, METI began an examination of whether to permit TCI to raise its stake. The press commented that concern was thought to focus on whether TCI would unfairly increase electricity charges or sell its shares in J-Power to 'foreign companies' – presumably meaning foreign power companies – potentially affecting the stable supply of electricity. The period of examination was in principle 30 days from the date of application, implying a decision by 13 February, but METI extended the period to mid-May 2008 (Nikkei, 2008g, 2008t, 2008v).

From this point, TCI appeared to exert a double pressure on J-Power's board, maintaining the potential threat of raising its shareholding, should permission be granted, while submitting new proposals. On 27 March 2008 it announced the submission to J-Power's board of a 127 page document of proposals to increase efficiency and urged the board to include all of them in its business plan. These included proposals calling for diversification of geographical spread by investing in newly established foreign electricity companies and benefiting from liberalisation policies, concentrating investments in emerging markets where there were prospects of high growth, such as China, India, and Russia, selling the company's cross-shareholdings, then valued at ¥68,000 million, and raising dividends (Nikkei, 2008c).

Requests by other non-residents in the past to exceed the 10 per cent limit on shareholdings in companies designated to be of national interest had not been considered contentious. However, on 8 April 2008, Amari Akira, the minister for METI, said in a conference that TCI's request to raise its stake in J-Power was different from these earlier cases because it impacted on both public order and national security. On 11 April, a special Subcommittee on Foreign Exchange and Other Transactions was convened. It summoned TCI to explain its intentions in increasing its shareholding in J-Power. On 14 April, TCI sent a document to METI and the Ministry of Finance proposing an alternative plan which addressed concerns about national security by offering to mandate a trust bank to manage TCI's increased shares in

J-Power and undertaking not to exercise its voting rights with respect to matters concerning either the Ōma nuclear power plant or power line facilities (Nikkei, 2008i, 2008n, 2008x).

On 16 April 2008, the ministries *advised* TCI not to raise its stake in J-Power, expressing concern that TCI's greater ownership could put at risk stable power supply for the nation and hinder the plan to construct a nuclear power plant in Ōma. In response to this, Ho said in a press conference on the same day that this response would have a negative impact on Japan. The Subcommittee on Foreign Exchange and Other Transactions was reported in the press to have several concerns. The first was that the 3–5 year investment horizon apparently associated with TCI could potentially disrupt the stable supply of electricity. Yoshino Naoyuki, a professor of economics at Keiō University who chaired the Subcommittee, said that investment in nuclear power plants had to be considered for a span of 20–25 years, and that long-term retained earnings were necessary for the purpose of maintenance and repair. Yoshino opposed TCI's investment plan to seek a higher dividend in a short period of time on these grounds. The second concern was that TCI might intend to become involved in the management of J-Power by seconding its nominees. The third concern, shared by all members of the Subcommittee, was one of opposition to TCI's most recent suggestion, that J-Power's high-cost nuclear power generation should be separated and run by the state, on the grounds that this would contradict the objective of J-Power's 2004 privatisation. Finally, the Subcommittee suspected that TCI would exit once it had achieved a capital gain, given TCI's past investment record elsewhere (Nikkei, 2008r; Nikkei Sangyō, 2008a).

Also on 16 April 2008, apparently in a parallel move, TCI announced that it had submitted resolutions for J-Power's next AGM in June 2008 calling for either an increased dividend of ¥120 per share or an increased dividend to the lower level of ¥80 per share; a ¥70,000 million share buy-back; limits on the value of cross-shareholdings to ¥5,000 million; and appointment of a minimum of three outside directors. The proposal to increase the dividend to ¥120 was justified as bringing J-Power into line with its peer companies. The other proposal, to raise the dividend only to ¥80, was aimed to give an alternative option to shareholders who might accept the board's argument that a more conservative dividend level was justified. Both proposals were publicised on TCI's Japanese website on 17 April. Regarding the proposal to limit cross-shareholdings, TCI called on J-Power to sell the shares valued at ¥68,000 million held as cross-shareholdings, including shares in Nippon Steel Corporation, Kajima Corporation, and Mitsubishi Heavy Industries. TCI indicated that it would vote against the proposal to re-elect Nakagaki as president at the forthcoming AGM in the event that J-Power's board refused to support these proposals (Nikkei, 2008u).

On 23 April 2008, J-Power's board announced that it would establish an external advisory board to advise the company's management. The press reported that this was a response to official urging that J-Power's board should be seen to be more accountable to its shareholders. This advice was apparently given to the company at the same time as the ministries urged TCI not to increase its stake in the company. In addition to the establishment of the advisory board, J-Power reiterated its intention to increase its IR activities specifically for retail shareholders and announced that it would strengthen the function of the board of corporate auditors. The board was also considering the appointment of external directors. Nakagaki said that moves to enhance J-Power's corporate governance were not specifically aimed to counter pressure from TCI; however, most commentators tended to link the two (Nikkei Sangyō, 2008h).

On the same day, TCI wrote to the UK government asking it to intervene and impose trade sanctions on Japan in response to the official stance on the recent request to increase its shareholding. This met a dismissive reaction from part of the UK business press. The UK government's reaction is not known but no action seems to have been taken. Two days later, on 25 April, TCI publicly challenged the Japanese authorities' advice not to raise its stake in J-Power. It alleged that the advice was mistakenly based, that the procedure for examination lacked transparency and fairness, and that the Subcommittee did not understand the market economics involved. TCI particularly criticised the timing of the advice, which had been issued only one day after the fund had submitted its revised proposal offering not to exercise voting rights for the extra shares. TCI contended that the examination was conducted with the decision already known, and accordingly urged the authorities to review their conclusions. Ho said that TCI had received several emails from J-Power's shareholders in support of the fund's claims. Comment in various Japanese financial magazines generally supported TCI's objectives at J-Power, often considering the affair to be a test case for wider problems in Japanese corporate governance. The authorities' leaning towards the use of the national interest defence to prevent TCI's further share purchases had immediately been queried by an editorial in *Nikkei* when it became publicly known in February 2008 (FT, 2008l; Independent, 2008; Nikkei, 2008aa, 2008b; Nikkei Sangyō, 2008k).

Allegations of misconduct

While the decision on the application to increase its shareholding was formally still pending – although it was already clear that the ministries were unhappy with the situation – TCI sought to apply pressure to J-Power's board through multiple initiatives which were increasingly confrontational. These suggested that J-Power's senior managers were guilty of misconduct. On 2 May 2008 TCI sent a letter to the statutory auditors of J-Power requesting an investigation into three issues: the basis on which J-Power had reduced charges for hydroelectric power and transmission facilities by 4 per cent; the reason behind a recent rise in cross-shareholdings held by the company which TCI believed would harm RoE and divert management attention from improving the core business; and the reason for J-Power's alleged failure to meet performance targets and to make the most of opportunities created by deregulation in the industry. TCI claimed that J-Power's board had given contradictory explanations of the reduction in charges, initially linking it to changes in the company's operating costs and cost of capital, even though such changes had apparently not occurred. TCI claimed that the reduced charges had caused a decline in annual operating profits of ¥6,000 million. On 13 May, J-Power's board revealed that TCI had formally requested J-Power's board of corporate auditors to investigate these points and to look into the possibility of legal action against 13 directors to recover this ¥6,000 million sum from them. On 24 June the board of corporate auditors announced that it had investigated the matter and had decided unanimously not to take legal action (Nikkei, 2008a).

While this was still continuing, on 8 May 2008, TCI sent a letter to Nakagaki effectively accusing J-Power of having unpublished commercial agreements with its cross-shareholding counterparties that could be contrary to the interests of other shareholders and requesting disclosure of any such agreements. On 9 May, J-Power's board strongly denied the existence of any such agreements linked to voting rights and commented that TCI's assertion was based on groundless and one-sided assumptions (Nikkei Sangyō, 2008j).

The national interest defence

On 13 May 2008, the ministries finally issued an official *order* that TCI should not increase its stake in J-Power beyond 10 per cent on the grounds that this could potentially lead to a freeze on the plan to build a nuclear power plant, reductions in expenditure for building power lines, and disruption of stable electricity supply. The official communication stated that TCI had not clearly explained how it would achieve its targets of 4 per cent RoA and 10 per cent RoE at J-Power. TCI did not specify immediately how it would respond. In the event, it did not publicly disclose whether it planned to accept the official ruling or to challenge it through the options open to it of a formal complaint or legal action until July, after a further J-Power AGM had been held at which its proposals announced on 16 April were submitted to the shareholders' vote (Nikkei, 2008h).

On 30 May 2008, in the course of J-Power's regular annual contacts with international investors, Kitamura Masayoshi, one of J-Power's deputy presidents (and subsequently Nakagaki's successor as president), commented in an interview with the *Financial Times* that his company was willing to seek compromises with investors provided that their proposals were sensible. He also mentioned that J-Power's board planned to consider the appointment of external directors during 2009 and emphasised that J-Power was not biased against foreign shareholders. However, he observed that in the case of TCI: 'We've exhausted the list of things we can talk about. The philosophy that we have as a company and TCI's philosophy [are] completely different.' When the *Financial Times* sought a comment from TCI in response, Ho said: 'In the face of management resistance, we are doing all we can to demonstrate how the legitimate requests will improve the broken corporate governance of J-Power.' It appeared that negotiation had effectively ceased (FT, 2008f).

On 21 May 2008, TCI had announced on its website that it would solicit shareholders' support against J-Power's board by requesting them to vote for its five proposals (in fact, four with one as two alternatives) and vote against two proposals put by J-Power's board to keep the dividend unchanged and to re-elect Nakagaki as president. Ho argued in a press conference on the same day that the management of J-Power did not listen to the fund's proposals and said that it was time for new personnel to take charge at J-Power. On 25 May, TCI held a meeting for J-Power's private shareholders to collect proxies to vote for its proposals. On 28 May, TCI was reported by *Kyōdō News* to have taken shareholdings in about ten Japanese companies which were shareholders of J-Power, including Mizuho Financial Group, Sumitomo Mitsui Financial Group, and Kajima Construction, apparently in an attempt to put pressure on J-Power's cross-shareholding arrangements. Ho explained the rationale for these investments: 'We want to hold them accountable for decisions they make and maximise the value of their investments.' Since these shareholdings all remained below 5 per cent it is not clear what happened to them thereafter. On 5 June, TCI sent letters to J-Power's shareholders stating that J-Power's cross-shareholdings and its alleged practice of employing retired government bureaucrats (popularly known as *amakudari*) only served the interests of the management. However, the latter accusation was justified on the basis of only two directors who were former METI officials and one proposed external corporate auditor from the FSA, which does not seem excessive for a company that had only been independent of ministerial control for less than four years at that stage (Institutional Investor, 2008; Nikkei-BP, 2008; Nikkei, 2008d, 2008e, 2008q; Nikkei Sangyō, 2008i).

The majority of J-Power's shareholders rejected TCI's proposals at the AGM on 26 June 2008 and the proposal to reappoint Nakagaki was approved. Ho, who had attended the meeting, claimed that the board had not paid enough regard to the interests of shareholders. Nakagaki said afterwards that the company endeavoured to engage in dialogue with institutional and retail shareholders and thereby strengthen their trust. He also called on TCI to understand the structural distinctiveness of the way that J-Power was run. The *Financial Times* – which had generally been supportive of TCI – reported that TCI had won between 20% and 40% of the vote for its five proposals and that TCI believed that about 40% of J-Power's voting rights were controlled by friendly cross-shareholders or suppliers. Comment from Nomura Securities was quoted to the effect that this outcome suggested that many shareholders were unhappy with management. However, data from sources closer to the company suggested that most of the proposals attracted support only at the lower end of this range (FT, 2008e, 2008j; Nikkei Sangyō, 2008b).

On 14 July 2008 (the final date on which it could have filed a statement of official dissatisfaction with the ruling), TCI accepted the official order barring it from increasing its stake in J-Power from 9.9% to 20%; it had apparently concluded that a contest with the Japanese administration would not be to its advantage (Nikkei, 2008f).

The aftermath

On 31 October 2008 it was reported that TCI had sold its 9.9 per cent holding in J-Power back to the company. J-Power stated that it had agreed to buy the entire stake, at TCI's request, for ¥3,830 per share, at a cost of some ¥63,000 million, compared with that day's closing price of ¥2,895. The *Financial Times* estimated that TCI had paid an average of ¥4,585 per share, implying a loss of some ¥12,500 million. However, as can be seen from Figure 8.8, the US$–Yen exchange rate was especially favourable for Yen investments liquidated in late 2008; we estimate from our own calculations that TCI may have made no major loss on its investment in J-Power before carrying costs and other expenses, provided that it had not previously covered its exchange position. However, we believe that most funds do not leave positions open.

The *Financial Times'* report gave no indication of any special background to this purchase, leaving the inevitable impression that J-Power had followed the traditional route of Japan's greenmailing targets and bought off an unwelcome investor. However, the Japanese press gave more detail and reported that TCI had taken advantage of a Japanese legal requirement that shareholders dissenting to any major realignment of assets could insist that their shares be purchased by the company at a fair price, usually negotiated against recent historical price trends by each side's lawyers. J-Power had undertaken a reorganisation of some of its subsidiary operations and TCI had filed opposition just before the regulatory deadline for dissent, on 29 September 2008. An un-named US investment banker was quoted by *Nikkei* observing that this had been merely an excuse to make a swift exit. Certainly it had been reported in the press in October that TCI's global investments had increasingly lost value throughout 2008 and that it had told investors that as recession approached, the fund would 'need investment to ride out this storm'. In April 2009 it was reported that Ho was leaving TCI to form his own fund (FT, 2008k, 2009c ; Nikkei, 2008w; WSJ, 2008b).

TCI's intervention had lasting effects on J-Power, but these were not what TCI had intended. Although Nakagaki consistently rejected suggestions that his board was responding to outside pressure in doing so, J-Power made limited moves to win the approval of foreign investors by appointing one external director and maintaining dividend increases, though not to the level demanded by TCI. In 2009 it introduced an anti-takeover defence, not as a specific mechanism but in the form of a statement that such a mechanism would be introduced in the event of investors accumulating shares with a view to influencing the company's strategy.[1] At the same time, management's move to restructure the company's share base in such a way as to reduce unsettling influences appears to have succeeded: the proportion of stock held by foreign shareholders declined sharply following the intervention, in favour of domestic investors. In March 2010 J-Power's foreign shareholder ratio was just under 17 per cent, still large in absolute terms but less than half its level before and during TCI's intervention.

9.4 Conclusion

In the Bull-Dog Sauce case, as in several of its other early interventions, Steel Partners demonstrated that it was possible to extract shareholder value from small and medium-sized Japanese listed companies, deploying a strategy of public engagement with calls for increased dividends and the use of tender offers to stimulate restructurings or pay-offs. Although these tactics succeeded in financial terms, they did not lead to a change in managerial attitudes in the companies that were targeted. In other companies they engendered a defensive reaction, based on concerns over greenmail and the uncertainty associated

---

[1] This statement, contained in J-Power's public disclosure to the Tokyo Stock Exchange dated 22 March 2011, emphasised the nature of the company as a utility on which the national economy relied for sustained electrical power supply and enjoined shareholders to accept this special situation. While emphasising support for the freedom of shareholders to trade their shares, the statement further noted that in the event of an investor appearing to accumulate shares with a view to controlling the company, if insufficient notice or explanation were forthcoming, suitable countermeasures would be taken within the parameters of the law to protect the best interests of the whole shareholder body and corporate value.

with hostile takeover bids. Steel Partners received limited support from other institutional investors. In official circles, rather than being praised for reducing agency costs and imposing financial discipline on firms, they were publicly vilified as an 'abusive acquirer'.

TCI's attempt to apply its 'large-cap' intervention formula in Japan had ended in an expensive failure. Despite the strong presence of foreign investors on J-Power's share register, in excess of 35 per cent, it had been unable to muster sufficient support for its resolutions at two successive AGMs. When it shifted its strategy to the accumulation of a larger shareholding, it had been drawn into a disagreement with the Japanese bureaucracy, in the course of which its nature as an investment fund seeking an influential holding in an economically important company had been publicly castigated as a threat to the national interest.

In both cases, there were some minority voices which were critical of the generally negative reaction to the interventions of the activist funds. As Yano Tomomi put it, when 80 per cent of the shareholders of Bull-Dog Sauce could vote in favour of the company's defence plan, the result was 'behaviour completely inexplicable in terms of economic rationality' (Yano, 2008, cited in Dore, 2009: 144). This response was at odds with the way that most investors had reacted to hedge fund activism in the USA and Europe hitherto and must have come as a surprise to the activists. In Chapter 10 we consider in more detail what we know of the reactions from management, investors, officials (including the judiciary), and the media.

10 | *Responding to activism: managers, investors, officials, and the media*

10.1 Introduction

In the USA and Europe, activist hedge funds obtained what they wanted from the companies they targeted when they were able to persuade boards of the validity of their arguments or, failing that, won the support of other shareholders. A general tolerance of their actions from government, regulators, and the courts was also important. This was often taken for granted in the USA but, as we have seen, the ability of the UK Takeover Panel to identify 'concert parties' arbitrarily and the persistent hostility of the Swiss Federal Banking Commission to Laxey's intervention in Implenia are two examples of how official stances could impede hedge fund activism. Where interventions involved public confrontations, the tone in which the media reported events could also become a factor in shaping public opinion and encouraging boards either to cooperate or resist. Hedge fund activism faced essentially the same situation in Japan. In order to succeed, it needed a degree of acquiescence from managers, support from other shareholders, and ideally a mixture of the two. Official attitudes and the tone of media reports were equally important to them in Japan as they were elsewhere in shaping public debate over activism. In this chapter we look at the nature of the responses they received from the boards of targeted companies and Japanese management in general; from other investors; from the official sector in the sense of government, bureaucracy, and the courts; and from the media, principally the financial press.

10.2 The responses of managers

The individuals most directly affected by activist hedge fund interventions were the directors and senior managers of the targeted companies: they met the fund managers, heard or received in writing their various requests and demands, and were called on to respond to their arguments. A substantial body of material relating to managers' responses is in the public domain and can be attributed to particular individuals. The Japanese financial press showed great interest in the events surrounding hedge fund activism and interviewed many board members and senior managers of the companies concerned, as well as managers at the funds. In addition to using this material, we draw on our own interviews, which are mostly but not exclusively reported on an anonymised basis (see Chapter 2 for an account of our research methods).

Initial shock

A common first reaction of management at the smaller companies targeted by activist hedge funds was one of surprise. In spite of the publicity already associated with the interventions of the Murakami Fund after 2000, some senior managers and board members had evidently not regarded their own companies as likely targets. As we have seen (Chapters 8 and 9 above), board members at Sotoh in December 2003 and at Bull-Dog Sauce as late as 2007 expressed surprise and shock when their companies were the subject of tender offers from Steel Partners.

Dealing with assertive shareholders seems to have been a worrying and unwelcome experience for some managers. As one director at a private equity fund put it to us: 'From the point of view of senior management at targeted firms, the reaction is that this is a problem, you see. Because in the past there was not much of this sort of thing with outside shareholders coming in and raising matters.' An officer at a business association, who was careful not to express opposition to foreign activist hedge funds as such and stressed that foreign investors were always welcome in the Japanese market, thought that exaggerated media reports were responsible for exciting undue public concern: 'The activists have brought all sorts of proposals to Japanese companies but the fact is that companies in Japan are still not used to this sort of thing. Then, because the media reports this in a very exaggerated way, one might say there is a feeling of concern – of caution – out of proportion to the real nature of it.'

A financial commentator felt that the concept of outsiders proposing ideas about the company's strategy was seen as unwelcome interference by most Japanese managers:

I think most Japanese managers simply don't believe that outsiders can possibly have better ideas for managing the company than they do. They have been with the company all their lives typically. It is true the life-time employment system isn't what it used to be but when you get to the top ranks of listed companies it is still the norm. And the people who have really spent their careers with this company, typically at the top management level, they've had posts in various positions throughout the organisation, different functions, different regions, and so on and they know the company well and they are convinced that an outsider couldn't possibly have anything useful to contribute. So the reaction – on the part of corporate executives – is always negative to the presence of these activists.

At larger companies, hedge fund interventions were greeted with less of a sense of shock. However, in some quarters, foreign activist hedge funds were seen from the outset as a destabilising influence. By the autumn of 2005, activist hedge fund interventions in Europe had been extensively reported in the Japanese press. TCI's campaign in the Deutsche Börse case, in the course of which it effectively forced out both the chairman and CEO, was familiar to the directors and managers of internationally orientated Japanese firms. As a senior officer at one targeted company put it to us: 'From the start we knew what sort of people they were so we were very cautious you see … We knew about the chairman – wasn't it? – at Deutsche Börse and how they made him resign, you see … Yes, we were very cautious about them.'

Limits to mutual learning: financial versus managerial perspectives

The funds saw what they were doing as normal investment practice which followed a familiar financial logic. While they were motivated by what they saw as a proper regard for self-interest, they viewed their activities as a mechanism by which firm performance could be improved. Wider benefits to the Japanese economy and society would follow the introduction of more efficient capital market practices. As a fund manager told us in 2008, 'Hopefully Japan will see that there is a lot of bottled up inefficiency, capital inefficiency, operating ineffi-ciency, and if it really wants a good future for its grandchildren, they need to change.'

There appears to have been an initial degree of acceptance among the managers of at least some target companies that the funds' interventions had merit. As one of them put it to us, 'For about the first year and a half I think there was a fairly constructive discussion about what kind of financial strategy we should pursue in order to utilise our capital as efficiently as possible and raise returns for the benefit of both investors and management.' The president of Yushiro, one of Steel Partners' first targets, commented publicly in January 2009 that the experience had been beneficial and had created an enduring creative tension in his company (Nikkei, 2009b).

However, in the end most managers found the funds' focus on shareholder returns as a mechanism for improving corporate performance to be unconvincing, thereby limiting what each side could learn from the other. Managers regarded hedge fund interventions as illegitimate to the extent that they were focused simply on making financial gains. A senior director at a targeted company told us:

We realise that, obviously, they chose [our company] as an investment target purely as a means to raise their own returns and that all this talk of 'improving the company' was just talk ... Now I ask myself exactly what were all those demands for capital efficiency that they developed over the past two years, or what they meant by talking about improving governance.

After a long and contentious intervention had ended, this director considered that the fund's financially driven approach was not compatible with the company's approach to planning for the long term:

You see, they are logical and they have extremely logical demands and ways of developing the situation and ways of saying things, but at the end of the day they are seeking a quick profit. I certainly don't go so far as to call them speculative but because they aim for very fast realisation of profit in a short space of time, in order to achieve this they say what we consider to be pretty unreasonable things. They tell us suddenly to double the dividend, they tell us to make a share buy-back, or else, irrespective of the fact that we consider ourselves to be one of the firms within our sector that, in a sense, makes the greatest use of financial leverage and in effect frequently has recourse to liabilities, they tell us to borrow even more loans: from our point of view as we seek to manage in a long-term, stable manner, this suggests that these people are only thinking in terms of about three or five years, so we feel that there is simply no common ground, you see.

Interviewed in 2009 after the onset of the global financial crisis, the same director considered that while lessons had been learned, these did not imply accepting the validity of the fund's approach. On the contrary, the crisis had vindicated his board's relatively conservative approach to gearing:

Do you know the expression *hanmen kyōshi* (someone who gives a bad example but effectively teaches by counter-example)? – [our President] said that they brought us very valuable experience, partly through this teaching by counter-example, and I agree with him … [the fund's managers] were always saying 'make use of borrowing, make use of borrowing' and that if we had the ability we should raise our gearing, but now everyone has realised that one big cause of the markets going funny was that sophisticated financial institutions raised their gearing too much. Now we feel again that what we were saying all along was right. It is obvious why shareholders should want to maximise the efficiency of shareholders' equity and to raise returns through this kind of approach. We understood that perfectly well. And so the idea was strengthened that when we made any investments we always had to check that capital efficiency was maximised and see whether this was a business that represented the most efficient use of capital: in that sense it was a valuable experience in that it caused our management to have a greater awareness of cost of capital.

Attitudes to dividends and leverage

The key issue over which this clash between managerial and financial views was played out was that of dividend increases. When they were asked to raise dividends by activist hedge funds, some boards of targeted companies accepted that the level of payments could be raised, but nevertheless queried the pace at which distributions to shareholders could be increased without damaging the company's business. Closely linked to this was the argument that payouts should be accommodated to the business's continuing investment needs. Management accused the funds of cutting across existing strategic plans in a clumsy and irresponsible way. They asserted that financial reserves which the funds argued to be surplus to requirements had already been allocated to specific projects. At two of the companies we visited, directors and senior managers were able to quote from business plans that appeared to predate the activists' interventions. Senior officers at one company explained:

Unconnected to their proposal, we already had put into our plans how we were going to dispose of our operating cash flow, you know … So we did not do all this in order to have a confrontation with them; it isn't a case either of doing things just because of this situation – all that happened is that we went ahead quietly doing what we originally felt should be done.

More generally, managers sought to assert their autonomy over the timing of cash disbursements. At several companies we were told a similar story of management's rejection of demands for an increased payout because of concerns about timing and sustainability:

Then, in the middle of this, all of a sudden, there was this matter that I've mentioned of raising the share price and all sorts of things. Suddenly came this talk of how we should increase dividends or have share buy-backs and so forth: we felt it was not appropriate for the time we are at now.

Management also stressed the importance of having sustainable plans for raising dividend levels:

Now, in this connection, [our company] itself, right from the start, had been considering increasing the dividend year by year and raising it like this in line with the company's performance, but our basic policy was to raise the dividend in a way that was as stable and sustainable as possible, not by raising it on one occasion only to lower it if our results deteriorated.

A senior director at another targeted company highlighted the company's opposition to the strategy of replacing equity with debt as a key point of difference with the fund:

Our position is that we shall pay the agreed dividend from our income but that the rest is needed for capital investment as the next phase of our investment expansion, so we want to allocate it to that. But [the fund] say that shareholders' funds – profits – belong to shareholders and that these are the most expensive form of funding. Borrowing is cheaper so they want us to take additional borrowing and apply that to capital investment, meanwhile returning our cash flow to the shareholders. This is where our opinions are completely opposed.

Attitudes to shareholders and other stakeholders

At the outset, some boards of companies targeted by activists in Japan gave the impression that they were focused on managing their businesses to the complete neglect of the interests of portfolio shareholders, as opposed to those who held their shares for business reasons. Other boards responded to activist interventions by stating publicly their willingness to be more responsive to investor needs in future. In an interview with *Nikkei* in February 2004, President Mabuchi of Sotoh said that his company had endeavoured to do business by sharing profits among its various stakeholders, including its employees and the community. When asked whether these principles had been made clear to shareholders who invested in Sotoh as a listed company, he conceded that perhaps they had not. Similarly, in an interview with *Nikkei Kinyū Shimbun* in February 2006, President Nagai of Yushiro said that he felt that the takeover attempt by Steel Partners had given Yushiro a stimulus to improve its investor relations (Nikkei, 2004d; Nikkei Kinyū, 2006b). There is evidence that companies which already had IR departments increased their efforts in this area after being targeted. As a senior officer at a target told us:

I think that we have learned a great deal from [a foreign activist hedge fund] becoming our shareholder on this occasion. We have realised with all the conversations we have held with them and all their demands that in this sort of situation unless we put out our message effectively, we cannot get all our various shareholders to understand our position.

However, this kind of heightened sensitivity to shareholder interests does not seem to have spread very far. The TSE has been analysing responses from companies quoted on its First Section, Second Section, and Mothers market on a bi-annual basis since 2007 and has published three sets of data covering returns submitted in 2006, 2008, and 2010 (TSE, 2007a, 2009, 2011a). These data, summarised in Table 10.1, illustrate the gap between First and Second Section companies in their attention to investors in general. Companies listed on the Mothers market are encouraged by the Exchange to hold investor meetings, which most likely explains their strong showing here. These data record a decline in all kinds of formal investor contact by the mostly smaller companies in the Second Section. These are precisely the sort

Table 10.1 *TSE survey on regular investor contact*

Regular seminars for investors:	Percentages of companies notifying compliance		
	2006	2008	2010
First section			
for individuals	22.3%	26.6%	25.6%
for analysts and institutional investors	76.8%	76.3%	78.1%
for overseas investors	19.7%	20.9%	18.9%
Second section			
for individuals	14.7%	19.5%	16.9%
for analysts and institutional investors	46.1%	43.3%	43.1%
for overseas investors	3.0%	2.4%	1.6%
Mothers			
for individuals	42.0%	47.2%	40.7%
for analysts and institutional investors	92.0%	89.7%	90.7%
for overseas investors	12.1%	9.2%	5.5%

Source: Tokyo Stock Exchange

of companies which could have expected to receive an approach from an activist hedge fund in the period of the TSE surveys. More than half of them do not seem to have felt it necessary to respond to the well-publicised experiences of Sotoh and Yushiro.

While some of the targets we spoke to accepted that hedge fund approaches had made them reconsider their relations with shareholders in general, they also expressed a desire to cultivate stable shareholders who would identify with the company's objectives, and, by implication, leave the board in peace to run the business. An officer at a financial infrastructure entity, speaking in 2008, described his view of the current situation as follows:

In Japan the original idea of a shareholder was something like a stable shareholder or a cross-shareholder, or else a bank from which funding was being received, and that is how many managers understand shareholders ... in the mind of management, these are the sort of people they think of as shareholders, and whom they value, so the result of all this is that, in their estimation, they just do not consider people who are doing it for the sake of short-term profit to be shareholders at all: I think it is probably all linked to this sort of preconception they hold.

The same desire for stable shareholders was apparent in discussions with senior management at a number of target companies. A senior manager we interviewed said:

Well, we are a publicly listed company so any shareholder who wants has the right to buy our shares, and we can't pick and choose. But, what we are saying now is that, fundamentally, we don't want to manage with any sort of short-term selling and buying of our shares that threatens to disrupt the company, with things taken to extremes whereby other shareholders wonder what is going on.

The same interviewee emphasised the importance of transparency and keeping shareholders well informed of the company's plans. At the same time, he expressed an interest in increasing the proportion of shares held by retail shareholders who, he felt, would also be likely to support management: 'Basically we want to increase the number of people – including private individuals – who understand about [our company]. These people may buy [our] products and we feel that they will read all sorts of press information about [us] too with interest.'

Another company which had been targeted by a foreign activist hedge fund, and which had a relatively high ratio of overseas shareholders, claimed to have no plans to avoid foreign shareholders in future, despite indications that some – though by no means all – of its foreign shareholders had supported the activists on at least some issues. Management's efforts were focused, instead, on the need to identify institutional shareholders – either foreign or Japanese – who would share its vision of the company:

Well, you see, we don't take the sort of view that our level of foreign shareholding is too big or too small … Whether they are foreigners or not, what's important is what sort of shareholders they are. Are they hedge fund-related? Are they shareholders who practice activism? Are they institutional shareholders who go for growth or value: what you might call 'orthodox institutional shareholders'? … If they are orthodox institutional shareholders then even if they are foreigners I think we can expect them to hold our shares without problems in the belief that our company will grow.

In order to achieve this, the board of this company planned to refocus its IR efforts on institutional shareholders which they considered supportive: 'But after this sort of experience our attitude is that we want a particular kind of investor like this to be our shareholders so – you might call it selective IR. We plan to increase the weight of IR to the investors we want as shareholders, not just to anyone at all.'

While formal attitudes to shareholders showed only minimal change, many managers in target companies explicitly rationalised their position of opposition to hedge fund interventions in terms of the defence of the interests of employees and customers. As the president of the engineering firm Hi-Lex, a company targeted by Steel Partners, observed to a reporter in 2006: 'There's not a single employee in our company who thinks he is working for the shareholders. The attitude is that this is all hard work and that we're doing it for our customers. That's how it all pulls together' (Kōbe Shimbun, 2006).

In the same year the president of another targeted company expressed his philosophy to us in these terms:

I always say that there are broadly speaking three sets of stakeholders in our company: one is the shareholders, another is the customers, and the third is the employees, including the management. I think the most important element of managing the company is to keep these three – this triangle – in balance. In order to maintain that stability and proceed with both growth and stability in balance with one another, a company, for example, that just pays attention to its shareholders and continually applies its profits to those shareholders will end up withering away at some stage in the future.

Shareholders were not denied a place in the company but they could not be accepted as its only important constituent.

Defending the company: 'poison pills' and related takeover defences

If the initial reaction to the activist funds was one of shock and, in some quarters, confusion, it was not long before an openly defensive position was adopted. Shortly after Steel Partners' tender offer for Sotoh was made, in April 2004, the Nagoya branch of UFJ Trust Bank gave a seminar on anti-takeover defences to representatives of local companies (Sotoh is based near Nagoya), and the press canvassed opinions

from those attending. An executive commented that he remained concerned, because the tendency of local companies to hold high reserves
made them ideal targets for this kind of attack. As the chief executive
of a food manufacturer, which was not identified, put it: 'the Sotoh
problem could be anyone's problem' (Nikkei Kinyū, 2004).

There was an upsurge in anti-takeover defences throughout the
listed company sector in Japan from 2005. These generally took the
form of rights plans allowing the target board to allocate shares or,
more frequently, warrants to receive shares, to friendly third parties
as a means of diluting the holdings of a raider or activist. In many
cases, the board's power to issue warrants was triggered once an
acquirer reached a certain threshold (such as 20 per cent) and was
either unable or unwilling to reassure the board or a board-appointed
committee of experts that its aims were compatible with the best
interests of the company. This 'pre-warning' (*jizen keikoku*) device
called to mind several features of US takeover defences of the kind
which had been sustained by the case law of the Delaware courts in
the mid-1980s. At the same time, in its emphasis on formal deliber-
ation by the board or an independent committee over the contents
of the potential acquirer's business plan, it represented a distinctively
Japanese variant of the original American form of the poison pill
(Milhaupt, 2009: 352). The evolution of new forms of poison pill in
Japan was assisted by legislation forming part of the new Companies
Act, passed in 2005, which made it easier for companies to issue
shares with limited transfer rights, which could be assigned to third
parties likely to support the board, and also to issue share warrants
which could be exercised only under certain conditions (Hayakawa
and Whittaker, 2009: 77).

The adoption of anti-takeover defences by listed Japanese companies for several years from 2005 was not solely a response to changes
in the law, nor to the activities of the hedge funds. Livedoor's bid for
Nippon Broadcasting System in early 2005, followed by Ōji Paper's
bid for Hokuetsu Paper in 2006, had helped to focus attention on
the issue (Buchanan and Deakin, 2009: 51–4). In October 2006, the
TSE reported that 131 companies on its exchange, or 5.6% of the
total, had defences in place. By August 2008 this had risen to 460
companies, or 19.4% of the total (TSE, 2007a, 2009). Take-up was
disproportionately high in companies which had been or were the

subject of hedge fund interest; as we have shown in Figure 8.7, take-over defence measures were introduced at 25 of the 34 companies in our sample of companies targeted by publicly confrontational hedge funds between 2005 and 2007, comprising nearly 74% of the total. In all but one case, this occurred after activists had emerged as sharehold-ers. In 2005, defences were adopted at two of the companies in our sample, both of which had activist shareholders at this stage. In 2006 there were adoptions at nine of our companies. In 2007 there were adoptions at 14 of them. If we include all the investments during the same period that we noted by funds classified only as 'public' rather than as overtly 'confrontational', the total of targeted companies rises to 48, of which 29, or 60 per cent, introduced such defences. However, at several of the companies involved, board spokesmen took care to describe their defences as being unrelated to the presence of activist shareholders: Fujitec's board stated that they did not view Dalton as a hostile acquirer when they announced measures in May 2007, Kyōsan Electric's board emphasised that they had already begun studying the concept before Dalton became a shareholder, and the board at Kikkōman, where Steel Partners had taken a shareholding, described its measures in June 2007 as only a general precaution (Nikkei, 2006e, 2007am; Nikkei Sangyō, 2006).

These anti-takeover defences were meant to be used to fend off unwelcome acquirers, and were sometimes successfully deployed to that effect. The pre-warning procedures gave boards the options of requiring would-be purchasers of substantial holdings to undergo a protracted examination of their objectives, and a science of obfus-cation developed whereby written requests and explanations were passed back and forth. As a hedge fund manager put it to us, 'They reject everything you say, thinking that they are doing all right; they try to put [forward] evidence to say that the issues you raise aren't really issues.' Evaluation of the fund's explanations would be under-taken either by an expert committee, nominally independent of the target company but in practice invariably appointed by its board, or by the board itself. Sapporo and Steel Partners, in particular, engaged in several years of this process before the fund sold its shares in late 2010, having made no progress in persuading the board or its advisers of the merits of its case for change (Bloomberg, 2010; Nikkei Kinyū, 2007a).

10.3 The attitudes of shareholders

As Kahan and Rock observed of hedge fund activism in the USA, 'In order to see their views prevail, however, hedge funds usually need the support of others' and one important constituency is that of other major shareholders (Kahan and Rock, 2007: 1089). As we have seen from the comments of Colin Kingsnorth at Laxey Partners in 2007, in the UK there is also a 'need to persuade, cajole and influence the other investors'. The same applies in Japan. A hedge fund manager operating there said to us in early 2008, 'Activism only works when you have pressure from shareholders; so in Japan that is the number one thing: you have enough shareholder votes and you win.' It was the lack of support from other shareholders which ultimately made activist strategies unworkable in the Japanese context. We consider below why investors were so reluctant to support activist interventions.

Japanese insurance companies: indifference to shareholder value?

Japanese insurance companies, and life insurers in particular, tend to regard their equity holdings as relatively stable, long-term investments. Some believe in having long-term investment horizons, to the exclusion of opportunities for short-term gain. An officer of a life insurer put it this way to us in 2009:

Some fund managing companies are more focused on total return over the next 3 months [but] life companies are considering, you know, 'our investment is 5 to 10 years', so we can probably accept some bumpy earnings for the next couple of years if we truly believe the management can do the right things for the shareholder.

Another factor in the indifference of Japanese insurance companies to shareholder value, as we have observed, is the tendency of some of them to use shareholdings to build up business relationships with their investee companies. A stable shareholding is seen as making it easier to sell insurance and related financial products to the company's employees. The chairman of a Japanese life insurance company told us in 2009, 'Most of our investments in Japanese corporations are not pure investment: they are relationship investments.' A hedge fund manager, speaking in 2008, had put it equally bluntly from the other side of the relationship:

The traditional life [insurers] don't interact with people like us at all, because they don't want to be seen as stepping out of line. Are they keeping time with what we do? I think there must be a small sense of that, meaning they have an obligation to the policy-holders so they can't just let the shares go to zero. But because of the history of their working relationships [with companies], I think they will find it difficult to speak up even if they may not agree ... So I think they are very conflicted on the many outcomes which are mutually exclusive, so it is a tough one for them. I don't think they are aligned with us and more likely they are just aligned with the company; they don't care about the share price, or they are stuck in the middle. We hope they migrate more to generating more return for the companies.

Another factor at work here may simply be the limited exposure of Japanese life insurers to the Japanese share market. As we saw in Chapter 6, Japanese life insurance companies hold a relatively small proportion of their total portfolios in Japanese equities. A life insurance manager, speaking to us in 2009, estimated the average level of equity holdings throughout his industry to be somewhere in the region of only 10 per cent. Officers of another life insurer estimated more generally that the level for all kinds of insurers then, including general and accident, was probably within the 5–20 per cent range. Looking at the declared values of domestic shares held on the unconsolidated balance sheet of Nippon Life, the largest Japanese life insurer, between 2005 and 2010, there is considerable fluctuation, and the overall level seems slightly higher than these estimates. However, the general trend is downward, from around 30 per cent in 2006 and 2007 towards around 20 per cent in 2010. This reduction means that returns from domestic equity investments are progressively less crucial to Japanese life insurers.

The non-life insurance industry in Japan also holds equity investments and faces conflicts of interest. A report from Fitch in August 2010 suggested that the six largest non-life companies are even more heavily committed to the domestic equity sector than many life companies, although progressive reductions in their holdings are expected. Fitch considered that these reductions were driven by an increasingly objective attitude to portfolio returns (Fitch, 2010). As this report stated:

Despite their strong capital positions, Fitch believes that the insurers' exposure to stock market volatility remains high, given that domestic stock investments accounted for nearly 30% of the six companies' aggregate total assets at end-March 2010. While policy stock holdings (i.e. holdings of stocks of companies with which the insurers have an insurance business relationship) have helped cultivate and maintain the inflow of insurance business, the insurers have been reducing such stock holdings as they have increasingly taken pure investment perspectives and become aware of risks. The introduction of IFRS[1] in the near future is expected to make such reductions easier in Japan. Fitch believes insurers are likely to speed up their reductions of stock holdings and plans to continue to monitor the speed and extent of these reductions.

Japanese pension funds

Japanese pension funds are not restricted by a perceived need to invest for business reasons, but few have been seen to take a confrontational stance with the boards of the companies in which they hold shares. The largest pension fund, the GPIF, held only 16.7 per cent of its total portfolio, an amount equivalent to ¥19,067,600 million worth of shareholdings, in domestic shares, as at 31 March 2007 (GPIF, 2007). It has since been reduced further. As we noted in Chapter 6, its insistence that it is a conservative 'beta investor', rather than an aggressive 'alpha investor', suggests an unwillingness to be associated directly with aggressive investment practices. This attitude is public knowledge, and few observers expect the management of the GPIF publicly to confront the boards of companies in which it holds shares or to align itself with activist hedge funds. A life insurance officer offered this view of the GPIF's position: 'The GPIF used to be considered as a government entity. A government entity cannot control a private company – should not be controlling a private company – therefore ... they're fairly hesitant to exercise a voting right even though they are a large shareholder because they are considered as a public [entity].'

Another large pension fund (although much smaller than the GPIF) is the PFA, to which we have already referred as a prominent critic of the corporate governance practices of Japanese companies, although it was not specifically an advocate of higher dividend payments. As

---

[1] International Financial Reporting Standards established by the International Accounting Standards Board (IASB).

at the end of March 2007 it held domestic equity assets valued at ¥3,628,433 million, equivalent to 27.5 per cent of its total portfolio, making it much less significant than the GPIF in terms of the value of its holdings, but still a potentially influential shareholder at least in those companies where it chose to concentrate its holdings (PFA, 2007). The PFA's emphasis on the direct management of at least part of its holdings brought it much closer to the managers and directors of companies in which it invested than was the case then with the GPIF. However, the PFA has gradually been reducing its domestic equity investments, which by 2010 were 17.1 per cent or roughly half their level in the early 2000s. The departure in July 2008 of its Executive Managing Director, Yano Tomomi, while not linked to any formal change in policy, was generally perceived in the market to have blunted its appetite for promoting governance reform. Even under Yano, the PFA's advocacy of corporate governance reform did not lead it to identify formally with the positions taken by activist hedge funds.

Fund managers and other institutional investors

If most insurers are conflicted and most pension funds uninterested in obtaining higher returns from the companies whose shares they hold, there should still be institutional investors or specialist fund managers in Japan prepared to press for better returns. Some private sector fund managers expressed public sympathy for the aims of the foreign activist hedge funds. A Japanese fund manager, writing in *Nikkei* in the context of Steel Partners' intervention in Myōjō Foods in late 2006, praised foreign funds operating in Japan, saying that the recent interventions at Myōjō Foods and other companies had triggered realignment within the industry and improved standards of management. But, at the same time, he was concerned that foreign funds such as Steel Partners were gaining outsize profits through tender offers, apparently considering this a step too far in the pursuit of shareholder value (Kubota, 2007).

There is some evidence that Japanese investors are beginning to focus more on returns from their portfolios. As a civil servant described the situation to us:

When it comes to requests to increase dividends, without making demands about how the company is run, particularly – things like dividends being too small even though there are big internal reserves or dividends being too small despite profits being achieved – then there is really not much opposition to such arguments. Well, maybe [managers] are not too happy about it, but I think other shareholders – Japanese shareholders – too, when they consider this, will feel that it is not such a bad idea and go along with the foreigners' proposals.

A board member at a company targeted by a foreign activist hedge fund acknowledged that increasing dividends was a move that had to be made, and expressed opposition only to what he characterised as the extreme nature of the fund's demands. He was well aware that even his company's long-standing Japanese institutional shareholders were interested in higher returns on their investment. He explained that his company was:

continually saying that it will amplify returns to shareholders progressively in line with its growth and this is something that they want and which they agree with; they are not saying that it has to be done immediately this year but they are looking forward to [our company] making the next return of value to shareholders as soon as it becomes possible. That was the way that the investors we contacted expressed it. After all, there's no such thing as an investor that says he does not want an increased dividend.

Even so, the question of how much dividend to pay soon becomes entangled in the question of what is judged to be appropriate for the firm's survival and growth. This is precisely the area where Japanese boards have been accustomed to taking decisions unaided by shareholders' opinions. Specific demands from shareholders for higher payouts continue to run the risk of seeming to infringe management's jealously guarded control over strategy and financial planning. An officer of the business association we spoke to offered this view in January 2008:

It is probably right to oppose [activist hedge funds] when their plan is to do things like push up dividends in the short term and to plunder medium to long-term value that has been nurtured over a long period. But in cases where things are not like this, where it is possible to pay more dividends, or where the payout is egregiously low compared to other, comparable companies so that it stands out as being very low in the context of the Japanese market, then it seems reasonable to ask for an increase in dividend. Indeed during the past three years the dividend payout level of Japanese companies has greatly increased. Many companies are raising their dividends to the extent that they have the capacity to do so and dividends are going up. The reason is that raising the dividend translates fairly directly into a rise in the share price so by raising their overall value they can conversely make themselves harder to acquire. If things go beyond that and shareholders demand unreasonable dividends or changes in the management, then I think that this becomes a scenario where they are acting as hostile acquirers rather than as shareholders.

The implication that we see in this informal opinion from an officer of a leading Japanese business association is that although shareholders can reasonably expect higher dividends provided that the company can safely afford to pay them, the decision on any increase rests entirely with the board: board autonomy is to be maintained. Moreover, any shareholder who challenges this autonomy and demands a bigger payout becomes a hostile acquirer and a threat to the company. While it is clear that a trend towards higher dividends is progressing and that Japanese investors seem to be applying at least some pressure to encourage it, the determination of management to control this process and their belief that this is an equitable situation seem to be deeply entrenched.

Overseas investors

Foreign institutional investors were more likely to be natural allies of activist hedge funds in Japan, as they had been in the USA and Europe. The public stance of at least a segment of overseas institutional investors in Japan is demonstrated by comments from the Asian Corporate Governance Association ('ACGA'), a group of internationally active institutional investors, many of them based in North America or the UK, with an interest in East Asian markets. The *ACGA White Paper on Corporate Governance in Japan*, published in May 2008, observed that:

While a number of leading companies in Japan have made strides in corporate governance in recent years, we submit that the system of governance in most listed companies is not meeting the needs of stakeholders or the nation at large in three ways:

- By not providing for adequate supervision of corporate strategy;
- By protecting management from the discipline of the market, thus rendering the development of a healthy and efficient market in corporate control all but impossible;
- By failing to provide the returns that are vitally necessary to protect Japan's social safety net—its pension system. (ACGA, 2008: 5)

ACGA's general secretary was quoted by the *Financial Times* on 12 May 2008 as saying: 'There is a high level of frustration among foreign and domestic investors about corporate governance and the slow pace of reform. We do feel that shareholders aren't being treated fairly and we are trying to seek a level playing field for shareholders.' The same *Financial Times* article offered its support, observing that 'Japan must improve its standards of corporate governance if it wants to stem the decline in investor confidence in the country, a group of the world's most influential institutional investors will warn this week'. The same article also commented negatively, as a related matter, on METI's recently announced rejection of TCI's application to increase its shareholding in J-Power (FT, 2008g).

Overseas investors expressly supported activists in a number of cases. At Aderans' 2008 AGM, Dodge & Cox, a US investor not generally noted for its adversarial behaviour and up to that point regarded as a 'friendly' shareholder by Aderans' board, aligned itself with Steel Partners to defeat a resolution for the re-election of Aderans' president and other directors. This was widely reported in the press as a shock for the board. *Nikkei* quoted an unnamed financial sector source as saying that Dodge & Cox's role was 'decisive' (Nikkei, 2008k). However, this was not necessarily a typical case; Aderans' board had become notorious for failing to deliver over several years on its promises of improved performance.

The relatively high proportion of votes cast in support of TCI's proposals at J-Power's AGMs in 2007 and 2008, while not enough to bring victory for the fund, implied that TCI had the backing of at least some of J-Power's shareholders. The general assumption was that these were non-resident institutional shareholders but this has not formally been confirmed. The announcement by J-Power's board in 2008 that it would establish an external advisory board and look into the appointment of an external director was viewed as a concession to the wishes of this constituency although when the financial press raised this matter with Nakagaki he denied that pressure from TCI had prompted this (Nikkei Sangyō, 2008h). In the end, however, the apparent disaffection of some overseas investors was not enough to deflect the company's management from its chosen strategy.

10.4 Civil servants and politicians

Some senior civil servants and government ministers commented directly on particular hedge fund interventions. As we reported in Chapter 9, public statements were made by both a minister and a civil servant following the Bull-Dog Sauce judgments in 2007. Earlier that year, when Steel Partners began to apply pressure to Sapporo's board to make strategic changes, a senior civil servant and a minister within METI had made their unease known. In a press conference on 19 February 2007, the same Kitabata Takao, Administrative Vice Minister of METI who later commented on the Bull-Dog Sauce case, said that Steel Partners should prove that they were not greenmailers. He accused them of gaining huge profits through selling shares and obtaining high dividends (which, of course, are Steel Partners' normal objectives as a fund). Subsequently, in a press conference on 20 February, Amari Akira, the Minister in charge of METI, said that he would 'keep his eye' on Steel Partners to see whether they had proposed their tender offer in order to enhance corporate value at Sapporo. He also expressed doubts about the fund's good intentions (Nikkei, 2007t, 2007al). However, there was no concerted political reaction against activist hedge funds. As Culpepper pointed out, politicians are only motivated to intervene in issues where voters are paying attention and corporate governance only occasionally attracts that attention for a sustained period (Culpepper, 2011: 189–90).

Nevertheless, there was an official reaction of a kind, principally through the civil service. Two significant official initiatives had a direct impact on the activist hedge funds' activities. The first of these was the official debate initiated in 2005 regarding anti-takeover measures, which although not aimed specifically at activist shareholders, came to affect the feasibility of activist strategies. The second was the response of METI to TCI's application to increase its shareholding above the 10 per cent limit for individual non-resident shareholders in companies operating in sectors of national importance.

Official guidance on anti-takeover defences

As we have seen, there was a jump in the use of poison pills and other takeover defences after the Livedoor bid for Nippon Broadcasting System in February 2005. Steel Partners had issued tender offers in the course of its interventions in Sotoh and Yushiro in 2003, and was to repeat the tactic at Myōjō Foods and Tenryū Saw in 2005, and again at Bull-Dog Sauce in 2007. On 27 May 2005 two reports were published, one in the name of the Corporate Value Study Group (*Kigyō Kachi Kenkyūkai*) ('CVSG'), an advisory group which METI and the Ministry of Justice had established the previous September under the chairmanship of a company law academic, Kanda Hideki, and the other, based on the CVSG's work, in the name of the two ministries.

The CVSG's report was entitled only 'Corporate Value Report' (*Kigyō Kachi Hōkokusho*) in its English translation but the original had the subtitle *Kōsei na kigyō-shakai no rūru keisei ni muketa teian* ('Proposals with a view to formulating equitable rules for the corporate community') (CVSG, 2005).[2] This was an extensive document of 128 pages in Japanese which examined the implications of the emergent takeover market in Japan and took as its starting point that:

Here in Japan, there is no common code of conduct in the business community with regard to what constitutes a non-abusive takeover and what constitutes a reasonable defensive measure ... Defensive measures against hostile takeovers, if they are used properly, can help enhance corporate value. But at the same time, there is a risk that defensive measures may be used to entrench corporate management.

This report examined the whole history and circumstances of takeovers in Japan and elsewhere before moving towards explicit recommendations.

The ministries' report was shorter and appeared to be derived from the CVSG document. It took the form of joint ministerial guidance to clarify the position on takeover defences and was entitled 'Guidelines regarding takeover defense for the purposes of protection

---

[2] We use the official indicative English translations for this and other Corporate Value Study Group reports, except in instances where no such translation exists.

and enhancement of corporate value and shareholders' common interests' (official title: *Kigyō kachi / kabunushi kyōdō no rieki no kakuho mata wa kōjō no tame no baishū bōei-saku ni kansuru shishin*) (the 'Guidelines'). In addition to their focus on 'protection and enhancement of corporate value and shareholders' common interests' the Guidelines sought to address the lack of consensus in Japan regarding what constituted a reasonable defensive measure in the event that a company's board received a takeover bid: their mission was 'to change the business community from one without rules concerning takeovers to one governed by fair rules applicable to all' (METI and MOJ, 2005). As a civil servant put it to us, they were a guide to assist boards in formulating responses to takeover attempts which would not overstep the limits that courts might be expected to impose. They were not seen as a precursor to future legislation. In one sense they were not designed to pre-empt the courts but in fact that is precisely what they did: 'At the end of the day this is a guideline – a guidance for people's reference – and it has no legal power of compulsion. But it sounds a warning bell for people at companies and is intended to make them understand that this is a topic where they need to make an effort not to be suspected of acting unlawfully.'

The Guidelines defined three main principles that were to be observed where defensive measures were under consideration:

1. Principle of preserving and increasing corporate value and shareholders' common interests (The adoption, implementation and termination of takeover defense measures should be undertaken with the goal of protecting and enhancing corporate value and, by extension, shareholders' common interests);
2. Principle of prior disclosure and shareholders' will (When takeover defense measures are adopted, their purpose and terms should be specifically disclosed and such measures should reflect the reasonable will of the shareholders); and
3. Principle of ensuring the necessity and reasonableness (Takeover defense measures that are adopted in response to a possible takeover threat must be necessary and reasonable in relation to the threat posed).

The Guidelines also noted the danger of managers using takeover defences to entrench their position and recommended the use of suitably experienced outsiders to evaluate any acquisition proposals: 'If provisions are included that give weight to the judgments of independent outside directors and auditors (independent outsiders) who are capable of closely monitoring any entrenchment behavior of inside directors, this should be effective in creating confidence among shareholders and the investment community that the decisions of the board of directors are fair.'

At the core of the Guidelines was the idea of 'corporate value' itself (*kigyō kachi*). This was defined as 'attributes of a corporation, such as assets, earnings power, financial soundness, effectiveness, and growth potential, etc., that contribute to the interests of the shareholders'. The Guidelines named shareholders as 'the real owners of a corporation' but defined their interests further as 'the interests of the shareholders as a whole' rather than the private interests of individual shareholders. Reference was made to the right of the company (*kabushiki kaisha*), rather than of the board, to defend itself should corporate value be threatened: 'Therefore, it is legitimate and reasonable for a joint-stock corporation to adopt defensive measures designed to protect and enhance shareholder interests by preventing certain shareholders from acquiring a controlling stake in the corporation.' The Guidelines implied that the board could defend the company against an unwelcome bid in circumstances where, even if shareholders might benefit financially from the terms of an offer, wider corporate value which contributed to their interests, as defined, would be undermined or destroyed. To this end, the Guidelines suggested a number of situations in which the use of takeover defences would be justified: these included greenmail, asset stripping, leveraged bids that sought to secure or repay debt with the company's assets, and effectively any acquisition by a bidder not interested in preserving the company over the longer term. This approach followed the classifications developed by the courts in the Livedoor litigation.

On 31 March 2006 the CVSG issued a further report entitled 'Corporate Value Report 2006: Toward the firm establishment of fair rules in the corporate community' (*Kigyō Kachi Hōkukusho 2006: Kigyō-shakai ni okeru kōsei na rūru no teichaku ni mukete*) (CVSG, 2006) which focused on disclosure of takeover defensive measures and listing rules; revisions of acquisition rules; and improving opportunities for communication between management and investors. Another report was issued on 2 August 2007 dealing specifically with issues arising from MBOs entitled *Kigyō kachi no kōjō oyobi kōsei na tetsuzuki kakuho no tame no keieisha ni yoru kigyō baishū (MBO) ni kansuru hōkokusho* ('Report on corporate acquisitions by management (MBOs) to promote the maintenance of equitable procedures which increase corporate value') (CVSG, 2007).

The Guidelines, as an at least semi-official document, had the greatest impact on the business community. As Milhaupt observed soon after their publication: 'The Takeover Guidelines, though technically nonbinding, are poised to have an immediate effect on Japan's institutional environment for corporate governance' (Milhaupt, 2005: 2200). The practical effect of the introduction of the idea of 'corporate value' was to legitimate takeover defences. Thus the boards of Myōjō Foods, Chūō Warehouse, Nōritz, Tenryū Saw, and Sapporo all spoke publicly of the need to preserve 'corporate value' when they rebuffed the approaches of activist hedge funds. When Hokuetsu published its rejection of Ōji's takeover offer in August 2006, just over a year after the issue of the Guidelines, it made no less than six references to 'corporate value' and 'the common interests of all shareholders' in combination, and two to 'corporate value' in isolation, in the course of a five-page defence document. Hokuetsu also emphasised that its defences were generally in accordance with the Guidelines (Hokuetsu, 2006). As the Guidelines had recommended, Hokuetsu's board set up an independent committee to evaluate Ōji's bid. It then went on to issue shares to friendly third parties at a discount of 20 per cent to the price offered by Ōji, thereby diluting Ōji's holdings and making its bid unfeasible, and effectively preventing the shareholders as a whole from deciding on the merits of Ōji's proposal. Yano, at the PFA, commented on these events to us soon after:

I think that this was a breach of fiduciary duty by the directors of Hokuetsu … This can be done just with a directors' decision in Japan – it's possible to increase capital through a big third-party allocation – and I think that the fact that this works in practice as a defensive strategy is a kind of hole in the Japanese system. The fact that these kinds of things can go through unhindered points to a lack of proper function in Japan with respect to the basic principles of joint stock companies and capitalist society. Well, this is something that one has to feel concerned about.

Notwithstanding doubts such as these, the phrase 'corporate value' appeared again in the judgments of the courts in the Bull-Dog Sauce litigation (see above in Chapter 9, and below in Section 10.5), where it was used to support the view that the company's warrants issue, which was designed explicitly to undermine Steel Partners' tender offer, was lawful. The CVSG issued a further report on 30 June 2008 (by now, its fourth) entitled *Kinji no sho-kankyō no henka o fumaeta baishū bōei-saku no arikata* (which was translated as 'Takeover defense measures in light of recent environmental changes' although 'arikata' usually implies a stronger meaning of 'the way that something should be') (CVSG, 2008). In April 2008 a change in the composition of the committee had been announced, replacing three of the six industrial members with two from the financial community so that nearly half of the committee now had a financial background of some kind. Dore observed that a change in the committee's tenor was to be expected (Dore, 2009: 146). The new report stressed that takeover defences were ultimately for the protection of shareholders; that hostile takeovers could have positive effects; that defences could deprive shareholders of opportunities to sell; and that defences to entrench management were unacceptable. It even noted that the independent committees on which so many takeover defences pivoted might not be an unassailable solution: 'There is an argument, however, that the responsibilities of such a committee are vague from the perspective of shareholders, and it should be recognized that formally establishing such a committee and following its recommendations will not immediately justify the decisions of the board of directors.'

Although this report appeared nearly one year after the Bull-Dog Sauce judgments, it was seen by some commentators as implicitly critical of them (Hayakawa and Whittaker, 2009: 85). It appeared to question the concept (which had not been proposed directly by any of the Bull-Dog Sauce judgments but could have been construed from them) that boards might discriminate freely against unwelcome shareholders as long as they could secure a majority shareholder vote to support them, observing in a footnote (footnote 5) that:

In the Supreme Court's decision on the Bull-Dog Sauce Co., Ltd. case (Supreme Court decision of August 7, 2007), the court ruled that 'when the gratis issue of stock acquisition rights to shareholders with differential terms is not for the purpose of maintaining corporate value and the interests of shareholders as a whole but mainly for the purpose of maintaining the control of directors managing the company or certain shareholders supporting such directors, such gratis issue of stock acquisition rights should in principle be understood as being issued according to a grossly unfair method'. The understanding that firm defense system can be established with the shareholder structure that would ensure formally passing a resolution of the general meeting of shareholders is inconsistent with these rulings in the judicial decision.

Dore observed a gradual retreat from the original emphasis on 'corporate value' in the CVSG's various reports (Dore, 2009: 159). However, the apparent element of shareholder value orientation in its 2008 report seems to have had little impact in practice. The successful countermeasures in the Hokuetsu and Bull-Dog Sauce cases had shown that takeover defences could be made to work in practice, and that a sufficiently determined board could use them to see off an unwelcome bid. In a commentary published on 7 June 2008 on whether the Guidelines issued by MOJ and METI might have affected the situation, *Nikkei* quoted Professor Ōsugi of Chūō University: 'They are being used in the fashion that happens to suit management' (Buchanan and Deakin, 2009: 54).

While not denying the Guidelines' impact, it is also important to put them into perspective. In our view, the Guidelines were a reaction to an underlying demand for protection by business rather than a decisive move by the bureaucracy. If there had been no Guidelines, the situation could well have proved more untidy but the basic determination of Japanese boards to defend their autonomy would still have created its own defences. Until the late 1990s, Japanese boards had two important ways to rebuff acquirers: stable shareholdings and dilution. Stable shareholdings, as we have seen, have not disappeared but have declined and are less reliable than they once were, while the rise of non-resident shareholders has introduced a further note of uncertainty. Dilution remained an option because most listed Japanese companies have authorised but unissued shares that can be issued at the board's discretion. Issue of these shares to accompany warrants only became possible from 2002 but previously they could be issued directly, as shares, to friendly parties. The courts had tended not to challenge boards' claims that new funds were genuinely needed for business purposes (the so-called *shuyō mokuteki rūru* or 'key objective rule'). But despite widespread complacence for many years among the business community regarding the courts' willingness to interpret this 'rule' loosely, there had been signs for some years that the situation was beginning to change. In 1989 dilutive tactics by Chūjitsuya and Inageya, two retailers which had attempted to block a takeover attempt from the real estate developer Shūwa by issuing stock cheaply to each other, had been prevented by the courts. Nine years later, in 1998, Madarame Rikihiro, founder and CEO of Nemic-Lambda, had been prevented by a court ruling from diluting his company's majority shareholder Siebe by issuing new shares (Huckaby, 1991; IIR, 1998). Subsequently, as discussed in Section 10.5 below, Nihon Broadcasting System was similarly prevented from diluting Livedoor's shareholding in 2005. A trusted defence mechanism had been found wanting and, although Bull-Dog Sauce's board subsequently prevailed with a related method in 2007, the circumstances of this case raised further doubts; boards that wished to preserve their autonomy needed more reliable methods to resist unwelcome acquirers. The Guidelines were clearly a convenient development but we see the most important influence here as being the general refusal of corporate boards to accept challenges to their autonomy and their determination to utilise any defences they could find.

METI's response to TCI's bid for J-Power

The nearest that activist hedge funds came to provoking a direct official reaction was when TCI requested permission to increase its shareholding in J-Power above the 10 per cent limit for individual non-resident shareholders, as described earlier in Chapter 9. Here, METI and the Ministry of Finance were responding to an application from TCI and acting within the parameters of existing legislation which had become an issue not because TCI was an activist investor but because it was a non-resident entity. However, the episode revealed official unease about the prospect of financial interests exercising influence over the strategies of companies which were deemed to be important to the national interest.

This concern was manifest from the very beginning, when Amari Akira, the same minister for METI who had expressed his doubts about Steel Partners' intentions at Sapporo, commented in a conference on 8 April 2008 that TCI's request to raise its stake in J-Power was different from similar cases, as it impacted both on public order and national security. A special sub-committee was convened to advise the ministries involved; this was a further indication that the J-Power situation was not an ordinary one. As the lawyer Nagasawa Tōru observed in an article in *Diamond Online*, shortly after the first ministerial *advice* to TCI not to proceed had been issued on 16 April 2008, 'in terms of procedure, the government side has taken a decision to consider whether or not to approve this shareholding increase under the Foreign Exchange Law, so there is no problem with the procedure at all'. However, as he pointed out in the same article, the real problem lay with the vagueness of the concerns expressed. Moreover, he noted, this was the first time that such a request had not quickly been approved (Diamond, 2008).

METI followed a publicised administrative process in this matter, in accordance with existing law and regulation, and the option to challenge its decision was available to TCI. As we noted earlier, an editorial in *Nikkei* had argued in February 2008 that invocation of the 'national interest' was not the best way to deal with TCI's desire to buy more J-Power shares. However, as we note later in Section 10.6, even the *Financial Times*' Lex column would subsequently concede that sensitivity over ownership of a nuclear power operator was not extraordinary by the standards of recent decisions relating to national interest in other countries.

In the event, the Subcommittee on Foreign Exchange and Other Transactions expressed disapproval of TCI's proposal, commenting critically on what it saw as TCI's 'short investment horizon'. Its conclusion that this would lead, in turn, to a quest for unreasonable short-term payouts was perhaps predictable since TCI had been arguing precisely for these ever since becoming a shareholder at J-Power. The Subcommittee apparently considered that with around 40 per cent of the total shareholding of J-Power then in foreign hands, an increase to 20 per cent in TCI's holding would put it in a position of effective control. The proposed increase might merely have absorbed existing shares held by non-residents but it could have resulted in a major increase in the net non-resident shareholding at J-Power. The Subcommittee's second point was that TCI might send nominees to J-Power's board and seek to influence strategy. This again was a response to TCI's own actions: it had earlier made several calls for external directors to be appointed at J-Power and had offered its own employees. The third point was that TCI's suggestion to segregate the nuclear business ran counter to the spirit of J-Power's recent privatisation. TCI had made this suggestion in order to make its approach seem less threatening; its offer of compromise was now being turned against it. The immediate message from this exchange was that from the point of view of the Subcommittee's members and the ministries it advised, TCI was not the sort of shareholder that was welcome at a Japanese company of national interest. However, Kawakami Keiichi at METI, speaking to the press following the initial decision in May, had stressed that Japan welcomed foreign investment and had noted that of 760 similar applications during the previous three years all had been approved within 30 days. He commented: 'Our concern about stable electricity supply never went away. That was our biggest concern' (Reuters, 2008).

As we have seen, TCI persisted in its efforts at J-Power and did not sell its shareholding until October 2008, after it had failed to win sufficient support from other shareholders to have its proposals adopted at the June AGM. However, this official rebuff was a severe discouragement. The ministries had not volunteered their views before TCI required them to do so by virtue of its application for permission to increase its shareholding but their final response, through the Subcommittee, had been officially to reject the concept of a hedge fund gaining power to influence any company that performed a function of national economic importance.

10.5 The courts

The courts are usually an expensive last resort for parties in a commercial dispute. In the USA, generally seen as a litigious environment, Brav *et al.* found that the hedge funds in their sample resorted to litigation in only 5.4 per cent of the cases studied (Brav *et al.*, 2008a: 1743). However, actual or threatened litigation is a useful lever for funds in situations where they find that their arguments are being frustrated or ignored, and they have taken their disputes to the courts in Japan. In doing so they entered a legal system which focuses on the social implications of each case as much as on the detail of the law. As Haley described it, judges, in common with other official players in Japan, 'see themselves as enforcing legal rules that serve the broad interests of the public in general and those groups whose loyalty and support is the most crucial. In the process, legal rules as enforced will similarly over time move toward community norms' (Haley, 1998: 210–11).

We are aware of five notable instances of litigation by activist funds during the period we are studying: the Murakami Fund's litigation against Tokyo Style's board in May 2004; the injunction sought by the SFP Value Realization Master Fund ('SFP') against Nireco's proposed anti-takeover defence in June 2005; Dalton's litigation against Sun Telephone regarding its board procedures for a discounted equity warrants issue in June 2006; Steel Partners' attempts to block Bull-Dog Sauce's dilutive defence measures between June and August 2007; and Silchester's attempt to prevent Autobacs Seven from issuing warrants to a third party with allegedly insufficient explanation in November 2007. Of these five examples, the Murakami Fund failed to win its lawsuit but was ultimately successful in obtaining a settlement in 2005, perhaps through threats of further litigation; SFP obtained its injunction and a higher court subsequently rejected an appeal by Nireco; Dalton obtained an injunction; Steel Partners' suits were rejected; and Silchester failed to obtain an injunction but was subsequently vindicated when the contentious warrants issue was abandoned amid doubts as to the purchaser's ability to pay. The lawsuits by the Murakami Fund, Dalton, and Silchester all dealt with alleged failures to observe formally determined procedures by the boards of the companies concerned. The lawsuits by SFP and Steel addressed the wider and more controversial question of the nature of minority shareholders' rights in Japan and the degree to which boards might impede them.

SFP's experience against the board of Nireco was a demonstration that the Japanese courts were willing to block egregious discrimination against shareholders. On 14 March 2005 Nireco's board had announced an anti-takeover defence to be triggered if any shareholder accumulated more than 20 per cent of its shares, citing the need to protect corporate value from 'abusive acquirers' in an environment where cross-shareholdings were declining. The mechanism of defence was to be a free distribution of non-transferable warrants valid for three years from June 2005 made only to shareholders registered as at 31 March 2005, at two warrants per share held, each warrant entitling the holder to purchase one new share at ¥1 in the event that the board decided to permit exercise, probably but not necessarily guided by an independent committee. The board reserved the right to deny exercise to shareholders considered to be greenmailers or otherwise likely to harm the company. SFP, which had held 6.92 per cent of Nireco since

November 2004 and was the most likely target of this defence measure, obtained an injunction to prevent the warrants issue from the Tokyo District Court on 1 June; a subsequent objection and an appeal against this decision to the Tokyo High Court on 15 June were both dismissed. The Tokyo District Court's decision stated that Nireco's board had not fulfilled any of the three requirements that the judge considered would normally justify defence measures: approval by the shareholders in general meeting, prevention of selfish implementation by the board, or causing loss to shareholders unconnected with any acquisition. The judge also criticised the warrants proposal in other respects, such as the vagueness of its criteria for defining unwelcome shareholders and the board's intention not to be bound by the independent committee's advice. The Tokyo High Court supported this decision, emphasising that the lack of consultation with shareholders made this defence measure inequitable (Tokyo District Court, 2005; Tokyo High Court, 2005b).

This was a successful outcome for SFP. Nireco's board was unable to proceed with its defence plan. Shimizu and Igi (translated by Kodama), commenting on the Tokyo District Court's decision soon afterwards, observed:

> It would be completely natural to regard the Nireco poison pill as a failure if one were to focus upon the final result in the courtroom. However, when viewed within the larger transition occurring within Japanese corporate governance, the Nireco poison pill also could be interpreted as a bold maneuver by a Japanese firm prompted by sheer necessity. And at some point in the future, it will probably be regarded as fulfilling a necessary role in the development of corporate defense measures for the practical lessons gleaned from the ensuing litigation. (Shimizu and Igi, 2007: 629)

The larger transition to which they referred was manifest particularly in two developments chronologically just on either side of the Nireco affair. The first of these was Livedoor's litigation to prevent the board of Nippon Broadcasting System from issuing dilutive warrants, which involved three hearings in March 2005. Prior to the Livedoor litigation, as we have seen, this tactic had often succeeded, although the Nemic Lambda case was a warning precedent. The final judgment in this case, delivered by the Tokyo High Court on 23 March 2005, defined the directors as 'persons fundamentally in receipt of the trust of the shareholders, who are the owners of the company' but, as we have seen, went on to accept that dilutive tactics might be employed against greenmailers, those seeking to plunder intellectual assets, those seeking to use the acquired target as security for other schemes, or asset-strippers. In such cases, where the acquirer had 'abusive' objectives, defensive action would be permissible, although the mere fact that the acquirer had adopted a hostile stance would not be sufficient (Tokyo High Court, 2005a).

The Nireco warrants issue had been announced only days before this decision and would surely have been formulated differently if Nireco's lawyers had been able to study it while they drafted the conditions. The presiding judge in the Livedoor case gave an interview in February 2006, after his retirement from the judiciary, in which he set out his understanding of shareholders' rights as follows (cited in Miyake, 2007: 166–71):

Shareholders have rights such as the right to submit proposals and to vote at shareholders' meetings. When it comes to participation in running the business, the furthest extent of their rights, if they assert themselves, is to change the board. Defensive measures that invalidate this kind of right cannot be permitted because they threaten shareholders' most basic position.

His approach can be thought of as impeccably orthodox, in emphasising, first, that shareholders' rights do not extend to a right to run the business and, second, that their right to replace the board should not be interfered with by management for the sake of its own protection. But he further commented:

In the case of an acquirer who is battening onto the company and is seeking to impair the profit of the shareholders as a whole, defensive measures are permissible. The responsibility to demonstrate that this kind of acquirer is involved rests with the target. However, even if one tries to prove that the acquirer's objectives, or whatever, are unreasonable, in practice it is quite possible that it will be difficult to make a judgement on this. I think that in future it will become a major point of contention for the courts whether in practice the duty of proof should move to the acquiring side.

The second development, which was not a court judgment but which was nevertheless to have a discernible influence on the development of the law, was the publication of the Corporate Value Study Group's Guidelines on 27 May 2005, which we have discussed already in this chapter in the context of the official reaction to hedge fund activism. The Guidelines' focus on 'corporate value' and 'shareholders' common interests' provided vocabulary not only for corporate boards and their lawyers but also for the courts. The effect of adopting the Guidelines, in contrast to more specific legislation on the subject of takeover defences, was to give the courts greater leeway to develop the law. The Guidelines drew on some of the distinctions between legitimate and illegitimate takeover defences first developed in the USA in the 1980s; a third of the members of the CVSG were academic lawyers who were familiar with the jurisprudence of the Delaware courts. By drawing on Delaware case law in this way, the CVSG implicitly invited the Japanese courts to become involved in contests for corporate control (Milhaupt, 2009: 357). At the same time, the emphasis in the CVSG's reports on 'corporate value' and 'shareholders' common interests' – implying that individual shareholders should defer to the common interest – created an effective alternative to shareholder value as a benchmark for evaluating takeover defences. It also suggested an emphasis on board autonomy in the face of shareholder pressure that went beyond Delaware's qualified support for poison pills (Hayakawa and Whittaker, 2009: 85). Where the Livedoor judgment by the Tokyo District Court in 2005 had referred frequently to 'corporate value' but only twice to 'shareholders' interests' rather than their 'common interests' (a pattern repeated by the Tokyo High Court in its judgment on the Livedoor case), the Bull-Dog Sauce judgments in 2007 referred frequently to both 'corporate value' and 'shareholders' common interests', often in tandem as a set phrase, almost exactly reproducing the phrasing of the Guidelines. Although the Guidelines used the expression 'abusive' mostly in the context of abuse of the board's powers, the Livedoor judge's prediction that the burden of proof would shift to the acquiring side largely came true in that 'abusive acquirer' became a stock expression to describe unwelcome acquirers. The Tokyo District Court used the expression in its Bull-Dog Sauce judgment, though not explicitly to describe Steel Partners and mostly in its review of submissions from Bull-Dog Sauce's lawyers, but the Tokyo High Court used it throughout and explicitly named Steel Partners as such, making clear the judge's view that discrimination against such an acquirer was justified.

A financial commentator to whom we spoke in early 2008 focused on this as the most controversial element of the Tokyo High Court's judgment:

The basic idea of the judgment is correct but it was a mistake to say that Steel Partners were abusive acquirers ... The scheme of it – the framework of the judgment – is universally correct, and so the mistake is in the application of it. Moreover, the part of Steel Partners' activity that was emphasised is wrong. So now everyone ignores the argument that Steel Partners were abusive acquirers. Most legal specialists and people connected with the market in Japan all say that it was a stupid judgment.

After the Bull-Dog Sauce judgments, target companies now knew that they could use the tactic of issuing dilutive warrants against an activist which did not have majority shareholder support. They could also deploy the 'pre-warning' poison pill to deflect pressure from an acquirer that did not have a refined plan for the development of the company's business. A plan to realise shareholder value through asset sales and share buy-backs would not suffice for this purpose. Above all, it was now possible to assume that an activist hedge fund focused solely on short-term returns would be labelled an abusive acquirer, with little hope of success in the courts.

10.6 The media in Japan and overseas

The wave of activist interventions that peaked in 2007 was widely reported in the Japanese popular media as well as in the financial press, and was discussed in the financial press in the USA and the UK. Some of this media commentary was a balanced account of events but some was more partisan. In Japan, the popular media tended to show activist hedge funds in an unflattering light as part of an undefined wave of speculators, creating a climate of opinion hostile to hedge fund activism. However, the financial press was more neutral in its coverage and there were some expressions of support for the financial ideas that were being promoted. The American and British financial press was generally dismissive of Japanese corporate governance and represented the activist hedge funds as proponents of overdue reform.

Popular media coverage in Japan

Wide media coverage ensured awareness that 'funds' were active in the Japanese market and the fact that they were perceived to be both foreign and disruptive did not help their image. A director of a private equity fund, which had no activist links, offered his view on how these funds were perceived:

... they don't have a very good image, generally speaking. 'What do they think they're doing?' is the general reaction. However, it obviously varies from person to person; there are those who are pleased when these funds come in and raise dividends, and at the same time there are those who think this business of making tender offers is appalling. Some feel that manage-ment were sleeping on the job and doing nothing so they needed a shock like this. I think there are all sorts of different views. But the general opinion from most Japanese people is: 'What's going on?' I think that most ordinary people see them as suddenly becoming shareholders, raising all sorts of mat-ters and disturbing the management.

A similar view was expressed by an officer at a body responsible for market infrastructure, who also noted the tendency to suspect these funds of links with murkier interests:

So it's really not clear what is going on. The impression that ordinary people like us have is that no one knows the true nature of these funds, so all these questions of whether these people have an activist history or whatever sort of history is all mixed up together, you see. The idea of 'funds' is all wrapped up together.

A key element in the nature of the general reaction was this aspect of confusion. As we have observed, even some boards were not ini-tially sure what the nature and motivations of the activist hedge funds were, or how they differed from corporate raiders or greenmailers. For the general public, the situation was even more confusing. In many ways the funds were seen as one more manifestation of the apparent collapse of the old economic order during the 1990s, in the course of which many hitherto admired institutions and practices had been found wanting.

In 2000 a group of investors led by the US private equity firm Ripplewood had purchased the distressed Long Term Credit Bank from the Japanese government for approximately ¥121,000 million and re-launched it as Shinsei Bank. Tensions arose when Shinsei Bank took advantage of contractual obligations undertaken by the government at the time of the sale to sell back certain distressed loans when their value fell below agreed limits,[3] resulting ultimately in the collapse of companies which were household names, including the Sogō Department Store and the Dai-ichi Hotel chain. Subsequently, in 2004, the bank raised ¥230,000 million in an IPO, realising a handsome profit for Ripplewood and its fellow investors. Although Ripplewood had not infringed any laws or agreements, there was a general feeling that foreign investors had battened onto the Japanese market and grown fat on the proceeds. As Nonomiya Hiroshi, Managing Director of Ripplewood Japan, observed at a Research Institute of Economy, Trade and Industry (RIETI) symposium in November 2002, 'there is always an allergy towards foreign – or apparently foreign – investment and I think it is hard to escape from this' (Nonomiya, 2002). Ripplewood continued to make a series of investments in Japan without arousing public disquiet thereafter but the unfolding of the Shinsei Bank affair at much the same time that the Murakami Fund and Steel Partners were attracting attention encouraged the view that 'funds' were targeting Japanese industry and commerce at a time of weakness.

In this context of growing public disquiet, some of the hedge funds' tactics backfired. The use of tender offers by Steel Partners encouraged the view of activist hedge funds as corporate raiders and asset strippers, a view which, as we have seen, even seems to have influenced the courts. Novels such as Ushijima Shin's *Daisan no Baishū* ('The Third Acquisition'), serialised in *President* magazine from January 2006 and subsequently published as a book in 2007, described the human tensions released by an audacious MBO proposal, and offered a counter-view of the business as a community belonging to its workforce, although the only foreign fund that enters the plot does so in a benign role. Mayama Jin's novels *Hagetaka* ('Vulture') and *Buyout*, published in 2006, were combined and adapted for a popular NHK drama series in 2007, also called *Hagetaka*. This described an imaginary transaction in which US-inspired buyout industry tactics clashed with traditional Japanese values.

---

[3] Defined as falling more than 20 per cent in value within three years.

Cases in which funds intervened to defend shareholders' interests against an apparently entrenched and aloof management were viewed more favourably. Following the failure of Tokyo Kohtetsu's board to secure approval of a special resolution for the merger with Osaka Seitetsu in the face of opposition organised by Ichigo Asset Management at Tokyo Kohtetsu's AGM, a private shareholder expressed his dissatisfaction with the board's attitude to the press after the meeting: 'Why do they have to bully minority shareholders like this? I'm glad the proposal was defeated' (Nikkei, 2007x). Similarly, as we have noted, Dalton's emphasis on MBOs and Perry's focus on the issue of subsidiary listings that had already attracted concern among the Japanese investment community appear to have protected them from some of the unfavourable comments received by Steel Partners and TCI.

Thus the main objection to foreign activist hedge funds in the public mind was that they single-mindedly pursued short-term financial profit, thereby threatening the livelihoods of employees and the well-being of customers. When, by contrast, the funds focused their efforts on companies that were seen to be underperforming, and a threat to employees and customers was less apparent, they received some support from the wider public and the media.

Press coverage in Japan

In the Japanese financial press, the shareholder value perspective pursued by the funds was by no means rejected out of hand. *Nikkei* commented, in the context of the Yushiro intervention in early 2004, that Steel Partners were not greenmailers, and that their kind of external intervention could prove a useful stimulus to managements that neglected their companies' share price (Nikkei, 2004c). On the other hand, some of Steel Partners' takeover bid tactics, in particular, attracted criticism even from the financial press. A foreign commentator described the general situation regarding Japanese media coverage at the time of the Myōjō intervention that came to a head in late 2006 as follows: 'The media coverage has been fairly awful, I have to say – it hasn't been helpful at all. Smaller companies often have no clue why they have been targeted. And media doesn't contribute: it is all "foreigners going after the food industries".'

Some sectors of the press expressed support for what the foreign activist hedge funds were trying to achieve. A director of an activist hedge fund felt that journalists at Japanese publications specialising in financial analysis had generally been willing to listen to his fund's arguments. He explained this in early 2008 in the particular context of a recent magazine article and more general coverage by *Nikkei*:

I think there is a pent-up demand for change and people know deep down inside that what we are doing – we may be brash, we may be a bit impertinent – but what we are doing is right and in some way very good for Japan and much needed for Japan to revitalise itself ... If you have a quick read of the [magazine] article it says: 'These guys are basically right'. You have people starting to say that. You have *Nikkei* saying that we are basically reasonable guys ...

Nikkei, in the editorial of 14 February 2008 on the subject of TCI's application to METI that we referred to earlier, which was entitled 'Is the bureaucracy seeking to open up Japan or close it off?', criticised the Japanese civil service strongly for its stance and urged it to take a more positive attitude to reform. The editorial queried METI's attitude, in advance of its final decision on TCI's application to increase its J-Power shareholding, and commented: 'There are all sorts of reasons for this and perhaps one cannot say that it is completely mistaken. However, the overall picture that emerges is of an introspective posture that pays too much attention to the profits of the established industrial community and shrinks from bold reform' (Nikkei, 2008aa).

Commentary on the disagreements between TCI and J-Power's board in Japanese financial publications tended to include at least some elements of support for TCI. In the January 2008 edition of *Sentaku* a commentator observed: 'certainly there are plenty of points where they have misunderstood the situation but the fact is that TCI's arguments include criticisms and pointers that identify structural problems within the Japanese electrical power sector' (Sentaku, 2008: 71). An article by Ōmae Kenichi, former head of McKinsey in Japan, in *Shūkan Post* ('Weekly Post') criticised the responses of J-Power's board to TCI, linked the case to wider issues about Japan's need to attract foreign investment, and said: 'What TCI are saying is sensible. Never mind that they are demanding this as activists: I think this is "global common sense"' (Weekly Post, 2008: 65).

Similarly, when Steel Partners orchestrated the removal of Aderans' board in May 2008, instead of accusing the fund of interfering in the

management of a Japanese company, *Nikkei* observed that Aderans'
management was to blame for its own predicament, having failed
to deliver on repeated promises for improved performance, and presented the affair as a demonstration that 'it is not the management
that chooses shareholders but shareholders that choose management'
(Nikkei, 2008l, 2008m).

Press coverage outside Japan

The reactions of the US and UK press tended to support the position
of the activist funds. The Asian edition of *The Wall Street Journal* published an article in April 2004 entitled 'Steel Partners' bold moves rattle
Japanese firms' which consisted mainly of a factual account but managed to imply that a dynamic investor was shaking the complacency of
inefficient Japanese management (AWSJ, 2004). In an article published
in June 2008 entitled 'Corporate Japan needs the activist touch', the
Financial Times commented: 'Japan needs activist shareholders more
than they need Japan. This is because the one thing activists can do in
Japan that others are not doing is to help unlock the intrinsic value of
inefficiently managed companies, thereby increasing their returns and
boosting returns to all shareholders' (FT, 2008a).

On 16 April 2008, *The New York Times* commented on METI's initial refusal of TCI's application to increase its shareholding in J-Power
to 20 per cent: 'The rejection is the latest in a series of setbacks for
foreign investors in Japan that have raised questions about the country's commitment to welcoming foreign investment and business.
Recently Japan has appeared adrift in economic policy, seeming to
waver between embracing the global economy, and erecting barriers
to keep it out' (NYT, 2008). The *Financial Times* published a leader
on 18 April 2008 that was generally hostile to J-Power's management,
and commented on this matter in a way that appeared to presume
that its board was complacent and inefficient, although no proof was
offered. It concluded: 'The Japanese government, meanwhile, needs to
decide which is the greater long-term threat to national prosperity and
security: allowing a foreign investor to own 20 per cent of an electrical
utility, or allowing management of Japanese companies to continue to
waste precious capital on low-return empire building' (FT, 2008d).

However, in the course of 2008 this support began to wane. *The
Independent* published the following comment on 26 April 2008,

following METI's initial decision and TCI's expression of disappointment, which included an implication that it planned to seek the assistance of the UK authorities in putting pressure on the Japanese government through trade sanctions:

The UK government should have no truck with Chris Hohn's ridiculous demand that trade sanctions be imposed on Japan in support of his so far thwarted bid to raise his stake in J-Power to 20 per cent. There are no doubt plenty of issues affecting Japan it is worth going to the barricades over, but Mr. Hohn's unedifying attempt to asset-strip one of Japan's leading power utilities is not one of them. (Independent, 2008)

Soon after this, the Lex column of the *Financial Times* queried TCI's persistence in demanding increased distributions from J-Power. It did not question TCI's arguments for a change of strategy at J-Power, but argued in an open letter to Hohn on 28 May 2008, presented as though coming from his own investment clients, that TCI was not pursuing a sensible investment policy by maintaining its efforts in the face of combined resistance from J-Power's management and the Japanese authorities:

We support plans to improve returns by upping debt and dividends and slashing cross-shareholdings. But may we humbly suggest that further efforts to force change on an unyielding management might prove as fruitless as the attempt to lift your stake to 20 per cent earlier this year? It was a safe bet that, in a world where French yoghurt and American ports are off limits, Tokyo might frustrate a big foreign holding in a company building a nuclear plant. (FT, 2008h)

As the reality of the global financial crisis became clearer, activist hedge funds provided less news on which to comment from Japan and the American and British financial press appears to have fallen silent about the inadequacy of corporate governance and the need to raise shareholder value in Japan.

10.7 Conclusion

In this chapter we have reviewed reactions to hedge fund activism. We first considered the responses of managers and investors, the two most immediately affected groups. The intransigence of boards and the indifference of most shareholders to the hedge funds' strategies were the main obstacles to their success. Some boards were initially willing to listen to the funds' arguments with an open mind, but their cooperation stopped once they discerned that the funds' objective was immediate financial gain rather than the long-term success of the company's business. After some early victories, the funds became increasingly hindered by managerial resistance. Even their successes at small companies took the form of payments to buy off an unwelcome presence, rather than triggering changes in corporate direction and strategy. When interventions were attempted at larger companies, more sophisticated and resourceful management proved adept at countering them. Listed companies progressively adopted anti-takeover defences which, while superficially similar to American 'poison pills', were intended to operate as a total deterrent against opportunistic hostile takeovers and were subsequently deployed to obstruct hedge fund interventions. Running through all these responses was the conviction that financial considerations should not dominate the practice of corporate governance, and that a clear distinction should be drawn between shareholders' financial interests and the sustainability of the company's business over the longer term. While it was predictable that management would take this position, the perspective was shared also by many shareholders, who viewed their investments in relational terms rather than purely as a financial portfolio, and were accordingly disposed to support the board. Foreign shareholders were more likely to support activist interventions, but they did not always do so and in many companies they were not sufficiently numerous to have a decisive voice.

We then looked at the responses of actors who were less immediately affected but whose attitudes were important because of their official powers. The response of politicians and the civil service to hedge fund activism did not take the form of specific regulation or legislation. Instead, the Guidelines, originally stimulated by purely domestic acquisition activity, developed into a primer for boards that wished to resist unwelcome shareholders such as activist hedge funds and influenced the courts in the same direction. When TCI provoked an official response to its arguments for a larger shareholding in a company of national importance it was rebuffed by METI's Subcommittee primarily not as a non-resident but as an unsuitable holder of such shares. When arguments about the legitimacy of the funds' interventions were brought before the courts, it was made clear that the practices of the community firm had resonance within the legal system. In the judgments issued in the course of the Bull-Dog Sauce litigation, companies were defined as being more than just sources of profit for their shareholders, and the objective of maintaining the long-run growth of the firm was seen as taking priority over short-term financial concerns. In the Bull-Dog Sauce judgments, the courts moved away from the qualified shareholder-value approach which had seemed possible after the Livedoor and Nireco cases and identified with the values of the community firm.

The reaction of the media in Japan was a mixture of popularisation and factual reporting. Although the popular media tended to portray 'funds' in a generalised and often negative light, the Japanese financial press reported events in a mostly balanced fashion throughout the period of our study, often acknowledging the logic of funds' demands or questioning official responses. The American and British financial press, by contrast, frequently preferred to promote shareholder primacy as a simple solution to the assumed defects of Japanese corporate governance. However, by the end of 2008, fewer newsworthy events were happening and general interest in hedge fund activism in Japan appeared to have decreased. Sustained by the apparent lesson of the financial crisis that financial capitalism and shareholder primacy were flawed objectives, Japan's rejection of confrontational activism across boards, investors, officials, and the courts, now seemed complete.

11 | *'Quiet activism': the future for shareholder engagement in Japan?*

11.1 Introduction

In the three preceding chapters we have examined hedge fund activism in Japan during most of the first decade of the twenty-first century. In Chapter 8 we analysed hedge fund activism in a broad sense, initially as captured by Thomson Reuters data, and then moved to consider first those funds that attracted public attention for one reason or another (the 'public' funds) before focusing on the more confrontational of them. In Chapter 9 we examined two interventions that proved to be turning points in the experience of hedge fund activism in Japan. In Chapter 10 we reviewed the responses to hedge fund activism, both in a general sense but especially with regard to the confrontational variety because this provoked the greatest public debate in Japan between advocates of the community firm's values and those who promoted the shareholder primacy approach to corporate governance. By 2010, publicly confrontational hedge fund activism seemed to have stopped. But this is not the only style of concerted engagement available to shareholders. Shareholder activism continues in Japan, but in a different form from the confrontational style which we have noted here. Some of the funds pursuing a quieter strategy were doing so all along; others have recently switched from a more adversarial approach. In this chapter we look at this alternative style of engagement, which we call 'quiet activism', and consider its implications for the future of corporate governance in Japan.

11.2 Continuing shareholder activism in the Japanese market

The period from 2000 to 2008 in Japan can be seen as an interlude during which confrontational shareholder activism erupted on to the market, caused turmoil at some targeted companies and attracted widespread attention, and then lost momentum until it faded away in the face of concerted opposition from the business community and the harsher climate of the global financial crisis. The various vehicles known as the Murakami Fund, which epitomised this approach among Japanese funds, were wound up in 2006. As we have seen, some of Murakami Yoshiaki's former colleagues continued to invest in the Japanese market from Singapore through Effissimo Capital Management but maintained a lower profile. Of the principal foreign funds that practiced this style of activism, Steel Partners had reduced the number and value of their investments and appeared not to have launched any fresh interventions since 2008, giving the impression that they retained many investments more for lack of a viable exit strategy than because they were still pressing for changes to unlock new value, and had only one investment above 5 per cent outstanding by early 2011; and TCI had made no further publicised investments in Japan after it sold its shareholding in J-Power in 2008 for several years (as we explain below, it had invested in Japan Tobacco by March 2010 but this did not attract attention until June 2011). Of the other three funds that we characterised as 'public', Perry had not made any investments in Japan of which we are aware since its exit from NEC Electronics in 2008 and only Ichigo and, to some extent, Dalton appeared to be committed to the Japanese market. Neither of these funds, as we observed in Chapter 8, had adopted confrontational strategies specifically to extract cash from Japanese targets, and both had sought to avoid giving the impression of a fund in search of purely financial gain at the expense of the target's non-shareholder stakeholders.

Figures 11.1 and 11.2 provide a comparison between 2007 and 2010 of the number of investments and the estimated capital outlays made by the five funds we have characterised here as 'public'.

From these comparisons we can see how Steel Partners' exposure to Japan had fallen, both in terms of number of investments and capital outlay. TCI decreased in terms of capital outlay but remained the same in unit terms because of the Japan Tobacco investment, which at the end of 2010 was being handled more privately than TCI's earlier investment in J-Power. Dalton and Perry are shown here to have no exposure at the end of 2010. In Perry's case we believe that this situation is still the same at the time of writing (August 2011) but we know from EDINET data that Dalton made at least two new investments in

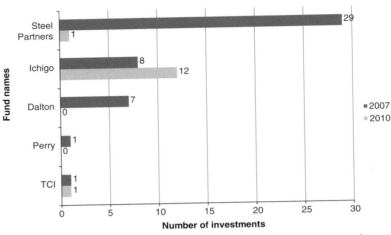

Figure 11.1 The five 'public' funds by number of investments comparing end 2007 to end 2010 (source: Thomson Reuters, EDINET)

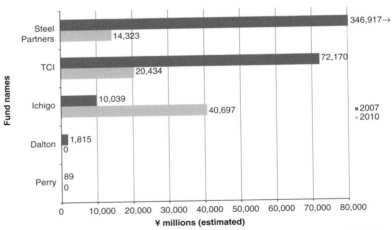

Figure 11.2 The five 'public' funds by capital outlay comparing end 2007 to end 2010 (source: Thomson Reuters, EDINET)

excess of 5 per cent during 2011, demonstrating that it is still present in the market. Ichigo, which was ranked as 'public' because of the attention it attracted through its Tokyo Kohtetsu investment but does not appear to have to have done so since, is the exception among these five funds: at the end of 2010 it had increased both the number and the capital value of its investments.

What is perhaps more significant is the large number of funds that have continued to invest in the Japanese market without attracting much public attention. Just as it did in 2007, Tower remained an important investor in 2010; in December 2007 we traced 42 investments in excess of 5 per cent by Tower with a capital value of ¥25,040 million, and in 2010 we traced 18 such investments with a capital value of ¥21,018 million, and there were probably many more below the 5 per cent limit for declaration. As explained in Chapter 8, it would seem that this firm is not overtly activist. Two other funds, Sparx Asset Management ('Sparx') and Taiyo Pacific Partners, operating as Taiyo Fund Management Co LLC ('Taiyo'), are not included in Thomson Reuters' database of activist funds, but were significant investors in Japan throughout the 2000s. As we have noted, these two funds were selected by CalPERS to handle an increasingly large part of its actively selected Japanese investments after 2003. Sparx had numerous investments in predominantly smaller companies at the end of both December 2007 and December 2010 and it would hold a predominant position in Figure 11.1 (number of investments) but a slightly lower position in Figure 11.2 (capital outlay) if it were included. Sparx, like Tower, is believed by market participants to operate mainly as a stock-picking 'value fund', which would generally not interfere in strategic matters but would wait until the company's intrinsic strengths had been reflected in a higher share price or the ability to fund higher payouts to shareholders. However, in 2007 it played an active part in calling for reinstatement of the president of the camera manufacturer Pentax, where it held a 24 per cent shareholding, when he was dismissed by a faction on the board that opposed a proposed merger with the optics company Hoya (FT, 2007e), a merger which went ahead in 2008. Taiyo is an American fund specialising in the Japanese market. In May 2011 its website described its approach as 'friendly activism' and emphasised that it 'works with management to protect, unlock, and create value'. We identified nine investments by Taiyo outstanding at the end of December 2007 and ten at the end of December 2010.

These data suggest that although public or confrontational activism had declined between 2008 and 2010, there was still a considerable amount of investment by hedge funds which can be described as activist to some extent: at the end of 2010, the Japanese market was evidently still attracting investors that perceived opportunities to obtain good returns from improvements at particular companies. However, these 'activists' were not publicly seeking to impose strategies on the boards of their targets, whatever might have been happening in private. Hedge fund activism in Japan no longer seemed to fit the template established by the Murakami Fund and Steel Partners.

Although some of the funds operating in Japan in this period seemed to be conducting their activism at a level that was barely detectable, closer to the 'value' end of the spectrum, there were others which were more clearly following an activist agenda, albeit one that favoured private engagement over public confrontation. Symphony Financial Partners ('SFP'), operating through a Cayman Islands vehicle called The SFP Value Realization Fund, were instrumental in two transactions which allowed them to sell their shareholdings at premia over the market: in June 2010 Marktec, a manufacturer of non-destructive testing materials, completed an MBO into which SFP sold their 18.14 per cent shareholding, and in March 2011 Hitachi Medical acquired Aloka, a manufacturer of medical equipment in which SFP held 9.0 per cent. SFP were involved in earlier buyouts and had sold into share buy-back schemes at companies in which they invested during the past several years, suggesting that they were able to shape corporate policies to some extent in their favour at the companies in which they invested. Surprisingly little attention was paid to these developments in the Japanese financial press which suggests first that they were achieved without public disagreement and second that there might have been more transactions of this kind taking place largely unnoticed. This lack of publicity does not mean that SFP were passive investors. As we have seen, they took legal action against the board of Nireco in 2005 to frustrate one of Japan's first examples of a 'poison pill' and challenged the board of Matsuya in May 2010 when they lodged a shareholder proposal – which proved unsuccessful – to remove anti-takeover defences (FT, 2010b; Nikkei, 2010). Interestingly, the *Nikkei* article reported the result of Matsuya's AGM vote without even naming SFP. What this suggests is that during the period of our study there was a middle layer of activist hedge funds which avoided public aggression but pursued a clearly activist strategy which could lead to public confrontation on occasions.

The same pattern of mostly private engagement with only occasional recourse to public action can be seen among some value funds which do not accept the description 'activist' and are not viewed in the market as confrontational. One example is Silchester International Investors, which described itself on its website (www.silchester.com) in August 2011 in the following terms: 'We see ourselves as value investors, working with the broad concept of "owning good companies at fair prices and fair companies at good prices"' but nevertheless took legal action against Autobacs Seven in 2007. Another example is Brandes Investment Partners ('Brandes'), a US investment manager and major investor in Japanese companies which did not appear in Thomson Reuters' database of funds with an 'activist orientation'. Brandes' main website (www.brandes.com) stated in August 2011, as part of the firm's '100 Year Vision': 'When it comes to results, value investing emphasizes the accumulation of wealth over the long term versus the pursuit of potentially fleeting short-term gains.' It had the equivalent of US$10,400 million, or nearly 23 per cent of its total assets under management, invested in Japan as at 31 March 2011. As its own policy statement suggests, Brandes was not considered in the market to be a confrontational investor but, between early 2007 and early 2009, its Japanese website showed that it issued public communications calling for higher payouts at four companies in which it was investing, triggering an immediate interest in the Japanese press. The incidence of articles mentioning Brandes in *Nikkei* rose from a maximum of two per year during the period 2000–6 to 20 in 2007, 14 in 2008, and 13 in 2009 before falling back to zero from the beginning of 2010 until the end of July 2011. Two of these exercises appear to have ended in compromises whereby Brandes reached agreement with the targeted boards over limited concessions and withdrew its formal demands. When we discussed these events with Brandes' officers they pointed out that these were only four cases among a much wider spread of investments by Brandes in Japan, many of which involved regular engagements with boards. They commented that although Brandes preferred to conduct discussions in private, there would always be exceptional situations where a degree of publicity might be appropriate to call the attention of other shareholders to the issues and made the further point that the interest of the Japanese press had probably been aroused by the novelty of seeing Brandes taking public positions in this way as much as by the content of Brandes' proposals.

Confrontational activism had not entirely disappeared from the Japanese market after 2008. On 9 June 2011, TCI was reported by the

Financial Times to have acquired a 1 per cent shareholding in Japan Tobacco and to have written to the Finance Ministry, which owned 50.01 per cent of the company, to raise concerns about its performance. The same article quoted the partner concerned at TCI, Oscar Veldhuijzen, as stating that Japan Tobacco was clearly being mismanaged. The initial reaction of some commentators was pessimistic. In the same article the *Financial Times* reported the views of an unnamed investor in Japan who said: 'They are going after the same people that will never listen', as well as those of Oguchi Toshiaki, representative director of Governance for Owners Japan, an organisation closely involved in monitoring corporate governance and board attitudes, who was quoted as saying: 'It's not what they say but the way they say it that was not accepted in Japan. So why are they doing it again?' (FT, 2011d).

TCI had opened a website entitled 'Japan Tobacco – the case for change' ('*JT o kaeyō*') where it invited other shareholders to register their support for its proposals. These were formulated in a related 13-page document dated June 2011 as three options involving different degrees of share buy-backs and dividend increases. The main thrust of TCI's criticism was that because Japan Tobacco's board was reducing debt rather than increasing returns to shareholders, even though finance was currently available at an interest rate of around 1 per cent p.a., and was investing in unproductive peripheral businesses rather than returning cash to shareholders, its poor cash management was depressing the company's share price compared with those of competitors, thereby destroying value for its whole shareholder base, including the government – and thus the public finances – of Japan (TCI, 2011a). These points were summarised in a letter dated 3 June 2011 sent to Noda Yoshihiko, then Minister of Finance, in which it called for the resignation of Japan Tobacco's CEO. In the same letter, TCI urged the Japanese government to reconsider its legal obligation to remain the majority shareholder in Japan Tobacco and to consider the contribution that a more financially orientated strategy at Japan Tobacco could make towards reducing the national budget deficit (TCI, 2011b).

In this letter, TCI stated that it held over 100,000 shares in Japan Tobacco or approximately 1 per cent of all shares outstanding. As at 31 March 2009 TCI did not appear among the major shareholders shown in Japan Tobacco's accounts but as at 31 March 2010 it was reported to hold 0.63 per cent. The following year, as at 31 March 2011, it was reported to hold 0.68 per cent (JT, 2010; 2011). Since the shareholding remains below 5 per cent it is not recorded by EDINET and indeed may have been outstanding at a level too low to register among Japan Tobacco's major shareholders before March 2010.

At the time of writing (August 2011) it was unclear how this matter would develop. In spite of the negative opinions expressed to the *Financial Times*, Okada Katsuya, Secretary General of the DPJ (*Minshutō* or Democratic Party of Japan), was quoted by *Nikkei* on 24 July as saying that the government was studying a reduction in the state's holdings in both NTT and Japan Tobacco. On the same day, *Nikkei Veritas* published an article effectively confirming many of the financial arguments made by TCI and agreeing that a sale of Japan Tobacco's shares by the government (which would probably result in an equivalent purchase by Japan Tobacco) should benefit the company's share price in the longer term (Nikkei, 2011; Nikkei Veritas, 2011). Once again, a strategy derived from the ideas of financial capitalism had been proposed publicly to a board that appeared to favour a more conservative and firm-centric approach.

11.3 The approach of the 'quiet' activists

Conversations we held with activist hedge funds operating in Japan in early 2010 reinforced the impression that they were not seeking publicity. An officer of one such fund told us: 'We are adopting a "submarine" approach. We never announce things officially.' A co-founder of SFP similarly stressed the need to keep a low public profile. As he put it: 'The idea is not to be in the media, don't make yourselves a target. So our job is not to make ourselves look good, it's to make money for our investors by having the share prices go up: share prices go up by having our companies look good. Well, don't make them look bad.'

A related theme that emerged was the need to avoid open conflict, in contrast to the more bellicose attitudes of Steel Partners, TCI, and others in earlier years. Two funds told us that if the boards of target companies refused to deal with them they would not pursue investments. Another co-founder of SFP focused particularly on what he saw as the the drawbacks of formalising disagreements by publicising letters to the boards of target companies, a tactic that Steel Partners and TCI had used widely and, as we have seen, even Brandes had attempted:

They are trying to sell themselves to the board and also publish that they're there. They can do that without publishing a letter – the letter will be marginalised. It's peculiar to Japan. If it's something very serious, they should go and meet and say it face to face, which is better communication and will come up with a better solution. [The board] will be embarrassed by the publicity: if you publish what you are saying or what communication you have with the management, that is a disaster. People won't talk to you any more.

However, quiet activism of this sort did not preclude public confrontation where no other solution was available. The partners of SFP told us that they had not hesitated to launch litigation where unreasonable barriers to minority shareholders had been proposed, as they demonstrated in the Nireco case. Although they regarded unnecessary publicity as counter-productive, they also saw activism as the lever to produce superior returns from their investments and were prepared to emerge into the public arena to protect their interests if necessary. Interestingly, SFP explained to us that they had not had a confrontation with the target's board at Nireco so much as with the company's lawyers, who had been determined to establish an impressive poison pill for their client.

Some funds active in the market in 2010 gave the impression of exercising the greatest care to avoid contentious topics in order not to appear to be challenging managerial perquisites, even in private meetings. One fund whose officers we met explained that they usually avoided talking about matters such as 'excess reserves' overtly, focusing instead on related matters such as the need to have a healthy return on equity, a point of view which they believed was already established as a legitimate cause of concern in Japanese management circles. Alternatively, they would simply propose the idea of using reserves to pursue investment opportunities. For the same reasons, they tended to avoid discussion of topics that could encourage their listeners to see them as short-termist, such as a focus on quarterly performance data, preferring to turn the discussion towards longer-term strategic issues. In this context they admitted that directors at some companies with good strategic records sometimes still refused to accept that outsiders could contribute anything of value, however politely suggestions were expressed. In such cases they simply chose not to invest.

The belief was expressed at two separate funds that the only way to make headway as an activist investor in Japan was to begin by creating confidence among the target company's management that having a hedge fund as a shareholder was potentially a positive development and not a threat to their company's ethos or their personal autonomy as its leaders. SFP told us of instances where they had even been asked for advice by board members after they had sold their shareholdings, and at another fund we heard of exchanges of gifts reminiscent of the relationships between banks and their long-standing commercial customers, implying a quite different sort of situation to the adversarial image usually associated with activist interventions.

The reactions to the mostly confrontational activism reported in Chapter 10 indicate managerial hostility to any public questioning by shareholders of the board's autonomy, but this does not necessarily describe management responses to shareholder activism of a non-confrontational kind. While public challenges to board autonomy are usually resisted strongly, there is evidence of a greater willingness to listen and to entertain proposals in private within certain limits. The finance manager of a company targeted by one of the quieter foreign funds, which sought to exert pressure at private meetings or through unpublicised letters, explained to us in early 2010 his instinctive reaction to the polite but persistent requests to raise shareholder value that he received periodically from the fund's representatives. Essentially, in his view, shareholder value was a valid topic for discussion, but not to the extent of being the driving force behind everything that happened in his company. Speaking in the presence of his president and the finance director, he emphasised that he was willing to concede the value of making improvements in the way that his company's finances were arranged, and even to consider outsiders' opinions in this respect, but not to concede that the company's performance should be judged solely or predominantly by reference to its contribution to shareholder returns: 'In a sense we can understand them very well at the level of their general conversation. It's not something like [the confrontations] we were discussing just now, but we do not think in terms of deciding the way we manage things or our dividend policy just on the basis of shareholder value.'

In the context of a company whose senior management was relatively open to the idea of shareholder engagement, this points to an environment in which it is unacceptable to see shareholder value as the main purpose of corporate activity, but in which suggestions for improvements to financial aspects of corporate structure could be the subject of dialogue between managers and investors. As long as the firm's business and its customers and employees are seen to benefit, there is no objection to engaging directly with shareholders. This may seem a weak concession from the point of view of investors educated to believe that companies are simply cash generating machines for shareholders, but it represents an advance from the point at which Japanese companies routinely rejected external advice and suspected any shareholder who expressed an opinion of being in league with extortionists. It suggests that Japanese boards are increasingly willing to listen to shareholders' opinions and to accommodate their desire for higher returns, but it also implies that any fund manager who refuses to concede that there may be more to the dynamics of a company in Japan than just shareholder value is unlikely to gain managers' trust and cooperation. 'Quiet' activism appears to operate largely within this zone, spilling out only occasionally into public conflict.

11.4 Conclusion

After the near complete disappearance of confrontational activism from Japan in the course of 2009 and 2010, quieter forms of activism that did not seek public confrontation appeared to be continuing. Many of the funds involved in this type of activism seemed closer to value funds than to the publicity-seeking funds that have been studied in the USA but, as the example of SFP shows, it was still possible to act decisively as an activist hedge fund in Japan without provoking the kind of opposition that had been seen so widely in interventions by the more adversarial funds. Dialogue between managers and investors over the creation and maintenance of shareholder value seemed to be acceptable in this context, but suggestions that returning value to shareholders was the sole objective of the company or that this outweighed the importance of 'corporate value' were liable to undermine trust. Equally, successful investors were careful to avoid suspicion of being focused too strongly on the shorter term, even though it might be obvious to all concerned that fund managers sought returns for their investors over both the short and long run. Above all, in this type of 'quiet activism', the autonomy of the board has to be respected when activists present their recommendations for change.

TCI's decision, in June 2011, to confront the board of Japan Tobacco publicly and to call upon the government for action, both as the majority shareholder and as custodian of the public finances, provides a contrast to this approach. In TCI's favour is the general perception within Japan that better fiscal discipline is required, particularly in the context of the damage inflicted by the tidal wave of March 2011 and the related nuclear power crisis. If this intervention were to succeed in its objectives and produce a return for the fund, it would imply that confrontational activism is still viable in Japan, at least in certain contexts. Whether the Japan Tobacco case is a sign of a revival of confrontational activism to the levels seen in the mid-2000s remains to be seen. For the time being, at least, it appears more to be an isolated event.

12 | Conclusions: hedge fund activism, Japanese corporate governance, and shareholder primacy

In this book we have used the case of hedge fund activism to illuminate larger trends within corporate governance. We have charted the rapid rise, temporary success, and eventual failure of confrontational hedge fund activism in Japan and used the reactions it provoked to examine the nature of the Japanese community firm. Corporate governance is the product of a complex institutional environment shaped by historical forces that are distinct to every national market. The globally ubiquitous legal structure of the joint stock company is an imperfect solution to the needs of disparate stakeholders cooperating to realise a surplus from joint production. Corporate governance systems at national level represent localised solutions designed to overcome the weaknesses of this organisational model. Similar legal structures do not necessarily lead to similar outcomes: because the institutional and historical environment of each national market varies, so too do its corporate governance practices.

We have expanded this theme to examine two divergent threads of corporate governance ideas that developed from the same starting point of the joint stock company, as loosely defined by law but adjusted by institutionalised practice: the shareholder primacy norm that emerged in the USA and the UK from the 1970s, on the one hand, and the community firm model that became pre-eminent in Japan after 1945, on the other. These are not the only variations to the basic corporate law model that have emerged throughout the world but they present a particular contrast to each other in the weighting that they apportion to the interests of different sets of stakeholders. This contrast is all the more compelling because the Japanese adoption of company law in the nineteenth century was a conscious imitation of European structures in order to achieve similar outcomes, subsequently amended by further input from the USA in the 1950s.

294

We then observed the development of hedge fund activism in the USA as an investment strategy that drew on the logic of shareholder primacy: if a corporate board was seen to diverge from this model, it created an arbitrage opportunity that activist investors could exploit. Unlike the demands of the earlier corporate raiders, hedge funds' interventions could be seen as a service to all shareholders and even to the whole national economy, since attention to shareholder value was recognised widely as a public good. This investment strategy spread to the UK, although, as we have seen, it did not function exactly as it did in the USA because the environment was not identical. Further expansion, to Continental Europe, produced some results outwardly suggestive of the US market but also a growing core of interventions in a more private style, as noted by Becht *et al.* (2010). At the same time, hedge fund activism was also entering the Japanese market.

This brings us to the main focus of our study: the attempt by activist hedge funds to transplant their investment strategies to Japan, often in an uncompromising manner. These strategies had been refined in the US market where shareholder primacy was taken for granted and were dependent on widespread acceptance of 'shareholder value' as the main objective of corporate activity. They were now applied in the Japanese market, where portfolio shareholders' interests had for many years been subordinated to those of other stakeholders and where many institutional shareholders justified their investments in terms of wider business interests rather than purely in terms of investment returns. The resultant clash of viewpoints between funds and corporate boards was not inevitable: a combination of political and economic pressures had already begun to change Japanese practices before the activist hedge funds arrived, and at least some of the funds' proposals were seen as addressing genuine financial weaknesses in the companies they targeted. However, the publicly confrontational style of activism which some funds championed tended to polarise opinions, drawing out the views on corporate governance of both sides into the public arena and thereby exposing to public view beliefs held by management that had seldom been enunciated in this way before. We analysed this clash of values and views in Chapter 8, successively in terms of activism in general, public activism, and activism where the uncompromising nature of the funds' approach to their targets' boards justified, in our opinion, the description 'confrontational'. We then examined two particular interventions that we consider both confrontational and influential in Chapter 9. Our review of the reactions to activism in Chapter 10 considered how the principal players in the Japanese market responded to all these manifestations of activism in general but especially to confrontational activism. The emergence of confrontational activism in Japan that we have observed here demonstrated a definitive and uncompromising statement of shareholder primacy in conflict with robustly established, contrary ideas. But it is also important to see this phenomenon in context and to take into account the extent to which other engagement strategies continued to be employed in the market, apparently with greater success. Chapter 11 looked at these quieter varieties of shareholder activism or engagement in Japan. These approaches may represent potentially a more sustainable strategy because of the implicit concessions they make to the logic of the community firm, although the initial moves we have described by TCI at Japan Tobacco in 2011 may yet show that an uncompromising approach based only on financial logic can prevail in particular circumstances.

In this chapter we start our review by drawing together our conclusions from Chapters 8–11 in Section 12.1 ('Corporate governance at the community firm') on what public and often confrontational hedge fund activism has shown about the fabric of Japanese corporate governance. In the subsequent three sections we examine the wider significance of this activism, beginning with its effects within Japan and then expanding our assessment to the global corporate governance debate. In Section 12.2 ('The impact of hedge fund activism in Japan') we ask what impact the activism we have observed had on the companies which it targeted and whether the funds ultimately changed anything through their efforts. In Section 12.3 ('Convergence and divergence in Japanese corporate governance') we ask what our findings contribute to the continuing debate on whether Japan's corporate governance is converging with US practice. Finally, in Section 12.4 ('The limits of shareholder primacy'), we use our findings to review the theory of shareholder primacy, treating it not as a universal standard but as a local phenomenon that has emerged from the specific conditions of the USA, the UK and other markets to achieve a degree of global recognition, and ask what these events in Japan show about its wider relevance.

12.1 Corporate governance at the community firm

The primary purpose of our research was to understand better the ideas and practices that underpinned corporate governance at Japanese companies as management encountered public or openly confrontational hedge fund activism. We have described Japanese corporate governance as 'firm-centric'. This term captures several features of the Japanese community firm: the marginal role played by shareholders, the 'internalist' focus of its board and senior managers, and its prioritisation of organisational interests and values over financial ones. The failure of confrontational hedge fund activism suggests that these core features of the Japanese model remain intact, perhaps surprisingly so given their apparent fall from grace during the post-bubble years and the outward enthusiasm for pro-shareholder corporate governance reforms which prevailed then. We consider below how certain key aspects of the community firm were revealed through our research.

The most fundamental of these aspects was simply that the company as an enduring organisational structure was considered to be more important than the investors who happened to hold its shares at any given time. The marginal role accorded to shareholders within the community firm is evident in the first responses of the relatively small companies targeted by Steel Partners in the early 2000s. The boards of these targets, such as Sotoh and Yushiro, were seen to be isolated from their companies' shareholders. They seemed to have had few if any established lines of communication with the shareholder body as a whole, of the kind which would have told them whether Steel Partners enjoyed wide support. The boards saw themselves primarily as having responsibility for the management of the business, with shareholder interests a strictly secondary concern. The reaction at larger companies approached at a later point in the cycle of these interventions by Steel Partners and TCI was different, but equally revealing of boards' attitudes to shareholders. Unlike those of Sotoh and Yushiro, the boards of these companies were less isolated from their shareholders and could gauge the likely level of support more easily. Companies like Nōritz and Sapporo felt sufficiently confident to assert the validity of their existing strategies and to engage in delaying tactics when they lacked better arguments. J-Power, as a company whose board was particularly attuned to the needs of its institutional shareholders following its IPO in 2004 and its sustained investor relations programme thereafter, responded to TCI's arguments promptly and in kind. But even at J-Power, the board reacted to these pressures ultimately not by conceding the logic of the fund's approach, but by reaffirming its existing strategic vision and seeking to strengthen relationships with shareholders who would be more amenable to this position in the future. Although *Nikkei* argued in its editorial of June 2008 on Steel Partners' Aderans intervention that it was shareholders who selected companies, not the other way around, this was not a view shared by the directors of many companies targeted by the hedge funds: from their perspective, the organisational unity and objectives of their companies should be preserved in any feasible way, even to the extent of reshaping the shareholder body itself.

Because the corporate governance of the community firm is firm-centric, the board's attention is normally devoted to the economic security of the business of the firm and its long-term survival as an organisation, rather than to the shareholders. Demands for the release of cash in the form of higher dividends or share repurchases were resisted on the grounds that reserves were set aside for the needs of the business, even where they had not been earmarked for any particular investment project. Targeted companies' boards can be categorised roughly into two groups in this context, neither of which showed sympathy for the funds' demands. At some companies – generally the smaller ones – the reaction of management to the lack of opportunities to invest excess cash in the business had been to accumulate it against the possibility that one day the company might need to draw on these resources for its survival. At others – generally the larger ones, which tended to have some degree of debt – positive cash flow was seen as an opportunity to reduce this debt and thereby strengthen the company's financial position. At these latter companies the problem was not so much a lack of financial sophistication as a divergence in opinion about whose interests the company should serve and how conservatively it should be managed. Arguments from the hedge funds that cash should automatically be paid to shareholders in the absence of specific investment projects or that borrowing should even be increased to fund payouts were strongly resisted because they cut across boards' fundamental belief in the need to underwrite the company's survival as a business first before considering any increase in distributions. Whether boards were hoarding cash or just pursuing conservative policies by reducing debt, the hedge funds saw this as lack of attention to the return on shareholders' capital. From the boards' point of view, they were simply prioritising the needs of the business. Financial moves that strengthened the position of the organisation, such as accumulation of reserves or lowering the level of debt, were generally assumed to be beneficial. Conversely, any manoeuvres that reduced this layer of protection were assumed to entail unacceptable risks, however much they might raise financial efficiency.

There was a striking lack of common ground or even shared language between these funds and the senior managers and board members of the companies where they intervened. Board members did not see fund managers as fellow-capitalists with a fiduciary duty to deliver returns to investors. When the funds told target boards that their objective was to improve corporate value – which has now become a widely used expression in Japan – but were then seen to promote their own immediate advantage, they were regarded with suspicion. In the USA or the UK the value of the company is usually understood to mean the value that the market places on a listed company's shares in aggregate, should any shareholder wish to sell – in effect, shareholder value – and 'corporate value' itself is defined variously as the sum of debt and shareholder value or simply as generated cash flows. But to the directors of the community firm, an ill-considered increase in payments to shareholders could weaken the company, even if the share price rose. In the USA or the UK it is likely that the funds' position would have been more readily understood by directors and senior managers who had themselves internalised a shareholder-value-based approach, as described by Roberts *et al.* (2006) in their study of the UK market. In Japan these common values were lacking.

An enduring feature of the Japanese community firm that emerged from the hedge fund interventions was a strong belief in managerial autonomy, and in particular in the autonomy of the board from shareholder pressure. The board, sitting at the apex of the managerial structure, tended to see itself as charged with preserving the firm as an organisational entity. When the debate over anti-takeover measures began, neither management nor the expert committees assembled by the ministries appeared to question the right of boards to determine tactics rather than putting the matter directly to shareholders. When we discussed the idea of allowing shareholders to decide how to respond to takeover approaches with the chairman of a financial company in September 2006, not long after the Ōji-Hokuetsu affair, he cited the example of a specific major manufacturer with a large foreign shareholding potentially receiving a takeover approach: '51% would raise their hands and that would be the end of it, wouldn't it? There's a huge risk of that, you see.' The fate of the company was simply too important to be entrusted to the whims of its shareholders. The fact that many of these shareholders might increasingly be foreigners evidently made the risk even greater. In the context of hedge fund activism this meant, as we have seen, resisting the transfer of the company's wealth to outsiders, even if they were also the shareholders. The more public the confrontation, and the more visible the challenge to board autonomy, the more determined some boards became in their resistance. Olcott, in a series of meetings with 22 current and former presidents and chairmen of mostly large companies in Japan (conducted as part of a joint study with Dore in 2007–8) found that sensitivity to the external world of the share price and shareholders' views had indeed increased but that these senior officers still had a principal focus on their firms and their actively participating stakeholders: 'The idea of the enduring nature of the company's existence, its status as a permanent fixture of Japan's economic and social landscape, is still powerfully imprinted on the minds of Japanese managers. Anything that threatens its existence, however much it may benefit its owners or enriches the managers themselves, will be strongly resisted by them' (Olcott, 2009: 218).

This 'internalist' or 'firm-centric' focus of the community firm is linked to a further characteristic of the community firm's corporate governance which was highlighted by the hedge fund experience, namely its focus on the need for good stewardship of the business. As we have noted above, 'corporate value' was perceived to be the intrinsic value of the company as an entity equipped to survive and prosper rather than its market price or any other financial benchmark. Tender offers in any country are commonly seen as challenges to incumbent management but in Japan they raised the further issue of stewardship. When hedge funds sought control in this way, boards opposed them partly on the grounds that it was not clear that the funds had the expertise to run the business. Statements by Steel Partners in June 2007 that they had no intention to interfere in the management of Bull-Dog Sauce after acquisition of the company proved counterproductive because they were taken as a sign of the fund's indifference to the company's underlying business. This attitude can also be found in press commentary on certain interventions and in the public and official discourse of the courts and ministerial advisory bodies. The 'corporate value' test of the company interest which was developed in the guidance drawn up by the Corporate Value Study Group and further elaborated by the courts in the Bull-Dog Sauce litigation echoed the organisational priorities of management, by stressing that the board was entitled to take steps to defend the company as a continuing concern in a situation where the bidder had no convincing business plan or was intent on breaking it up through an asset sale or otherwise exploiting it. Companies which implemented defences reminiscent of American 'poison pills' in large numbers from 2005 onwards justified their actions as resistance to what were viewed as opportunistic and value-destroying bids, while TCI's attempt to take a further 10 per cent stake in J-Power was blocked by official intervention partly because of concerns that a financially motivated investor should not be permitted to take what could amount to an effective controlling stake in a company of strategic importance to national energy policy.

The willingness of boards to adopt these defensive measures was an indication of their determination to defend their companies. Because tender offers were seen as attacks on the organisational integrity of the firm, and because the perceived opinion of the bureaucracy and the courts appeared to favour preservation of this integrity, boards felt greater freedom to respond to bids or the threat of them with defensive measures. Cross-shareholdings were in decline and confidence in traditional dilution tactics had progressively been undermined by court judgments such as that on the Nippon Broadcasting System affair. When the Corporate Value Study Group issued its guidance on justifiable defence measures in May 2005, boards were quick to take advantage of the protection that this offered, adding mechanisms of obfuscation and delay through expert committees and written exchanges, such as the interminable and inconclusive exchange of questions and answers that developed between Steel Partners and Sapporo during a six-year-long intervention. The expensive campaign by the board of Bull-Dog Sauce to resist Steel Partners in 2007 explored the limits of this strategy but was in keeping with the spirit of the process. The aim of these anti-takeover defences was to ensure that boards rather than shareholders would determine whether bids could proceed. By these means, 'corporate value' as defined and adjudicated by the board became the benchmark to set against the funds' promotion of 'shareholder value'.

From the viewpoint of agency theory, directors who instituted anti-takeover defences would be suspected of acting in defence of their own prerogatives, and this danger was noted also by the Corporate Value Study Group. That is not how senior Japanese managers themselves saw it; we believe that boards which promoted defence measures in Japan did so in the genuine belief that they were defending their companies' best interests and that this represented their duty as directors. But this illustrates an intrinsic weakness of the community firm; its internal focus encourages boards to exclude external influences and, although the system monitors itself in many respects, there is little protection against a well-intentioned but inept board. Under pressure from real or imagined threats from activist hedge funds, many companies chose to erect barriers to external interference that potentially interrupted the gradual process of change within their companies, and equipped boards to retreat into defensive postures. However well intended these moves might have been, they brought risks; as Culpepper observed in the context of French and German appetite for defences: 'If protection against takeover were costless, all managers would want it – takeover protection is tantamount to a job protection law for senior managers' (Culpepper, 2011: 51). In France and Germany, the market's negative perception of such defensive measures was seen as the main cost. In Japan, the danger of a retreat into introspection and lack of accountability has become a major concern.

In one sense, the debate about whether the activist hedge funds had convincing business plans for the companies in which they intervened and sometimes sought to acquire missed the point. The funds almost certainly were not interested in taking full control of their target companies; they used tender offers as a tactic to induce restructuring and payouts, or in the hope that third parties might emerge to outbid them, as happened at Myōjō Foods in 2006. But the very public arguments over hedge fund intentions nevertheless crystallised wider concerns over the model of corporate governance which they represented. In managerial practice, as well as in public discourse, the Japanese community firm was understood to be more than the collection of tradable securities that the activist hedge funds implicitly believed it to be.

Calls from the funds for the appointment of external directors were received with little enthusiasm, although some were appointed.

Agency theory sees externally appointed and ideally independent directors as an important resource to monitor executive behaviour and to guard against excess. In the community firm, where monitoring is internalised, external directors are acceptable as advisers but any of them who sought to exercise strategic authority would tend to be seen to be arrogating the functions of the 'real' executive board. Even at some companies that have made a conscious effort to introduce external directors and to empower them, we found that the board's executive core still seemed to run the business at all levels. Against this background, few boards were likely to accede willingly to calls from funds that were mistrusted from the start to appoint their candidates as external directors.

Board members in the companies that were targeted also had strong personal incentives to resist hedge fund interventions. Within most listed Japanese companies, including those targeted by the hedge funds, turnover among permanent employees remains low and there is continuity of executive management promotion within the organisation through to board level. Companies prefer to nurture their own managers and seldom appoint outsiders over them; mobility of managers between companies is limited. Executive directors cannot usually respond to a change of control at their company that may disrupt their career prospects by leaving, because they are unlikely to find similar employment elsewhere. In this environment, a tender offer is a direct threat to the personal livelihoods of the directors and of many senior managers too. The strong resistance offered by boards to hedge fund interventions is thus tied to the attachment that most senior managers, up to and including board members, continue to feel to the companies which employ them – an attachment which is underpinned by clear economic interests.

All of these factors contributed to encourage boards to defend the community firm. Their behaviour can be rationalised through agency theory as the reaction of self-interested executive management to the threat of financial discipline and effective monitoring but our interview-based research suggests that quite different dynamic factors were at work. The starting point to understand these reactions is the community firm, its structure, its internal pressures, and the obligations it imposes on its members. Hitherto these had usually been accepted tacitly as simply 'the ways things were done' but through these interventions and the reactions they provoked, Japanese corporate governance was delivered into the public view to an unusual extent. The issues were defined in terms of the limits beyond which management would resist shareholders' influence, the importance of board autonomy, and the priority of operational considerations over purely financial ones. At the same time, these practices received a new intellectual underpinning to rival the theory of 'shareholder value': the twin concepts of 'corporate value' and 'shareholders' common interests' were the first steps towards a philosophy aimed at sustaining the corporate governance of the community firm.

12.2 The impact of hedge fund activism in Japan

We now consider what hedge fund activism achieved in Japan during the period of our study in terms of fostering sustained change. In the USA, hedge fund activism represented the latest and, many argued, the most advanced stage in the process of refining capital market 'discipline' over corporate management (Macey, 2008). Yet its enduring impact in Japan, despite the attention it attracted, seems to have been much weaker.

As we have noted, 'hedge fund activism' covers a variety of engagement strategies. We have concentrated on the most public and confrontational variety because it has been instrumental in demonstrating the dynamics of corporate governance at the community firm. This form of activism failed in Japan in the sense that it was unable to bring about the transformation of corporate practice that was required for the funds' investment strategies to be successful over the longer term. Early successes by Steel Partners often took the form of payouts which target companies' boards saw as a price worth paying to retain their autonomy: there was no fundamental acceptance of the principles of shareholder primacy or shareholder value. Our analysis in Chapter 8 provided evidence that boards of companies targeted by these funds subsequently accelerated the pace of increase in dividend payments and reduced cash reserves slightly, but there was no sign of fundamental strategic change towards a financially driven model with reduced capital investment or greatly increased leverage in response to these interventions. Comparison of market capitalisation and Tobin's Q between targeted companies and selected peer samples over the following two years produces equivocal results but there is no decisive evidence that the market began to value these companies more highly than comparable firms in the market. In a later phase, from around 2005, confrontational funds faced concerted resistance from management and were much less successful in securing payouts. From our survey of 34 interventions by Steel Partners and TCI between 2002 and 2008, we estimate that only a few of the interventions initiated from late 2004 onwards produced satisfactory returns, as we have defined them, partly because of this opposition. There was increasingly also an official dimension to the reaction to hedge fund activism during this later period, which took the form of bureaucratic and judicial resistance. Consequently the strategy of confrontational activism had already reached its effective limits even before the full onset of the global financial crisis in 2008, which independently triggered a need on the part of many funds to liquidate investments, reducing both their holdings and their capacity for aggressive new moves in the Japanese market.

The stability of the community firm model in the face of pressure from external forces and the failure of confrontational activism to influence this model in a sustained fashion are what emerge most clearly from this process. But it does not follow that the model is unbendingly rigid or that confrontational activism had no impact on it. Japanese companies have been amending their formal governance structures in response to the new environment of the post-bubble economy, and practical market pressures have been growing in Japan for many years now to improve returns to shareholders and to deliver more detailed information to them. This phenomenon has been described as the 'new community firm', as it combines a continued commitment to stable employment with newly flexible forms of managerial decision-making (Inagami and Whittaker, 2005), and as the 'hybridised' Japanese firm, which accepts a greater role for hitherto peripheral elements such as external directors and financially motivated shareholders while seeking to maintain high levels of investment in research and development and in firm-specific skills and capabilities (Aoki, 2007; Jackson and Miyajima, 2007).

As we have seen, these processes of change sometimes involve less genuine modification of practice than appearances suggest. The company with committees system is one example of this, where several such companies to whose officers we spoke appeared to have kept most aspects of the community firm intact, even to the extent of preserving its internal focus. Many boards accepted a greater role for outside directors not in order to bring about more effective external supervision, but as part of a process of streamlining managerial decision-making and rendering the internal management of corporate risks more transparent (Buchanan and Deakin, 2008; Lawley, 2008). However, many of the changes that are shaping the 'new community firm' are not superficial. Perceptions that institutional investors who buy parcels of a company's shares should be kept informed through sustained IR exercises, that contact with all shareholders can provide useful feedback and guard against sudden attacks by unwelcome acquirers, and that streamlined internal management structures can make the company more effective, are all the results of changes in the market environment and of managers' practical experience and response to those changes. These are all reactions to changing circumstances within the markets in which these companies operate and they are as robust as the pressures that shape them.

Some of the demands made by the more confrontational activists complemented these pressures. Their calls for higher payouts reinforced the trend to higher dividends that was already evident in the Japanese market. Their calls for more attention to be paid to shareholders' interests complemented the growth of IR and the increasing awareness that shareholders were no longer a resource that could be taken for granted. Their attempts to extract cash and to impose financial discipline, although motivated by their own interests and those of their investors, highlighted the lack of financial sophistication of many Japanese boards and their tendency to hoard cash without any strategy beyond a desire to protect their companies against unforeseen problems. By adding elements of confrontation and tension, and by provoking crises at the companies they targeted, these activists helped to emphasise these issues and to publicise them in the Japanese context in a way that no amount of theoretical argument about the merits or demerits of shareholder primacy could have achieved. In this sense, the confrontational activist hedge funds had an impact on Japanese corporate governance, not by introducing much that was genuinely new, but by giving fresh impetus to debates about the interests that companies served.

Yet a greater sensitivity to shareholder interests and to issues of capital efficiency does not mean that Japanese boards necessarily accepted the idea of shareholder primacy. Although it appears that the hedge funds' interventions prompted increased communication between boards and shareholders, this should not be equated with the downgrading of organisational values in favour of financial ones. Rather, it signifies a realisation among directors and other managers that hitherto subordinated issues needed to be given greater priority, and a determination to incorporate these concerns within the wider organisational logic of the community firm. This implies a renewal of the community firm model, but with a more explicit recognition of the place of shareholders within it. Similarly, the message that cash should not be hoarded blindly did not translate into a belief that it should be distributed to shareholders by default; this overdue awareness of capital efficiency was seen as something to contribute to 'corporate value', with all that this concept implies in Japan for the prioritisation of the community firm over the interests of any of its constituents.

On the evidence that we have presented, confrontational hedge fund activism failed as a sustainable investment strategy in Japan: from this, one could infer that any kind of activist approach is simply inappropriate to the Japanese context and the nature of its corporate governance. However, this may be misleading, for two reasons. On the one hand, aspects of these funds' diagnosis of the problems of Japanese corporate governance may not have been entirely incorrect; as we have argued above, their interventions reinforced changes associated with the gradual evolution of the community firm model. Meanwhile, on the other hand, there is evidence that less confrontational forms of shareholder activism may be successful for the funds which practice them and also, on occasion, beneficial for the companies targeted. We look further at these two aspects below.

From the 1990s and throughout the period of our study, many commentators within Japan and beyond took the view that there were problems in the management and performance of Japanese firms that could be addressed through mechanisms of corporate governance. In 2004 the authors of a study on corporate governance produced for METI by Nissei Kenkyūjo, Waseda University's Finance Kenkyūjo, and UFJ Sōgō Kenkyūjo observed that 'among the causes of our country's decreased industrial competitiveness is the fact that the so-called Japanese industrial model of long-term employment with a main bank system that was admired until the 1980s has ceased to function since the 1990s' (METI, 2004). Four years later, after a period of more sustained economic growth, the Keizai Dōyūkai produced a publication entitled *Creating a new style of Japanese management*, in the course of which it argued that 'although the Japanese economy seems to have broken free of the long period of stagnation that followed the burst of the so-called "bubble economy" and to have returned to a path of stable growth, Japan's relative economic standing internationally is gradually declining and its presence in the world is weakening' (Dōyūkai, 2008). A widely held view was that Japanese industry's initial success after the Second World War had been driven by a perceived need to catch up with other economies, a target that had now been achieved but not replaced by anything equally inspirational for the future. In his book *Japan: The system that soured*, Richard Katz observed:

The root of the problem is that Japan is still mired in the structures, policies and mental habits that prevailed in the 1950s-60s. What we have come to think of as the 'Japanese economic system' was a marvellous system to help a backward Japan catch up to the West. But it turned into a terrible system once Japan had in fact caught up. (Katz, 1998: 4)

Katz focused on the macroeconomic context of the Japanese economy and the effect of government policies, but for many his critique could be extended to the level of individual companies which were cash-rich but conservatively managed and not making optimal use of their reserves. From this point of view, the activist hedge fund objective of releasing free cash flow through dividends and related restructurings had the potential to release capital to more efficient uses, thereby stimulating economy-wide gains, as well as exposing corporate managers to disciplinary pressures of the kind which were becoming generally accepted in North America and Western Europe.

If these issues had attracted such attention, it is appropriate to consider why the confrontational activists' interventions only reinforced existing trends and failed to promote greater changes to the core of Japanese corporate governance, to the benefit of the wider economy. There was clearly concern in Japan that the economy had lost its way and, as we have seen, a common reaction was to blame corporate governance for this. On at least some occasions, the confrontational activists were targeting boards that were seen to lack financial and strategic acumen. Nevertheless, even in these cases, as well as more generally, they failed to bring about the fundamental changes in corporate strategy that they had sought. The critical issue here seems to have been the

openly confrontational tactics they employed. By attacking managerial autonomy they confronted the natural hierarchy of the community firm; by challenging this hierarchy they were seen to threaten the
organisational continuity of the firm and all its dependants; although
they were effectively demanding that core features of the community
firm be dismantled, on those occasions when they were asked to provide an alternative business plan – in a context where governance and
running the business were held to be almost identical – both Steel
Partners and TCI denied any intention of wishing to run the businesses they were targeting, which was an answer that would have been
understood perfectly in the USA or the UK but suggested immediately
to their Japanese audiences that they were asset strippers or greenmailers. Their position of arguing, on the one hand, for greater efficiency
of capital allocation, while also seeking (and in the early cases gaining)
high returns on their own investments, placed them at odds with public opinion and prompted a growing general hostility despite otherwise supportive comment from elements of the financial press.

But if confrontational hedge fund activism did not work in Japan,
some kinds of activism seem to be feasible for the funds pursuing them, and these may, in turn, bring about wider changes to the
Japanese economy. As we have seen, funds continuing to operate in
Japan after the onset of the global financial crisis stressed the need
to avoid public confrontation and indeed publicity in general. SFP's
record, for example, in executing MBOs and other transactions with
minimal publicity during the past few years suggests that it is possible
to drive situations to successful conclusions through a degree of activism, provided that it is done without posing a public challenge to the
board's autonomy or threatening the organisational logic of the community firm. This is a further sign that Japan may therefore be moving
in the direction of a model of engagement based on dialogue and possibly partnership between active shareholders and the boards of their
targets, an approach that may have some parallels in the Continental
European experience described by Becht *et al.* (2010).

The strategy of publicly demanding higher payments to shareholders from accumulated cash or through increased leverage does not
seem to be a viable method in Japan. However, the 'quiet activism'
that we identified in Chapter 11 as potentially playing a sustained role
in the Japanese market is aligned with the continuing trend towards
transparency of managerial goals and objectives, greater attention to

shareholders, and the acceptance of increased financial discipline. If this trend leads to greater acceptance of the logic of capital efficiency in resource allocation and corporate planning, some will see it as a belated vindication of at least some of the ideas associated with confrontational hedge fund activism.

12.3 Convergence and divergence in Japanese corporate governance

In 1997 the Japan Corporate Governance Forum observed in its Interim Report that 'the compatibility of corporate governance practices with global standards has also become an important part of corporate success' (JCGF, 1997). In this, it was anticipating the ideas that were subsequently published by Hansmann and Kraakman (2001), to the effect that convergence on an essentially American pattern of shareholder primacy was not only economically beneficial but also inevitable. This debate continues but the view that Japanese corporate governance practice will eventually converge on the essentials of the shareholder primacy approach is no longer being confidently asserted within Japan itself. In late 2008 Nakatani Iwao, economist and former chairman of Sony, and previously a strong advocate of financial capitalism, wrote in the introduction to a book aimed at general readership that stimulated much discussion among corporate managers: 'It is not that I have come to deny the whole idea of structural reform itself. However, I have reached the point where I cannot accept reform that fosters a widening of disparities and turns a blind eye to the sort of things that destroy the social values which Japanese society has nurtured hitherto' (Nakatani, 2008: 32).

Nakatani's reference to social values implies that the Japanese community firm is the product of widely held assumptions about the nature of companies which differ from those held elsewhere. While this may be so, reference to 'social' or 'cultural' conditions should not divert attention from the material interests which the community firm continues to serve. As we have seen, it enjoys legitimacy because it is seen as delivering material benefits to a number of groups, including management and core employees but also many shareholders. If this ceased to be true, convergence of the Japanese system on the essentials of the shareholder value model would be a more likely possibility.

It is possible to view the generally negative reaction in Japan to confrontational hedge fund activism as the defensive response of particular vested interests, such as senior managers. This explanation would fit well with agency theory and be compatible with the idea that convergence can be postponed but not prevented because it is driven by the greater good of the whole economy. However, if shareholders in Japanese companies had seen it as in their interests to support the activist hedge funds against managerial insiders, they could easily have done so. It was not simply Japanese shareholders with business links to target companies, but overseas shareholders and other portfolio investors who declined to support activist interventions in sufficient numbers. It is implausible to see such shareholders as part of a conspiracy with management against the public good. It is more plausible to take the view that they saw value, in both the short and long term, in supporting management strategies. Japanese community firms have proved rather more durable than conventional wisdom, influenced by US and UK patterns in the corporate governance field, had thought possible.

The durability of the community firm arose from its effectiveness as a mechanism to draw stakeholders together in effective business units to support their livelihoods and to deliver national prosperity. It still delivers these results. What has changed since the early days of the community firm in the post-war era is that it now needs to serve portfolio investment needs that are more extensive and socially more important than those that existed then. Data focused on the 2010 census published by the Statistics Bureau of the Ministry of Internal Affairs and Communications (*Sōmu-shō, Tōkei-kyoku*) show that Japan had the highest proportion of elderly citizens (defined as those aged 65 or more) in a sample of 13 similarly developed or highly populated countries. It also had the lowest percentage of population under 15 years of age, suggesting that this trend will intensify. In 2010, those aged 65 or more comprised 23.1 per cent of the total population, a figure that is forecast by the Statistics Bureau to rise to 39.6 per cent by 2050 (MIC, 2011).

Returns from portfolio investment income, as opposed to the profitability of companies' operations and the benefits they generate purely for their active stakeholders, will become increasingly important. An article in *Financial News*, published in September 2011, quoting a pensions specialist, pointed out that the GPIF's portfolio had begun to shrink in Yen terms, despite recent positive investment returns, because its inflows of capital had shrunk with the decline of the national work-force and had begun to be overtaken by its contracted outflows, imply-ing a growing need for higher returns henceforth (Financial News, 2011). This, rather than theories about shareholder primacy, is likely to drive demand for higher dividends and generally higher distribution policies in Japan during coming years.

In this sense, a degree of convergence is already happening and is likely to continue. But this is still not a total convergence on the shareholder primacy model. It is a form of what Gilson called 'func-tional convergence' where 'existing governance institutions are flexible enough to respond to the demands of changed circumstances without altering the institutions' formal characteristics' (Gilson, 2001: 356). The community firm has survived and is adjusting itself, so far with a degree of apparent success.

The idea that vested interests are resisting the forces of convergence also misses the significance of the adjustments within the Japanese model of corporate governance since the late 1990s, to which we have already referred. Corporate governance reform has been seen in Japan as a means to an end, and the end is the modernisation of the commu-nity firm, not its replacement by a different model. Large Japanese com-panies still appear to be dominated by internally appointed managers, and to prioritise loosely defined worker and community interests over those of shareholders, in much the same way as they did in the 1960s or 1970s. Beneath the surface, however, the managerial structure of the community firm has been changing in response to what Japanese managers see as the need to improve the speed and effectiveness of decision-making. Almost all of the larger and more successful compan-ies have taken a number of linked steps over the past decade: reducing the size of boards, enhancing the role of outside advisers (in some cases, but not all, as external directors), and clarifying the distinction between supervision, as the function of the board, and execution, as the function of executive officers, many of whom are now outside the board (Buchanan and Deakin, 2008). This process was described in 2009 in the following terms by a senior officer of the Toshiba group: 'What Toshiba's experience shows is that corporate governance is about much more than just the behavior of the board of directors. If it is to be effective, it needs to have a comprehensive approach that covers all considerations of board structure, the supervisory role of the board, management systems, and execution, internal controls, attention to stakeholders, and CSR' (Fuwa, 2009: 265).

By contrast, corporate governance in the USA or the UK is very much focused on the behaviour of the board of directors, which is supposed, among other things, to monitor the conduct of management on behalf of the shareholders. It is precisely the internal emphasis on organisational unity within the Japanese community firm which ensures divergence from the American or British models of accountability, both based on a mixture of external resources such as independent boards, assertive shareholders, and capital market pressures, and reduces the likelihood of future convergence. Market forces will continue to refine Japanese practice and it is possible that they will eventually produce a result that is closer to the shareholder primacy model than it is at present. But for the foreseeable future the core values of the community firm seem intact and likely to resist anything but a gradual prioritisation of shareholders' interests within the existing framework.

12.4 The limits of shareholder primacy

So far we have considered what public or overtly confrontational activism has revealed about the practices and beliefs that underlie Japanese corporate governance, what impact it has had on them, and what conclusions can be drawn about the likelihood of convergence between the Japanese and the US or similar models. We now examine a wider aspect of the hedge fund activism phenomenon, with implications beyond Japan. As we have seen, shareholder primacy and its attendant ideas of agency theory and shareholder value have been promoted by some commentators as global standards, and as the most economically beneficial way to run a company. The reactions in Japan to confrontational hedge fund activism that we have seen demonstrated that a majority of Japanese managers, as well as investors, bureaucrats, and jurists, do not agree. Here we review some differences and interactions between the shareholder primacy and the community firm models and ask what the experience of confrontational activism in Japan until 2008 has shown about them.

We have suggested that the entry of activist hedge funds into Japan triggered a tournament of corporate governance ideas, in which the contrast between competing conceptions of the firm was displayed with unusual clarity: was the company an enduring productive entity where the prime concern of management was the survival of the organisation and its underlying business, or was it to be seen as an item of shareholder property, a collection of tradable assets and securities? We have suggested that the tension between these two views is inherent in the legal structure of the joint stock company and has only partially been remedied by the mixture of formal and informal institutionalised practices that is corporate governance. In the USA and the UK, from the 1970s through to the global financial crisis, the pendulum swung in favour of shareholder primacy and the financial model of the firm. This development was driven by a variety of localised forces in both of these markets, and the results were not uniform across them, despite their many structural resemblances. In Japan, efforts to resolve the inherent contradictions of the corporate form took a different course. In the post-war period, the rise of the community firm made the company synonymous with the business and its active stakeholders, as captured by the idea of 'enterprise' or 'corporate value'. But neither shareholder primacy nor the community firm was a culturally embedded phenomenon. From the early years of the twentieth century until the 1970s, the power of executive management, rather than that of shareholders, appears to have been the defining characteristic of both the US and British corporate environments. Conversely, before the Second World War, large Japanese companies appear to have been run primarily with the interests of their shareholders – often the controlling families – in mind. The rise of the shareholder primacy model in the USA and elsewhere, and the rise of the community firm in Japan, were responses to particular sets of conditions. They are evidence of path dependencies of the kind that can be ascribed to institutional rigidities, but they also demonstrate the flexibility of corporate governance systems in response to the changing needs of their local markets.

There has long been a tendency, at least among commentators, to compare these different models and to identify relative strengths and weaknesses that are held to be inherent in them, rather than to see them principally as the result of prevailing local economic conditions. During the period of Japanese economic ascendancy in the 1980s, it was common to question the economic systems of the USA and of many other industrialised countries, comparing them unfavourably with those of Japan, although the emphasis was generally on Japanese working practices and organisational structures rather than on corporate governance. But growth in the US economy from the 1990s, which coincided with stagnation and lack of confidence in Japan following the collapse of the investment bubble, suggested to many observers that the US economic model was now the key to success. Moreover, US corporate governance was singled out as the crucial factor in this model. It was against this background of confidence in US practice that the activist hedge funds made their entry into the Japanese market. The financial crisis that was evident by 2008 undermined their position, not just because it required them to liquidate some of their holdings, but also because it was widely seen in Japan as discrediting many of their arguments for lean financial structures, which could now be categorised as 'instruction through bad example' or *hanmen kyōshi*. Across the world, companies with accumulated cash were seen to be best positioned to survive the recession that was expected to follow the financial crisis (FT, 2009a). This was clear encouragement for the majority of Japanese managers, who had not accepted the funds' arguments, to conclude that their conservative approach had been vindicated.

What this process of fluctuation in the reputations of both models best demonstrates is that corporate governance generally does not determine economic outcomes. The causality is mostly the other way around, with economic and societal conditions tending to influence corporate governance. Mitarai Fujio, then president of Canon, put this viewpoint to us in October 2003 in a discussion of the relevance of US practices to Japan:

I think that American corporate governance is something that developed against the background of America and American society, and which functions in that context. Meanwhile, our kind of governance in Japan is based on a Japanese context. So I do not think that one can say which is the right way. I have worked in both countries but when it comes to comparing the two systems, I would say it was a case of 'apples and oranges' as the English expression has it. This is because companies are part of the societies of the countries where they operate. And their employees are citizens of those countries. So one cannot escape from the structure of those countries' laws, customs, culture and whatever. Indeed, there is no need to escape from them. It is rational to operate in accordance with them ... I think that it is illogical to import the American system to Japan. I think it would be equally illogical to import the Japanese system to America.

It is easy to exaggerate the rigidity of corporate governance 'models', which ultimately are compiled from the conclusions of observers watching boards in action. Where similarities in economic forces are present, companies will tend to be run in a similar way, irrespective of their nationality. John Ward, Professor of Family Enterprise at the Kellogg School of Management in the USA, was quoted by the *Financial Times* in 2008 in a discussion about successful US family enterprises (in the particular context of Paccar). He said that these companies 'see their primary stakeholders as employees and customers, rather than shareholders and managers. There is a whole attitude that the institution is worthy in itself and belongs to lots of people, not just the owners' (FT, 2008c). This is at least a partial manifestation of the community firm, although far from Japan.

Rather than see corporate governance in terms of rigid models, it is more accurate to view it as a delicate balancing of interests by corporate boards in order to promote the interests of the business and its stakeholders. If we return to Kester's definition of corporate governance, quoted in Chapter 3, as 'the entire set of incentives, safeguards, and dispute-resolution processes used to order the activities of various corporate stakeholders, each seeking to improve its welfare through coordinated economic activity with others' it is clear that this must be a flexible process. The Japanese company president whom we quoted in Chapter 10 saw it as a balancing of interests between the triangle of shareholders, customers, and employees, including management. Jensen, whom we quoted in Chapter 4, writing in defence of agency theory, conceded that 'managers must pay attention to all constituencies that can affect the value of a firm'. With such a strong consensus in favour of balance, the greatest danger seems to be a lack of balance in boards' approach to corporate governance, rather than the adoption by companies or countries of any particular model of corporate governance.

Concern about balance within the shareholder primacy model has been expressed in both the USA and the UK. In Chapter 4 we noted Davis' observation that by the end of the 1990s, it was generally understood that 'the corporation existed to create shareholder value; other commitments were means to that end'. A very different understanding of the implications of growing financialisation had dominated discussion only a few years before. As late as 1996, it was argued that the US system of corporate investment was 'failing' by virtue of a short-term emphasis on share price returns at the expense of long-term corporate value. The result was a 'distortion of corporate investment priorities' that was putting 'American companies in a range of industries at a serious disadvantage in global competition and, ultimately, threatens the long-term growth of the US economy' (Porter, 1997: 5). The basis for this claim included evidence that aggregate investment in plant, R&D, and, above all, intangible assets such as employee training and human resource development, were lower in US firms than at their German and Japanese counterparts; that US firms' R&D portfolios had fewer long-term projects than European and Japanese equivalents; and that the hurdle rate implied by US investment evaluation procedures was higher than the true cost of capital. The country with 'the most efficient capital markets of any nation' was producing 'apparently suboptimal behavior' because of the stress on current stock price as the principal benchmark of corporate value (Porter, 1997: 8).

Concern was also expressed more recently in the UK – not for the first time – about the excessive role of the stock market in British industry and the endemic short-termism of shareholders in British companies. Writing in the *Financial Times*, its former editor, Richard Lambert, described a report from the Bank of England in May 2011 identifying investors' short-termism as a form of market failure. He quoted Sir Ralph Robbins, former CEO and later chairman of Rolls-Royce: '"What do you want", Sir Ralph would ask. "A world-leading company in a dozen years' time, or a bigger pay-out today?" Time and again, the reply would come: "Give us the money"' (FT, 2011c).

Arguments like these pose a direct challenge to the view that capital markets are informationally efficient, but they were put to one side once the boom in high-technology stocks began to get underway in the late 1990s and were not revived when the stock market bubble burst in 2000, as an asset-price boom in residential property securities, encouraged by low interest rates, took the place of the one in equities. In the wake of the financial crisis that gathered momentum from 2008, it has been argued that 'the finance based theory of the corporation has lost credibility' (Davis, 2009: 41). But for these critics, it was nevertheless impossible to return to the 'organization society' which financialisation had displaced. The local economic forces present in the US and UK markets are too strong to allow imposition of, for example, the Japanese community firm model to solve these problems. As Davis argued subsequently in his paper, quoted above: 'we cannot go back to a system of corporate-sponsored welfare capitalism any more than we can return to feudalism'.

'Excess' was arguably also present in Japan. The accumulated reserves that activist hedge funds like Steel Partners identified at some of their first Japanese targets and the intense focus of some boards on their companies' operations, to the exclusion of financial concerns or attention to shareholders, were seen by some in Japan as well as overseas as illustrations of how the community firm could degenerate when management lost its sense of balance. The funds saw the solution to these problems to be adoption of shareholder primacy ideas but, just as US companies might find it difficult to solve their problems by returning to 'feudalism', so Japanese companies could not accept solutions that diverged from their local institutional framework of corporate governance.

The account we have given of the confrontational activist hedge fund episode in Japan does not show that a shareholder primacy approach could never work there, nor that it is unsuitable for other systems, such as that of the USA. But the clash of models that we have described throws into sharp relief the limitations of corporate governance mechanisms outside their home environments. In Japan the funds were confronting not capricious arrangements sustained by self-interested management, but the operation of a system that was robust because it had evolved successfully to deliver consistent returns to its key participants. The funds' interventions revealed weaknesses but they also exacerbated some potentially problematic developments, such as the spate of defence measures adopted across Japanese listed companies in the wake of the Nippon Broadcasting System judgment. What they did not do was to change the underlying model of Japanese corporate governance, although the pressure they applied may have helped to reinforce existing trends such as the tendency to pay greater attention to shareholders and increase dividends. Official pressure for enhanced external supervision, for example, is likely to return to the corporate law reform agenda from time to time, as it did in the context of the debate over the company with committee reforms in the early 2000s. There were indications that the DPJ government that took power from late 2009 intended to implement various reforms to corporate governance practices, either by direct legislation or by imposing soft regulation through stock exchange rules. These initiatives may bear fruit at some later stage but no major reforms had been achieved as of August 2011.

We offer three broad conclusions from this experience with regard to the exportability of corporate governance systems in general and the global relevance of shareholder primacy ideas in particular. Our first conclusion is that it highlights the distinctiveness of all national corporate governance models. Corporate governance regimes across the world are still enormously varied (Aguilera and Jackson, 2010). In a global context, both shareholder primacy and the community firm are rooted in specific environments and will only be duplicated where the same conditions are faithfully reproduced. Most national systems do not have strong institutional investor ownership, a market for corporate control, or a large cadre of non-executive directors to populate the boards of listed companies: they are therefore unlikely to provide a welcoming environment in the near future for the values of shareholder primacy precisely as it operates in the USA or the UK. Similarly, most national systems lack Japan's post-war experience of rebuilding an economy under the leadership of largely autonomous managers at widely owned companies financed mainly by banks: they are unlikely to mimic the community firm exactly.

Our second conclusion is that the tendency of corporate governance researchers and policy makers to treat the US case as the benchmark against which other systems are measured is in danger of becoming a barrier to understanding. Hedge fund activism involving public confrontation is an example of a distinctively American practice which has been confused with a global one. Confrontational activism originated in the USA because it was sustained by a particular local environment where it could arbitrage deviations from the strict observance of shareholder primacy. When it left that environment behind it had of necessity to operate differently, first in the UK and then in Continental Europe. When it came to Japan, it faced a superficially similar structural environment but with even greater practical impediments than in the UK and Europe. By contrast, quieter forms of activism that accommodate themselves more to the demands of the community firm may be succeeding better. The failure of confrontational activism to make headway in Japan is hard to explain if the convergence of systems on US practice is seen as inevitable, but much more straightforward if we take seriously evidence of the resilience of national systems in the face of globalising influences (for example Boyer, 1996; Wade, 1996).

Our third conclusion concerns the role played by corporate governance arrangements as a source of competitive advantage or disadvantage, and the way in which situations in different national markets will develop in coming years. The defining characteristic of the Japanese model of corporate governance is not that boards simply hoard cash, or even that they prioritise worker or managerial interests over those of shareholders. They often do all of these things but it would be more accurate to think of Japanese companies as orientated internally towards the organisational structure of the enterprise and externally towards competitive success in product markets, as opposed to achievement of the financial benchmarks set by capital markets. Their competitive position in product markets is the primary benchmark by which Japanese firms measure their own success, and maintaining successful relations with the various corporate constituencies, including but not confined to shareholders, is a means to this end. By contrast, the managerial strategies of most listed companies in America or Britain are openly orientated towards capital market benchmarks. This is the outcome of a corporate governance system in which, to an increasing degree from the 1980s onwards, 'the main purpose of those who controlled corporations was no longer making profits from production and trade but rather to assure that the liabilities of the corporations were fully priced in the financial market' (Minsky, 1993: 112). The competitive success of these companies depended critically on being able to maintain a high and rising share price, a condition which made it possible for the more successful to grow by acquisition, eventually on a global scale. The perception that this might have involved a confusion of means and ends may explain Jack Welch's observation in 2009 that making shareholder value the sole objective of the company was 'a dumb idea' (FT, 2009e). It remains to be seen whether companies which built their strategic position on a capital-market orientated strategy will prosper in the near future in a context likely to be far removed from the buoyant financial conditions of the mid to late 2000s.

Against this background, we may question whether the organisational values associated with the joint stock company in Japan are really as outmoded as some commentators, even in the aftermath of the global financial crisis, have suggested. It has perhaps been too easily assumed, particularly on the basis of US or UK experience, that a public listing on securities markets cannot be combined with an enduring organisational identity for the firm and a commitment to return value to a range of corporate constituencies. In Japan, the company of the future will not be exactly the same as the community firm of the immediate post-war decades. Managerial structures are changing and the respective roles of boards and senior managers are being recast. Shareholder voice will play a more prominent role than it has in the past. However, shareholder activism of any sort will make little headway in the Japanese setting as long as it is seen as undermining the board's capacity for strategic decision-making and hence the long-term competitiveness of the company. National corporate governance systems are distinct to their particular environments and therefore not easily exportable. Thus we do not believe that the community firm is a universally valid solution to the imperfections of the joint stock company, any more than is shareholder primacy. However, its focus on the organisational sustainability of the underlying business of the company may come to resonate well with corporate governance priorities in the aftermath of the global financial crisis. Shareholder primacy ideas, by contrast, have become identified with a financialised variant of capitalism which, as exemplified by the approach of the more confrontational activist hedge funds, views businesses primarily as commodities and as opportunities for short-term gain, a position which is coming under renewed scrutiny as the global financial crisis continues (Williams and Zumbansen, 2011).

The experience of hedge fund activism in Japan suggests that there always were limits to shareholder primacy as the driver of corporate governance ideas and practices. How far we can expect to see the unravelling of the shareholder primacy norm in the aftermath of a crisis which has put the logic of financial capitalism into question remains to be seen. The roots of the crisis lie in the structures and tendencies of the preceding period which began with the 'deal decade' of the 1980s and culminated in the shareholder-driven capitalism of the 2000s, of which hedge fund activism was the clearest expression. We have sought to throw light on that period through a study which demonstrates that, in one significant national context, the logic of the shareholder primacy norm was exhausted, even before the financial crisis brought one phase of the cycle to an end and initiated another, with results which are as yet unknown.

Data appendix

Interview data

Table A.1 presents details of the entities visited, broken down by sector, and shows data on the number of meetings for each sector. Table A.2 provides specific information on the corporate visits, in an anonymised form.

As explained in Chapter 8, a data set was identified of targeted companies and related hedge funds as at the end of December 2007, which was refined into a list of 119 companies targeted by 19 funds. This was further divided, according to the attention that each hedge fund received from *Nikkei*, into 39 interventions by 5 funds following 'public' strategies (as defined) and a further 80 investments by funds that were characterised as 'non-public'. The 119 company list is shown in Table A.3.

Table A.1 *List of meetings held 2003–10*

	2003–4		2006		2007–8		2009		2010		2003–10	
	entities	meetings	entities	meetings	entities	meetings	entities	meetings	entities	meetings	entities	meetings
Manufacturers	11	26	3	4	1	1	2	2	0	0	17	33
Services	4	7	3	3	2	2	3	3	1	1	13	16
Financial	2	7	2	3	0	0	0	0	0	0	4	10
Investors	7	7	1	1	4	4	3	3	2	2	17	17
Others[1]	11	11	13	13	6	6	6	6	4	4	40	40
Totals	**35**	**58**	**22**	**24**	**13**	**13**	**14**	**14**	**7**	**7**	**91**	**116**
Repeat visits[2]	*23*		*5*		*6*		*9*		*5*		*48*	
Net entities	*12*		*17*		*7*		*5*		*2*		*43*	

Notes:

1. 'Others' primarily covers associations, ministries, market infrastructure providers, lawyers, commentators, and academics.
2. 'Repeat visits' indicates either multiple meetings with representatives of the same entity in 2003–4 or meetings thereafter at entities already visited in earlier years.
3. Total of manufacturers, service companies, and financial companies visited 2003–10 after excluding repeat visits was 20.

Table A.2 *Manufacturing, services, and financial companies visited 2003–10 (analysed by characteristics at time of contact)*

	Sector	Company with committees	Executive officers	External directors	IR effort	Foreign exposure	Foreign ownership
1	Construction		x				<10%
2	Machinery	x	x	x	x	x	>10%
3	Machinery			x	x	x	>10%
4	Trading						<10%
5	Transport			x			<10%
6	Chemical		x	x	x		>10%
7	Machinery		x	x	x	x	>10%
8	Financial	x	x	x	x	x	>20%
9	Trading		x	x	x	x	>10%
10	Utility				x	x	>20%
11	Chemical				x	x	>10%
12	Chemical		x			x	>20%
13	Machinery			x		x	>20%
14	Transport		x	x	x	x	<10%
15	Utility		x	x	x	x	>10%
16	Electrical				x	x	>20%
17	Financial		x	x	x	x	>20%
18	Electrical	x	x	x	x	x	>10%
19	Electrical	x	x	x	x	x	>20%
20	Machinery		x		x	x	>10%

Table A.3 *List of investments by funds categorised as 'active orientation' by Thomson Reuters at 31 December 2007*

Company name	Ownership % 31 Dec. 2007		Fund names and percentages from EDINET and company accounts
	Thomson Reuters	31 Dec. 2007	
Tokyo Kohtetsu Co Ltd	34.64	24.71	Ichigo Asset Mgmt Int'l Pte Ltd ('Ichigo') 24.71%
Nikki Co Ltd	31.73	23.20	Ichigo 23.20%
Aderans Holdings Ltd (now Uni-hair)	24.69	24.69	Steel Partners Japan Strategic Fund (Offshore) LP ('Steel Partners') 24.69%
Sansei Yusōki Co Ltd	24.57	24.57	Steel Partners 24.57%
A & D Co Ltd	23.76	18.11	Liberty Square Asset Mgmt LP ('Liberty') 6.94%, Tower Tōshi Komon KK ('Tower') 11.17%
Crymson Co Ltd	21.33	21.57	Tower 21.47%
Ōhashi Technica Inc	20.91	20.38	Ichigo 5.01%, Tower 15.37%
Shōfū Inc	20.13	20.44	Steel Partners 10.31%, SFP Value Realization Master Fund Ltd ('SFP') 10.13%
IK Co Ltd	19.18	19.65	Tower 19.65%
Takada Kikō Co Ltd	19.11	19.11	Liberty 19.11%
Nissin Foods Holdings Co Ltd	18.99	18.99	Steel Partners 18.99%
Nōritz Corp	18.98	18.60	Steel Partners 18.60%
Sapporo Holdings Ltd	17.55	19.28	Steel Partners 19.28%
Aval Data Corp	16.31	17.66	SFP 17.66%
Sanjō Machine Works Ltd	16.09	16.18	SFP 16.18%
DC Co Ltd	16.08	16.29	Blue Sky Capital Management Pty Ltd ('Blue Sky') 16.29%
Maruichi Steel Tube Ltd	15.96	15.26	Steel Partners 15.26%

Table A.3 (*cont.*)

Company name	Ownership % 31 Dec. 2007		
	Thomson Reuters	Fund names and percentages from EDINET and company accounts	
Maezawa Kyūsō Industries Co Ltd	15.73	17.91	SFP 17.91%
Fujitec Co Ltd	15.30	15.30	Dalton Investments LLC ('Dalton') 15.30% (until 14 Dec 2007, then 4.13%)
Kuraudia Co Ltd	15.09	15.10	Tower 15.10%
Ezaki Glico Co Ltd	15.08	14.44	Steel Partners 14.37% + Liberty 0.07%
Tekken Corp	15.01	15.10	Blue Sky 15.01%
Ebara-Udylite Co Ltd	14.97	15.13	Tower 15.13%
Asahi Broadcasting Corp	14.43	14.43	Liberty 14.43%
Nireco Corp	14.20	15.25	SFP 15.25%
Tiemco Ltd	14.13	13.77	SFP 13.77%
Fukuda Denshi Co Ltd	14.09	14.09	Steel Partners 14.09%
Yushiro Chemical Industries Co Ltd	13.69	13.69	Steel Partners 13.69%
Nihon Tokushu Toryō Co Ltd	13.37	13.38	Steel Partners 13.38%
Nakakita Seisakusho Co Ltd	12.96	19.82	SFP 6.77%, Steel Partners 13.05%
Citizen Holdings Co Ltd	12.62	12.62	Steel Partners 12.62%
Tōmen Electronics Corp	12.57	12.57	Tower 12.57%
Chūō Warehouse Co Ltd	12.22	12.22	Steel Partners 12.22%
Brother Industries Ltd	11.98	10.23	Steel Partners 10.23%

Company			
Matsuya Co Ltd	11.55	12.46	SFP 12.46%
Takara Printing Co Ltd	11.46	11.49	Liberty 11.49%
Tenryū Saw Mfg Co Ltd	11.36	11.36	Steel Partners 11.36%
Toba Yōkō	11.36	11.36	Ichigo 11.36%
Nippon Information Development Co (NDI)	10.19	10.19	Tower 10.19%
CDG Co Ltd	10.05	10.05	Tower 10.05%
J-Power	9.90	9.90	TCI 9.90%
Watts Co Ltd	9.88	9.99	Tower 9.99%
King Jim Co Ltd	9.78	10.42	SFP 10.42%
Hikari Business Form Co Ltd	9.56	11.12	Dalton 6.28%, JMBO Fund Ltd 3.28%, Altma Fund SICAV Plc 1.56% (all Dalton)
Airtech Japan Ltd	9.32	9.29	Tower 9.29%
New Cosmos Electric Co Ltd	9.27	9.25	Steel Partners 9.25%
Denki Kōgyō Co Ltd	9.23	9.84	Steel Partners 9.84%
Paltek Corp	9.20	9.20	Tower 9.20%
Tomoe Corp	8.96	8.96	Gandbara Master Fund Limited ('Gandbara') 8.96%
Tenma Corp	8.79	8.37	Liberty 8.37%
Kyōsan Electric Mfg	—	8.73	Dalton 8.73%
Maezawa Industries Inc	8.63	8.48	SFP 8.48%
Tōei Animation Co Ltd	8.57	8.57	Liberty 8.57%
House Foods Corp	8.55	7.94	Steel Partners 7.94%
Daito Gyorui Co Ltd	8.53	8.53	Halberdier Capital Management Pte Ltd 8.53%
Gunze Ltd	8.50	7.83	HBK Investment LP 7.83%
Nagawa Co Ltd	8.43	9.29	SFP 9.29%

Table A.3 (*cont.*)

Company name	Ownership % 31 Dec. 2007		
	Thomson Reuters		Fund names and percentages from EDINET and company accounts
Hi-Lex Corp	8.37	8.37	*Steel Partners 8.37%*
Mitsui Sōko Co Ltd	8.25	8.25	*Liberty 8.25%*
Yagi & Co Ltd	8.22	8.22	*Tower 8.22%*
Pla Matels Corp (Puramatels)	7.87	7.87	*Tower 7.87%*
Ihara Science Corp	7.83	11.68	*Capital Guardian Trust Co. 5.54%*
Inaba Denkisangyō Co Ltd	7.72	7.09	*Steel Partners 7.09%*
Saison Information Systems Co Ltd	7.69	7.69	*Tower 7.69%*
Hisaka Works Ltd	7.64	7.64	*Steel Partners 7.64%*
Zuikō Corp	7.64	8.12	*SFP 8.12%*
Karakami Kankoh	7.52	7.52	*Elmwood Advisors Pte Ltd 7.52%*
Hakuseisha Co Ltd	7.41	7.02	*SFP 7.02%*
Japan Transcity Corp	7.40	7.40	*Liberty 7.40%*
Fujita Kankō Inc	7.37	7.37	*Blue Sky 7.37%*
ITC Networks Corp	7.31	7.30	*Tower 7.30%*
Parco Co Ltd	7.26	7.26	*Wesley Capital Mgmt LLC 7.26%*
Jeans Mate Corp	7.11	7.11	*Liberty 7.11%*
Warehouse Co Ltd	7.03	7.03	*Tower 7.03%*
PCA Corp	7.02	7.02	*Tower 7.02%*
Eikoh Inc	6.97	6.97	*Tower 6.97%*

Company			
Aiphone Co Ltd	6.90	6.90	Ichigo 6.90%
Nippon Ceramic Co Ltd	6.84	12.02	SFP 7.02%
Ishihara Chemical Co Ltd	6.77	6.77	Steel Partners 6.77%
Agro-Kaneshō Co Ltd	6.74	6.94	SFP 6.94%
Miraca Holdings Inc	6.72	6.57	Steel Partners 6.57%
LEC Inc	6.57	6.57	Tower 6.57%
Ishihara Sangyō Kaisha Ltd	6.49	6.76	Indus Capital Partners LLC ('Indus') 6.76%
Meitō Sangyō Co Ltd	6.46	7.10	SFP 7.10%
Nisshinbō Industries Inc	6.35	5.05	Steel Partners 4.46%, Liberty 0.59%
Daiichi Kensetsu Corp	6.25	6.25	Tower 6.25%
JP-Holdings Inc	6.06	5.95	DKR Sound Shore Oasis Fund Ltd 5.95%
Yōmeishu Seizō Co Ltd	6.04	6.05	SFP 6.05%
NEC Electronics (now Renesas Electronics)	—	6.03	Perry 6.03%
Systems Design Co Ltd	5.99	5.99	Tower 5.99%
Amano Corp	5.98	5.98	OZ Management LP ('OZ Mgmt') 5.98%
Kuriyama Corp	5.90	5.90	Tower 5.90%
TTK Co Ltd	5.85	5.82	Steel Partners 5.82%
Meihō Facility Works Ltd	5.83	5.83	Tower 5.83%
Kikkōman Corp	5.82	5.65	Steel Partners 5.65%
Nippon Fine Chemical Co Ltd	5.71	19.73	Dalton 14.02%, JMBO Fund 5.71% (all Dalton)
Chūōkeizai-Sha Inc	5.64	6.07	SFP 6.07%
Happinet Corp	5.56	5.56	Ichigo 5.56%
Fuji Corp	5.52	5.52	Tower 5.52%
Ajis Co Ltd	5.42	5.42	Tower 5.42%

Table A.3 *(cont.)*

Company name	Ownership % 31 Dec. 2007		
	Thomson Reuters	Fund names and percentages from EDINET and company accounts	
Raito Kōgyō Co Ltd	5.36	5.36	*Halberdier Capital Research 5.36%*
Trans Cosmos Inc	5.16	5.16	*Dalton 5.16%*
Shibusawa Warehouse Co Ltd	5.11	5.11	*Liberty 5.11%*
Tsuzuki Denki Co Ltd	5.08	5.08	*Tower 5.08%*
Descente Ltd	5.06	6.07	*Indus 6.07%*
Shimachū Co Ltd	5.05	5.05	*OZ Mgmt 5.05%*
Asics Corp	5.03	5.03	*Gandhara 5.03%*
Prap Japan Inc	5.00	5.00	*Liberty 5.00%*
Kaneshita Construction Co Ltd	4.99	5.55	*Steel Partners 5.55%*
Hitachi Zōsen Corp	4.98	4.98	*Indus 4.98%*
Siix Corp	4.89	4.89	*Tower 4.89%*
Chiyoda Integre Co Ltd	4.81	5.14	*Ichigo 5.14%*
Tigers Polymer Corp	4.74	5.02	*SFP 5.02%*
Nihon Kaiheiki Industries Co Ltd	4.68	4.45	*SFP 4.45%*
Bull-Dog Sauce Co Ltd	4.40	4.40	*Steel Partners 4.40%*
Tsurumi Manufacturing Co Ltd	3.72	7.37	*Dalton 7.37%*
Taikisha Ltd	1.93	13.30	*Silchester International Investors Ltd. 13.30%*
Central Security Patrols Co Ltd	1.83	2.12	*SFP 1.83% + associates 0.29%*
Tōa Valve Holding Co	1.80	1.80	*Tower 1.80%*

Source: Thomson Reuters (adjusted)

EDINET

EDINET is the abbreviation of 'Electronic Disclosure for Investors' NETwork'. It operates through the servers of the Cabinet Office (*Naikaku-chō*) but is controlled by the Financial Services Authority (*Kinyū-chō* or 'FSA'). Its purpose is to bring together obligatory filings from listed companies and investors in a format accessible to the public. In the FSA's explanation accompanying the launch of a new version of the system in March 2008 it stated: 'EDINET is an electronic corporate disclosure system under the Financial Instruments and Exchange Act, and all listed or major fund-raising companies and investment funds in Japan are required to file their disclosure documents using the system. The corporate disclosure documents submitted by these entities are publicly available on the Internet through EDINET' (FSA, 2008).

Our main use of EDINET has been to inspect disclosures by funds of shareholdings in excess of 5 per cent in Japanese listed companies. Under amendments to the Securities and Exchange Law in 1990 (see Chapter 6), public disclosure was required of all beneficial share ownership in excess of 5 per cent in Japanese listed companies. These data are available to the public for approximately five years but older submissions can often be traced through commercial share data websites.

The current underlying legislation is contained in Chapter II–III, Article 27, of the 2007 amendments to the Financial Instruments and Exchange Act or *Kinyū Shōhin Torihiki Hō* (formerly the Securities and Exchange Law or *Shōken Torihiki Hō*).

The reporting obligations vary depending on whether the investor declares its objectives to be pure portfolio investment or making 'important suggestions' (*jūyō teian kōi nado*). The funds that we are studying generally fall into the second category. The FSA described the system in an introduction to the then planned changes published in September 2006. The default process is as follows: 'If total shareholdings in a listed company reach above 5%, the shareholder must submit a "report on large shareholdings" within 5 business days from the date of the purchase. (If the holdings increase or decrease by 1% or more at a later date, a "report on changes" must also be submitted within 5 business days)'. This captures the majority of cases in which we are interested, although some earlier investments by, for example, the Murakami Fund, did not follow it. Less rigorous requirements apply

to pure portfolio investors: 'However, in consideration of the administrative workload for institutional investors engaged in a large volume
of trading as part of their daily business activities, a lower frequency
of reporting will be required (special reporting system)'. The timing
for such pure portfolio investors was formerly every three months, by
the 15th of the following month, but from the 2006/7 amendments
became 'roughly every 2 weeks, within 5 business days' (FSA, 2006).

Bibliography

Abe, N., and Jung, T. (2004). 'Cross-shareholdings, outside directors, and managerial turnover: the case of Japan'. *Hitotsubashi University Hi-Stat Discussion Paper Series*, No. 38, 1–34.

ABN AMRO. (2008). ABN AMRO Bank N.V. company website. Retrieved from www.abnamro.com, 15 January 2008.

ACGA. (2008). *ACGA white paper on corporate governance in Japan*. Hong Kong: Asian Corporate Governance Association.

Acheson, G., Hickson, C., and Turner, J. (2010) 'Does limited liability matter? Evidence from nineteenth-century British banking'. *Review of Law & Economics*, 6(2), 99–125.

Adams, R. (2009). 'Governance and the financial crisis'. *ECGI Finance Working Paper*, No. 130/2009.

Aguilera, R., and Cuervo-Cazurra, A. (2009). 'Codes of good governance'. *Corporate Governance: An International Review*, 17(3), 376–87.

Aguilera, R., and Jackson, G. (2010). 'Comparative and international corporate governance'. *The Academy of Management Annals*, 4(1), 485–556.

Ahlering, B., and Deakin, S. (2007). 'Labor regulation, corporate governance, and legal origin: a case of institutional complementarity?'. *Law & Society Review*, 41(4), 865–908.

Ahmadjian, C. L. (2003). 'Changing Japanese corporate governance'. In U. Schaede and W. W. Grimes (eds.), *Japan's managed globalization: adapting to the twenty-first century* (215–40). New York: M. E. Sharpe.

(2007). 'Foreign investors and corporate governance in Japan'. In M. Aoki, G. Jackson and H. Miyajima (eds.), *Corporate governance in Japan: institutional change and organizational diversity* (125–50). New York: Oxford University Press.

AIMA. (2008). *AIMA's roadmap to hedge funds*. London: The Alternative Investment Management Association.

Aoki, M. (1994). 'Monitoring characteristics of the main bank system: an analytical and developmental view'. In M. Aoki and H. Patrick (eds.), *The Japanese main bank system* (109–41). New York: Oxford University Press.

(2001). *Toward a comparative institutional analysis.* Cambridge, MA: MIT Press.

(2007) 'Conclusion: whither Japan's corporate governance?' In M. Aoki, G. Jackson and H. Miyajima (eds.), *Corporate governance in Japan: institutional change and organizational diversity* (427–48). New York: Oxford University Press.

(2010). *Corporations in evolving diversity: cognition, governance and institutions.* New York: Oxford University Press.

Arlington. (2009). Arlington Capital Investors Limited company website. Retrieved from www.acil.co.uk, 16 July 2009.

Armour, J., and Gordon, J. (2008). 'The Berle-Means corporation in the 21st century', paper presented to University of Pennsylvania Law School seminar, 'Understanding Business Law Scholarship', 6 November 2008.

Armour, J., and Skeel, D. (2007). 'Who writes the rules for hostile takeovers, and why? The peculiar divergence of US and UK takeover regulation'. *Georgetown Law Journal*, 95, 1727–94.

Armour, J., Deakin, S., and Konzelmann, S. (2003). 'Shareholder primacy and the trajectory of UK corporate governance'. *British Journal of Industrial Relations*, 41, 531–55.

Armour, J., Deakin, S., Lele, P., and Siems, M. (2009a) 'How do legal rules evolve? Evidence from a cross-national comparison of shareholder, creditor and worker protection'. *American Journal of Comparative Law*, 57, 579–630.

Armour, J., Hansmann, H., and Kraakman, R. (2009b). 'What is corporate law?'. In R. Kraakman, J. Armour, P. Davies, L. Enriques, H. Hansmann, G. Hertig, H. Kanda and E. Rock (eds.), *The anatomy of corporate law: a comparative and functional approach* (1–34). New York: Oxford University Press.

Aronson, B. (2010). 'Postwar reform of corporate law and corporate governance in Japan: under the Occupation and the Japanese reaction'. In the International House of Japan and the Blakemore Foundation (eds.) *Law and practice in postwar Japan: the postwar legal reforms and their influence* (59–65). Tokyo: International House of Japan.

Asahi Shimbun. (2008). '買収攻防、情と法の正義 (Bid tactics: the right balance of emotion and the law)'. 朝日新聞 (*Asahi Shimbun*), 16 April 2008.

AWSJ. (2004). 'Steel Partners' bold moves rattle Japanese firms'. *Asian Wall Street Journal*, 15 April 2004.

Bainbridge, S. M. (2010). 'Shareholder activism in the Obama Era'. In F. S. Kieff and T. A. Paredes (eds.), *Perspectives on corporate governance* (217–34). New York: Cambridge University Press.

Bauer, R., Braun, R., and Clark, G. L. (2008). 'The emerging market for European corporate governance: the relationship between governance and capital expenditures, 1997–2005'. *Journal of Economic Geography*, 8(4), 441–69.

BBC. (2005). 'Deutsche Boerse chief quits post'. *BBC News*. Retrieved from http://news.bbc.co.uk, 23 November 2011.

(2006). 'NYSE and Euronext in $20 billion merger'. *BBC News*. Retrieved from http://news.bbc.co.uk, 23 November 2011.

Becht, M., Franks, J., and Grant, J. (2010). 'Hedge fund activism in Europe'. *ECGI Law Working Paper Series in Finance*, No. 283/2010.

Becht, M., Franks, J., Mayer, C., and Rossi, S. (2009). 'Returns to shareholder activism: evidence from a clinical study of the Hermes UK Focus Fund'. *The Review of Financial Studies*, 22(8), 3093–3129.

Beltratti, R., and Stulz, R. (2010). 'Why did some banks perform better during the credit crisis? A cross-country study of the impact of governance and regulation'. *Fisher College of Business Working Paper*, No. 2009-03-012.

Berle, A. A., and Means, G. C. (1932). *The modern corporation and private property* (1991 edn). New Brunswick, NJ: Transaction Publishers.

Black, B., and Coffee, J. (1994). 'Hail Britannia? Institutional investor behavior under limited regulation'. *Michigan Law Review*, 92, 1997–2087.

Blair, M. (2003) 'Locking in capital: what corporate law achieved for business organizers in the nineteenth century'. *UCLA Law Review*, 51, 387–455.

Blair, M., and Stout, L. A. (1999). 'A team production theory of corporate law'. *Virginia Law Review*, 85(2), 248–328.

Bloomberg. (2006a). 'Fukui sold fund after losing confidence in Murakami'. *Bloomberg.com*.

(2006b). 'Murakami arrested on suspicion of insider trading'. *Bloomberg.com*.

(2007). 'Japan stocks rally loses steam on shareholder concern (Update 1)'. *Bloomberg.com*.

(2008). 'J-Power delays Oma nuclear plant start by 2½ years'. *Bloomberg.com*.

(2009a). 'Dalton to merge Japanese units, seek acquisitions'. *Bloomberg.com*.

(2009b). 'Steel Partners seeks to convert biggest fund to public company'. *Bloomberg.com*.

(2009c). 'TCI's John Ho said to leave U.K. fund for new venture'. *Bloomberg.com*.

(2009d). 'TCI said to plan fee cut, ease withdrawal limits'. *Bloomberg.com*.

(2009e). 'Steel Partners wins Cayman Island court case versus plaintiff investors, including Carl Icahn affiliate'. *Bloomberg.com*.

(2010). 'Lichtenstein's Steel Partners sells its entire stake in Sapporo Holdings'. *Bloomberg.com.*

Bolton, A. (2007). 'Cadbury sends a bad message to corporate raiders'. *Financial Times* (Letters), 10 June 2007.

Boyer, R. (1996). 'The convergence hypothesis revisited: globalization but still the century of nations?'. In S. Berger and R. Dore (eds.), *National diversity and global capitalism* (29–59). Ithaca, NY: Cornell University Press.

Bratton, W. (2002). 'Enron and the dark side of shareholder value'. *Tulane Law Review*, 76, 1275–1361.

(2007). 'Hedge funds and governance targets'. *The Georgetown Law Journal*, 95(5), 1375–1433.

Brav, A., Jiang, W., Partnoy, F., and Thomas, R. (2008a). 'Hedge fund activism, corporate governance, and firm performance'. *Journal of Finance*, 63(4), 1729–75.

(2008b). 'The returns to hedge fund activism'. *Financial Analysts Journal*, 64(6), 45–61.

Buchanan, J., and Deakin, S. (2008). 'Japan's paradoxical response to the new "global standard" in corporate governance'. *Zeitschrift Für Japanisches Recht/Journal of Japanese Law*, 13(26), 59–84.

(2009). 'In the shadow of corporate governance reform; change and continuity in managerial practice at listed Japanese companies'. In D. H. Whittaker and S. Deakin (eds.), *Corporate governance and managerial reform in Japan* (28–69). New York: Oxford University Press.

Bughin, J., and Copeland, T. E. (1997). 'The virtuous cycle of shareholder value creation'. *McKinsey Quarterly*, 2, 156–67.

Businessweek. (2006). 'The battle for the bourses: two hedge funds are pressuring Paris-based Euronext to hook up with either the Deutsche Börse or the New York Stock Exchange – or else'. *Businessweek*, 22 May 2006.

Cadbury, A. (1992). *Report of the committee on the financial aspects of corporate governance*. London: Gee and Co. Ltd.

(2002). *Corporate governance and chairmanship: a personal view*. Oxford University Press.

Callen, T., and Ostry, J. D. (eds.). (2003). *Japan's lost decade: policies for economic revival*. Washington: International Monetary Fund (IMF).

Callon, S. (2007). 'Ichigo's Scott Callon leads Japan's first successful shareholder revolt'. Retrieved from www.japansociety.org, 23 November 2011.

Carlton, W. T., Nelson, J. M., and Weisbach, M. S. (1998). 'The influence of institutions on corporate governance through private negotiations: evidence from TIAA-CREF'. *The Journal of Finance*, 53(4), 1335–62.

Chatterjee, S. (2007). 'Warren Lichtenstein heads Steel Partners'. *Wall Street Activist.* Retrieved from www.wallstreetactivist.com, 6 November 2009.

Cheffins, B. (2008). *Corporate ownership and control: British business transformed.* Oxford University Press.

Cheffins, B., and Armour, J. (2011). 'The past, present and future of shareholder activism by hedge funds'. *University of Cambridge Legal Studies Research Paper*, No. 38/2011.

Chen, X., Yao, T., and Yu, T. (2007). 'Prudent man or agency problem? On the performance of insurance mutual funds'. *Journal of Financial Intermediation*, 16(2), 175–203. (Published online in December 2006.)

Chernow, R. (1993). *The Warburgs.* New York: Random House (First Vintage Books).

Chūbu Electric. (2007). *The policy on shareholder return.* Nagoya: Chūbu Electric Power Co., Inc. (press release).

Clifford, C. P. (2008). 'Value creation or destruction? Hedge funds as shareholder activists'. *Journal of Corporate Finance*, 14(4), 323–36.

Coase, R. H. (1937). 'The nature of the firm'. *Economica (NS)*, 4, 386–405.

 (1988). 'The problem of social cost'. In R. H. Coase, *The firm, the market and the law*. University of Chicago Press.

Conference Board. (2008). *The 2008 institutional investment report: trends in institutional investor assets and equity ownership of US corporations.* New York: The Conference Board.

Connor, G., and Woo, M. (2004). *An introduction to hedge funds.* London School of Economics and International Asset Management.

Culpepper, P. D. (2011). *Quiet politics and business power: corporate control in Europe and Japan.* New York: Cambridge University Press.

CVSG. (2005). 企業価値報告書〜公正な企業社会のルール形成に向けた提案 (Corporate Value Report: Proposals with a view to formulating equitable rules for the corporate community). Tokyo: 企業価値研究会 (Corporate Value Study Group).

 (2006). 企業価値報告書2006〜企業社会における公正なルールの定着に向けて (Corporate Value Report 2006: Toward the firm establishment of fair rules in the corporate community). Tokyo: 企業価値研究会 (Corporate Value Study Group).

 (2007). 企業価値の向上及び公正な手続き確保のための経営者による企業買収(MBO)に関する報告書 (Report on corporate acquisitions by management (MBOs) to promote the maintenance of equitable procedures which increase corporate value). Tokyo: 企業価値研究会 (Corporate Value Study Group).

(2008). 近時の諸環境の変化を踏まえた買収防衛策の在り方 (Report of takeover defense measures in view of recent environmental changes). Tokyo: 企業価値研究会 (Corporate Value Study Group).

Davies, P. (2008) *Gower and Davies' principles of modern company law* (8th edn). London: Sweet and Maxwell.

(2010). *Introduction to company law* (2nd edn). Oxford University Press.

Davis, G. F. (2009). 'The rise and fall of finance and the end of the society of organizations'. *Academy of Management Perspectives, 23*(3), 27–44.

Deakin, S. (2002). 'The many futures of the contract of employment'. In J. Conaghan, M. Fischl and K. Klare (eds.), *Labour law in an era of globalization: transformative practices and possibilities* (177–96). Oxford University Press.

(2003). 'Enterprise-risk: the juridical nature of the firm revisited'. *Industrial Law Journal, 32*, 97–113.

(2011a). 'What directors do (and fail to do): some comparative notes on board structure and corporate governance'. *New York Law School Law Review, 55*, 525–41.

(2011b) 'The juridical nature of the firm'. In T. Clarke and D. Branson (eds.), *Handbook of corporate governance* (113–35). London: Sage.

Deakin, S., and Carvalho, F. (2011). 'System and evolution in corporate governance'. In P. Zumbansen and G-P. Calliess (eds.), *Law, economics and evolutionary theory* (111–30). Cheltenham: Edward Elgar.

Deakin, S., and Hughes, A. (1999). 'Economic efficiency and the proceduralisation of company law'. *Company, Financial and Insolvency Law Review, 3*, 169–89.

Deakin, S., and Konzelmann, S. (2004). 'Learning from Enron'. *Corporate Governance: An International Review, 12*(2), 134–42.

Deakin, S., and Slinger, G. (1997). 'Hostile takeovers, corporate law and the theory of the firm'. *Journal of Law and Society, 24*, 124–50.

Deutsche Börse. (2005a). *Announcement: change in supervisory board.* Frankfurt: Deutsche Börse AG.

(2005b). *Annual general meeting report.* Frankfurt: Deutsche Börse AG.

(2008). *Shareholder structure (2000–2007).* Frankfurt: Deutsche Börse AG.

Diamond. (2008). '「Jパワー問題」が象徴する、経産省官僚の外資アレルギー (The METI bureaucracy's allergy to foreign capital is symbolized by the "J-Power problem"'. *Diamond Online.* 18 April 2008. Retrieved from http://diamond.jp, 8 March 2011.

DiMaggio, P. J., and Powell, W. (1983). 'The iron cage revisited: institutional isomorphism and collective rationality in organizational fields'. *American Sociological Review, 48*(2), 147–60.

DIR. (2006). 会社法下の保有割合と株主の権利 (Shareholding percentages and shareholder rights under the Company Law). Tokyo: 大和総研 (Daiwa Institute of Research).

Dore, R. (2000). *Stock market capitalism: welfare capitalism*. New York: Oxford University Press.

(2008). 'Financialization of the global economy'. *Industrial and Corporate Change*, 17(6), 1097–1112.

(2009). 'Japan's conversion to investor capitalism'. In D. H. Whittaker and S. Deakin (eds.), *Corporate governance and managerial reform in Japan* (134–62). New York: Oxford University Press.

Dōyūkai. (1996). 第12回企業白書主文(要旨)、日本企業の経営構造改革、コーポレート・ガバナンスの観点を踏まえた取締役会と監査役会のあり方 (White Paper no. 12 summary: Reform of the management structures of Japanese business: how the board of directors and the board of corporate auditors should be constituted from a corporate governance viewpoint). Tokyo: 経済同友会 (Keizai Dōyūkai: Japan Association of Corporate Executives).

(2008). *Creating a new style of Japanese management* (English translation): Keizai Dōyūkai (Japan Association of Corporate Executives).

DTI. (2002). *Company Law Steering Committee: modern company law for a competitive economy: developing the framework*. London: Department of Trade and Industry (Department for Business, Enterprise and Regulatory Reform from June 2007).

Easterbrook, F., and Fischel, D. R. (1991). *The economic structure of corporate law*. Cambridge, MA: Harvard University Press.

ECGI. (2007). 'Hedge funds and activism'. *Research Newsletter*, Vol. 4, Spring/Summer 2007.

Economist. (2007). 'Leader of the swarm: Christopher Hohn, like his hedge fund, is powerful, feared – and generous'. *The Economist*, 12 July 2007.

Eichengreen, B., and Mathieson, D. (1999). 'Hedge funds: what do we really know?'. *Economic Issues*, 19, 1–14. Retrieved from http://imf.org, 23 November 2011.

Eisenberg, M. (1989). 'The structure of corporation law'. *Columbia Law Review*, 89, 1461–1525.

EIU. (2009). *Mountains of money? Asset management in Japan*. London: Economist Intelligence Unit.

Enriques, L., and Volpin, P. (2007). 'Corporate governance reforms in continental Europe'. *Journal of Economic Perspectives*, 21(1), 117–40.

Erkens, D., Hung, M., and Matos, P. (2009). 'Corporate governance in the 2007–8 financial crisis: evidence from financial institutions worldwide'. *ECGI Finance Working Paper*, No. 249/2009.

Eurex. (2007). 'Eurex Circular 191/07'. Retrieved from www.eurexchange. com, 23 November 2011.

Fahlenbrach, R., and Stulz, R. (2010). 'Bank CEO incentives and the credit crisis'. *Journal of Financial Economics*, 99, 11–26.

Fairbank, J. K., Reischauer, E. O., and Craig, A. M. (1965). *East Asia: the modern transformation* (third impression, 1969 edn Vol. II). London: George Allen & Unwin Ltd.

Fama, E. (1970). 'Efficient capital markets: a review of theory and empirical work'. *Journal of Finance*, 25, 383–417.

Fama, E., and Jensen, M. (1983). 'Separation of ownership and control'. *Journal of Law and Economics*, 26, 301–25.

Ferran, E. (2011). 'The regulation of hedge funds and private equity: a case study in the development of the EU's regulatory response to the financial crisis'. *ECGI Law Working Paper*, No. 176/2011.

Ferreira, D., Kirchmaier, T., and Metzger, D. (2010). 'Boards of banks'. *ECGI Finance Working Paper*, No. 289/2010.

FINalternatives. (2010). 'TCI profit plummets 80%'. Retrieved from www. finalternatives.com, 23 November 2011.

Financial News. (2011). 'World's largest pension passes a tipping-point'. *Financial News*. Retrieved from www.efinancialnews.com, 23 November 2011.

Fischel, D. R. (1982). 'The corporate governance movement'. *Vanderbilt Law Review*, 35(6), 1259–92.

Fitch. (2010). *Japan special report: Japanese non-life insurance sector: outlook stable on healthier fundamentals*. New York and London: Fitch Ratings.

Flexnews. (2006). 'Japan's Nissin bids for Myōjō to block US fund'. *Flexnews/ Reuter*. Retrieved from www.flex-news-food.com, 15 January 2007.

Freeman, E. R., and McVea, J. (2001). 'A stakeholder approach to strategic management'. In M. Hitt, E. Freeman and J. Harrison (eds.), *The Blackwell handbook of strategic management* (189–207). Oxford: Blackwell Publishing Ltd.

Freudmann, A. (2007). 'Not just barking at the moon'. *IR Magazine*. 1 January 2007. Retrieved from www.insideinvestorrelations.com, 23 November 2011.

Froud, J., Haslam, C., Johal, S., and Williams, K. (2000). 'Shareholder value and financialization: consultancy promises, management moves'. *Economy and Society*, 29(1), 80–110.

FSA. (2006). *New legislation framework for investor protection*. Tokyo: Financial Services Agency, September 2006.

  (2008). *FSA launches new electronic corporate disclosure system (EDINET)*. Tokyo: Financial Services Agency, 17 March 2008.

FT. (2002). 'Laxey Partners increases British Land stake to 9%'. *Financial Times*, 16 July 2002.

    (2003). 'British Land siege paid off for Laxey'. *Financial Times*, 15 September 2003.

    (2005a). 'D Börse acts to heal TCI rift'. *Financial Times*, 21 April 2005.

    (2005b). 'Deutsche Börse forced to drop its bid for London exchange'. *Financial Times*, 7 March 2005.

    (2005c). 'Divided spoils put an end to Laxey-Wyevale battle'. *Financial Times*, 22 December 2005.

    (2005d). 'Fund calls on Börse to drop bid for LSE'. *Financial Times*, 3 February 2005.

    (2005e). 'Standard Life tests Börse on LSE bid'. *Financial Times*, 24 January 2005.

    (2006a). 'Laxey demands Saurer clear-out'. *Financial Times*, 30 August 2006.

    (2006b). 'Laxey move turns up heat on Saurer'. *Financial Times*, 3 March 2006.

    (2006c). 'Steel Partners Japan exodus'. *Financial Times*, 21 June 2006.

    (2006d). 'Unaxis vague on details of deal for Saurer'. *Financial Times*, 7 September 2006.

    (2006e). 'Wyevale suitor reviews options'. *Financial Times*, 18 January 2006.

    (2007a). 'ABN at six-year high as TCI raises hopes of shake-up'. *Financial Times*, 22 February 2007.

    (2007b). 'Implenia accuses Laxey of short-termism'. *Financial Times*, 20 November 2007.

    (2007c). 'Laxey launches bid for Swiss group'. *Financial Times*, 3 November 2007.

    (2007d). 'TCI calls for scalp of ABN chief as battle turns personal'. *Financial Times*, 2 May 2007.

    (2007e). 'Sparx in call for Pentax board shake-up'. *Financial Times*, 1 May 2007.

    (2008a). 'Corporate Japan needs the activist touch'. *Financial Times*, 25 June 2008.

    (2008b). 'Generali shrugs off demands from activists'. *Financial Times*, 6 February 2008.

    (2008c). 'How Paccar bucks a family business trend'. *Financial Times*, 8 July 2008.

    (2008d). 'J-Power failure'. *Financial Times*, 18 April 2008.

    (2008e). 'J-Power investors reject TCI proposals'. *Financial Times*, 27 June 2008.

(2008f). 'J-Power spat has made Japan "nervous" '. *Financial Times*, 30 May 2008.

(2008g). 'Japan told to improve its corporate governance'. *Financial Times*, 12 May 2008.

(2008h). 'A letter to TCI'. *Financial Times* (Lex Column), 28 May 2008.

(2008i). 'Swiss regulator calls for action against Laxey'. *Financial Times*, 11 March 2008.

(2008j). 'TCI high and dry'. *Financial Times*, 27 June 2008.

(2008k). 'TCI sells out of J-Power at a loss'. *Financial Times*, 31 October 2008.

(2008l). 'TCI defies Japan over J-Power bid'. *Financial Times*, 25 April 2008.

(2009a). 'Companies learn to care for cash'. *Financial Times*, 2 October 2009.

(2009b). 'Fears of record hedge fund withdrawals'. *Financial Times*, 23 March 2009.

(2009c). 'Ho leaves TCI after ill-fated J-Power deal'. *Financial Times*, 15 April 2009.

(2009d). 'TCI quits fight for CSX with share sale'. *Financial Times*, 27 April 2009.

(2009e). 'Welch slams the obsession with shareholder value as a "dumb idea" '. *Financial Times*, 13 March 2009.

(2010a). 'Hedge funds enjoy biggest asset boost in 3 years'. *Financial Times*, 19 October 2010.

(2010b). 'Fund seeks to block Matsuya's poison pill'. *Financial Times*, 24 May 2010.

(2011a). 'Laxey steps up pressure on Alliance Trust'. *Financial Times*, 17 April 2011.

(2011b). 'Nat Express strikes truce with activist hedge fund'. *Financial Times*, 10 May 2011.

(2011c). 'Sir Ralph's lessons on short-termism'. *Financial Times*, 22 May 2011.

(2011d). 'TCI ready to relight investor activism in Japan'. *Financial Times*, 9 June 2011.

Fuwa, H. (2009). 'Management innovation at Toshiba: the introduction of the company with committees system'. In D. H. Whittaker and S. Deakin (eds.), *Corporate governance and managerial reform in Japan* (254–65). New York: Oxford University Press.

Galaskiewicz, J. (1991). 'Making corporate actors accountable: institution-building in Minneapolis-St. Paul'. In W. W. Powell and P. J. DiMaggio (eds.), *The new institutionalism in organizational analysis* (293–310). University of Chicago Press.

Galbraith, J. K. (1954). *The great crash 1929* (1961 edn). Boston, MA: Houghton Mifflin.

Gelter, M. (2010). 'Taming or protecting the modern corporation? Shareholder-stakeholder debates in a comparative light'. *ECGI Law Working Paper*, No. 165/2010.

Generali. (2009). Generali Group company website (14 July 2009 update). Retrieved from www.generali.com, 15 December 2009.

Gerlach, M. L. (1992). *Alliance capitalism: the social organization of Japanese business*. Berkeley, CA: University of California Press.

Gigerenzer, G. (2010) *Rationality for mortals. How people cope with uncertainty*. New York: Oxford University Press.

Gillan, S. L., and Starks, L. T. (2007). 'The evolution of shareholder activism in the United States'. *Journal of Applied Corporate Finance*, 19(1), 55–73.

Gilson, R. (2001). 'Globalizing corporate governance: convergence of form or function'. *American Journal of Comparative Law*, 49(2), 329–57.

Gilson, R., and Milhaupt, C. J. (2005). 'Choice as regulatory reform: the case of Japanese corporate governance'. *American Journal of Comparative Law*, 53, 343–77.

Global Pensions. (2006). 'Interview with Nobu Shimizu of GPIF: GPIF faces challenges of independence'. *Global Pensions*, 14 August 2007.

Gordon, A. (1998). *The wages of affluence: labor and management in post-war Japan*. Cambridge, MA: Harvard University Press.

Gordon, J. N. (2007). 'The rise of independent directors in the United States, 1950–2005: of shareholder value and stock market prices'. *Stanford Law Review*, 59(6), 1465–1658.

GPIF. (2007). 平成18年度業務概況書 (*Review of operations in fiscal 2006*). Tokyo: 年金積立金管理運用独立行政法人 (Government Pension Investment Fund).

(2011). 平成23年度第一半期運用状況 (*Statement of operations in first quarter of fiscal 2011*). Tokyo: 年金積立金管理運用独立行政法人 (Government Pension Investment Fund).

Greenwald, B., and Stiglitz, J. (1986). 'Externalities in economies with imperfect information and incomplete markets'. *Quarterly Journal of Economics*, 101, 229–64.

Greenwood, R., and Schor, M. (2009). 'Investor activism and takeovers'. *Journal of Financial Economics*, 92(3), 362–75.

Guardian. (2005). 'Börse rebel threatens to derail LSE bid'. *The Guardian*, 17 January 2005.

(2007). 'Barclays finds an ally in China in struggle for ABN Amro'. *The Guardian*, 24 July 2007.

Haley, J. O. (1998). *The spirit of Japanese law* (2006 edn). Athens, GA: The University of Georgia Press.

Hamao, Y., Kutsuna, K., and Matos, P. (2011). 'US-style investor activism in Japan: the first ten years (5 February 2011 version)'. SSRN: id1785281.

Hamilton, R. W. (2000). 'Corporate governance in America 1950–2000'. *The Journal of Corporation Law*, Winter 2000, 349–73.

Hanazaki, M., and Horiuchi, A. (2004). 'Can the financial restraint theory explain the postwar experience of Japan's financial system?'. In J. P. H. Fan, M. Hanazaki, and J. Teranishi (eds.), *Designing financial systems in East Asia and Japan* (19–46). London: RoutledgeCurzon.

Hannah, L. (2007). 'The "divorce" of ownership from control from 1900 onwards: re-calibrating imagined global trends'. *Business History*, 49(4), 404–38.

Hansmann, H. (1996). *The ownership of enterprise*. Cambridge, MA: Belknap Press.

Hansmann, H., and Kraakman, R. (2000). 'Organizational law as asset partitioning'. *European Economic Review*, 44, 807–17.

(2001). 'The end of history for corporate law'. *The Georgetown Law Journal*, 89(2), 439–68.

Hansmann, H., Kraakman, R., and Squire, R. (2006). 'Law and the rise of the firm'. *Harvard Law Review*, 119, 1333–1403.

Harris, R. (2000). *Industrializing English law: entrepreneurship and business organization 1720–1844*. Cambridge University Press.

Hayakawa, M., and Whittaker, D. H. (2009). 'Takeovers and corporate governance: three years of tensions'. In D. H. Whittaker and S. Deakin (eds.), *Corporate governance and managerial reform in Japan* (70–92). New York: Oxford University Press.

Hayashi, F., and Prescott, E. C. (2002). 'The 1990s in Japan: a lost decade'. *Review of Economic Dynamics*, 5, 206–35.

Hedgetracker. (2009). 'Children's Investment Fund cutting fees, scaling back'. *Hedgetracker.com*.

(2010). 'Steel Partners settles lawsuit with Carl Icahn'. *Hedgetracker.com*.

(2011). 'Steel Partners – Investor Profile'. *Hedgetracker.com*.

Hendry, J., Sanderson, P., Barker, R., and Roberts, J. (2006). 'Owners or traders? Conceptualizations of institutional investors and their relationship with corporate managers'. *Human Relations*, 59 (8), 1101–32.

(2007). 'Responsible ownership, shareholder value and the new shareholder activism'. *Competition & Change*, 11(3), 223–40.

Hermes. (2009). Hermes Pensions Management Limited company website. Retrieved from www.hermes.co.uk, 21 July 2009.

Hokuetsu. (2006). 王子製紙株式会社による公開買付けの反対に関する お知らせ (Announcement regarding opposition to Ōji Paper's public tender offer). Niigata: 北越製紙株式会社 (Hokuetsu Paper Mills, Ltd.).

Hoshi, T. (1994). 'The economic role of corporate grouping and the main bank system'. In M. Aoki and R. Dore (eds.), *The Japanese firm: sources of competitive strength* (285–309). New York: Oxford University Press.

Huckaby, S. T. (1991). 'Defensive action to hostile takeover efforts in Japan: the Shuwa decisions'. *Columbia Journal of Transnational Law*, 29, 439–71.

Ichigo. (2007). 'Ichigo Asset Management takes 10.96% stake in steel maker Tokyo Kohtetsu, seeks dialogue with management to remedy poor terms for shareholders in proposed share exchange'. Ichigo Asset Management website. Retrieved from www.ichigoasset.com, 15 January 2007.

IFSL. (2010). *Hedge Funds 2010*. London: International Financial Services London.

IHT. (2005). 'Deutsche Börse defends offer for London exchange'. *International Herald Tribune*, 18 January 2005.

IIR. (1998). 'A Japanese-UK proxy story'. *IR Magazine*, 1 December 1998. Retrieved from www.insideinvestorrelations.com, 23 November 2011.

Ikeda, M., and Nakagawa, Y. (2002). 'Globalization of the Japanese automobile industry and reorganization of keiretsu-suppliers'. *Actes du Gerpisa*, 33, 29–40.

Imai, T. (2001). 新たな経済社会の構造 (*Building a new economic society*): 経団連 (Keidanren: Chairman's speech at Imperial Hotel, Tokyo, 20 June 2001).

Implenia. (2009a). Implenia AG company website. Retrieved from www. implenia.com, 29 October 2009.

(2009b). 'Laxey backs itself into a corner'. Implenia AG company website. Retrieved from www.implenia.com, 1 June 2011.

Inagami, T. (2009). 'Managers and corporate governance reform in Japan: restoring self-confidence or shareholder revolution?'. In D. H. Whittaker and S. Deakin (eds.), *Corporate governance and management reform in Japan* (163–91). New York: Oxford University Press.

Inagami, T., and Whittaker, D. H. (2005). *The new community firm: employment, governance and management reform in Japan*. Cambridge University Press.

Independent. (2007). 'Hedge fund TCI lobbies for break-up of bank giant ABN Amro'. *The Independent*, 22 February 2007.

(2008). 'J-Power thwarts TCI's ambitions'. *The Independent*, 26 April 2008.

Institutional Investor. (2008). 'TCI buys up stakes in J-Power owners.' *Institutional Investor*, 28 May 2008.

Ishiguro, T. (1991). 'Japan amends its securities laws.' *International Financial Law Review*, 25–8.

Iwai, K. (2008). 会社はこれからどうなるのか (What will become of the company henceforth?). Tokyo: 平凡社 (Heibonsha).

Jackson, G., and Miyajima, H. (2007). 'The diversity and change of corporate governance in Japan'. In M. Aoki, G. Jackson, and H. Miyajima (eds.), *Corporate governance in Japan: institutional change and organizational diversity* (1–47). New York: Oxford University Press.

Jacoby, S. (2005a). *The embedded corporation: corporate governance and employment relations in Japan and the United States*. Princeton University Press.

(2005b). 'Corporate governance and society'. *Challenge*, 48(4), 69–87.

(2009). 'Foreign investors and corporate governance in Japan: the case of CalPERS'. In D. H. Whittaker and S. Deakin (eds.), *Corporate governance and managerial reform in Japan* (93–133). New York: Oxford University Press.

Japan Times. (2009). 'Murakami's sentence suspended'. *The Japan Times*, 4 February 2009.

JCAA. (2009). 委員会設置会社リスト・委員会設置会社に移行した会社 (Companies with committees list: companies that have transferred to become companies with committees). Tokyo: 日本監査役協会 (Japan Corporate Auditors' Association), www.kansa.or.jp.

(2010). 委員会設置会社リスト・委員会設置会社に移行した会社 (Companies with committees list: companies that have transferred to become companies with committees). Tokyo: 日本監査役協会 (Japan Corporate Auditors' Association), www.kansa.or.jp.

JCER. (2005). *Investment funds target cash rich firms* (JCER Researcher Report No. 67 by Maezawa Hirokazu). Tokyo: Japan Center for Economic Research.

JCGF. (1997). *Corporate governance principles – a Japanese view (Interim Report)*. Tokyo: Japan Corporate Governance Forum, www.jcgf.org.

(2001). *Revised corporate governance principles*. Tokyo: Japan Corporate Governance Forum, www.jcgf.org.

Jensen, M. (1986). 'Agency costs of free cash flow, corporate finance, and takeovers'. *American Economic Review*, 76(2), 323–9.

(2001). 'Value maximization, stakeholder theory, and the corporate objective function'. *Journal of Applied Corporate Finance*, 14(3), 8–21.

(2005). 'Agency costs of overvalued equity'. *Financial Management*, 34, 5–19.

Jensen, M., and Meckling, W. (1976). 'Theory of the firm: managerial behavior, agency costs and capital structure'. *Journal of Financial Economics*, 3, 305–60.

Johnston, A. (1980). *The City Take-over Code*. Oxford University Press.

J-Power. (2008). *Fact Book 2008*.

JT. (2010). 有価証券報告書、第25期 (Annual securities report, period no. 25). Tokyo: 日本たばこ産業株式会社 (JT Group).

(2011). 有価証券報告書、第26期 (Annual securities report, period no. 26). Tokyo: 日本たばこ産業株式会社 (JT Group).

Kahan, M., and Rock, E. B. (2007). 'Hedge funds in corporate governance and corporate control'. *University of Pennsylvania Law Review*, 155(5), 1021–93.

Katz, R. (1998). *Japan: the system that soured – the rise and fall of the Japanese miracle*. New York: M. E. Sharpe, Inc.

Kawakita, H., and Miyano, R. (2007). 村上ファンドの投資行動と役割、標的となった企業の特徴に関して (The investment behaviour of the Murakami Fund and its role: characteristics of its target companies). Tokyo: ニッセイ基礎研究所 (NLI Research).

Keidanren. (1997). *Urgent recommendations concerning corporate governance*. Tokyo: Nippon Keidanren (Japan Business Federation).

Kennedy, A. (2000). *The end of shareholder value*. London: Orion Business (The Orion Publishing Group Ltd.).

Kester, W. C. (1991). *Japanese takeovers: the global contest for corporate control*. Boston, MA: Harvard Business School Press.

(1996). 'American and Japanese corporate governance: convergence to best practice?'. In S. Berger and R. Dore (eds.), *National diversity and global capitalism* (107–37). New York: Cornell University Press.

Klein, A., and Zur, E. (2006). 'Hedge fund activism'. *ECGI Working Paper Series in Finance*.

(2009). 'Entrepreneurial shareholder activism: hedge funds and other private investors'. *The Journal of Finance*, 64(1), 187–229.

(2011). 'The impact of hedge fund activism on the target firm's existing bondholders'. *Review of Financial Studies*, 24(5), 1735–71.

Knight Vinke. (2009). Knight Vinke Asset Management LLC company website. Retrieved from www.kvamllc.com, 16 July 2009.

Kōbe Shimbun. (2006). 'カイシャ異変、第1部、誰のためにあるのか、1. ヒルズ族、「株式重視」その先に― (Changes in the company, part 1: Who is it there for? 1. The financial crowd – the future course of "attaching importance to shareholders")'. *神戸新聞* (*Kōbe Shimbun*), 1 January 2006.

Kochan, T., and Rubinstein, S. (2000). 'Toward a stakeholder theory of the firm: the Saturn partnership'. *Organization Science*, 11, 376–86.

Koslowski, P. (2000). 'The limits of shareholder value'. *Journal of Business Ethics*, 27, 137–48.

Kritzer, H. (1996). 'The data puzzle: the nature of interpretation in quantitative research'. *American Journal of Political Science*, 40, 1–32.

Kruse, T. A., and Suzuki, K. (2011). Steel Partners' activism efforts at United Industrial, Ronson, and BKF Capital: the good, the bad, and the ugly (earlier version available on SSRN www.ssrn.com). Unpublished manuscript.

Kubota, M. (2007). '現代版「泣いた赤おに」(A modern version of "The red ogre who cried")'. 日経金融新聞 (*Nikkei Kinyū Shimbun*), 20 February 2007.

Lane, C. (2003). 'Changes in corporate governance of German corporations: convergence to the Anglo-American model?' *Competition & Change*, 7(2–3), 79–100.

Lawley, P. (2008). 'Panacea or placebo? An empirical analysis of the effect of the Japanese committee system corporate governance law reform'. In L. Nottage, L. Wolff, and K. Anderson (eds.), *Corporate governance in the twenty-first century. Japan's gradual transformation* (129–54). Cheltenham: Edward Elgar.

Lazonick, W., and O'Sullivan, M. (2000). 'Maximizing shareholder value: a new ideology for corporate governance'. *Economy and Society*, 29(1), 13–35.

Learmount, S. (2002). *Corporate governance: what can be learned from Japan?* Oxford University Press.

Leigh-Pemberton, R. (ed.). (1990). *Creative tension?* London: The National Association of Pension Funds Ltd.

Lichtenstein, W. (2007). Letter to President Ikeda of Bull-Dog Sauce, dated 11 May 2007.

Lindsell, M. (2007). 'Where to find exceptional value in Japan'. *MoneyWeek*, 1 February 2007. Retrieved from www.moneyweek.com, 22 November 2011.

Lintstock. (2005). *Hedge fund engagement with UK plcs*. London: Lintstock Ltd.

Lobban, M. (1996). 'Corporate identity and limited liability in France and England 1825–67'. *Anglo-American Law Review*, 25, 397–440.

London Stock Exchange. (2003). *Investor relations: a practical guide*. London: The London Stock Exchange plc and collaborating institutions.

Loomis, C. J. (1966). 'The Jones that nobody keeps up with'. *Fortune*, April 1966, 237–47.

Mace, M. L. (1971). *Directors: myth and reality*. Boston, MA: Harvard University.

Macey, J. (2008). *Corporate governance: promises kept, promises broken.* Princeton University Press.

Manne, H. (1965). 'Mergers and the market for corporate control'. *Journal of Political Economy*, 73, 110–20.

MarketWatch. (2009). 'UK hedge fund Laxey says no loss on Implenia stake'. *MarketWatch Inc.*, 14 November 2009. Retrieved from www.marketwatch.com, 9 June 2010.

(2010). 'Hedge-fund activists eyeing a comeback'. *MarketWatch Inc.*, 9 October 2010. Retrieved from www.marketwatch.com, 23 November 2011.

Matsumoto, K. (1983). *The rise of the Japanese corporate system* (T. I. Elliott, trans. 1994 revised edn). London: Kegan Paul International.

METI. (2004). コーポレート・システムに関する研究報告書 (*Study report on the corporate system*). Tokyo: 経済産業省 (Ministry of Economy, Trade and Industry).

METI and MOJ. (2005). 企業価値・株主共同の利益の確保又は向上のための買収防衛策に関する指針 (Guidelines regarding takeover defence for the purposes of protection and enhancement of corporate value and shareholders' common interests). Tokyo: 経済産業省 (Ministry of Economy, Trade and Industry) and 法務省 (Ministry of Justice).

MIC. (2010). 労働力調査 長期時系列データ (*Labour Force Survey, Long-term Time Series Data*). Tokyo: 総務省 (Ministry of Internal Affairs and Communications).

(2011). 第六十回 日本統計年鑑 平成23年 (*The Statistical Handbook of Japan 2011*). Tokyo: 総務省、統計局 (Ministry of Internal Affairs and Communications, Statistics Bureau).

Milhaupt, C. J. (2005). 'In the shadow of Delaware? The rise of hostile take-overs in Japan'. *Columbia Law Review*, 105(7), 2171–2216.

(2009) 'Bull-Dog Sauce for the Japanese soul? Courts, corporations and communities – a comment on Haley's view of Japanese law'. *University of Washington Global Studies Law Review*, 8, 345–61.

Milhaupt, C. J., and Pistor, K. (2008). *Law and capitalism: What corporate crises reveal about legal systems and economic development around the world.* Chicago University Press.

Milhaupt, C. J., and West, M. D. (2004). *Economic organizations and corporate governance in Japan: the impact of formal and informal rules.* New York: Oxford University Press.

Minsky, H. (1993). 'Schumpeter and finance'. In S. Biasco, A. Roncaglia and M. Salvati (eds.), *Market and institutions in economic development* (103–15). Basingstoke: St Martin's Press.

Mitarai, F., and Niwa, U. (2006). 会社は誰のために (*Who is the company for?*). Tokyo: 文藝春秋 (Bungei Shunjū).

Miwa, Y., and Ramseyer, J. M. (2005). 'Who appoints them? What do they do? Evidence on outside directors from Japan'. *Journal of Economics & Management Strategy*, 14(2), 299–337.

(2006) *The fable of the keiretsu: urban legends of the Japanese economy*. University of Chicago Press.

Miyajima, H., and Kuroki, F. (2007). 'The unwinding of cross-shareholding in Japan: causes, effects, and implications'. In M. Aoki, G. Jackson, and H. Miyajima (eds.), *Corporate governance in Japan: institutional change and organizational diversity* (79–124). New York: Oxford University Press.

Miyake, S. (2007). 市場と法、いま何が起っているのか (The market and the law: what is happening now?). Tokyo: 日経BP社 (Nikkei BP-sha).

Morck, R., and Nakamura, M. (1999). 'Japanese corporate governance and macroeconomic problems'. *Harvard Institute of Economic Research*, Discussion Paper no. 1893.

Morikawa, H. (1992). *Zaibatsu: the rise and fall of family enterprise groups in Japan*. University of Tokyo Press.

Nakatani, I. (2008). 資本主義はなぜ自壊したのか (*Why did capitalism self-destruct?*). Tokyo: 集英社インターナショナル (Shūei-sha International).

National Stock Exchanges. (2004). 平成15年度株式分布状況調査の調査結果について (Results of shareholding distribution survey for 2003). Tokyo: 全国証券取引所 (National Stock Exchanges).

(2011). 平成22年度株式分布状況調査の調査結果について (Results of shareholding distribution survey for 2010). Tokyo: 全国証券取引所 (National Stock Exchanges).

Nielsen, L. B. (2010). 'The need for multi-method approaches in empirical legal research'. In P. Cane and H. Kritzer (eds.) *The Oxford handbook of empirical legal research* (951–75). Oxford University Press.

Nikkei-BP. (2005). '村上ファンドが新日本無線にTOB、日清紡のTOB条件に異議 (Murakami Fund makes bid for New Japan Radio and contests terms of Nisshinbō's bid)'. *Nikkei Business Publications*, 22 November 2005.

(2008). 'TCI、Jパワー株主に「天下り」問題視する書簡 (TCI sends letter to J-Power shareholders raising issue of "Amakudari")'. *Nikkei Business Publications*, 6 June 2008.

Nikkei. (1989). 'ピケンズ氏、増配打診、小糸製・ブーン社の第一会談終える―焦点は株肩代わり (Pickens raises issue of dividend increase: first meeting between Koito and Boone Company concluded – focus on greenmailing)'. 日本経済新聞 (*Nihon Keizai Shimbun*), 21 April 1989.

(2003a). 'ソトー、突然のTOB、戸惑い隠せず (Sotoh: sudden takeover bid – unable to hide surprise)'. 日本経済新聞 (*Nihon Keizai Shimbun*), 20 December 2003.

(2003b). '米国型統治まず36社 (American style governance: initially 36 companies)'. 日本経済新聞 (*Nihon Keizai Shimbun*), 15 June 2003.

(2004a). 'ソトー巡りTOB合戦、株式買い付け価格、米系ファンドが大幅引き上げ (The takeover struggle surrounding Sotoh: US fund raises tender price sharply)'. 日本経済新聞 (*Nihon Keizai Shimbun*), 26 January 2004.

(2004b). 'ソトー買収劇終幕、TOB応募、株式の1%弱 (The curtain comes down on Sotoh's takeover drama: response to tender less then 1% of shares)'. 日本経済新聞 (*Nihon Keizai Shimbun*), 24 February 2004.

(2004c). '米系ファンドの買収に対抗策－日本企業、資本効率の改善急務 (Japanese firms need to improve their capital efficiency quickly to respond to takeovers from US funds)'. 日本経済新聞 (*Nihon Keizai Shimbun*), 16 January 2004.

(2004d). 'ソトー、ＴＯＢ白熱－馬淵社長、株式非公開化、やむを得ない (TOB climax: Sotoh's President Mabuchi says no alternative to delisting shares'. 日本経済新聞 (*Nihon Keizai Shimbun*), 6 February 2004.

(2005a). 'TOBの基礎知識(3)敵対的買収増え規制強化も(マネーレッスン)終 (Basic knowledge about TOBs: (3) regulations strengthen along with the increase in hostile bids)'. 日本経済新聞 (*Nihon Keizai Shimbun*), 28 April 2005.

(2005b). '経団連会長「堀江氏はもっと説明すべき」(Keidanren Chairman: "Mr. Horie should explain more clearly")'. 日本経済新聞 (*Nihon Keizai Shimbun*), 24 February 2005.

(2006a). 'サンテレの新株予約権、差し止め処分、株主が申し立て (Shareholder requests interim restraining order against Sun Telephone's new share warrant issue)'. 日本経済新聞 (*Nihon Keizai Shimbun*), 23 June 2006.

(2006b). 'サンテレホン、TOB提案に反対、米系ファンド「敵対的でない」 (Sun Telephone opposes TOB proposal: US fund maintains "non-hostile")'. 日本経済新聞 (*Nihon Keizai Shimbun*), 20 October 2006.

(2006c). 'サンテレホンMBO実施、米系ファンドとの攻防幕、別連合と、溝埋まらず (Sun Telephone MBO implemented – conflict with US fund comes to an end – agreement with other grouping – no sign of bridging gap)'. 日本経済新聞 (*Nihon Keizai Shimbun*), 21 December 2006.

(2006d). 'サンテレホン株、TOBへの応募9割－ダルトン、出資比率4割弱に (90% response to TOB for Sun Telephone's shares – Dalton's shareholding just under 40%)'. 日本経済新聞 (*Nihon Keizai Shimbun*), 9 November 2006.

(2006e). '京三、買収防衛策を導入 (Kyōsan introduces anti-takeover defence strategy)'. 日本経済新聞 (*Nihon Keizai Shimbun*), 5 December 2006.

(2006f). '日清、明星に出資交渉、「白馬の騎士」最大手浮上―即席めん、シェア五割に (Nissin, Myōjō in negotiations for capital participation: sector leader emerges as "white knight" – 50% market share in instant noodles)'. 日本経済新聞 (*Nihon Keizai Shimbun*), 10 November 2006.

(2006g). '明星食品、米スティール、保有比率ゼロ (Myōjō Foods: Steel of the USA reduces holding to zero)'. 日本経済新聞 (*Nihon Keizai Shimbun*), 19 December 2006.

(2006h). '村上ファンド近く解散、出資金返還にメド (Murakami fund to be wound up shortly: plans in hand to return cash to investors)'. 日本経済新聞 (*Nihon Keizai Shimbun*), 7 November 2006.

(2007a). 'Jパワー、個人株主開拓を積極化―説明会など開催、筆頭株主TCI意識か (J-Power puts big effort into increasing private shareholders: holds presentations etc. – awareness caused by lead shareholder TCI?)'. 日本経済新聞 (*Nihon Keizai Shimbun*), 26 December 2007.

(2007b). 'Jパワー、英ファンドの役員派遣拒否、年内にも回答、「業績低下は誤認」 (J-Power refuses secondment of directors from UK fund: will respond within this year on "erroneous fall in results arguments")'. 日本経済新聞 (*Nihon Keizai Shimbun*), 8 December 2007.

(2007c). 'Jパワー社長、株主提案に反論、「減収減益で増配ふさわしくない」 (J-Power's president argues against shareholder's proposal: "inappropriate to raise dividend when revenues and profits are falling")'. 日本経済新聞 (*Nihon Keizai Shimbun*), 15 May 2007.

(2007d). 'Jパワー社長、英ファンドの増配要求応じず (J-Power's president does not agree to UK fund's demand for increased dividend)'. 日本経済新聞 (*Nihon Keizai Shimbun*), 2 April 2007.

(2007e). 'NECエレの海外大株主2社、親子上場見直し要求、NECに「保有株50%未満に」 (Two major foreign shareholders in NEC Electronics demand review of listed subsidiary situation: ask NEC "to reduce holding below 50%")'. 日本経済新聞 (*Nihon Keizai Shimbun*), 29 May 2007.

(2007f). 'イカリソース従業員、ブルドックへのTOBに反対 (Ikari employees oppose Bull-Dog's takeover)'. 日本経済新聞 (*Nihon Keizai Shimbun*), 12 June 2007.

(2007g). 'サッポロHD、時間稼ぎ批判かわす、スティールに再び質問状 (Sapporo Holdings sends another question list to Steel: effort to ward off playing for time accusations)'. 日本経済新聞 (*Nihon Keizai Shimbun*), 23 November 2007.

(2007h). 'スティール、ブルドック株TOB価格、1700円に引き上げ (Steel raise Bull-Dog offer price to ¥1,700)'. *日本経済新聞 (Nihon Keizai Shimbun)*, 15 June 2007.

(2007i). 'ブラザー工業の小池新社長に聞く、スティール提案否決成長戦略どう描く (Interview with Brother's new President Koike: how does he see his growth strategy in the light of the rejection of Steel's proposal?)'. *日本経済新聞 (Nihon Keizai Shimbun)*, 30 June 2007.

(2007j). 'ブルドック、TOB対抗へ新株予約権－スティールと対決姿勢、法廷闘争もにらむ (Bull-Dog opposes bid with share options – takes confrontational stance with Steel: legal tussle in the offing)'. *日本経済新聞 (Nihon Keizai Shimbun)*, 8 June 2007.

(2007k). 'ブルドック、スティール、初会談は物別れ (Bull-Dog and Steel meet for first time but fail to reach agreement)'. *日本経済新聞 (Nihon Keizai Shimbun)*, 13 June 2007.

(2007l). 'ブルドック、総会検査役の選任申し立て－従業員一同がTOB反対声名 (Bull-Dog: call for appointment of shareholders' meeting inspector – employees unanimous in opposing bid)'. *日本経済新聞 (Nihon Keizai Shimbun)*, 9 June 2007.

(2007m). 'ブルドックソース、TOBに引き続き反対 (Bull-Dog Sauce maintains opposition to takeover)'. *日本経済新聞 (Nihon Keizai Shimbun)*, 9 August 2007.

(2007n). 'ブルドックの買収防衛策容認、東京地裁の可処分決定要旨 (Bull-Dog's defence strategy approved: summary of Tokyo District Court's judgment permitting the action)'. *日本経済新聞 (Nihon Keizai Shimbun)*, 29 June 2007.

(2007o). 'ブルドック株TOB、応募1.89%－スティール、買収できず (Bull-Dog shares tender: 1.89% acceptances – takeover fails)'. *日本経済新聞 (Nihon Keizai Shimbun)*, 24 August 2007.

(2007p). 'ブルドック株TOB価格上げ、法廷闘争と二正面作戦－スティール、対決姿勢鮮明に (Increase in offer price for Bull-Dog shares: Steel make hostile stance clear with dual strategy and legal tussle)'. *日本経済新聞 (Nihon Keizai Shimbun)*, 16 June 2007.

(2007q). 'ブルドック買収、「自ら経営、ない」－スティールが回答書 (Bull-Dog takeover: Steel reply in writing 'no plan to manage business ourselves')'. *日本経済新聞 (Nihon Keizai Shimbun)*, 2 June 2007.

(2007r). '「ブルドック買収」終幕、防衛策、最高裁も容認－最高裁決定要旨 ("Bull-Dog acquisition" comes to an end: Supreme Court also approves defence strategy – summary of Supreme Court judgment)'. *日本経済新聞 (Nihon Keizai Shimbun)*, 8 August 2007.

(2007s). 'ブルドック防衛策承認、「株主利益」巡り応酬(07株主総会) (Bull-Dog's defence strategy approved: response that this concerns "shareholders' profits" – 2007 AGM)'. 日本経済新聞 (*Nihon Keizai Shimbun*), 25 June 2007.

(2007t). '「乗っ取り屋でない」、スティール明示を―サッポロ巡り、経産次官 (Vice Minister calls for Steel to demonstrate that they are not raiders with regard to Sapporo)'. 日本経済新聞 (*Nihon Keizai Shimbun*), 20 February 2007.

(2007u). '事前警告型買収防衛策、ブルドックが導入、再度のTOBを警戒 (Bull-Dog to introduce advance warning anti-takeover defence as precaution against further bids)'. 日本経済新聞 (*Nihon Keizai Shimbun*), 31 August 2007.

(2007v). '企業価値を探る・非開示なら株主軽視 (In search of corporate value; lack of transparency means contempt for shareholders)'. 日本経済新聞 (*Nihon Keizai Shimbun*), 24 March 2007.

(2007w). '「企業価値高めるストーリー示せ」イチゴアセットを批判 (Criticism of Ichigo Asset Management: "Show me how this raises corporate value")'. 日本経済新聞 (*Nihon Keizai Shimbun*), 5 March 2007.

(2007x). '個人、実質半数「ノー」 (Effectively half of private individuals say "no")'. 日本経済新聞 (*Nihon Keizai Shimbun*), 23 February 2007.

(2007y). '「敵対的」TOB相次ぐスティール、ブルドックに開始、経営には関心示さず (Steel progress to 'hostile' bid for Bull-Dog: show no interest in management involvement)'. 日本経済新聞 (*Nihon Keizai Shimbun*), 19 May 2007.

(2007z). '英TCI、中部電株すべて売却 (UK TCI sells all its Chūbu Electric shares)'. 日本経済新聞 (*Nihon Keizai Shimbun*), 21 November 2007.

(2007aa). '英ファンドTCI、中部電株も1％取得 (UK fund TCI takes 1% of Chūbu Electric's shares)'. 日本経済新聞 (*Nihon Keizai Shimbun*), 15 March 2007.

(2007ab). '第三部こんなに変わった(3)イエと資本と経営と(株主とは) (Part 3: How things have changed – family, capital and management: how do they fit with shareholders?)'. 日本経済新聞 (*Nihon Keizai Shimbun*), 28 January 2007.

(2007ac). '経営陣、従業員による企業買収、フジテック拒否へ、米ファンドに (Fujitec tells US fund it rejects MEBO)'. 日本経済新聞 (*Nihon Keizai Shimbun*), 14 December 2007.

(2007ad). '腰かけから鉄の女へ(4)ブルドックソース社長池田章子氏(人間発見) (From stopgap job to Iron Lady (4) President Ikeda Shōko of Bull-Dog Sauce – Discovering the human side)'. 日本経済新聞 (*Nihon Keizai Shimbun*), 8 November 2007.

(2007ae). '米スティール、ブルドックにTOB提案、敵対的買収に発展も (Steel of the USA plan tender offer for Bull-Dog – possibility that this will develop into hostile takeover)'. 日本経済新聞 (*Nihon Keizai Shimbun*), 17 May 2007.

(2007af). '米スティール、ブルドック株、TOB開始 (Steel of the USA begin tender offer for Bull-Dog's shares)'. 日本経済新聞 (*Nihon Keizai Shimbun*), 18 May 2007.

(2007ag). '腰かけから鉄の女へ(1)ブルドックソース社長池田章子氏(人間発見) (From stopgap job to Iron Lady (1) President Ikeda Shōko of Bull-Dog Sauce – Discovering the human side)'. 日本経済新聞 (*Nihon Keizai Shimbun*), 5 November 2007.

(2007ah). '経産省、北畑事務次官、ブルドックソース買収防衛策容認「意義ある」 (Kitabata, METI Vice Minister: "Approval of Bull-Dog Sauce defence strategy significant")'. 日本経済新聞 (*Nihon Keizai Shimbun*), 10 August 2007.

(2007ai). '経産省次官、買収者助長を懸念 (METI Vice Minister concerned that measures will encourage acquirers)'. 日本経済新聞 (*Nihon Keizai Shimbun*), 4 September 2007.

(2007aj). '経産省研究会、敵対的買収者、出現後の防衛策、導入ルール検討 (Corporate Value Study Group to study introduction of rules for post-event defence strategies against hostile acquirers)'. 日本経済新聞 (*Nihon Keizai Shimbun*), 27 October 2007.

(2007ak). '新任役員の気がかり、能率協調査、「吸収合併」倍増の23% (Concern among newly-appointed directors: Nōritsu Kyōkai survey finds "absorption by merger" doubled to 23%)'. 日本経済新聞 (*Nihon Keizai Shimbun*), 3 August 2007.

(2007al). '甘利経産相、「サッポロ買収の推移見守る (Minister of Economy Trade and Industry Amari: "will keep an eye on developments in Sapporo acquisition")'. 日本経済新聞 (*Nihon Keizai Shimbun*), 20 February 2007.

(2007am). '買収防衛策をフジテック導入 (Fujitec to introduce defence strategy)'. 日本経済新聞 (*Nihon Keizai Shimbun*), 12 May 2007.

(2007an). '第七部新しい素顔（1）ファンドは悪役なのか（株主とは） (No.7: A new aspect (1) So are funds bad for shareholders?)'. 日本経済新聞 (*Nihon Keizai Shimbun*), 03 August 2007.

(2007ao). '投資冷え込み、金融相「ない」、スティール抗告棄却で (No adverse effect on investment says Finance Minister as Steel's appeal is dismissed)'. 日本経済新聞 (*Nihon Keizai Shimbun*), 10 July 2007.

(2007ap). 'Jパワーとファンド、配当巡り株主に手紙合戦、多数派工作が本格化 (J-Power and fund competing to send letters to shareholders – manoeuvring for majority becomes serious)'. 日本経済新聞 (*Nihon Keizai Shimbun*), 9 June 2007.

(2008a). 'Jパワー、TCIに通知、取締役13人提訴、監査役会認めず (J-Power notifies TCI that board of corporate auditors has not authorised prosecution of 13 directors)'. 日本経済新聞 (*Nihon Keizai Shimbun*), 25 June 2008.

(2008b). 'Ｊパワー株買い増し問題、政府、来月に中止命令、不服申し立て焦点 (The J-Power shareholding increase issue – government order to desist next month: attention focuses on formal complaint)'. 日本経済新聞 (*Nihon Keizai Shimbun*), 26 April 2008.

(2008c). 'Ｊパワーに提言書、英ファンド、効率化求め (UK fund sends proposal to J-Power demanding greater efficiency)'. 日本経済新聞 (*Nihon Keizai Shimbun*), 28 March 2008.

(2008d). 'Ｊパワー問題、個人株主向けにTCIが説明会 (J-Power problem: TCI holds presentation for private shareholders)'. 日本経済新聞 (*Nihon Keizai Shimbun*), 24 May 2008.

(2008e). 'Ｊパワー株、委任状争奪戦、TCIが表明 (TCI makes clear its position: proxy fight over J-Power shares)'. 日本経済新聞 (*Nihon Keizai Shimbun*), 22 May 2008.

(2008f). 'Ｊパワー株の買い増し中止命令、TCI、受け入れへ、政府との対立回避 (TCI accepts J-Power share purchase desist order – avoids confrontation with government)'. 日本経済新聞 (*Nihon Keizai Shimbun*), 14 July 2008.

(2008g). 'Ｊパワー株の買い増し問題、審査延長を決定－経産省、英ファンドに説明要求 (Increased J-Power share purchases problem: decision to extend study period – METI requires explanations from UK fund)'. 日本経済新聞 (*Nihon Keizai Shimbun*), 14 February 2008.

(2008h). 'Ｊパワー株買い増し、TCIに中止命令－政府、申し出を却下 (Purchase of extra J-Power shares: TCI ordered to desist – application rejected)'. 日本経済新聞 (*Nihon Keizai Shimbun*), 14 May 2008.

(2008i). 'Ｊパワー株買い増し、変更、中止勧告へ、外為審、英ファンドから聴衆 (Increased J-Power share purchase: moving towards recommendation to amend or stop – Foreign Exchange Committee hears explanations from TCI)'. 日本経済新聞 (*Nihon Keizai Shimbun*), 12 April 2008.

(2008j). 'アデランス、多難の再出発、新経営体制が発足―強まる「スティール色」 (Aderans: a tumultuous relaunch – new management structure makes a start – Steel's influence stronger)'. 日本経済新聞 (*Nihon Keizai Shimbun*), 10 August 2008.

(2008k). 'アデランス取締役の再任否決、2位株主、大勢決める、「友好」から一転 (Aderans directors denied reappointment: no. 2 shareholder the main decider: the switch from "friendly")'. 日本経済新聞 (*Nihon Keizai Shimbun*), 3 June 2008.

(2008l). '一般株主も「再任ノー」－アデランス経営陣、七人否決 (08株主総会) (Ordinary shareholders say "no" to re-election for Aderans' management: seven rejected – 2008 AGM)'. 日本経済新聞 (*Nihon Keizai Shimbun*), 30 May 2008.

(2008m). '日本企業は株主とどう向き合うか(社説) (How should Japanese firms relate to their shareholders?)'. 日本経済新聞 (*Nihon Keizai Shimbun: Editorial*), 8 June 2008.

(2008n). '甘利経産相、Jパワー「一般と違う」 (Minister Amari on J-Power: "different from the usual")'. 日本経済新聞 (*Nihon Keizai Shimbun*), 8 April 2008.

(2008o). '米ダルトン、フジテック株11%分売却へ (US Dalton moves to sell 11% of Fujitec)'. 日本経済新聞 (*Nihon Keizai Shimbun*), 9 January 2008.

(2008p). '経産省、大間原発の設置許可、Jパワーに、来月にも着工 (METI approves Ōma nuclear plant: authorisation to begin construction likely to be given to J-Power next month)'. 日本経済新聞 (*Nihon Keizai Shimbun*), 23 April 2008.

(2008q). '英TCI、Jパワー株主に書簡、持ち合いなど批判 (UK TCI sends letter to J-Power shareholders – criticises cross holdings etc.)'. 日本経済新聞 (*Nihon Keizai Shimbun*), 6 June 2008.

(2008r). '英ファンド、Jパワー株買い増し、短期利益志向を懸念、外為審「反対」 (UK fund's increased purchase of J-Power shares: Foreign Exchange Committee worried by short-term profit focus – "opposed")'. 日本経済新聞 (*Nihon Keizai Shimbun*), 16 April 2008.

(2008s). '英ファンド、新たに3役員枠要請、社外第三者、Jパワーに書簡 (UK fund sends new letter to J-Power demanding appointment of three independent external directors)'. 日本経済新聞 (*Nihon Keizai Shimbun*), 23 February 2008.

(2008t). '英ファンド、買い増し検討、Jパワー株「20%」へ届出、外資規制の対象 (UK fund studies further purchases: notifies plan to go to 20% – falls under foreign exchange regulations)'. 日本経済新聞 (*Nihon Keizai Shimbun*), 16 January 2008.

(2008u). '英ファンドTCI、Jパワーに圧力強める－拒否なら社長再任反対 (UK fund TCI increases pressure on J-Power: will oppose re-election of president if proposals rejected)'. 日本経済新聞 (*Nihon Keizai Shimbun*), 18 April 2008.

(2008v). '英ファンドのJパワー株買い増し、経産省、中止、修正要求も (UK fund's further purchases of J-Power shares: METI's power to demand cessation or adjustment)'. 日本経済新聞 (*Nihon Keizai Shimbun*), 20 January 2008.

(2008w). '英投資ファンドTCI、Jパワー株売却へ、通らぬと判断 (UK fund TCI moves to sell J-Power shares – abandons calls for increased dividend)'. 日本経済新聞 (*Nihon Keizai Shimbun*), 1 November 2008.

(2008x). '英投資ファンドTCI、Jパワー株買い増しへ新提案、信託活用で議決権凍結 (UK fund TCI issues new proposal re buying extra

J-Power shares: freeze voting rights through discretionary mandate)'. 日本経済新聞 (*Nihon Keizai Shimbun*), 15 April 2008.

(2008y). 'ダイワボウ情報、ダイワボウがTOB、ファンドから株取得、完全子会社に (Daiwabō makes bid for Daiwabō Information System, buys all fund's shares and makes company 100% subsidiary)'. 日本経済新聞 (*Nihon Keizai Shimbun*), 10 September 2008.

(2008z). '筆頭株主エフィッシモ、学研社長の解任提案へ (Lead shareholder Effissimo moving towards proposal for resignation of Gakken's CEO)'. 日本経済新聞 (*Nihon Keizai Shimbun*), 23 April 2008.

(2008aa). '霞が関は日本を開くのか、閉じるのか (Is the bureaucracy seeking to open up Japan or to seal it off?)' 日本経済新聞 (*Nihon Keizai Shimbun*), 14 February 2008.

(2008ab). '企業年金連合会、買収防衛策への判断基準厳格に (PFA increases severity of its standards for takeover defences)'. 日本経済新聞 (*Nihon Keizai Shimbun*), 26 March 2008.

(2008ac). '米スティール、ブルドック全株売却、買収劇から完全撤退 (Steel of the USA sell all their Bull-Dog shares: complete withdrawal from this acquisition drama)'. 日本経済新聞 (*Nihon Keizai Shimbun*), 18 April 2008.

(2009a). 'エフィッシモ、産車体を提訴、日産自子会社への融資、「低金利で逸失利益出る」 (Effissimo sues Nissan Shatai: loan to Nissan subsidiary "is at low interest and causes opportunity cost loss")'. 日本経済新聞 (*Nihon Keizai Shimbun*), 18 July 2009.

(2009b). 'ユシロ化学工業長井禧明-経営のスピードが上がった ("The speed of our management has risen" – Nagai Yoshiaki, President of Yushiro Chemical)'. 日本経済新聞 (*Nihon Keizai Shimbun*), 20 January 2009.

(2009c). '村上元代表に猶予判決、インサイダー二審も有罪、重要事実の基準修正 (Former principal Murakami receives deferred sentence – still guilty of insider trading at second judgment – amended interpretation of material events)'. 日本経済新聞 (*Nihon Keizai Shimbun*), 4 February 2009.

(2010). '松屋、買収防衛策、12%が反対 (Matsuya: 12% oppose anti-takeover measures)'. 日本経済新聞 (*Nihon Keizai Shimbun*), 1 June 2010.

(2011). '岡田幹事長、政府保有株売却を検討' (Secretary-General Okada: disposal of government shareholdings under study). 日本経済新聞 (*Nihon Keizai Shimbun*), 24 July 2011.

Nikkei Business. (2007). '日本企業に相次ぎTOB攻勢米スティール・パートナーズ代表「サッポロに取締役派遣も」 (The representative of Steel Partners of the USA who have launched successive takeover assaults on Japanese firms: "We may well send directors to Sapporo")'. *Nikkei Business*, 21 May 2007.

Nikkei Kinyū. (2004). '名古屋発－TOB対策、金融機関が指南、経営者の危機感商機 (From Nagoya: guidance from a financial institution in anti-takeover strategy, taking the opportunity of unease among management)'. 日経金融新聞 (*Nikkei Kinyū Shimbun*), 13 April 2004.

　(2005). 'ユシロ、TOB回避から1年－安定株主拡大の手緩めず(IR追跡) (Yushiro: one year after evading takeover – no relaxation in expansion of stable shareholders – pursuit of IR)'. 日経金融新聞 (*Nikkei Kinyū Shimbun*), 25 January 2005.

　(2006a). '米ダルトン日本法人社長佐野順一郎氏(プライムインタビュー) (Mr. Sano Junichirō, president of US Dalton's Japanese subsidiary – "Prime Interview")'. 日経金融新聞 (*Nikkei Kinyū Shimbun*), 20 October 2006.

　(2006b). 'ユシロ化学工業社長長井禧明氏－米ファンドTOB転機（トップが描くＩＲ戦略) (Nagai Yoshiaki, President of Yushiro Chemical – US fund's TOB was a turning point (Top management describe IR strategy)'. 日経金融新聞 (*Nikkei Kinyū Shimbun*), 7 February 2006.

　(2007a). 'サッポロ、新たな買収防衛策－法知識で神経戦 (Sapporo: a new anti-takeover strategy – war of nerves using legal knowledge)'. 日経金融新聞 (*Nikkei Kinyū Shimbun*), 19 February 2007.

　(2007b). 'ブルドック、総会は勝利、市場の信任は－特定株主排除に懸念、「企業が株主選ぶ」 (Bull-Dog's success at AGM – Market reservations about excluding specific shareholders: "the firm choosing shareholders")'. 日経金融新聞 (*Nikkei Kinyū Shimbun*), 25 June 2007.

　(2007c). '中部電総会、「安定配当」に風圧－増配要求一割が賛成 (Chūbu Electric AGM: pressure on "stable dividend" – 10% in favour of demand for increased dividend)'. 日経金融新聞 (*Nikkei Kinyū Shimbun*), 28 June 2007.

　(2007d). '市場が問う親子上場(下)求心力と遠心力の黄金比 (The market questions listings of parent controlled subsidiaries (part 2) The ideal balance between centripetal and centrifugal forces)'. 日経金融新聞 (*Nikkei Kinyū Shimbun*), 3 December 2007.

　(2007e). '「日本改革」の大合唱　　　－　　外国人、企業統治で瀬踏み (The great chorus for "reforming Japan": foreigners test the water on corporate governance)'. 日経金融新聞 (*Nikkei Kinyū Shimbun*), 14 November 2007.

　(2007f). '防衛策、企業価値を破壊？－ブルドックの手法に批判も (Defence strategies: harmful to corporate value? Also some criticism of Bull-Dog's approach)'. 日経金融新聞 (*Nikkei Kinyū Shimbun*), 18 June 2007.

　(2007g). '個人アナリスト始動の予兆－中小型株への「集合知」探る（スクランブル) (The first signs of individuals as analysts beginning to stir: investigating the Wisdom of the Crowds towards SME shares)'. 日経金融新聞 (*Nikkei Kinyū Shimbun*), 16 January 2007.

Nikkei Sangyō. (2000). '昭栄にTOB, 広がるか？株主資本主義―オリックス全面支援 (TOB for Shōei: will this trend spread? ORIX, the supporter of shareholder primacy, giving its full support)'. 日経産業新聞 (*Nikkei Sangyō Shimbun*), 25 January 2000.

(2003a).'「モノ言う」株主とは (Who are these shareholders who express opinions?)'. 日経産業新聞 (*Nikkei Sangyō Shimbun*), 25 June 2003.

(2003b). '米国型統治、是か非か (Yes or no to American-style governance?)'. 日経産業新聞 (*Nikkei Sangyō Shimbun*), 24 June 2003.

(2004). 'TOB攻防、ソトー68日の軌跡―株主との関係に一石 (Takeover battle: Looking back on Sotoh's 68 days – a new element enters investor relations)'. 日経産業新聞 (*Nikkei Sangyō Shimbun*), 25 February 2004.

(2005). '東京スタイル社長、村上ファンドと、株主代表訴訟、一億円支払いで和解 (Tokyo Style president reaches compromise with Murakami Fund on derivative action paying ¥100m)'. 日経産業新聞 (*Nikkei Sangyō Shimbun*), 18 October 2005.

(2006). 'キッコーマンが買収防衛策導入 (Kikkōman introduces anti-takeover defences)'. 日経産業新聞 (*Nikkei Sangyō Shimbun*), 27 October 2006.

(2007a).'Jパワー、増配提案否決、将来の増配に含みも―安定株主確保狙う(07株主総会) (J-Power: dividend increase proposal defeated: possibility of future increases – search to secure stable shareholders)'. 日経産業新聞 (*Nikkei Sangyō Shimbun*), 28 June 2007.

(2007b). 'TCI幹部、増配要求で、Jパワー、「資金調達効率化を」 (TCI's senior directors in demand for higher dividend: "move to greater efficiency in fund-raising")'. 日経産業新聞 (*Nikkei Sangyō Shimbun*), 30 May 2007.

(2007c). 'フジテック、株主ダルトン、欧米事業巡り対立―知名度向上に欠かせない (Fujitec and Dalton in confrontation over US/European business: need to raise market profile)'. 日経産業新聞 (*Nikkei Sangyō Shimbun*), 22 June 2007.

(2007d). 'フジテック株15.97%取得、米オーチスの親会社、UTCが筆頭株主 (US Otis' parent company UTC as lead shareholder: holds 15.97% of Fujitec)'. 日経産業新聞 (*Nikkei Sangyō Shimbun*), 26 December 2007.

(2007e).'ブルドック、防衛策承認、賛成票8割超す―社長「企業価値向上粛々と」 (Bull-Dog's defence strategy approved: over 80% of votes in favour – President: "Moving carefully towards corporate value")'. 日経産業新聞 (*Nikkei Sangyō Shimbun*), 25 June 2007.

(2007f). 'ブルドックソース、スティールがTOBへ――株1584円、全株取得めざす (Bull-Dog Sauce: Steel moving towards tender offer aiming to acquire all shares at ¥1,584 per share)'. 日経産業新聞 (*Nikkei Sangyō Shimbun*), 17 May 2007.

(2007g). 'ブルドックソース、スティールがTOB開始—うまみは売却益か配当か (Steel's bid for Bull-Dog Sauce: disposal profit or dividends as the attraction?)'. 日経産業新聞 (*Nikkei Sangyō Shimbun*), 21 May 2007.

(2007h). 'ブルドックとスティール、TOB巡り、トップ会談物別れ (Bull-Dog and Steel hold top level meeting regarding bid but fail to reach agreement)'. 日経産業新聞 (*Nikkei Sangyō Shimbun*), 14 June 2007.

(2007i). 'ブルドックの新株予約権、きょう効力発生、一株につき3個割り当て (Bull-Dog's rights issue implemented today: 3 for 1 allotment)'. 日経産業新聞 (*Nikkei Sangyō Shimbun*), 11 July 2007.

(2007j). '太陽誘電、昭栄子会社を買収—キャパシター、大容量分野に進出 (Taiyō Yūden acquires Shōei subsidiary: capacitors – makes entry into high capacity sector)'. 日経産業新聞 (*Nikkei Sangyō Shimbun*), 5 February 2007.

(2007k). '日本精化、MEBOで、米ダルトンの提案を拒否 (Nippon Fine Chemical rejects US Dalton's proposal involving MEBO)'. 日経産業新聞 (*Nikkei Sangyō Shimbun*), 31 October 2007.

(2007l). '踊る投資家経営陣のむ (Active shareholders overcome management)'. 日経産業新聞 (*Nikkei Sangyō Shimbun*), 23 February 2007.

(2008a). 'Jパワー株買い増し、TCIに中止勧告、政府、安定供給影響を懸念 (Government advises TCI to desist from further purchase of J-Power shares: fears about stable supply)'. 日経産業新聞 (*Nikkei Sangyō Shimbun*), 17 April 2008.

(2008b). 'Jパワー総会、TCI提案を否決、中垣社長は再任 (J-Power AGM: TCI proposals defeated and President Nakagaki re-elected)'. 日経産業新聞 (*Nikkei Sangyō Shimbun*), 27 June 2008.

(2008c). 'NECエレ株主総会、携帯向け半導体で対立、攻防20分、経営陣、米ペリー (NEC Electronics' AGM: disagreement over semiconductors for mobiles – 20 minute exchange between management and US Perry)'. 日経産業新聞 (*Nikkei Sangyō Shimbun*), 27 June 2008.

(2008d). 'スティールの買収提案、サッポロHDが反対 (Sapporo Holdings opposes Steel's acquisition proposal)'. 日経産業新聞 (*Nikkei Sangyō Shimbun*), 27 February 2008.

(2008e). 'ノーリツ、スティールの買収提案に難色、ちらつく防衛策発動 (Nōritz raises difficulties for Steel's takeover proposal: mobilisation of anti-takeover defences adds to confusion)'. 日経産業新聞 (*Nikkei Sangyō Shimbun*), 20 October 2008.

(2008f). '日本精化株5%、米ダルトン売却、自社株買い応じる (Dalton sells 5% of Nippon Fine Chemical in response to buyback)'. 日経産業新聞 (*Nikkei Sangyō Shimbun*), 7 February 2008.

(2008g). '株主軽視？アデランスの油断―役員再任否決、再び波乱の総会 (Lack of attention to shareholders? Aderans' carelessness – rejection of directors' re-election – once again a tempestuous AGM)'. 日経産業新聞 (*Nikkei Sangyō Shimbun*), 30 May 2008.

(2008h). '経営諮問機関を設置、Jパワーが企業統治強化策 (J-Power to establish management advisory body – policy of strengthening corporate governance)'. 日経産業新聞 (*Nikkei Sangyō Shimbun*), 24 April 2008.

(2008i). '英TCI、「委任状争奪戦に」、総会に向け、Jパワー経営陣と (UK TCI moves towards AGM with proxy fight – clash with J-Power management)'. 日経産業新聞 (*Nikkei Sangyō Shimbun*), 22 May 2008.

(2008j). '議決権行使巡りTCIに抗議、Jパワー「事前合意ない」 (J-Power strongly criticises TCI regarding question of exercise of voting rights: "no prior agreements exist")'. 日経産業新聞 (*Nikkei Sangyō Shimbun*), 12 May 2008.

(2008k). 'TCI Jパワー株買い増し中止勧告拒否、「事実誤認」政府を批判 (TCI rejects advice to desist from increasing J-Power shareholding; criticises government: "lack of understanding about the realities")'. 日経産業新聞 (*Nikkei Sangyō Shimbun*), 28 April 2008.

Nikkei Veritas. (2008). 'NECエル株売買を拒否、変わりたくないNEC ― 米ファンド攻勢で見えた戦略不在 (NEC refuses to trade shares: struggle between change-resistant NEC and US fund reveals lack of strategy)'. 日経ヴェリタス (*Nikkei Veritas*), 17 February 2008.

(2011). 'ＪＴ、新興国開拓に「一服」なし―株価、極めて割安な水準'. (JT: no let-up in developing markets push – share price at very low level). 日経ヴェリタス (*Nikkei Veritas*), 24 July 2011.

Nikkei Weekly. (2008). 'Kinder, gentler Steel Partners? Lichtenstein talks strategic shift'. *The Nikkei Weekly*, 29 September 2008.

NLI Research. (2004). 株式持合い状況調査、2003年度版 (*Cross-shareholding survey 2003*). Tokyo: ニッセイ基礎研究所 (NLI Research).

Nonomiya, H. (2002). '日本企業の事業再編とプライベートエクイティ・ファンドの活用 (Business restructuring in Japanese industry and the role of private equity funds)'. Paper presented at RIETI conference.

North, D. C. (1990). *Institutions, institutional change and economic performance* (2002 edn). Cambridge University Press.

NRI. (2008). 経営用語の基礎知識 (*Basic knowledge of economic terms*). Tokyo: 野村総合研究所 (Nomura Research Institute), (Last updated April 2008). Retrieved from www.nri.co.jp, 24 November 2011.

NYT. (1990). 'A Pickens drama, far from Texas'. *The New York Times*, 29 June 1990.

(2008). 'Japan bars investment by British hedge fund'. *The New York Times*, 16 April 2008.

(2009). 'Perry Partners apologizes for first loss'. *The New York Times*, 2 February 2009.

O'Sullivan, M. A. (2000). *Contests for corporate control*. Oxford University Press.

Odaka, K. (1999). ' "Japanese-style" labour relations' (S. Herbert, Trans.). In T. Okazaki and M. Okuno-Fujiwara (eds.), *The Japanese economic system and its historical origins* (145–79). New York: Oxford University Press.

OECD. (2004). *OECD principles of corporate governance*. Paris: Organisation for Economic Co-operation and Development.

Okazaki, T. (1996). 'The Japanese firm under the wartime planned economy'. In M. Aoki and R. Dore (eds.), *The Japanese firm: sources of competitive strength* (350–78). New York: Oxford University Press (Clarendon).

(1999). 'Corporate governance' (S. Herbert, Trans.). In T. Okazaki and M. Okuno-Fujiwara (eds.), *The Japanese economic system and its historical origins* (97–144). New York: Oxford University Press.

Okazaki, T., and Okuno-Fujiwara, M. (1999). 'Japan's present-day economic system and its historical origins' (S. Herbert, Trans.). In T. Okazaki and M. Okuno-Fujiwara (eds.), *The Japanese economic system and its historical origins* (1–37). New York: Oxford University Press.

Okuno-Fujiwara, M. (1999). 'Japan's present-day economic system: its structure and potential for reform' (S. Herbert, Trans.). In T. Okazaki and M. Okuno-Fujiwara (eds.), *The Japanese economic system and its historical origins* (266–82). New York: Oxford University Press.

Olcott, G. (2009). 'Whose company is it? Changing CEO ideology in Japan'. In D. H. Whittaker and S. Deakin (eds.), *Corporate governance and managerial reform in Japan* (192–221). New York: Oxford University Press.

ONS. (2010). *Share ownership survey 2008*. London: Office for National Statistics.

Orrù, M., Biggart, N. W., and Hamilton, G. G. (1991). 'Organizational isomorphism in East Asia'. In W. W. Powell and P. J. DiMaggio (eds.), *The new institutionalism in organizational analysis* (361–89). University of Chicago Press.

Ōsaki, S. (2006). 'The Murakami Fund incident and future fund regulation'. *Nomura Capital Market Review*, 9(3), 1–15.

Park, D. (2008). 'The year of the activist hedge fund'. *FINalternatives*, 11 March 2008. Retrieved from www.finalternatives.com, 23 November 2011.

Partnoy, F., and Thomas, R. S. (2007). 'Gap filling, hedge funds, and financial innovation'. In Y. Fuchita and R. E. Litan (eds.), *New financial instruments and institutions: opportunities and policy challenges* (101–40). Baltimore, MD: Brookings Institution Press.

PFA. (2007). 平成18年度(2006年度)年金資産運用状況 (2006: Situation of pension assets under management). Tokyo: 企業年金連合会 (Pension Fund Association).

Pickens, T. B. (1989). 'Remarks to the Chicago World Trades Association'. *Oklahoma State University Electronic Publishing Center and University Archives*. Retrieved from http://digital.library.okstate.edu, 24 February 2005.

Pistor, K. (2011). 'On the plasticity of corporate law.' Paper presented to the 16th IEA World Congress, Tsinghua University, Beijing, July 2011.

Porter, M. E. (1992). 'Capital disadvantage: America's failing capital investment system'. *Harvard Business Review*, Sept–Oct 1992, 65–82.

   (1997). 'Capital choices: changing the way that America invests in industry'. In D. Chew (ed.), *Studies in international corporate finance and governance systems: a comparison of the US, Japan, & Europe* (5–17). New York: Oxford University Press.

Poteete, A., Janssen, M., and Ostrom, E. (2010). *Working together: collective action, the commons, and multiple methods in practice.* Princeton University Press.

Rappaport, A. (1986). *Creating shareholder value: the new standard for business performance.* New York: The Free Press.

Renesas. (2009). *NEC Electronics and Renesas to integrate business operations – establishment of the world's third largest semiconductor company.* Kawasaki: Renesas Technology Corp.

Reuters. (2005). 'New Japan Radio Co., Ltd.'s 19,754,000 common shares transferred to Nisshinbo Industries'. *Reuters.com.*

   (2007a). 'Hermes attacks "noise" from activist hedge funds'. *Reuters.com.*

   (2007b). 'Implenia says views Laxey's stake as hostile'. *Reuters.com.*

   (2008). 'Japan blocks TCI attempt to boost J-Power stake'. *Reuters.com.*

   (2009a). 'Algebris fund sells Generali stake – report'. *Reuters.com.*

   (2009b). 'Icahn seeks support in case against Steel Partners'. *Reuters. com.*

   (2009c). 'Japan GPIF picks 14 funds to manage foreign stocks'. *Reuters. com.*

   (2009d). 'Japan GPIF: 2008/09 investment losses ¥9.667 trin'. *Reuters. com.*

   (2009e). 'Steel Partners cuts stakes in Japan firms by $1.7 billion'. *Reuters. com.*

Robé, J-P. (2011). 'The legal structure of the firm'. *Accounting, Economics and Law*, 1, Article 5 (www.bepress.com/ael.vol1/iss1/5).

Roberts, J., Sanderson, P., Barker, R., and Hendry, J. (2006). 'In the mirror of the market: the disciplinary effects of company/fund manager meetings'. *Accounting, Organizations and Society*, 31(3), 277–94.

Roe, M. J. (1993). 'Takeover politics'. In M. Blair (ed.), *The deal decade* (321–47). Washington, DC: Brookings Institution.

(1996). 'Chaos and evolution in law and economics'. *Harvard Law Review*, 109(41), 641–68.

Röhl, W. (ed.). (2005). *History of law in Japan since 1868* (Vol. XII). Leiden: Brill.

Rosenstein, B. (2006). 'Activism is good for all shareholders'. *Financial Times* (Letters), 9 March 2006.

Ryūtsū Shimbun. (2007a). ブルドック、TOB反対表明、池田章子社長会見－「新株予約権に株主賛同確信」 (Bull-Dog announces opposition to bid – interview with President Ikeda Shōko: "confident that shareholders will support share options")'. 流通新聞 (*Ryūtsū Shimbun*), 10 June 2007.

(2007b). 'ブルドックTOB賛否留保、「強い懸念有する」、スティールに質問状、警戒感にじむ。(Judgment reserved on Bull-Dog bid – "strong concerns": written questions to Steel and sense of apprehension)'. 流通新聞 (*Ryūtsū Shimbun*), 28 May 2007.

Sako, M. (2005). 'Does embeddedness imply limits to within-country diversity?'. *British Journal of Industrial Relations*, 43(4), 585–92.

Sentaku. (2008). 'Jパワー(電源開発)ファンドに狙われる電力卸会社 (J-Power, the electricity wholesaler stalked by a fund)'. 選択 (*Sentaku* Magazine), 68–71.

Sheard, P. (1994). 'Interlocking shareholdings and corporate governance in Japan'. In M. Aoki and R. Dore (eds.), *The Japanese firm: sources of competitive strength* (310–49). New York: Oxford University Press.

Sheldon, C. D. (1958). *The rise of the merchant class in Tokugawa Japan, 1600–1868: an introductory survey*. Locust Valley, NY: J. J. Augustin.

Shimizu, T., and Igi, T. (2007). 'The Nireco poison pill: the impact of a court decision (trans. Christopher. J. Kodama from New Business Law Journal no. 812)'. *Pacific Rim Law & Policy Journal*, 16(3), 613–30.

Shishidō, Z. (2001). 'Reform in Japanese corporate law and corporate governance: current changes in historical perspective'. *The American Journal of Comparative Law*, 49(4), 653–77.

Siems, M. (2008). *Convergence in shareholder law*. Cambridge University Press.

Simon, H. (1955) 'A behavioral model of rational choice'. *Quarterly Journal of Economics*, 69, 99–118.

Skeel, D. (2010) 'The new financial deal: understanding the Dodd-Frank Act and its (unintended) consequences'. Institute for Law and Economics, Research Paper No. 1-21, University of Pennsylvania Law School.

Sloan, A. P., Jr (1965). *My years with General Motors*. London: Sidgwick and Jackson.

Smith, A. (1776). *The wealth of nations: books IV–V* (Vol. II). 1999 edition. London: Penguin Books.

Strine, L. (2008). 'The role of Delaware in the American corporate governance system, and some preliminary musings on the meltdown's implications for corporate law'. Paper presented at the Conference on Governance of the Modern Firm, 13 December 2008, Molengraaff Institute for Private Law, Utrecht University (copy on file with authors).

Summers, L. (2001). *London Stock Exchange Bicentennial Lecture*, London (copy on file with authors).

Sun Telephone. (2006). 株主による仮処分の申し立てに関する決定のお知らせ (Notification on decision regarding shareholder's request for interim restraining order). Press Release: 30 June 2006.

Supreme Court. (2007). 平成19年(許)30株主総会帰結禁止等仮処分命令申立却下決定に対する抗告棄却決定に対する許可抗告事件 (Case of appeal with permission against decision to dismiss appeal against decision to reject application for interim order to prohibit resolution of a general shareholders' meeting. Ref. 2007 (Kyo) 30). Tokyo: Supreme Court: 7 August 2007.

Szymkowiak, K. (2002). *Sokaiya: extortion, protection, and the Japanese corporation*. Armonk, NY: M. E. Sharpe.

Tachibanaki, T. (ed.). (1998). *Who runs Japanese business?* Cheltenham: Edward Elgar.

Takeover Panel. (2010). *The Takeover Code*. London: The Panel on Takeovers and Mergers.

TCI. (2011a). *Japan Tobacco – the case for change*. The Children's Investment Fund Management (UK) LLP, June 2011 (www.jtchange.com).

(2011b). *Letter from Oscar Veldhuijzen to the Minister of Finance*. The Children's Investment Fund Management (UK) LLP, 3 June 2011 (www.jtchange.com).

Teubner, G. (2001). 'Legal irritants: how unifying law ends up in new divergences'. In P. A. Hall and D. Soskice (eds.), *Varieties of capitalism: the institutional foundations of comparative advantage* (417–41). New York: Oxford University Press.

Tokuda, A. (2002). 'The origin of the corporation in Meiji Japan'. *CeFiMS Discussion Paper (DP21)*. Retrieved from www.cefims.ac.uk, 23 November 2011.

Tokyo District Court. (2005). 平成17年(モ)第6329号・平成17年(ヨ)第20050号・新株予約権発行差止仮処分命令申立事件 (Application for provisional disposition to prevent issue of new share warrants: Refs. 2005 (mo) no. 6329 and 2005 (yo) 20050). Tokyo District Court: 1 June and 9 June 2005.

(2007). 平成19年(ヨ)第20081号株主総会決議禁止等仮処分命令申立て事件 (Application for provisional disposition to prohibit decision of shareholders' meeting. Ref. 2007 (yo) no. 20081). Tokyo District Court: 28 June 2007.

Tokyo High Court. (2005a). 平成17年(ラ)第429号・新株予約権発行差止仮処分決定認可決定に対する保全抗告事件 (Appeal against decision on temporary restraining order to prevent issue of new share warrants: Ref. 2005 (ra) no. 429). Tokyo High Court: 23 March 2005.

(2005b). 平成17年(ラ)第942号新株予約権発行差止仮処分決定認可決定に対する保全抗告 (Appeal regarding decision to grant provisional disposition to prevent issue of new share warrants: Ref. 2005 (ra) no. 942). Tokyo High Court: 15 June 2005.

(2007). 平成19年(ラ)第917号株主総会帰結禁止等仮処分命令申立却下決定に対する広告事件 (Appeal regarding dismissal decision on application for provisional disposition to prohibit decision of shareholders' meeting etc. Ref. 2007 (ra) no. 917). Tokyo High Court: 9 July 2007.

Tokyo Kohtetsu. (2007). 大阪製鐵株式会社との株式交換契約の失効について (*re lapsing of share swap agreement with Osaka Steel*). Retrieved from www.kohtetsu.jp, dated 22 February 2007.

Tricker, R. I. (1984). *Corporate governance – practices, procedures and powers in British companies and their boards of directors*. Aldershot, Hants.: Gower Publishing.

(1994). 'Case studies: Koito Manufacturing Company'. *Corporate Governance: An International Review*, 2(1), 30–5.

TSE. (2007a). *TSE-listed companies white paper of corporate governance 2007*. Tokyo Stock Exchange, Inc.

(2007b). 上場制度総合整備プログラム2007 (*Comprehensive Improvement Program for Listing System 2007*). Tokyo Stock Exchange, Inc.

(2009). *TSE-listed companies white paper of corporate governance 2009*. Tokyo Stock Exchange, Inc.

(2010). *Main board monthly report.* Tokyo Stock Exchange, Inc.

(2011a). *TSE-listed companies white paper of corporate governance 2011.* Tokyo Stock Exchange, Inc.

(2011b). 投資部門別株式保有率の推移(長期統計 (*Movements in share-holding levels by investor categories – long-term statistics*). Tokyo Stock Exchange, Inc.

Turnbull, N. (1999). *Internal control: guidance for directors on the combined code.* London: The Institute of Chartered Accountants in England and Wales.

Uchida, K., and Xu, P. (2008). 'US barbarians at the Japan gate: cross border hedge fund activism'. *Bank of Japan Working Paper Series*, No. 08-E-3.

UKCGC. (2010). *UK Corporate Governance Code (June 2010).* London: Financial Reporting Council.

Vergne, J-P. (2008). 'The social construction of competitive advantage and the origin of global capitalism: the case of the Dutch East India Company'. *Academy of Management Proceedings*, 1–6.

Viénot, M. (1995). 'Rapport sur le conseil d'administration des sociétés cotées'. *Revue de droit des affaires internationales*, 8, 935–45.

Vogel, E. F. (1979). *Japan as no. 1* (1999 edn). Cambridge, MA: Harvard University Press.

Wade, R. (1996). 'Globalization and its limits: reports of the death of the national economy are greatly exaggerated'. In S. Berger and R. Dore (eds.), *National diversity and global capitalism* (60–88). Ithaca, NY: Cornell University Press.

Walker, D. (2008). 'Hedge fund fees under fire as performance dives'. *Financial News*, 27 October 2008. Retrieved from www.efinancial-news.com, 23 November 2011.

Webley, L. (2010) 'Qualitative approaches to empirical legal research', in P. Cane and H. Kritzer (eds.), *The Oxford handbook of empirical legal research*. Oxford University Press.

Weekly Post. (2008). 'ジャングルで勝ち抜く戦闘力をつける「ビジネス新大陸」の歩き方 (The progress of the "new territory for business" that gives strength to win in the jungle)'. 週刊ポスト (*Shūkan Post*), 64–5.

West, M. D. (2001). 'The puzzling divergence of corporate law: evidence and explanations from Japan and the United States'. *University of Pennsylvania Law Review*, 150(2), 527–601.

Westney, E. D. (2000). *Imitation and innovation: the transfer of western organizational patterns in Meiji Japan.* Cambridge, MA: Harvard University Press.

Williams, C. and Zumbansen, P. (eds.). (2011). *The embedded firm: corporate governance, labor, and finance capitalism*. New York: Cambridge University Press.

Williamson, O. E. (1985). *The economic institutions of capitalism: firms, markets, relational contracting* . New York: The Free Press.

(1996) *The mechanisms of governance*. New York: Oxford University Press.

Winter, S. (1993). 'Routines, cash flows, and unconventional assets: corporate change in the 1980s'. In M. Blair (ed.), *The deal decade* (74–9). Washington, DC: Brookings Institution.

WSJ. (2008a). 'Hedge fund Perry Capital lays off 20 to 30 staffers in equities'. *The Wall Street Journal*, 16 October 2008.

(2008b). 'TCI calls for patience after third-quarter loss of 15.6%'. *The Wall Street Journal*, 15 October 2008.

Xu, J., and Li , Y. (2010). 'Hedge fund activism and bank loan contracting'. *AFA 2011 Denver Meetings Paper*. Retrieved from www.ssrn.com, 11 February 2012.

Yomiuri. (1989a). '小糸製作所　米社が20％を所有、筆頭株主に　M＆Aの"仕掛け人" (US company holds 20% of Koito Seisakusho: M&A "operator" as largest shareholder)'. 読売新聞 (*Yomiuri Shimbun*), 3 April 1989.

(1989b). '株を買い占めたブーン社が役員派遣を希望、初会談で小糸製作所側は拒否 (At the first meeting, Koito Seisakusho side rejects call to send board members from Boone's organisation which has accumulated its shares)'. 読売新聞 (*Yomiuri Shimbun*), 21 April 1989.

(1991).'ピケンズ氏が小糸株売り戻し 元の保有者麻布建物に 事実上の買い占め敗北宣言 (Pickens sells back Koito shares to original owner, Azabu Tatemono, and declares effective failure of accumulation exercise)'. 読売新聞 (*Yomiuri Shimbun*), 29 April 1991.

(2005a). '日本無線、日清紡に新日本無線株を売却　TOB成立　村上氏側が強く反発 (Japan Radio sells its New Japan Radio shares to Nisshinbō: Murakami side opposes bid strongly)'. 読売新聞 (*Yomiuri Shimbun*), 9 December 2005.

(2005b). '［阪神電鉄の研究］(中)手堅い社風 長期的な企業価値優先(連載) (Study on Hanshin Electric Railway (2): hard-headed company ethos, priority to long-term corporate value)'. 読売新聞 (*Yomiuri Shimbun*), 17 November 2005.

(2006). '検証・攻防「阪神株」インサイダーで幕切れ　村上元代表、突然の退場 (Murakami's arrest for insider trading causes sudden exit from studies and tussles over Hanshin stocks)'. 読売新聞 (*Yomiuri Shimbun*), 21 June 2006.

(2007). '村上被告、実刑2年、インサイダー事件 (Murakami given 2 year custodial sentence in insider case)'. *読売新聞* (*Yomiuri Shimbun*), 19 July 2007.

Yoshimori, M. (2005). 'Does corporate governance matter? Why the corporate performance of Toyota and Canon is superior to GM and Xerox'. *Corporate Governance: An International Review*, 13(3), 447–57.

Zingales, L. (1998). 'Corporate governance'. In P. Newman (ed.), *The new Palgrave dictionary of economics and the law* (497–503). London: Palgrave Macmillan.

Index